COMPUTER FUNDAMENTALS
With BASIC Programming

WEST'S
Computer Education Series

COMPUTER FUNDAMENTALS
With BASIC Programming

Steven L. Mandell

Colleen J. Mandell

WEST PUBLISHING COMPANY

St. Paul   New York   Los Angeles   San Francisco

Copyediting: Editing, Design, and Production
Text design: Christy Butterfield
Cover design: Christy Butterfield
Cover art: Dick Cole
Creative art—text: John Shank
Composition: IPS Publishing, Inc.

Disclaimer of Warranties and Limitation of Liabilities

The author has taken due care in preparing this book and the programs in it, including research, development, and testing to ascertain their effectiveness. The author and the publisher make no express or implied warranty of any kind with regard to these programs or the supplementary documentation in this book. In no event shall the author or the publisher be liable for incidental or consequential damages in connection with or arising out of the furnishing, performance, or use of any of these programs.

TRS-80 is a trademark of the Radio Shack Division of Tandy Corporation. Apple is the registered trademark of Apple Computer, Inc. Commodore 64 is a trademark of Commodore Business Machines. IBM PC is a trademark of International Business Machines Corporation.

Photo Credits

3 Courtesy of NOAA; 4 Courtesy of Bethlehem Steel; 8 Courtesy of Honeywell Inc,; National Center for Atmospheric Research/National Science Foundation; 9 J. Martin Natvig; 15,16,17,18,20,21, Courtesy of International Business Machines Corporation; 22 Iowa State University Information Service; 23,24 Courtesy Sperry Corporation; 25, 26, 27 Courtesy of International Business Machines Corporation; 28 Courtesy of Philips; 36 National Center for Atmospheric Research/National Science Foundation; Courtesy of Control Data Corporation; 37 Courtesy of NCR Corporation; 38 Courtesy of International Business Machines Corporation; 39 Courtesy of Hewlett-Packard; 52 Courtesy of the Internal Revenue Service; 54,55 Courtesy of BASF Systems Corporation; 56 Courtesy of Chromatics, Inc.; 57 Courtesy of New England Telephone; 60 Used with permission of Recognition Equipment Company, Inc.; 62 The Voice Connection; 63 Norma Morris; 64 The Mouse House, Inc.; 65 Koala Technologies; 66 Courtesy of Qume Corporation, a subsidiary of ITT Corporation; 67 Courtesy of Mannesmann Tally Corporation; 69 Courtesy of Universal Data Systems; 81 Courtesy of International Business Machines Corporation; 82 Courtesy of Texas Instruments; 93 Matt Rothan, Columbus College of Art and Design; 94 Courtesy of Intergraph Corporation; Reprinted with permission from Computervision Corporation, Bedford, Massachusetts; 95 Courtesy of International Business Machines Corporation; Courtesy of Chromatics, Inc.; Samurai by Image Resource; 106 Courtesy of Chrysler Corporation; 107 Courtesy of Bethlehem Steel; Courtesy of Chrysler Corporation; 108 Courtesy of Chrysler Corporation; 110 Jim Winkler, Medical College of Ohio; 112 Ariel Computerized Exercise System; 114 Courtesy of International Business Machines Corporation; 115 The Voice Connection; 117 Courtesy of Philips; Courtesy American Satellite Company, Rockville, Maryland; 119 U.S. Air Force Photo; 120,128 Courtesy of International Business Machines Corporation; 129 Courtesy of National Semiconductor Corporation; 130 Courtesy of Hewlett-Packard; 132 Courtesy of Sperry Corporation; 133 Courtesy of Hewlett-Packard; 134 Robin DeLoach-Fieldcrest Mills, Inc.; 137 Courtesy Marathon Oil Company; 139 Courtesy Sperry Corporation; 150 Courtesy of Lanier, a Harris Company; 151 Courtesy of Heath Company; 153 Courtesy of Androbot.

Authors:

Colleen J. Mandell, B.S., M.S. Ed. D.; Educator; Software Developer, Psychometrist; Associate Professor, College of Education, Bowling Green State University

Steven L. Mandell, B.S., B.S.Ch.E., M.B.A., D.B.A., J.D.; Computer Book Author; Software Developer; Computer Lawyer; Associate Professor of Computer Systems, Bowling Green State University

Educational Consultant

Julie G. Fiscus, B.A., M.A.; Computer Educator

Content Specialists

Sarah S. Basinger, B.A.; Computer Educator; Writer

Barbara Applebaum, B.A., M.A.; Computer Educator; Writer

Laura J. Bores, B.S., M.B.A.; Computer Educator; Writer

Donna M. Guinard, B.S.; Systems Analyst

Gay N. Jones, Ph.D.; Educator in Library and Educational Media

Duane E. Whitmire, Ph.D.; Lecturer in Computer Science

Critical Evaluators For West's Computer Education Series

Bruce Don Bowen
Davis Country School District,
Data Processing Department
Layton, Utah
Charles M. Bueler
Assistant Superintendent for
Instruction
Hannibal Public Schools
Hannibal, Missouri
Dr. Tom Burnett
Assistant to Superintendent
for Computer Technology
Lincoln Public Schools
Lincoln, Nebraska
Sharon Burrowes
Wooster City Schools
Wooster, Ohio
Bruce B. Burt
West Chester School District
West Chester, Pennsylvania
Vincent Cirello
East Meadow High School
Curriculum Center
East Meadow, New York
Don M. Cochran
Bartlesville High School
Bartlesville, Oklahoma
Dr. George E. Cooke
Assistant Superintendent, Indiana
Area School District
Indiana, Pennsylvania
Carolyn Cox
Virginia Beach City Public Schools
Office of Curriculum and Staff
Development
Virginia Beach, Virginia

Joseph Crupie
North Hills High School
Pittsburg, Pennsylvania
Charles R. Deupree
Ionia Public Schools
Ionia, Michigan
Dr. Helen Ditchazy
Assistant Superintendent
Jackson Public Schools
Jackson, Michigan
Dr. John H. Emhuff
Assistant Superintendent
Instruction
Mt. Vernon, Indiana
Ms. Carol Haynes
Prospect School
Learning Center Director
Hinsdale, Illinois
Ken Hendrickson
Oak Park Elementary School
Newbury Park, California
Dr. Sandra Howe
Kalamazoo Public Schools
Kalamazoo, Michigan
Monica Ilas
Media Specialist for Lakewood
Public Schools
Lakewood, Ohio
Doris Kassera
Media Specialist
Eau Claire Elementary Schools
Eau Claire, Wisconsin
Colvin Kindschi
Oak Park Elementary School
Newbury Park, California

Douglas Krugger
Computer Operations Center
School District of the City of Erie
Erie, Pennsylvania
Mary E. Larnard
Newburyport High School
Newburyport, Massachusetts
Wally Leech
The Media Center
Greater Johnstown School District
Johnstown, Pennsylvania
Letitia Martin
Indian Hills Elementary School
North Little Rock, Arkansas
Marilyn Mathis
Murfreesboro City Schools
Murfreesboro, Tennessee
Dr. Judith K. Meyers
Lakewood City Schools
Coordinator Media Services
Lakewood, Ohio
Mark A. Mitrovich
Principal
Clarkston High School
Clarkston, Washington
Willis Parks
Coordinator of Computer
Education
North Canton City Schools
North Canton, Ohio
Bette Pereira
Harrison High School
Harrison, Ohio

The following people have reviewed portions of **Computer Fundamentals with BASIC Programming**:

A Note on the Reading Level

The reading level of **Computer Fundamentals with BASIC Programming** has been checked and verified to fall within the seventh through ninth grade span. Nine samples of approximately 100-150 words were checked. The following indexes were used: Estimated Dale, Fog Index, Flesch Grade Level, Smog Index, and the Frye.

Preface

West's Computer Education Series

The computer revolution has excited the education profession more than any other technological advancement. It is clear that students must be able to master computer skills if they are to survive in a technology-based world. The goal of West's Computer Education Series is to provide the necessary learning packages to support the classroom teacher in accomplishing the objectives of the computer curriculum.

Before embarking on West's Computer Education Series, great care was taken to plan the overall concept of a fully integrated series as well as to assess the particular requirements for each individual text. An extensive survey of computer educators was done across the country in the very early stages of development. After the basic plans for the series were established, many teachers and computer coordinators were asked to comment on the general scope of the series and the specific content for each of the texts. The manuscripts were read and evaluated by many computer educators, and student and teacher feedback was obtained through field testing. Computer professionals were then assigned the task of technically verifying all of the material. Many changes and refinements were incorporated throughout the development of each text, and great care was taken to maintain the integrity of the series each step along the way. The result of this very careful development and review process is a product the authors and the publisher are proud and confident to present to the educational community.

Three additional factors were given top priority during this project: Reading level, pedagogical design and teacher materials. Students must be presented material at the appropriate reading level if educational objectives are to be accomplished. Grade spans have been kept to a maximum of three years, thus enabling a close targeting of both level and relevancy of examples. The pedagogical design of each book was carefully developed based on grade level and subject matter. Additionally, the series was developed with an overall pedagogical plan, making it very easy for the teacher and the students to move from one text to the next. We have employed outlines, learning objectives, vocabulary lists, learning checks, summary points, test, glossaries and other devices appropriate to specific titles to enhance the educational process for the student.

The teachers' manuals that accompany each text in West's Computer Education Series are complete, thorough and easy to use for teachers at any level of computer expertise. The manuals offer an extensive package of materials to assist the teacher in reinforcing the concepts introduced in the texts.

About This Text

Students face increased exposure to computers at school and at home. Their knowledge of hardware, software, and programming can determine their attitude toward computer use. **Computer Fundamentals with BASIC Programming** provides an integrated look at many aspects of computer use. The first nine chapters present computer uses, history, hardware, software, careers and ethics. Chapters ten through eighteen cover the fundamentals of BASIC programming. The BASIC programs were written to run on the Apple family of microcomputers, but microcomputer differences are noted for the IBM PC, Commodore 64 and TRS-80.

Each chapter contains standard pedagogical devices: A chapter outline, learning objectives, and introduction provide a framework for material in the chapter. Learning checks for self-testing, summary points, chapter test, and chapter glossary give students an opportunity to evaluate their level of mastery of the material. Within the first nine chapters, highlights emphasize computer use relating to the chapter content. Issues provide a forum for discussion about topics of concern to students, teachers, and parents.

The programming chapters contain programming examples, hands-on exercises which encourage students to use computers at home or at school, and comprehensive programming problems which review material covered in each chapter. Students can also test their knowledge by trying additional programming problems that are available at the end of each chapter.

A keyboarding appendix at the back of the text can aid an entire class or individual students unfamiliar with working at a computer keyboard. Ten enrichment topics cover a variety of additional computer literacy and programming topics, allowing a maximum amount of flexibility in teaching this course.

The teacher's manual to support this book is divided into two parts: Classroom Administration and Additional Teacher Materials. Each chapter of the manual includes a chapter overview, outline, vocabulary list, lesson plans with activities, answers to all tests and answers to worksheets. In the first nine chapters, the manual includes additional discussion questions. Solutions to all programming problems are included for chapters ten through eighteen. Chapter 18 of the teacher's manual emphasizes structured programming and provides an aid to programming in modules. A separate section with supplemental programming problems and solutions is also included. The second portion of the manual includes black-line masters to use as transparencies, tests, and worksheets, a resource list, and a glossary.

To the Student

In writing **Computer Fundamentals with BASIC Programming**, the authors' goal was to help you learn to understand and use computers. The first half of this text covers computers in the world around you, how they work, and how they are used. In the second half of the book you will learn the BASIC programming language and the skills needed to program a computer.

The chapters in this text were written in a way that will make learning easier:

Chapter Outline
Each chapter begins with an outline that gives you an overall picture of what the chapter is about and prepares you to read the chapter.

Learning Objectives
This list tells you what you will achieve by studying and understanding the chapter.

Learning Checks
Following each section within the chapter you will find questions. If you stop to answer the questions as you study, you will be able to check your progress. If you are able to answer the learning check questons correctly, you are ready to go on to the next section.

Highlights
The first nine chapters in this text are about computers in the world around you. Included in these chapters are Highlights, short, interesting features about uses of computers.

Issues
Also included in the first nine chapters are Issues, which look at both sides of a question relating to computers.

Programming Examples
The second half of this text is about programming in the BASIC language. In these chapters there are many examples that will help you to understand the chapter and learn to write your own programs.

Hands-On Exercises
Where you see the words *Now Try This* followed by an arrow, there will be an exercise you can practice on the computer.

Summary Points

A point-by-point summary at the end of each chapter restates the important ideas in the chapter to help make studying and remembering easier.

Vocabulary List

A list of the important new terms with their definitions is included at the end of each chapter as another study aid. The glossary at the back of the book gives a complete list of all the important terms.

Chapter Test

Taking the chapter tests will let you check how much of the material you remember and understand.

Programming Problems

By doing the complete programming problems after the programming chapters, you can build your BASIC skills.

Acknowledgments

Many individuals have been involved in the development of the material for West's Computer Education Series. These professionals have provided invaluable assistance for the completion of a series of this magnitude: Greg Allgair, Kim Girnus, John Gregor, Steve Hoffman, Craig Howarth, Rhonda Raifsnider, and Jeff Sanborn on student material; Mike Costarello, Margaret Gallito, Sara Hosler, Gloria Pfeif, and Jennifer Urbank on instructor material; Norma Morris and Donna Pulschen on manuscript development; Shannan Benschoter, Linda Cupp, Charles Drake, Lisa Evans, Janet Lowery, Sally Oates, Valerie Pocock, Brian Sooy, Candace Streeter, Nancy Thompson, and Michelle Westlund on manuscript production; and Meredith Flynn and Kathy Whitacre on photographs.

The production management of all of the books in the series is a tribute to the many talents of Marta Fahrenz. The educational surveys and teacher communications were designed and maintained by editor Carole Grumney, a very special person. Debora Wohlford, sales manager for elementary/high school texts, has been extremely important in market research and in helping to shape the scope of the series. One final acknowledgment goes to our publisher and valued friend, Clyde Perlee, Jr., without whose support the project would never even have been attempted.

Contents

Chapter **4**   **Communication and Its Tools**   **50**

Chapter **9**　　**Ethical Issues and Computers of Tomorrow**　　**143**

Chapter **14**   **Testing the Program**   **241**

COMPUTER FUNDAMENTALS
With BASIC Programming

Chapter 1

Computers and Their Impact

Learning Objectives

After reading this chapter, you should be able to:

1. Name five ways computers affect our lives, society, and language.

2. List three factors that describe a computer's power.

3. Distinguish between data and information.

4. Describe the flow pattern in electronic data processing.

5. Contrast batch and interactive processing.

6. Explain the terms *hardware* and *software*.

Introduction

Using computers is much like eating potato chips or watching television. The extent of use quietly builds up. All of a sudden you realize just how many chips you have eaten, just how many hours of TV you have watched, or just how many times you have run across computers in your daily lives.

Of course, you can always close the bag of chips or turn off the TV. But you can rarely avoid computers. When you buy jeans or a sandwich, your purchases are rung up on a point-of-sale terminal. If you watch football on TV you see pictures that spin and shrink through the use of computer graphics. Your favorite music may be produced with the help of computers. Maybe you will buy a Coke from a talking vending machine. If you put money in the bank, chances are your savings account is updated by computer. Even the jargon of computers—bits, bytes, number-crunching, on-line, "garbage-in, garbage-out," joystick—cannot be escaped.

Computer A machine with uses limited only by the creativity of the humans who use it.

Computers are general-purpose machines limited only by the humans who use them. They can increase the quality of your life. They can be fun to use. They make time-consuming chores easier and faster.

Yet, computers stir feelings of doubt. Many people fear they will become only numbers in the computer age. They are afraid their jobs may be taken over by computers. And they are afraid of the very worst pictures described by science fiction writers—a tragic computer error that will plunge the world into nuclear war or a systems failure that will paralyze society.

Willing or not, society is being led into the computer age. Let's find out about the power of computers.

Computers Today

Computers do many jobs. Some jobs seem simple. Others are a surprise. But you can see how computers affect your daily lives.

Figure 1-1. *This computer console displays weather systems.*

Computers may improve the safety of travel. Scientists build computer models of airplane crashes. Knowing the "crash behavior" of the planes will help aircraft designers. They will plan safer seats, windows, and fabrics to decrease fire dangers. New chemicals can stop fires from spreading after a crash.

In many places, computers control traffic lights. Imagine what would happen if these computers failed!

Credit card bills and payments are entered into computers. When a bill is not paid, the computer records the fact. The credit card company may not be the only company that knows the bill was not paid. The record may be copied into data lists that belong to banks, loan companies, or other credit card companies. The problem arises when the bill is paid. Sometimes not all of the lists are updated, and customers wonder why they cannot get more credit.

Computers can affect our lives in a less direct way, too. The railroad cars that transport products and food are sorted at railroad yards. Computers scan the codes on the sides of the cars and switch as many as 2,500 cars at one time.

Nature is also monitored by computers. Computers check weather patterns. An unusual weather pattern may show a storm brewing or a drought coming (see Figure 1-1). Newscasts can warn people to prepare for very heavy rains, high winds, and lightning.

When elk travel, computers can trace their paths. Scientists study the patterns to find out what problems in the environment affect the elk.

Computers help to check problems like acid rain. Once scientists know where the pollution comes from, the conditions can be corrected (see Figure 1-2).

Figure 1-2. *Using the latest advances and computer controls, Bethlehem Steel Corporation's "A" coke battery has many complex environmental control devices.*

Even language is affected by the computer age. Look at these common words: *bit, boot, bug, chip, down, bus, menu*. Yes, they still mean what you think they do. But they also have new meanings. Take *boot*, for example. When talking about computers, a boot is not a high-topped leather shoe. It is a way to start a computer. *Down* does not mean depressed, or even underneath. It means the computer is not working. You can travel by *bus*, but so can bits!

Just think of the many roles this modern wonder plays in your life! What makes the computer so powerful? In the next section we discuss the things that make the computer so powerful.

The Power of Computers

Science fiction has given computers human powers. Isaac Asimov's *Robbie* tells the story of a robot who babysat for an 8-year-old girl. He was human enough to save her life when she was in danger. Computers in movies, however, are sometimes evil. They try to take over the world.

After reading about computers with superhuman powers, would you believe computers can perform only a handful of functions? Today's machines cannot reason as humans do. They cannot think or act like humans. What they can do is perform arithmetic calculations, make comparisons, and store and retrieve facts. They get most of their amazing power from three features: speed, accuracy, and memory.

Here you are—learning all about trailer values, GOTO statements, and IF/THEN statements! If your parents do not use computers, that is enough to create a generation gap. Maybe you should send them to computer camp. After all, they may have sent you to Girl Scout camp, Boy Scout camp, music camp, YMCA camp, or church camp. Now you can return the favor and narrow the generation gap at the same time. Your parents can learn enough at camp to keep up with what you are learning about computers in school!

Not only that—they can learn about computers in a relaxed setting on the beach, in the woods, after using a hot tub, or after a swim. Some camps are set in exotic places like Mexico, Hawaii, or Lake Tahoe. One camp is housed on the Mississippi Queen, a river boat on the Mississippi River. Another, Mount Rainier Computer Camp, is perched near Crystal Mountain, Washington. Still others are less like camp and more like school. The Summer Computer Institute at Amherst College in Massachusetts fits this kind of camp.

Wherever they are, the camps are becoming more popular. They present computers in a less frightening setting. If you want to know more about which camp would best suit your mother and father, check with Benton's *The Complete Guide to Computer Camps and Workshops*. You might even find a camp for the whole family, such as Family Computer Camp in Potsdam, New York. At this camp, campfire nights and ice cream sundae evenings mix with bits and bytes and BASIC.

Speed

Computers obey instructions very quickly. Unless a breakdown occurs, speed is the one feature that we can be sure a computer has.

Today's computer can act in a matter of nanoseconds. A **nanosecond** is one-billionth of a second. Electricity can travel at about the speed of light, 186,000 miles in one second. In one nanosecond, electricity will travel 11.8 inches. The smaller the distances in the electronic circuitry of a computer, the shorter the time needed for electricity to travel those distances. That is why circuits etched on tiny chips increase the power of computers.

Accuracy

The same type of current passed through the same electrical circuits will yield the same result each time. The computer is very reliable because its circuitry is reliable. The computer follows instructions and performs math calculations and comparisons accurately. It will add long columns of numbers, make out hundreds of paychecks, and even record your attendance in school. Such chores might be very boring for humans. The same operation is required over and over and over...

Of course, if the data or the instructions are not correct, the computer will not be able to produce correct results. This is called "**garbage in-garbage out**." It means if a computer is "fed" the wrong facts, the answer will be useless.

Memory or storage A computer part that provides the ability to recall information.

Retrieve Finding stored information.

Memory

The part of a computer that stores data is called **memory** or **storage**. Computers can store huge amounts of data. They can **retrieve** the data at super fast speeds. A computer can store data in much less space than paper files take. The amount of storage in a computer system often depends on the user's needs.

 LEARNING CHECK 1-1

1. The three features that give computers their power are _____, _____, and _____.

2. What is a nanosecond?

3. What is the phrase that explains that what you put into a computer must be accurate or the computer cannot give accurate results?

1. speed, accuracy, memory 2. one-billionth of a second 3. garbage in-garbage out

Data Processing

Data processing is not a new idea. People have performed data processing ever since they have had anything to count. **Data processing** is the collecting, handling, and passing out of data to achieve a goal.

The speed, accuracy, and memory of computers make data processing faster. Data processing by computer is called **electronic data processing**, or **EDP**. What is data? And how does a computer process it? This section answers these questions.

Data and Information

We have used the word "data" without defining it. Data and information are often used to mean the same thing. This chapter contrasts the two in order to explain data processing.

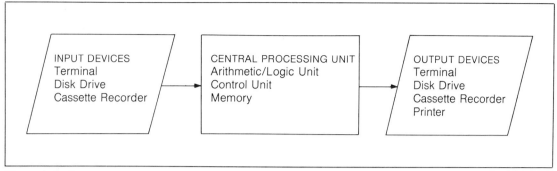

Figure 1-3. *Data processing follows the same basic flow.*

Data are raw facts. The number "365" is a fact. It is a fact until you think of it as a piece of useful information. For example, you might immediately think of it as the number of days in a year. But it might be the amount of money you need to buy a bike or the number of jelly beans in a jar for a guessing game. Once you know what "365" is and have a use for the number, it becomes **information**. Information must be accurate, timely, and complete. Information increases understanding and helps people to make decisions.

Data Raw facts that have not been organized.

Information Data that have been organized and processed so that they are meaningful.

Input, Processing, and Output

All data processing follows the same basic flow: input, processing, and output (see Figure 1-3). **Input** is the step in which data are collected, checked for accuracy, and coded so the computer can understand them. (The computer usually does the coding.)

During **processing**, the computer may handle the data in one or more of five ways: classifying, sorting, calculating, summarizing, and storing. The computer classifies data by grouping them into categories. For instance, at a bank the computer may look at your deposit and "decide" whether your money goes into your savings account or into your Christmas Club fund. Then the computer sorts the data, perhaps by account number. Next, the computer performs math calculations. The bank's computer will add your deposit to bring your account up to date. The bank needs summaries of data, so the computer then provides reports of totals for all the day's deposits, including yours. Finally, the computer stores the data for future use.

The results are now available for output. **Output** means the computer retrieves or brings back the data and changes it back into a form that you can understand. Output may appear in printed form or on a screen. If the data mean something to you, they become information.

Input The step in the data processing flow in which data are collected and coded.

Processing Handling input to produce information.

Output Information that results from processing.

Figure 1-4. *Interactive processing (left) in the workplace versus batch processing (right) with magnetic tape drives.*

Batch and Interactive Processing

Two types of computer processing can occur. One type is batch processing. In **batch processing**, data are collected over time in a separate file and processed all at once.

Taking a test is an example of batch processing. Over a period of a month or a semester, you collect facts about a subject, perhaps plant life. When the teacher announces a test, you open the plant life file in your brain and study it. On test day, you process all the facts at once. The facts become information because you use them to increase understanding about plant life or to make decisions about answering test questions.

The other type of processing is **interactive processing**. During interactive processing, a user enters input while the processing is going on. Usually the input is entered by keyboard, but other devices may be used.

A class discussion shows how interactive processing works. The teacher's questions about the subject, which is plant life, make you think about what you know. You may answer a question, but you can also ask a question about something you do not understand (see Figure 1-4). You may even offer some new facts.

Hardware, Software, and People

Any equipment that is used in the computer data processing steps is called **hardware**. Computer hardware consists of more than just a computer. Devices are needed to input and output data or to transfer data to a storage medium. These devices support the computer system but are outside the main computer. They are called **peripheral devices**. The hardware you are probably most familiar with is the **microcomputer** (see Figure 1-5).

Figure 1-5. *Students show their creativity on the Apple Macintosh microcomputer.*

Users enter and receive data by using some type of hardware device. That device is called a **terminal**. Some terminals are called **input/output devices** because they can allow data both to enter and to exit. A common type of terminal consists of a keyboard and a television-like screen.

Users may get output in a form that is temporary. It is displayed on the television-like screen of a terminal. As soon as the terminal is turned off or new information is requested, the old information vanishes. This copy is called **soft copy**.

Hard copy can be read without using the terminal or computer. It is usually paper copy and is produced by a printer.

To use computer hardware, the user needs software. **Software** is the **program** or set of programs that make the computer do its work. The game *Zork* is software. A program that permits the user to write stories or letters is software. Software, or programs, tell the computer exactly what to do. The people who write the instructions are called **programmers**.

Both software and hardware are becoming more **user-friendly**. User-friendly computer tools are easy to use. You do not have to be a computer expert to understand user-friendly material.

Terminal A point in a computer system where data can enter or exit.

Soft copy Data displayed on a television-like screen.

Hard copy Printed output.

Program Step-by-step instructions that tell the computer what to do.

You might have thought of many ways computers are used. But I bet you have not thought of this one! A new computer system controls the feeding of cows! The system is made by Alfa-Laval of Kansas City. It remembers special diets for each cow in a dairy herd. The diets help the cows to produce more milk.

Each cow wears some computer hardware. The hardware is an electronic "necklace." Tags on the necklaces transmit radio signals to a computer whenever the cows pass antennas on the stalls. When the cow enters her own stall, the computer recognizes her. The computer checks its memory to determine whether the cow is due for a feeding. If she is, the computer triggers a mechanism, and food is dumped into the cow's trough. Of course, the food is specially mixed for each cow.

If a cow waits longer between meals, more food is dispensed. The system prevents both underfeeding and overfeeding.

Perspective   *We are becoming more dependent upon computers. As we study about them, we become more comfortable with them. We learn more about how we can continue to benefit from computers, yet control the problems their use creates. And we may wonder how all this started in the first place!*

✦ **LEARNING CHECK 1-2**

1. The conversion of data into information is called
   a. processing
   b. classifying
   c. changing
   d. batching

2. The three steps of data processing are _____, _____, and _____.

3. The type of processing in which the user can enter data while processing is going on is called _____.

4. TRUE   FALSE   The programs are the sets of instructions that tell the computer exactly what to do, while the software is the package the programs come in.

5. Who is the person who writes computer programs?

6. Hardware that supports the main computer but is not part of it is called _____ equipment.

1. a 2. input, processing, output 3. interactive 4. FALSE 5. programmer 6. peripheral

---

Electronic bulletin boards enable a computer user to send messages to and receive messages from other computer users without seeing the people face-to-face. Electronic college courses give students the chance to read information, ask and answer questions, and see other students' answers without going to a classroom or speaking to the other students. Home computers and video games may encourage parents and children to spend all of their free time in front of the computer.

Will computers prevent us from forming friendships, talking to our families, or participating in outdoor activities?

When video games in arcades became popular, many people worried that children would be hypnotized by playing the games. Video games are not as popular as they once were. Children who spent all their time and money at the arcades are finding other things to do with computers.

One thing a person can do with the computer is to use a modem and phone lines to enter and receive messages on an electronic bulletin board. You might feel more relaxed "talking" to another person through a computer rather than meeting that person face-to-face.

Research at Carnegie-Mellon University in Pittsburgh examines how communications by electronic means have affected human interaction. In one study, discussions were held using computers as a way of communication. Other discussions involved face-to-face group meetings. The discussions by computer took longer. Arguments were common, and students were often rude to one another. However, the computer discussions were fairer than the face-to-face discussions. Each person had an equal share of time. People who were always talking in the face-to-face situation did not dominate when using the computers.

Computers may affect not only how a person acts in a group. They may also affect how families behave. Perhaps a husband or wife feels a spouse spends too much time with the computer.

Perhaps the children will no longer want to communicate with other family members. Yet in other families, members may gather around the computer for a common activity, such as a game or educational program.

Computers also discourage the kinds of activities that children do to build physical strength. While playing with computers, users tend to sit almost motionless. Teachers, parents, and counselors at computer camps are becoming more aware of this problem. They are forcing children to turn in their disks for regular exercise and play with other young people. Fortunately, most young people seem to know when they need to get up and exercise.

Will computers cause users to form relationships with new people? Or will computers so hypnotize the users that they no longer care to interact with people? What decides the outcome? Is the computer at fault? Or does the computer only bring out a characteristic in a person that was there in the first place? What do you think?

SUMMARY POINTS

- Computers affect our lives in many ways. They help improve travel, assist in billing, and direct railroad cars. They help scientists forecast weather, study animals, and control pollution. They even affect the meanings of words in our language.

- Computers get most of their power from three features: speed, accuracy, and memory.

- Computers are useful in processing data electronically. Data are raw unorganized facts. Information consists of facts organized in a useful manner.

- All data processing follows the same flow: input, processing, output. Batch processing involves processing groups of data at different periods. Interactive processing allows a user to enter input during processing.

- Hardware is the physical components that make up a computer system. Peripheral devices support the computer system, but they are outside the main computer. A terminal is the point in a computer system at which data can enter or exit.

- Soft copy consists of data displayed on the computer's screen. It is temporary and does not last. Hard copy is output printed on paper.

- Software consists of a program or set of programs that make the computer do its work. The person who writes the programs is called a programmer.

CHAPTER TEST

Vocabulary

Match the number of the term in the left column with the correct definition in the right column.

1. Input   **a.** Raw facts that have not been organized.

2. Information   **b.** The step in the data processing flow in which data are collected and coded for computer use.

3. Retrieve   **c.** A person who writes a program.

4. Soft copy   **d.** Data displayed on a television-like screen; not a permanent record of output.

5. Programmer   **e.** The part of the computer that provides the ability to recall information.

6. Terminal   **f.** Data that have been organized and processed so they are meaningful and can be used to increase understanding or make decisions.

7. Output   **g.** Fetching stored information so that it can be examined.

8. Memory   **h.** The handling of data provided as input in order to produce information; includes calculating, classifying, sorting, summarizing, and storing.

9. Data   **i.** Information that comes from the computer as a result of processing.

10. Processing   **j.** A point in a computer system where data can enter or exit.

Questions

1. What is one way that computers are used to improve the safety of our travel?
2. If incorrect data is entered into a computer, the results may be incorrect but accurate. Explain why this is so.
3. What is the term that means processing data by computer?
4. What is the difference between data and information?
5. What basic flow does all data processing follow?
6. Which stage of data processing involves having the computer bring back information and put it into a form that the user can understand?
7. What type of processing allows the user to enter input while the processing is going on?
8. Name some examples of computer hardware.
9. Why are terminals called input/output devices?
10. What is the difference between hard copy and soft copy?

DISCUSSION QUESTIONS

1. Which words associated with computers do you already know? Find out what the word *jargon* means. Contrast some ordinary words that have new meanings in context with computers.
2. Discuss how owning a computer might affect your life. If you do own one, perhaps you can analyze any changes that have occurred in your behavior. Why do you think a computer changes behavior?
3. Have you ever heard your parents talk about mistakes the computer has made? Do you remember the circumstances? Discuss some real situations when "garbage in" might have resulted in "garbage out."

ACTIVITIES

1. Watch for articles on computers in magazines and newspapers. See how many you can collect in one week. Be sure to photocopy the article if the magazine or newspaper does not belong to you.
2. Use computer magazines. Locate pictures and product information about as many computer products for one brand of microcomputer as you can. The brand may be the computer that your family owns or your school uses for classroom purposes. Photocopy the material if the magazines are not yours.
3. Review computer magazines or other sources of information about computers. Be sure they are current, within the past year. Write a HIGHLIGHT on some interesting aspect of computers, computer use, or computer users that you found. The class can compile the highlights in booklet form and photocopy it. Try not to duplicate the ones found in the text. Possible sources are *Family Computing, Popular Computer, ENTER, InfoWorld*, or *Creative Computing*.

Chapter 2

Computers and Their Beginnings

Learning Objectives

After reading this chapter, you should be able to:

1. Explain how the need for faster, more reliable data processing and calculations led to the development of the computer.
2. Name the features of the first, second, third, and fourth generations of computers.

Introduction

Humans have always sought ways to figure, sort, compile, store, and control data. Ancient peoples tied knots in pieces of rope or laid out pebbles to keep an exact count of their belongings. Merchants once carved records on clay or stone tablets. Then came the abacus, a device made of beads on wires, which was used for addition and subtraction (see Figure 2-1). Slide rules, adding machines, journals, ledgers, and file cabinets helped our parents and grandparents perform calculating and record-keeping duties. All of these methods called for direct human action. What events led to automatic data processing?

The Pascaline

In the mid-1600s, Blaise Pascal, a French mathematician, invented an adding machine called the Pascaline. This machine was based on the decimal system (see Figure 2-2). Much like an odometer keeps track of a car's mileage, the Pascaline used a series of eight rotating gears, or notched wheels. Each wheel stood for one place—the ones place, tens place, hundreds place, and so

Figure 2-1. *The Abacus*

In the early 1600s, John Napier, a Scottish mathematician and clergyman, designed a portable multiplication table called Napier's Bones.

The device was made of ivory rods that looked like bones. You could slide these "bones" up and down against each other and match the numbers

printed on them to multiply and divide. Napier's idea led to the invention of the slide rule in the mid-1600s.

on. As the first wheel counted out ten digits (one complete turn), a pin on its edge would turn the next wheel, which stood for the number of tens. This second gear would rotate the next, and so on.

Unfortunately, a market for the Pascaline never grew. Only fifty Pascalines were built. Pascal was the only person who could repair his machine. Not only that—clerks and accountants wouldn't use the machine. They were afraid it might do away with their jobs!

Today we honor Pascal's role in computer history. The computer language, Pascal, was named after him.

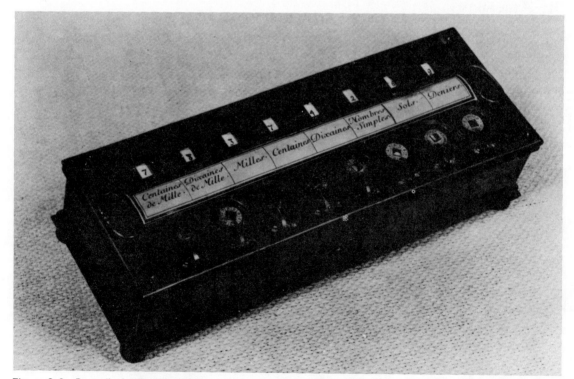

Figure 2-2. *Pascal's Adding Machine*

Figure 2-3. *Jacquard's Loom*

Blaise Pascal's machine would only add and subtract. The German mathematician Gottfried von Leibnitz improved Pascal's invention. He designed a model that would also multiply, divide, and figure square roots. Yet, both machines needed to be changed by hand for each different math operation.

The Punched-Card Concept

Jacquard's Loom

The first machine to be controlled by precoded directions was a loom. Loom operators had to constantly change the settings of their machines to make different woven patterns in fabric. The process was tiresome and time-consuming.

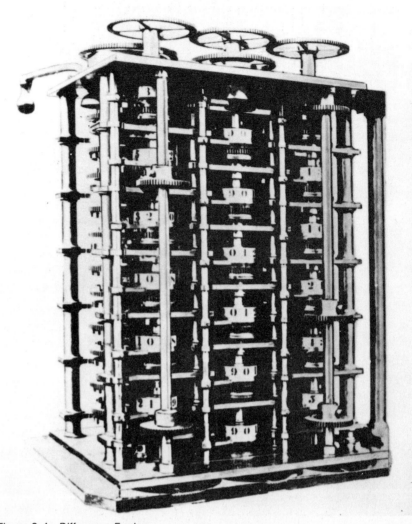

Figure 2-4. *Difference Engine*

Punched cards A
storage method in
which data is repre-
sented by the pre-
sence or absence
of holes.

In the late 1700s in France, Joseph Jacquard designed a loom
that could read sets of **punched cards**. The cards changed the
loom settings to create different patterns (see Figure 2-3). These
sets of punched card instructions were the forerunners of computer programs. They told the machine what to do without
changing the machine in any way.

Babbage's Analytical Engine

Charles Babbage, an English mathematician, was the first to plan
automatic calculating machines. He wanted his machines to build
tables showing the results of complex math operations quickly
and accurately. In 1822, Babbage built a working model of his
first idea, called the difference engine (see Figure 2-4). However,
he was unable to build a larger version. Parts for the larger
machine were too hard to make in Babbage's day. Even slight

Even before computers were invented, a woman became the first "programmer." She was Ada Augusta Byron, Countess of Lovelace and the daughter of the Romantic poet Lord Byron. She was also a genius in math. She began working with Charles Babbage in 1842, planning sets of coded card programs for his analytical engine and writing about his work. She added her own ideas, too.

One of the ideas introduced the loop. Certain instructions often repeated the same sequence of steps. Therefore, Lady Lovelace coded the program to loop back and repeat the steps when needed. This loop would decrease the number of directions that would have to be written. She also suggested to Babbage that he use the binary system of ones and zeros in his machine rather than the more common decimal system.

In honor of her work, a high-level programming language used chiefly by the U.S. government was named Ada.

---

flaws in the brass and pewter rods and gears threw the difference engine out of whack.

Babbage lost interest in this project when he began designing a new machine, the analytical engine. This steam-powered machine would have gotten its instructions and input through coded punched cards. It would have been able to add, subtract, multiply and divide. It also would have stored the results and printed them automatically.

Babbage died before he could construct a working model of the analytical engine. His son built a model of the machine. But the analytical engine was also too advanced for its time.

Because of his ideas, Babbage is known as "the father of computers."

Hollerith's Code

Dr. Herman Hollerith, a statistician, planned a new use for punched cards. He worked for the U.S. Census Bureau. Counting the 1880 census by hand had taken 7½ years. The population was even larger for the 1890 census, and the job looked impossible. So Hollerith invented a "tabulating machine" that would read and sort data from punched cards (see Figure 2-5). These Hollerith cards were forerunners of what almost everyone knows as the standard computer card. They were punched in a code known as the **Hollerith Code**. This code is still used today.

Using Hollerith's machines, the government finished the 1890 census in 2½ years, despite an increase of three million people.

Hollerith Code A method of data representation punched onto cards named for the man who invented it.

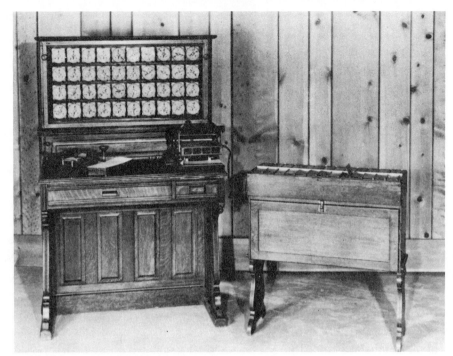

Figure 2-5. *Hollerith's "Census Machine"*

The new method took one-eighth the time of manual processes.

Hollerith's company, the Tabulating Machine Company, later became the International Business Machine Corporation (IBM).

Key-driven and hand-cranked adding machines were invented at this same time. During the late 1920s and early 1930s, more advanced accounting machines evolved. These machines could read from punched cards, keep records, and handle many other jobs. But the mechanical parts just worked too slowly to handle the growing loads of data.

LEARNING CHECK 2-1

1. What was the first machine to be controlled by precoded instructions? Who invented this machine?

2. Charles Babbage was called "the father of computers" because _____.
   a. his tabulating machine company became IBM
   b. his difference and analytical engines used the basic principles of modern computers
   c. his machine was the first to use punched cards
   d. he created the Pascaline

3. TRUE FALSE Hollerith's role in the 1890 census was to invent a tabulating machine that could sort and count data automatically from punched cards.

1. a loom, Joseph Jacquard 2. b 3. TRUE

Figure 2-6. *The Mark I Calculator*

The First Electronic Computers

Mark I

By 1944, a team headed by Howard Aiken at Harvard University produced the Mark I (see Figure 2-6). The machine was controlled by paper tapes and read data from punched cards. The Mark I consisted of seventy-eight accounting machines and contained 500 miles of wiring. It was three times as large as a living room and weighed five tons.

The Mark I was an automatic calculator, not a computer. It could multiply ten-place numbers in three seconds. Its mechanical parts made a loud, clacking noise. The U.S. Navy used it to figure data needed to design and fire weapons until the end of World War II. In many ways, the Mark I was like the analytical engine first drafted by Charles Babbage more than 100 years earlier.

The Atanasoff-Berry Computer

Several years before the Mark I was finished, John Vincent Atanasoff and his assistant, Clifford Berry, had built a true computer (see Figure 2-7). A professor of math at Iowa State University, Atanasoff needed a machine that would solve large, complex equations. Existing calculators were too slow and inaccurate.

Atanasoff's device, the Atanasoff-Berry Computer (ABC), was the first electronic digital computer. But for many years, other people got the credit for his ideas. Atanasoff was unable to sell or to patent his computer.

Figure 2-7. *The ABC Computer*

The ENIAC

World War II led to demands for machines that could keep track of war equipment and thousands of military men and women. Also needed were machines that would solve weaponry and decoding problems. In England, Alan Turing began work as early as 1939 on an electronic digital computer called Colossus and code-named ULTRA. This machine could decode secret German war messages churned out by Germany's mechanical encoder, Enigma. Many people believe ULTRA's power won the war for the Allies.

In Philadelphia, J. Presper Eckert, Jr., and John Mauchly built a computer based on Atanasoff's ideas. Backed by the U.S. Army and assisted secretly by Turing, the two men built the Electronic Numerical Integrator And Calculator, the ENIAC (see Figure 2-8).

The ENIAC was huge. It weighed thirty tons and covered as much floor space as half a tennis court. It could perform in three-thousandths of a second a problem that the Mark I could do in three seconds. The ENIAC was so fast that scientists thought just seven computers like it could handle all of the calculations the world would ever need.

ENIAC was built to compute at high speeds the complex numbers needed to aim and fire weapons accurately. But the war ended in 1945 before ENIAC was finished. The U.S. government used the computer to predict weather, study cosmic rays, and learn about atomic energy. It was the first electronic digital computer put to long-term, working use.

The ULTRA, the ABC computer, and the ENIAC all depended on electric currents rather than moving mechanical parts. Electric

Figure 2-8. *The ENIAC*

currents have only two states—"on" and "off." Thus, the **binary number system**, a system based only on the digits one and zero (on and off), was used to make these machines work. All numbers, letters, and characters must be coded in combinations of ones and zeros. This system, "the language of the computer," is called **machine language**. It is the only language a computer can directly understand and act upon.

Binary number system The numeric system that uses the digits 0 and 1 and has a base of 2.

Machine language A language based on combinations of 1s and 0s.

EDVAC

The ENIAC could not store instructions as modern computers can. Instead, it was programmed by setting many switches by hand. John von Neumann suggested writing step-by-step instructions in the on-off electronic code. Then the instructions could be stored in the computer's memory.

This **stored program** idea was used in the EDVAC (Electronic Discrete Variable Automatic Computer) in the late 1940s. Now one machine could do many tasks. With built-in instructions, a computer could easily switch to a different program. EDVAC and a similar English-built computer marked the start of the computer age.

Stored program Instructions kept in the computer's memory in electronic form.

🖐 LEARNING CHECK 2-2

1. What kind of machine was the Mark I?

2. Which two men working separately in the United States and England developed the first electronic digital computers?

a. Alan Turing and Howard Aiken
b. Howard Aiken and John Mauchly
c. John Atanasoff and J. Presper Eckert, Jr.
d. John Atanasoff and Alan Turing

3. The new idea used in EDVAC and a similar English computer was the _____ concept.

Family Trees: Generations of Computers

The First Generation: 1951-1958

Vacuum tube A fragile glass case that contains circuitry to control the flow of electricity.

First-generation computers were very large, expensive, and often undependable. **Vacuum tubes** controlled their electrical operations. Vacuum tubes are light bulb-like devices through which electricity can pass. They can be found in old radios and televisions.

The ENIAC contained more than 18,000 of these tubes. The masses of vacuum tubes took up a lot of space and gave off much heat. Special air conditioning had to be installed to cool the tubes.

Vacuum tubes could switch on and off thousands of times per second. But one tube would fail about every fifteen minutes. Time was wasted hunting for the burnt-out tube.

Figure 2-9. *A First-Generation Computer—The UNIVAC I*

Figure 2-10. *A Second-Generation Computer*

Although the first-generation computers were much faster than earlier devices, they were slow compared with today's computers. Their internal storage was limited. Yet for the first time, business firms saw how they could use computer data processing. One first-generation computer, the UNIVAC I (UNIVersal Automatic Computer), did business data processing (see Figure 2-9). The most popular uses for it were payroll and billing.

Before UNIVAC I, computers had been one-of-a-kind machines built for special scientific and military work. These uses earned for computers the nickname "number crunchers."

Writing programs for computers using the ones and zeros of machine language was time-consuming. During this period, the **symbolic language** was developed to make it easier to program the machines. The computers translated the symbols into machine language. Instructions and data were entered into these machines by way of punched cards.

Symbolic language Also called assembly language; consists of symbols that stand for words or ideas.

The Second Generation: 1959-1964

When the bulky, hot vacuum tubes were traded for tiny **transistors**, the technology race began. Transistors did the same job as vacuum tubes. They were much smaller, solid-state devices. Transistors were mounted close together and connected with tiny, flat wires on small cards called circuit boards.

With the use of transistors, the second-generation computers were smaller, faster, and more reliable than earlier models (see Figure 2-10). They needed less power to run, and their transistors gave off much less heat. The computers also had more storage space. They could store more data internally and send data to storage outside the main system. New English-like programming languages made programming easier.

Transistor A type of electronic component used to control the flow of electricity.

Figure 2-11. *A Third-Generation Computer*

The Third Generation: 1965-1971

Integrated circuit
Electronic circuits
etched on a silicon
chip.

Silicon chip Solid
state circuitry on a
piece of silicon, a
material found in
quartz and sand.

Remote terminal
A device used at
another location to
communicate with
the main computer.

Integrated circuits—electronic circuits etched on **silicon chips**—greatly reduced the size of transistors and other electronic parts in the 1960s. The compact circuits made third-generation computers smaller and more powerful. Less money bought more reliable, faster computing power. As many as 50 million additions could be done in one second on these computers.

During this period, the advances in electric circuits led to the development of **minicomputers** (see Figure 2-11). These computers had the same features of full-sized computers but on a smaller scale.

Another third-generation idea was the use of the **remote terminal**. A terminal at one place could send data for processing to the main computer at another location. Many users could use a central computer at the same time, receiving results almost instantly.

Families of computers were designed to support many jobs in an organization. IBM introduced the System/360 computers for all types of processing. The series could support forty different external devices.

The software industry began to emerge. Programs to do payroll, billing, and other business tasks became available at fairly low costs. Yet software was certainly not free of "bugs" or errors. Because of rapid growth during this period, skilled programmers were scarce. Programs did not always process data cor-

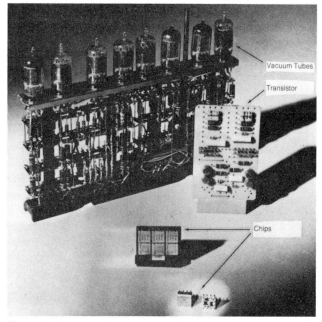

Figure 2-12. *Four Generations of Computer Components*

rectly. The computer industry had "growing pains" as the software industry lagged behind advances in hardware technology.

The Fourth Generation: 1972-?

Computers of the fourth generation offered better performance and prices. In these computers, the size of electronic parts was further reduced through **large-scale integration (LSI)** (see Figure 2-12). Thousands of transistors could fit on a single quarter-inch square of silicon. An entire computer's internal circuitry could be placed on one chip.

LSI technology led to the very small computer called a microcomputer. Some microcomputers are also called home computers or personal computers. It is this computer that you are most likely to use at home and in school.

The microcomputer's "brain" is the **microprocessor**, a chip that contains many closely packed circuits (see Figure 2-13). In third-generation computers, chips could only be used for one job. As engineers studied LSI, they made general-purpose chips called microprocessors. These chips did computing and the logic work of a computer. Besides being used in microcomputers, microprocessors control the functions of microwave ovens, sewing machines, thermostats, and automobiles.

Through **very large-scale integration (VLSI)**, even more circuits are placed on a chip. Imagine a map showing every street in Los Angeles on the head of a pin. Now you have an idea of how many circuits can be placed on a single silicon chip.

Large-scale integration (LSI) A method of packing circuits with thousands of transistors on a single silicon chip.

Microprocessor The "brain" or governing unit of a microcomputer.

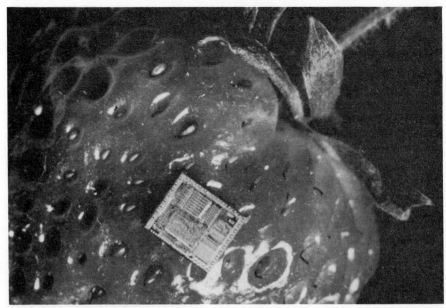

Figure 2-13. *A Bell Lab Microprocessor*

LEARNING CHECK 2-3

1. What made the first-generation computers work?

2. Second-generation computers were smaller than first-generation computers because they used _____.

3. The major feature of third-generation computers was
   a. VLSI
   b. symbolic language
   c. the use of integrated circuits
   d. the development of microcomputers

4. What made microcomputers possible?

1. vacuum tubes 2. transistors 3. c 4. large-scale integrated circuits

Perspective *Today's computers are very fast and reliable. They can store billions of characters (letters, numbers, and special symbols). Their chips rarely fail, perhaps once every 33 million hours of use. A single chip is far more powerful than the ENIAC of the 1940s.*

Computer manufacturers are stressing ease of use. They want their computers to be user-friendly. People can sit down at computers and, within a very short time, learn how to make them do many wonderful tasks.

The computers will calculate, compare, and sort facts. They will store and retrieve information. And they will simulate, or copy, real-life events. Yet they cannot perform any task without instructions from humans. They have IQs of zero.

Throughout the history of computers, only a very few women have made an impact in the field. Ada Augusta Byron, Countess of Lovelace, was known as "the first programmer" for her work in 1842 with Charles Babbage and his analytical engine. Navy Commodore Grace Murray Hopper was a leader in planning the first operational high-level language for business programs.

Today, many women work as programmers, including one mother/daughter team familiar to readers of computer magazines. The mother, Leslie Grimm, is a computer programmer for The Learning Company, which produces educational software. Her daughter, Cori, designs computer graphics.

Genevieve Cerf, an instructor in electrical engineering at Columbia University, believes women make better programmers than men do. She says women are more organized, more verbal, and more likely to keep the user in mind while writing programs.

Yet, educators are concerned that women are not entering the computer arena as readily as men are. In the past, men who worked with computers were engineers, scientists, and businessmen. Since women did not enter these professions often, they were not involved in the studies that led to advances in computer technology.

Women may avoid computers for several reasons. One stumbling block is the fear of math. Often, schools add computer studies to the math courses. Girls who have been led to dislike math may transfer that dislike to computers. Yet studies show that girls are very excited about computers, especially the word processing, graphics, and research aspects.

Another roadblock is that girls tend to gather with girls and boys tend to gather with boys, except when dating. Who often clusters around the computers in a classroom? The boys do. And the girls may be less bold about claiming a computer. One study noticed that while girls would wait their turn, boys would interrupt girls working at a computer by punching keys, making noises, and jiggling the chairs where the girls were sitting.

In addition, software packaging has been directed toward males. Boys and men appear on the package designs much more often than girls and women. Not only are the packages designed to attract males, but the programs are geared toward males. Attack-and-hit activities are common. Some studies show that boys like games with fast, violent, and noisy action, while girls prefer fantasies, word-oriented rewards, and completion tasks (where the object of the game is to finish something). The only arcade game that was equally popular with girls and boys is *PAC MAN*, a completion task game.

Women may find going into computer stores another barrier to learning about computers. In the past, computers and electronic parts were sold in electronics stores. The salesmen spoke "compu-terese," so women avoided the shops. Yet Karenn Jagoda, a computer saleswoman in Washington, D.C., has noticed that women ask smart questions about computers and take buying a computer very seriously.

Finally, parents may encourage their sons, but not their daughters, to play with computers. These parents may not even be aware of their attitude. But studies show that parents are more apt to buy computers for their sons and are more apt to send sons to computer camps. The girls that do go to camp attend less expensive, less advanced camps. After all, some people think that girls are not supposed to like computers and electronic gadgets.

But these trends are turning around. More girls are attending computer camps. Elementary-aged girls are doing more programming. Games and other software are being designed to appeal to girls. Parents are beginning to buy computers for their children, not only for their sons. Teachers are checking who uses the school computers, for what purpose, and for how long.

More parents and teachers are encouraging girls to take math, science, and computer courses.

Perhaps the computer field will no longer be dominated by men, as it has been in the past. Women should no longer avoid the field by giving in to popular beliefs.

SUMMARY POINTS

- Humans have always looked for ways to figure the answers to problems and keep track of the results. Devices that show this search include the abacus, Pascal's and Leibnitz's calculating machines, and Babbage's analytical engine.

- The weaving industry was the first to use a programmable machine, with punched cards to instruct looms. Hollerith later used this concept to process census data. He invented machines that could read data from punched cards.

- The Mark I was the first automatic calculator, while the ABC computer, ULTRA, and the ENIAC were the first true electronic computers.

- Von Neumann suggested storing instructions in computer memory by using electronic code, or machine language. The first two computers that used stored programs were EDVAC and a similar English computer.

- Electronic computers at first depended on vacuum tubes for their internal circuits. These first-generation computers were huge, slow, and unreliable. The development of transistors increased computer speed and reliability and decreased computer size. Transistors marked the second generation of computers.

- Etching of electronic circuits on silicon chips led to third- and fourth-generation computers. Today's computers rely on large-scale integrated circuits and offer improvements in size, speed, and reliability.

CHAPTER TEST

Vocabulary

Match the term from the numbered list with the description from the lettered list that best fits the term.

1. Machine language

a. Devices used at another geographical location to enter data and communicate with the main computer.

2. Remote terminals	**b.**	The number system, used in computer operations, that uses the digits zero and one and has a base of two.
3. Transistor	**c.**	The "brain" or governing unit of a microcomputer.
4. Hollerith code	**d.**	A method of data representation named for the man who invented it.
5. Integrated circuit	**e.**	The only set of instructions that a computer can run directly.
6. Punched cards	**f.**	Electronic circuits etched on a small silicon chip.
7. Binary number system	**g.**	A commonly used storage method in which data is represented by the presence or absence of holes.
8. Stored program	**h.**	A type of electronic component used to control the flow of electricity.
9. Symbolic language	**I.**	Also called assembly language.
10. Micro-processor	**J.**	Instructions stored in the computer's memory in electronic form.

Questions

1. Why were Babbage's machines ahead of their time?
2. What contributions did each of these men make toward the development of computers?
   a. Hollerith
   b. Atanasoff
   c. von Neumann
3. What is meant by a stored program?
4. What kinds of data processing needs led to the development of these machines?
   a. Hollerith's tabulating mechine
   b. Mark I
   c. ABC Computer
   d. ENIAC
5. Why has the development of large-scale integrated circuits had such a great impact on the computer industry?
6. What are the characteristics of each of the four generations of computers?

DISCUSSION QUESTIONS

1. Trace the development of punched cards throughout the history of the computer. Make a list of the developments in sequence.
2. List the data processing needs that each development fulfilled, judging from the material in the text.
3. Discuss some things that you think computers will be able to do in the future.

ACTIVITIES

1. Look in some arithmetic or math textbooks or other math sources. Find how to make a set of paper Napier's Bones. Make the set and learn how to use them.

2. Collect an abacus, slide rule, adding machine, calculator, and classroom computer. Make up some multiplication and division problems and try them on each instrument. What happened?

3. Draw a time line beginning with the year 1900. Enter important dates for your grandparents, parents, and your lives with birth dates, high school graduation, marriage, children, current time, and other important events. Now mark the computer developments from this text. Do extra research to mark the development of other important inventions, such as radio, television, and automobile.

Chapter 3

Hardware and Its Work

Learning Objectives

After reading this chapter, you should be able to:

1. Contrast digital and analog computers with respect to internal operations.

2. Distinguish between dedicated and general-purpose computers with respect to types of jobs performed.

3. Name the chief features of each of the four groups of computers discussed in the chapter.

4. Describe the functions of each part of the central processing unit.

5. Explain the difference between RAM, ROM, and registers.

6. Discuss how data are represented in the binary number system.

Introduction

Not all computers are alike. They range in size from very small, portable computers with limited storage to huge machines capable of storing millions of bits of data. Yet, while size, storage capacity, and power differ among computers, they do share some common features. All computers must be given data before processing can begin. And all computers must be able to output the results of processing so that people can understand them. In this chapter we discuss the types of computers and find out how they work.

Types of Computers

Computers function in different ways and do different types of jobs. Analog and digital computers differ in the way they measure and represent data. Dedicated and general-purpose computers differ in the types of jobs they do. The next section explains the differences between analog and digital computers and dedicated and general-purpose computers.

Analog and Digital Computers

If you have pumped gasoline into a can for your lawn mower, or if you have watched an odometer on your family's car, you have seen how an analog device works. When you pump gasoline, a device measures the amount and price of the gasoline. As more gasoline is pumped, the amount and price change on the display. As your car travels down the road, the increase in miles traveled is shown on the odometer. The rotation of the wheels is changed into numbers that show how many miles you have gone. An **analog computer** works in much the same way. It measures a continuous condition such as pressure, temperature, length, rotations, or flow.

A **digital computer**, on the other hand, works by on and off states in electric current. Just as a light goes on and off when you flick a light switch, a digital computer records the on and off states of groups of switches. In various combinations, these groups of switches stand for letters, numbers, and characters. In this book, our discussion is limited to digital computers.

Dedicated and General-Purpose Computers

You may have a microcomputer in your own home without knowing it. Microcomputers are not just the typewriter-and-television-like units you may see sitting on a desk. They may be **dedicated computers**. Dedicated computers each do one special job.

Some dedicated computers protect against intruders by using cameras and sensing devices. They automatically dial the police if a break-in occurs. Others monitor smoke detectors for fire prevention, control temperature for efficient energy use, or turn lights on and off when someone enters or leaves a room.

Appliances such as sewing machines, microwave ovens, and stereos may be controlled by dedicated computers. One product hooks into the telephone and stops unwanted calls. Your car may contain a dedicated computer to mix air and fuel or to control the firing of the spark plugs.

Even game computers are dedicated. They use only game cartridges and cannot handle word processing or financial packages. Families now realize that for just a little more money, they can buy personal computers that can do much more than play games. These personal, or **general-purpose computers** appear on desks, crowd the dinner table, and are tucked into study corners at home. They are general-purpose computers because they can do many things, depending on the software used.

Most larger computers are general-purpose machines, too. The next section describes the types of computer systems.

Computer Systems

The four groupings of computers are supercomputers, mainframes, minicomputers, and microcomputers. Although you will be working mainly with microcomputers, you should be able to describe features of the others.

Analog computer
A computer that measures continuous physical or electrical states.

Digital computer
A type of computer that operates by changing data to on or off states.

Dedicated computer A computer that has a special job determined by its hardware.

General-purpose computer A computer used for many applications.

Figure 3-1. *Supercomputers such as this CRAY-1 are the most expensive and powerful computers.*

Supercomputers

Supercomputer A
very powerful, fast,
and efficient com-
puter.

Supercomputers are the fastest and most efficient computers. Their prices range from $4 million to $15 million. Most companies cannot afford supercomputers, nor do they need the kind of power supercomputers provide. The CRAY 1 computer, built by Cray Research, Inc., is a supercomputer (see Figure 3-1). It weighs 10,500 pounds—twice as much as an IBM System/370 Model 168 (a large mainframe computer) and 400 times as much as an Apple II.

Figure 3-2. *Mainframe computers are less complex than supercomputers and are used by organizations that have large processing needs.*

Figure 3-3. *Minicomputers have the same features as mainframe computers, but have less storage.*

Supercomputers such as the CRAY 1 are used for figuring lengthy and complex math problems. Scientists in weather forecasting, aircraft design, and energy conservation use these computers. The federal government uses them for nuclear weapons research, cryptography (studying codes), and nuclear reactor safety analysis. Large oil companies may use supercomputers to improve production in oil fields. Digital Productions used a CRAY X-MP to create computer art for the movie *Starfighter*.

The giant computers may perform up to one billion computations per second. The CRAY-MP is packed with 240,000 silicon chips so that it can perform at these speeds. The circuitry in supercomputers is so densely packed and so fast that it must be kept cool with a liquid coolant to prevent parts from melting.

Mainframe Computers

Mainframe computers are smaller than supercomputers. They are less powerful and cost less. Mainframes are used chiefly by large businesses, hospitals, universities, and banks with large processing needs (see Figure 3-2).

A mainframe can process large amounts of data at high speeds. It can support many peripheral devices. Printers, remote terminals, and external storage devices are all peripherals.

A mainframe creates a fair amount of heat and cannot be plugged into a standard electrical outlet. It may rest on a special

Figure 3-4. *Today's microcomputers are much faster and store much more data than the room-sized ENIAC did in 1946.*

platform so that its wires and cables can be housed beneath it. These factors add to its cost. To use a mainframe, companies must have special electical wiring, cooling systems, and platforms.

Minicomputers

Minicomputers are much like mainframes but on a smaller scale. Minicomputers store less data and do not work as fast (see Figure 3-3). The prefix *"mini-"* comes from the word "minimal," which means least or smaller. Many uses of computer power do not need the vast amounts of power provided by mainframe computers. Often only a little computer power is needed. That is why minicomputers were developed.

Early minicomputers performed special tasks. These tasks included figuring equations for engineers; controlling heat, pressure, flow rates, and motor speeds of machines in factory settings; and adjusting mixtures of chemicals. Many of today's minicomputers are used in business. Payroll and accounting are two common uses. The smaller computers bring computer power to companies that neither need nor can afford mainframes.

Minicomputers can be plugged into standard electrical outlets. They often do not need special air conditioning and can be linked to each other from several locations. They do not use as much floor space as mainframes and do not need platforms.

Figure 3-5. *This woman uses a portable computer on a train.*

Microcomputers

Large-scale integration and microprocessors made microcomputers possible. Typical microcomputers store in memory 1,000 times what ENIAC did and process data 100 times faster. Yet, microcomputers do not have as much storage or speed as minicomputers.

Most computers used in homes are microcomputers. They are small enough to fit on a desk. They are powerful enough for jobs like word processing, financial planning, and games (see Figure 3-4). Some businesses and industries link microcomputers to their mainframe systems. Users can do small data-processing jobs without the mainframe or can link with the mainframe to get data from its memory.

A new portable computer, the Sharp PC-5000, contains a bubble memory! Today's computers store data in bit cells, which can be in on or off electrical states, located on silicon chips. A bubble memory device stores data as tiny bubbles of magnetism on a chip.

Bubble memory was invented in the 1970s by Andrew Bobeck of Bell Laboratories. Bubble memory devices are very fast and very small. A bubble memory module that is only slightly larger than a quarter can store 10,000 characters of data! But high costs prevent bubble memory from being widely used.

With the use of bubble memory in the Sharp portable computer, bubble memory may again compete against other devices. The makers of microcomputers may decide that bubble memory will help sell their products.

Microcomputers may be small, but they are still awkward to carry. An even more recent phase in computer technology has brought about portable "lap" computers. Many are small enough to put in a briefcase (see Figure 3-5). The portables weigh from nine to twenty-eight pounds. They use flat screens instead of the usual rounded, television-like screens. The lighting in a room can make a flat screen hard to read. Once problems with the flat screens are solved, the flat screens may replace the current rounded screens.

As changes continue, the differences between the groups of computers become less distinct. Advanced microcomputers can do what the less powerful minicomputers can do. The more powerful minicomputers overlap the capabilities of the less powerful mainframes.

⟩ LEARNING CHECK 3-1

1. An analog computer measures a(n) _____,such as pressure, temperature, or flow.

2. What type of computer does only one special job?

3. Which of the following statements is not true about mainframe computers?
   a. They are smaller and less powerful than supercomputers.
   b. They cannot be plugged into standard electrical outlets.
   c. They do not need special air-conditioning systems.
   d. They rest on a special platform so wires and cables may be housed under the computer.

4. The development of _____ made microcomputers possible.

5. TRUE FALSE There is a clear difference between the groups of computers.

The Central Processing Unit

Every computer system has basic components. They include the central processing unit, the input devices, and the output devices. Input and output devices are discussed in chapter 4.

The **central processing unit (CPU)** processes data. It is the "brain" of the system. The CPU has three parts: the **control unit**, the **arithmetic/logic unit (ALU)**, and the **primary storage unit** (see Figure 3-6). Each unit performs its own unique functions. The CPU also has storage locations called registers. Often the CPU is placed on the piece of hardware known as the microprocessor.

Control Unit

The control unit is the boss of the computer. It controls what happens in the CPU. It does not process or store data. It directs the order of operations. The control unit retrieves one instruction at a time from the storage unit. It interprets the instruction and sends signals to the ALU and storage unit for the instruction to be done.

Central processing unit (CPU) The brain of the computer.

Control unit The section of the CPU that governs the actions of the computer.

Arithmetic/logic unit (ALU) The section of the CPU that handles arithmetic calculations and logical comparisons.

Primary storage unit A section of the CPU that holds instructions and data during processing.

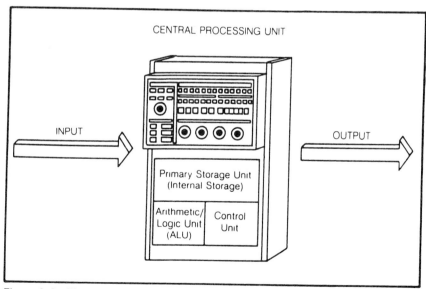

Figure 3-6. *The CPU consists of three units.*

Bit short for BInary
digiT; a zero or one
for off or on electri-
cal impulses.

Byte A group of
bits, generally eight,
that operates as a
unit.

The control unit repeats the process until all instructions have been completed and the data is processed.

The numbers, letters, and characters of the instructions and data are stored one **bit** at a time in bit cells (bit for BInary digiT.) Tiny circuits etched on silicon chips contain bit or storage cells that are electrically charged. Each cell is either on or off. The "on" state stands for a one and the "off" state stands for a zero. The control unit of the CPU "reads" memory by testing the electrical contents of each cell, or bit. A bit is the smallest unit of information a computer handles. A group of eight bits next to each other is called a **byte**.

The control unit also communicates with input and output devices and transfers instructions and data into and out of storage.

Arithmetic/Logic Unit

The arithmetic/logic unit (ALU) handles calculations. It does not store data. Calculations include arithmetic operations (addition, subtraction, multiplication, and division) and logic operations. Logic operations are comparisons such as greater than, less than, and equal to. Since most internal processing involves figuring and comparing, the power of a computer often depends on the design of its ALU.

Primary Memory

Primary memory (main storage, primary storage, or internal storage) holds all instructions and data needed for processing. Any intermediate and final results in calculations are stored there, too. After all of the data have been processed, the results stay in memory until the control unit causes them to be erased. This normally occurs after the results are sent to some output device or storage medium.

To locate data or to use instructions, the control unit (or CPU) must be able to find them in storage. Therefore, each area in storage is assigned an address. A simple way to understand this idea is to picture computer storage as a large group of mailboxes. Each can hold one item of information. Since each place has its own address, the computer can find items by using stored-program instructions that give the address.

Although primary storage can be located on a microprocessor chip, it also comes on other chips. The major kinds of primary storage are random-access memory (RAM) and read-only memory (ROM).

When you were little, you probably scuffled along the carpet to build up static electricity. Then you zapped somebody! Ten steps on a nylon rug can build up 10,000 to 20,000 volts of static electricity in your body. If you discharge the static electricity near a computer, you could destroy a microprocessor chip! Even a low-voltage discharge that humans do not feel can cause blips, glitches, and gremlins in microchips!

Static can be sent to a computer in two ways. Contact charging occurs when a person touches the computer, or perhaps the keyboard. Induction charging comes from electric fields radiating from items such as clothing or polyethelene bags. Some common sources of static electricity are waxed, painted, or varnished surfaces; vinyl tile floorings; synthetic garments; styrofoam; copying machines; spray cleaners; and plastic-covered chairs and desks. A shirt sleeve, for example, can produce enough static electricity to destroy some kinds of memory chips.

Static can be reduced by keeping room humidity at 50 percent or higher. You can also use anti-static mats or sprays. And before you sit at your computer, ground yourself by touching a metal object—a metal part on a chair, a pipe, even a doorknob. Anything that gives you a zap will ground you—and help protect your computer system!

RAM

Random-access memory (RAM) is memory into which data or instructions can be stored, or from which data can be retrieved easily and in any order. This process is called writing to and reading from memory. RAM is the working area of the computer. To begin work, data and programs are written into RAM. Usually, the data in RAM memory come from a program that is input by the user. The program can be read from many times, or it can be changed. When the power is shut off, RAM memory is erased from the computer.

Random-access memory (RAM) Storage that allows data to be quickly stored or accessed.

ROM

Another kind of memory is **read-only memory (ROM)**. ROM cannot be changed. The on and off states in ROM always remain the same, so the current always travels the same path. Because of this feature, ROM is called hard-wired memory. The only way to change ROM's contents is to rebuild the circuitry. ROM remains intact even after the power to the computer is turned off.

ROM usually contains instructions for the basic operations of the computer. Directions like how to figure math problems or how to send data to peripherals are part of ROM. These built-in directions are fast and accurate. Some companies are building

Read-only memory (ROM) Program circuitry that is hard-wired into the computer.

software (programs that often come on disks or tapes) into ROM chips. This practice will help to prevent illegal copying of software because ROM cannot be accessed or changed.

Think of RAM and ROM in terms of your own memory. If your central nervous system is working correctly, the "ROM" of your brain tells your body how to breathe, digest food, walk, blink, and so forth. You do not have to tell your brain to do this. On the other hand, if you are taking a test, you may access RAM. You may want to pull out of storage the new material you learned. As time goes on, facts stored in "RAM" may disappear!

While you are studying for a test, you may think your brain cannot hold one more fact. But your brain really will remember more facts because it does not have defined limits. The main memory of a computer has limits. The amount of memory in a computer is expressed in **kilobytes** (K). One K of storage consists of 1,024 bytes. Usually this is rounded to 1,000 bytes. Thus, a microcomputer that contains 64K holds 64,000 (really 65,536) bytes of data. In very large computers, a megabyte is used to measure storage. A megabyte is one million bytes.

The amount of RAM and ROM memory, as well as any other primary storage, makes up the total K a computer has. Sometimes extra RAM or ROM chips can be added to a computer to increase storage.

Registers

Register A temporary storage area located in the CPU.

The CPU also contains special storage areas that act as high-speed "loading zones." These areas are called **registers**. They are not part of primary storage. The contents of registers can be located and retrieved much faster than the contents of primary storage. Just before processing, data and program instructions are loaded into these locations.

There are several kinds of registers. They include the instruction register, the address register, the storage register, and the accumulator. The instruction register contains the instruction that is to be processed next. It is decoded by the control unit. The address register holds the address of the data that is needed. The storage register temporarily holds information being sent to or taken from the primary storage unit. The accumulator stores the results of ongoing arithmetic operations. For instance, results of subtotals are accumulated into this register.

W LEARNING CHECK 3-2

1. TRUE   FALSE   The part of the CPU that directs the order of operations is the arithmetic/logic unit.

2. What is a bit cell?

3. Another name for read/only memory is _____.

Data Representation

We have discussed how the computer can understand only two states: on and off. This means that every piece of data must be entered in some form of on and off states. The number system that allows for only two states or digits is the binary number system. The decimal system is based on groups of tens. The binary system is based on groups of twos.

Let's review how the decimal system works first. Each digit place in the decimal system (the ones, the tens, the hundreds, and so on) stands for a power of ten. As we move to the left, the powers of ten get larger, as shown below:

10^4	10^3	10^2	10^1	10^0
10,000	1,000	100	10	1

The decimal number 316 can be taken apart as follows:

$$
\begin{array}{l}
316 \\
\quad \text{base 10} \\
\quad 6 \times 10^0 = 6 \times 1 = 6 \quad\quad \text{or} \quad 3 \quad 1 \quad 6 \\
\quad 1 \times 10^1 = 1 \times 10 = 10 \\
\quad 3 \times 10^2 = 3 \times 100 = \underline{300} \quad\quad\quad 10^2 \ 10^1 \ 10^0 \\
\quad\quad\quad\quad\quad\quad\quad\quad\quad\quad\quad 316
\end{array}
$$

In **binary representation**, the same idea is true, but each position in the number stands for a power of two. Shown below are the positions and powers of the binary number system:

Binary representation A method of using 0s and 1s to represent off and on electrical states in a digital computer.

2^7	2^6	2^5	2^4	2^3	2^2	2^1	2^0
128	64	32	16	8	4	2	1

The value of the decimal number 14 is shown in binary notation on the next page:

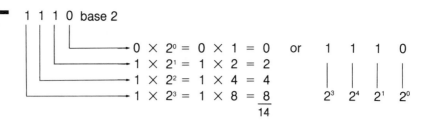

$$1 \times 2^3 = 1 \times 8 = \underline{8}$$
$$14$$

Now consider again the decimal number 316. The binary equivalent is:

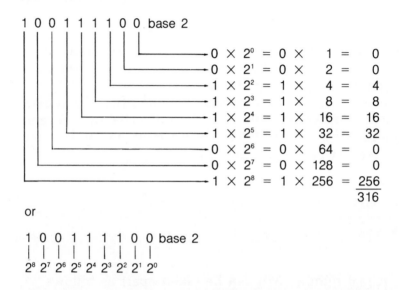

or

But how does this fit in with computers? Each digit position in a binary number is called a bit (short for BInary digiT). A 1 in a bit position indicates the presence of a power of two. A 0 in a bit position shows the absence of a power.

A computer reads these bits, or ons and offs, in groups. Sometimes bits are grouped in fours and sometimes in eights, called bytes. If your microcomputer is called an 8-bit computer, that means it can handle 8 bits, or one byte, at a time. If your computer is a 16-bit computer, it can handle 16 bits at a time. Larger computers deal with 32 or 64 or 128 bits at a time. Of course, the larger the amount of data handled at one time, the faster the computer!

A byte of data can stand for a number, a letter, or a character. In one system of computer coding, for instance, A is 1100 0001, B is 1100 0010, C is 1100 0011, and so forth.

Just think how time-consuming and confusing it would be if you had to use hundreds of 1s and 0s to talk with your computer!

 LEARNING CHECK 3-3

1. What two electrical states exist in a computer's circuits?

2. The number system that matches the two states in a computer's circuitry is called the _____.

3. Convert these binary values to decimal numbers:
   a. 10010100
   b. 11111
   c. 1001101

4. TRUE   FALSE   The number forty-six in the decimal number system can be changed to the binary number 101110.

Perspective   *Powerful supercomputers work at phenomenal speeds and perform functions that need huge amounts of memory. They are used by scientists and the government for solving complex math problems. But they are just tools. Their mind-boggling power remains in the control of human beings. Human beings decide what goes into a computer and what comes out. Human beings decide what devices are used to enter and retrieve data. Human beings decide how computers are used.*

ISSUE/WHO WILL WIN THE RACE FOR SUPERCOMPUTER TECHNOLOGY?

Supercomputers are used for very large data-processing jobs. Up to this time, the United States has been the only nation to build and sell supercomputers. But now the Japanese have promised to build supercomputers that will outdo supercomputers built by the United States.

The market for supercomputers is small, but there are other reasons for the United States to maintain its lead in supercomputer technology. First, supercomputer research has given the United States the lead in overall computer technology. Some of the ideas used in building supercomputers have been carried out in other computers. Second, supercomputers are very useful in studying aerospace, semiconductors, and oil. And third, supercomputers are very important in national defense. They are used in nuclear weapons research.

The Japanese are working hard to produce their own supercomputers. They plan to build supercomputers that will use many of the same programs used in mainframe models like those built by International Business Machines Corporation (IBM). This could mean more customers for the Japanese computers. Companies can buy more powerful computers without having to rewrite all of their programs to match the circuitry of supercomputers. The Japanese also plan to decrease the costs and increase the speeds of supercomputers.

Speeds in supercomputers are measured in megaflops. One megaflop equals one million "floating-point operations" (a kind of math calculation) per second. A current model produced by Cray Research, Inc., will work at 300 megaflops. The Japanese hope to built super-computers that will work at speeds of 10,000 mega-flops by 1990. Yet ETA Systems Inc. says its computer will run at 30,000 megaflops by 1990.

To compete, U.S. companies must develop computers with greater speeds. They must come up with new designs. They must also be able to make many (perhaps as many as sixty-four) supercomputers work together to solve a problem. Can these companies stay ahead of Japan? U.S. companies believe they can. They say they have more experience and more success in testing. They just want to be sure they have 30,000 megaflops by 1990, not millions of dollars worth of superflops!

SUMMARY POINTS

- Analog computers measure a continuous state, such as temperature, pressure, length, rotations, or flow. Digital computers run by on and off electrical states.

- Four types of digital computers are supercomputers, mainframes, minicomputers, and micro-computers. The differences are mainly in speed and storage.

- The central processing unit (CPU) has three parts—the control unit, the arithmetic/logic unit, and the primary storage unit. The control unit maintains order and controls the operations of the computer; the arithmetic/logic unit performs calculations and comparisons; and the primary storage unit stores instructions and data during processing.

- RAM is random-access memory. It is memory in which data can be stored or from which data can be retrieved easily and in any order. ROM is read-only memory. ROM is hard-wired so that the instructions stored there cannot be changed or accessed.

- Since computers operate by the electrical states of on and off, the binary number system is used for data representation. The binary number system has two digits, one and zero, for on and off, respectively. Each digit position in binary notation is called a bit, for BInary digiT. A bit is the smallest amount of data a computer can store. The computer stores bits in bit cells. Eight of these bits are a byte.

CHAPTER TEST

Vocabulary

Match the term from the numbered column with a description from the lettered column that best fits the term.

1. Digital computer	**a.**	A temporary holding area located inside the CPU and used for holding data or instructions; material held there can be processed very quickly.
2. Primary storage	**b.**	An extremely powerful computer; very fast and very efficient; often used for scientific applications.
3. Super-computer	**c.**	Storage that allows data to be quickly stored or accessed.
4. Bit	**d.**	The smallest unit of information that a computer handles.

5. Read-only memory (ROM)	**e.**	The CPU of a microcomputer; fits on a silicon chip.
6. Micropro-cessor unit.	**f.**	A group of bits that operates as a unit.
7. Byte	**g.**	A type of computer that measures continuous physical or electrical conditions, such as flow, temperature, or pressure.
8. Central Pro-cessing Unit (CPU)	**h.**	A section of the central processing unit that holds instructions, data, and intermediate and final results during processing.
9. Register	**i.**	The "brain" of the computer, composed of three sections—the control unit, arithmetic/logic unit, and primary storage.
10. Random-access	**j.**	The part of computer hardware in which the circuits are hard-wired.

Questions

1. What are the three parts of the central processing unit and what does each do?
2. What is the difference between RAM and ROM?
3. Why does the binary number system work well with digital computers?
4. Change these binary values to decimal numbers.
   a. 100001
   b. 1100100
   c. 110
5. Change these decimal numbers into binary code.
   a. 16
   b. 892
   c. 103

DISCUSSION QUESTIONS

1. Can you think of some ways that dedicated computers affect your everyday life? Are they used in your home, school, or family car?
2. Do you think the race against the Japanese to develop supercomputer technology is really important for the United States to win? Why?
3. If you could have any type of computer from one of the four groups discussed in the chapter, what would it be? What would you do with it?

ACTIVITIES

1. Practice changing numbers from the decimal number system to the binary number system and vice versa.
2. Draw a diagram showing the flow of an instruction as it travels through the central processing unit.
3. Visit a computer store and look at some of the latest models of portable computers.

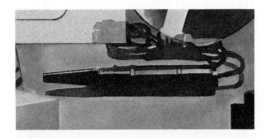

Chapter 4

Communication and Its Tools

Learning Objectives

After reading this chapter, you should be able to:

1. Describe how the computer communicates with its parts.

2. Explain where the computer gets data and instructions that are not in primary storage.

3. Describe how the user can enter data and receive information from the computer.

4. Discuss how the user can get data and information from sources outside the immediate computer system.

Introduction

The microprocessor, the "brain" of the microcomputer system, would be just like a human brain if it were kept outside the body. It would have no "body" to control, no way to communicate, and no way to receive data from the outside. It would just sit alone and collect dust.

If the computer is to work, it must have devices for data to be input and output. It must also have ways of storing instructions and data outside the primary storage area. Finally, it must have electrical hookups for all its parts.

Bus

Some of you may travel to school on a bus. Data and instructions in a computer travel by **bus**. A bus carries data between the parts of the CPU and input/output devices. Bus is the term given to all the wires and cables that connect the parts of the computer.

Microcomputer owners can often buy add-on busses for their computers. Extra busses allow owners to connect more peripherals, such as printers, disk drives, or film projectors to the computer.

Bus The term given to the wires and cables that connect the parts of the computer.

Secondary Storage

Data and special instructions are often located in secondary storage. **Secondary storage** is storage outside the main computer. The most common types of secondary storage are magnetic tapes and disks. These secondary storage media cost much less than primary storage. Data placed in secondary storage can be accessed as needed for processing. However, getting data from secondary storage is much slower than from primary storage. Data can also be written onto these tapes and disks.

Secondary storage Storage outside the main computer or CPU.

Figure 4-1. *Magnetic tapes are being loaded on tape drives.*

Magnetic Tape

A **magnetic tape** is a plastic strip wound on a reel, like the tape used in reel-to-reel tape recorders. The plastic base of the tape is treated with a magnetizable coating. Data are stored on the tape by magnetizing small spots on its surface. Large volumes of data can be stored on a single tape because the data can be stored compactly.

To read the tape, the reel is mounted on a **tape drive** (see Figure 4-1). The drive moves the tape past a **read/write head** that detects the magnetic spots (see Figure 4-2). Pulses are sent from the head to the computer. The computer translates the pulses into data. To write to the tape, the head magnetizes spots. Any data already stored in the magnetic area are erased.

Magnetic tape cassettes were designed to use with small computer systems. The tapes are run on cassette recorders like the

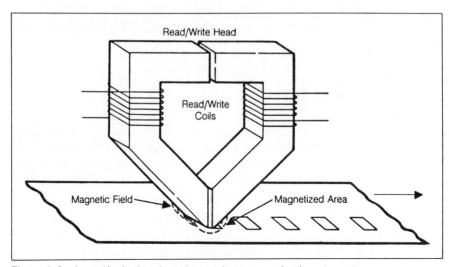

Figure 4-2. *A read/write head reads or writes magnetized spots on tape.*

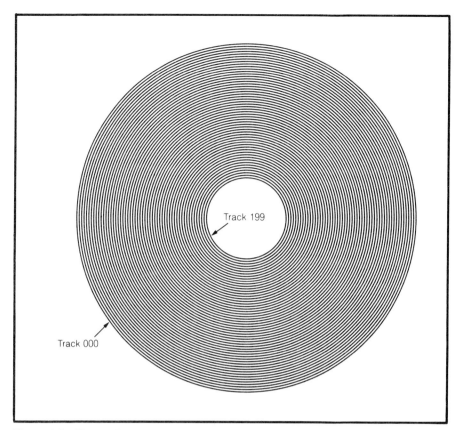

Figure 4-3. *The tracks on a disk never touch each other.*

recorders used in audio recording. The tapes used for storing data are of higher quality and density than those used in sound recording.

Magnetic tapes provide **sequential access storage**. For the computer to find data on a tape, it must read through the tape from the beginning until it finds the proper data or instructions. A lot of time can be wasted in this process.

Sequential-access storage Secondary storage from which data are read in order until the needed data are found.

Magnetic Disk

A **magnetic disk** is a platter similar to a record. It is coated with a magnetizable material. Data are stored by magnetizing spots on the disk's surface. Phonograph records have grooves. Disks for computers have tracks. These tracks cannot be seen. They are just paths that the recorded data follow (see Figure 4-3).

A **disk drive** rotates the magnetic disks, and a read/write head reads the data. The head will move across the disk until it finds the right track for the data. The drive rotates the disk until the data are found on the track. In this fashion, the computer can locate the data directly without searching through the whole disk. Therefore, the disks are a form of **direct-access storage**.

Disks for larger computers are metal. They are coated on both

Direct-access storage A method of storing data so they can be retrieved in any order.

Figure 4-4. *A disk pack stores hard disks on a rigid spindle.*

sides with material that can be magnetized. Several disks are combined to form a disk pack (see Figure 4-4). A center shaft connects the disks. They are rotated and read at the same time. Special arms hold the read/write heads.

Microcomputers use flexible, or floppy, disks. They are made of plastic and are enclosed in a jacket that protects the disk (see Figure 4-5). They are coated with magnetizable material. Some disks are coated on both sides.

Cartridges

Cartridges are mainly used for video games. They simply plug in, much as an eight-track tape is inserted into a tape player. Cartridges can contain random-access memory (RAM) and read-only memory (ROM). Game cartridges use ROM to protect the game from damage.

Laser Disks

Laser disks need concentrated beams of light to store data. The beam makes marks on the thin layer of metal or polymer (a synthetic substance) that coats the disks. These marks are read by a computer.

Laser disks hold much more data than magnetic disks hold. They also resist the wear, fingerprints, and dust that can harm magnetic disks. The disks are read in an optical disk drive by laser beams.

Figure 4-5. *Floppy disks in two sizes are enclosed in protective jackets.*

When pictures are stored on laser disks, they are called videodisks. Images stored on videodisks are high quality. Combined with microcomputers, the disks are used in education. Programs for hearing-impaired children contain better pictures. A set of programs called LaserSoft is used much like a video encyclopedia in some schools. LaserSoft is not just a movie. With the program, students can ask the computer questions as well as answer questions.

The state of Alaska's Department of Public Safety has fingerprint files stored on optical disks. In less than five minutes, 2,750 prints can be checked. All images are as clear as fingerprints stored on cards.

Most laser disk microcomputer programs are in a read-only form. Advances in technology will soon offer laser disks that can be written to and erased.

 LEARNING CHECK 4-1

1. What job does the "bus" do for a computer system?

2. Name four kinds of secondary storage. Why are they secondary storage?

3. Sequential access is
   a. a storage medium that can be accessed only by reading from the beginning of the storage medium to the place where data are stored
   b. faster than direct-access storage
   c. used mainly with disk storage
   d. used chiefly with disk packs

1. provide a pathway on which data can travel 2. magnetic tape, magnetic disk, cartridges, and laser disk; they are outside the main computer 3. a

Figure 4-6. *The visual display terminal consists of a screen (cathode ray tube) and keyboard.*

Input Devices

Visual display terminal (VDT) A terminal that displays data on a television-like screen (CRT).

To communicate with the computer, you must use an input or output device. **Visual display terminals (VDTs)** with keyboards are common input devices (see Figure 4-6). Keyboards allow users to "key in" data, requests, or instructions. Most keyboards have keys that you press just as you would the keys on a regular typewriter. Some keyboards are membrane keyboards. They have flat, pressure-sensitive surfaces with areas that respond to touching rather than to striking (see Figure 4-7). The output appears on a **cathode ray tube** (CRT) or monitor.

There are many other input and output devices. We discuss input devices first.

Card Reader

The oldest way to enter data into a computer system is by punched card. The standard punched card has 80 vertical columns and 12 horizontal rows (see Figure 4-8). One data character can be stored in each column by punching a set of holes. The pattern of holes used to code characters is called the Hollerith code, after Herman Hollerith. At the very top of the card, the data are shown as letters and numbers.

Figure 4-7. *The computer used with this public telephone has a membrane keyboard.*

Data are recorded on punched cards with the use of a keypunch. An operator presses keys on a keyboard that is similar to a typewriter. The proper holes are punched into the card. The devices that read the holes are called card readers. Some card readers "sense" the data when little metal brushes pass over the holes. Others use a light source.

Today, punched cards are used for things like time cards, utility bills, and government checks. Cards are inexpensive, but they are bulky to store and can be damaged easily ("Do not fold, bend, or spindle.").

Key-to-Magnetic Devices

Magnetic tapes and disks provide secondary storage that takes up much less space and is faster to access than are punched cards. Data on tapes or disks can also be changed or replaced.

A key-to-tape device is used to store data on magnetic tape. The name suggests that the operator is "keying data to the tape."

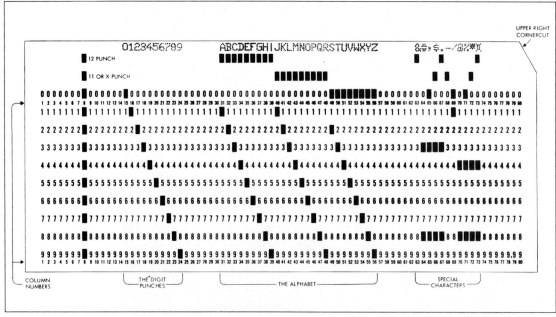

Figure 4-8. *An 80-column punched card is arranged to code digits, letters, and special characters.*

When data are stored on a disk, a key-to-disk device is used. Data are entered directly onto the disk or the tape.

Source-Data Automation

Data can be processed electronically at high speeds. More time is required to prepare and enter data into a computer system than to process it. Many times data must be sent from a source, such as a sales receipt, to the computer. The extra steps can be time-consuming and costly.

Source-data automation is more efficient. Source-data automation collects data about an event in computer-readable form when and where the event takes place. It improves the speed, accuracy, and efficiency of data processing. It does away with the paperwork.

Each method of source-data automation requires special machines. The machines read data and change them into machine-readable form. Common methods are magnetic-ink character recognition, optical recognition, and voice recognition.

Magnetic-Ink Character Recognition Magnetic ink helps the banking industry process checks. The magnetic-ink characters are read by both humans and machines. Data such as the bank number, the account number, and the check amount are printed in magnetic ink on the bottom of the check. The characters

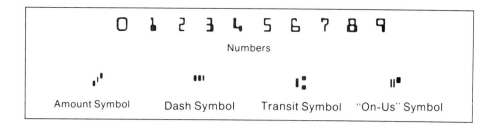

Numbers

Amount Symbol   Dash Symbol   Transit Symbol   "On-Us" Symbol

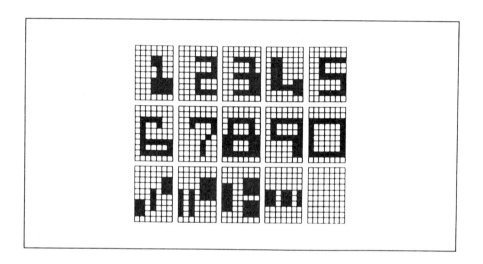

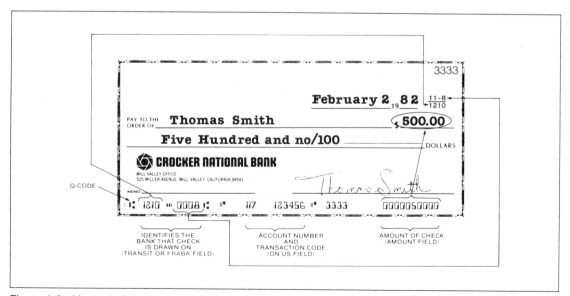

Figure 4-9. *Magnetic ink characters are used to identify checks.*

Name _____ Student No. _____

Subject _____ Teacher _____

Date _____ Hour _____

Scores	
Part 1	
Part 2	
Type	

Directions:
Use a No. 2 pencil to fill in completely the lettered box corresponding to your answer. For example, if you believe the correct answer relates to box c, fill in box c as follows:
Example: ⟨a⟩ ⟨b⟩ ■ ⟨d⟩ ⟨e⟩
To change your answer, erase completely and re-mark.

Error →

Do not mark in this shaded area. It is reserved for the error-indicating function of the Test Scorer.

Rescore

Visual Products Division/3M
© MINNESOTA MINING and MANUFACTURING CO. 1975
U.S. PATENT NO. 3,516,440. PATENTED IN CANADA, 1971
MADE IN ACCORDANCE WITH U.S. PATENT NO. 3,806,408.
PATENTED IN CANADA, 1974.   PRINTED IN U.S.A.

Number Correct   L-2S

Feed ⟶

Figure 4-10. *When answers are marked with a No. 2 pencil on this answer sheet, an optical mark reader will interpret the marks.*

appear in a special pattern. When the check is processed through a magnetic ink character reader, the magnetic characters are read. This is called magnetic-ink character recognition (MICR) (see Figure 4-9).

Optical Recognition Optical recognition devices can read marks or symbols coded on paper and change them to electrical pulses

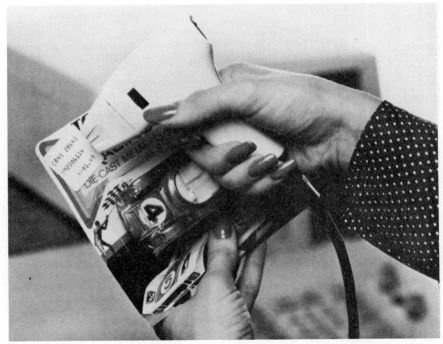

Figure 4-11. *Using a hand-held scanner makes data entry easier and more accurate at a retail store.*

How do you know that the pair of Levi jeans you bought are really Levis? What about other designer clothing or records or tapes? How can you be sure that the items you buy are not counterfeits?

Billions of dollars of counterfeit products are sold each year to customers who think they are buying the real thing. One way companies can beat the counterfeiters is to call Light Signatures, Inc., in Los Angeles. This company "fingerprints" products with a high-intensity light beam and a computer. Invisible codes are imprinted in a product's label. No two imprints are exactly alike. The system can code 100,000 labels per hour. A record of all the imprints is kept by computer.

If a manufacturer suspects that a store is selling counterfeit products, they can buy samples and test them through this computer system. Levi Strauss and Chrysalis Records are using this system.

It's not nice to fool the computer!

for the computer. The simplest approach is optical mark recognition (OMR). OMR is often used for machine scoring of exams (see Figure 4-10). The computer reads the pencil marks as they pass under a light. The presence of marks in certain places indicates right or wrong answers.

A bar-code reader reads lines or bars that stand for data. The bars vary in width. Grocery items contain bars in a code called the Universal Product Code (UPC). The UPC and other product codes are read by fixed scanners or hand-held wands at point-of-sale terminals (see Figure 4-11).

Optical-character recognition (OCR) devices read the shapes of characters (see Figure 4-12). Even though OCR devices can recognize several shapes, handwritten shapes must follow a certain pattern. Some OCRs are used along with a machine that will "speak." The system scans the printed text and reads it aloud.

ABCDEFGHIJKLMN
OPQRSTUVWXYZ,.
$/*-1234567890

Figure 4-12. *Characters to be read by optical character recognition must be uniform.*

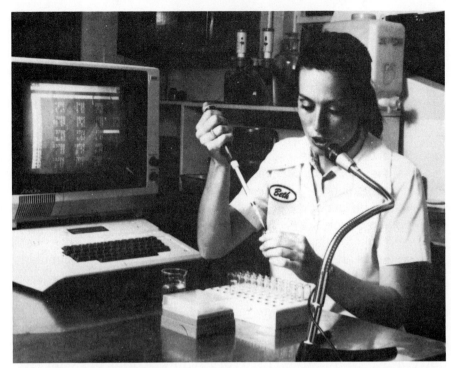

Figure 4-13. *This lab technician uses a voice recognition system to enter data. Her hands are free for other tasks.*

Voice Recognition   A **voice recognition system** is an input method in which the computer recognizes spoken words. The computer must be "trained" to know your voice and also the words you will be speaking. Voice recognition works best with short-answer data. So far, the computer recognizes only limited patterns.

The system is faster than entering data by hand, but it has its limits. The computer may interpret one word as some other word. This can ruin a message! Also, the computer may fail to recognize a word that was entered into its "vocabulary."

A pilot may use voice recognition to change radio frequencies. In a business or manufacturing process, workers can use voice recognition to enter data while using their hands to do other jobs (see Figure 4-13).

Remote Terminals   The source, in source-data automation, is usually in another place away from the central computer. It is remote. Devices that collect data at their source and send them to a central computer for processing are called remote terminals. These devices are **on-line** because they are in direct communication with the computer. Generally, data travels by some form of telecommunication equipment.

Some remote terminals are called **dumb terminals** because they cannot be programmed. Their jobs are preset. Point-of-sale terminals are dumb terminals. They capture sales data and act like

On-line In direct communication with the computer.

Dumb terminals Terminals that cannot be programmed.

Keyboard, you're being displaced! Make way for the new electronic gadgets! Today's technology allows data to be entered into a computer with a blink of an eye, a twitch of a forehead.

Of course video enthusiasts can have fun with games that let them control objects on the screen with a muscle twitch here and there. One such device is *Mindlink*, designed by Atari. A headband that fits over your forehead picks up muscle movements and sends the signals to a receiver located in the computer or video game console.

Similar equipment enables handicapped people to control their environment through sensing devices attached to computers. Victims of muscular dystrophy, cerebral palsy, or stroke can change room temperature, flick television channels, or make a phone call by blinking an eye or twitching a cheek muscle. The sensing device sends electrical signals generated by the body to the computer and in an instant the job is done.

Peter A. McWilliams has prepared a book called *Personal Computers and the Disabled*, published by Quantum Press, which outlines ways that computers can benefit people with specific handicaps. With computers, people who are confined to their homes can invite the world into their living rooms with a twinkling of an eye.

---

cash registers. A touch-tone device is a dumb terminal that sends data over common phone lines. Most have special keyboards, and some are combined with voice recognition systems.

Intelligent terminals are remote terminals that can be programmed to do certain things. Data can be edited or handled in some way at these terminals. Most intelligent terminals have a CRT and/or printer built into them.

Figure 4-14. *Joysticks can be used to control the movement of the cursor on the screen.*

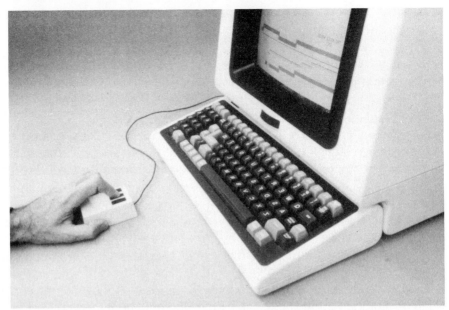

Figure 4-15. *By rolling this "mouse" on a smooth flat surface and clicking the button, a user can bypass the keyboard to make choices and give commands.*

Special Input Devices

You can use special input devices to enter data into a computer. The devices include joysticks, mice, light pens, touch screens, and graphics tablets. These tools allow you to bypass the keyboard and command the computer to follow certain instructions.

If you have played a video game, you may already have used a **joystick** (see Figure 4-14). The joystick and the mouse simply control the movement of cursors on the screen. A **cursor** is a mark that shows where you are on the screen. Sometimes it is a rectangle, or an arrow, or a flashing light. Controlling the cursor with a keyboard can involve pushing and holding down several keys. A joystick moves the cursor by shifting the position of a stick mounted on a base. It is somewhat like the floor-mounted stick shift in a car. While the gear shift has certain slots into which it can be moved, the joystick moves freely.

A **mouse** is a device about the size of a box of jello (see Figure 4-15). On the bottom is a small ball like a roller bearing. The mouse rolls along any smooth, flat surface to make the cursor move. Both the joystick and mouse are connected to the computer with input cords. Both have push buttons to activate a command.

Light pens allow you to draw and alter designs on the display terminal. You touch the screen with the device to make it work. Light pens are sometimes used with a **graphics tablet**, a pad on which you can draw electronically (see Figure 4-16). One light pen can be used directly on a table top, exactly like the mouse.

With touch screens and pads, you use your own fingers to

Cursor A mark on the screen that shows the user's current location.

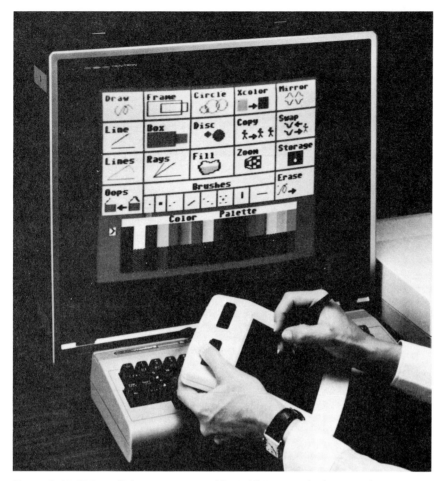

Figure 4-16. *Using a light pen on a graphics tablet can make input to the computer easier.*

command the computer. The KoalaPad is one example of a pad that will send your commands to the computer. You can draw pictures or you can tell the computer to sound a note or chord of music. Some pressure-sensitive pads have overlays with pictures or words on them. You can see which section of the tablet surface you need to press to make something happen on the screen.

Output Devices

Printers, plotters, computer output microfilm, and CRTs provide computer output that you can read. We discussed the soft copy that CRTs produce. The problems with CRTs are that they show only small amounts of data at a time and the output is not portable. The other devices produce hard copy in paper or film form.

Paper copy provides a permanent record. Copies are easily passed to other readers. They also provide back-up copies. Paper copies are made with two basic kinds of printers—impact and nonimpact (see Figure 4-17).

Figure 4-17. *This printer prints onto continuous forms which can then be torn apart.*

Impact printers will print either one character at a time or one line at a time. Printer-keyboards and dot-matrix printers are the two principal character-at-a-time devices. A metal hammer engraved with a character strikes a print ribbon, pressing the image of the character onto paper. Fully formed characters like those made with a typewriter can be made with the printer-keyboard. One of the most popular devices for producing this quality of type is the daisy wheel printer. Daisy wheel printers are called letter-quality printers because they produce high-quality images (see Figure 4-18).

Dot-matrix printers produce characters by moving a vertical row of pins. Although some dot-matrix printers will print very high-quality output, most will print characters in which the dots are distinct (see Figure 4-19). These printers are much faster than the printer-keyboard devices.

Some printers contain raised characters mounted on chains or drums. They can print one line at a time. They are faster printers than the printers that print one character at a time.

Nonimpact printers make no hammer motion to produce images. Since there is no mechanical movement, printing occurs much faster. Some methods are similar to the xerographic process in copying machines. The nonimpact printers depend on electrical fields, heat, magnetically charged areas, and lasers to create images. These devices are faster and more reliable than impact printers. They also offer a wider choice of character shapes.

Because of the speeds with which the different kinds of printers operate, printers are grouped in low-speed and high-speed categories. The low-speed printers type from 10 to 300 characters per second. They are usually impact printers. High-speed nonimpact printers can print up to 20,000 lines per minute.

A **plotter** also produces output, but it can draw pictures! Its pens can create lines, curves, and complex shapes in color. Plot-

Figure 4-18. *A daisy wheel offers high-quality type and is often used on printers for professional quality printing.*

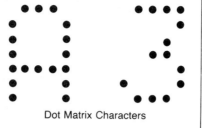

Solid Characters   Dot Matrix Characters

Figure 4-19. *Some printers print dot matrix characters rather than solid characters.*

ters are used to produce bar charts, graphs, pie charts, and maps. The shapes are created as pens move across the paper (see Figure 4-20).

One form of common computer output saves space when hard copy is needed. It is called **computer output microfilm (COM).** This method produces tiny photographed images by computer on microfilm or four-by-six-inch pieces of film called microfiche. The reader then uses a special magnifying machine to read what is on the film.

 LEARNING CHECK 4-2

1. What is the term for data collection in computer-readable form when and where an event takes place?

2. Name four special input devices.

3. A printer that prints by means of a hammer striking a ribbon is a(n) _____.

1. source-data automation 2. joystick, mouse, light pens, touch sensitive screens 3. impact printer

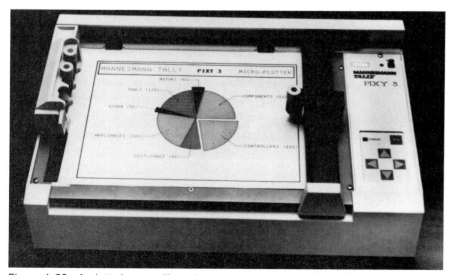

Figure 4-20. *A plotter's pen will produce graphic output such as this pie chart.*

We have water pollution and air pollution as a result of insecticides, exhaust from automobiles, garbage dumps, woodburning stoves, and weed killers. Now there is a new form of pollution—electric "hash."

As the use of computers and other electrical equipment increases, "hash" or "noise" increases. Electrical devices give off impulses that travel through the air as radio waves. Worldwide, these impulses increase at a rate of fifty percent a year. These im-

pulses interfere with radio transmissions and computer operations. Any unwanted impulses or signals are called "hash" or "noise."

For instance, the electronic "noise" from video games interfered with radio transmissions of the Nevada Highway Patrol. In cities, stray radio waves from commercial radio and television transmitters on top of skyscrapers caused breakdowns in nearby computer systems. Some companies are installing

costly screens to shield computer hardware from this "noise."

One airline banned portable computers and electronic games on planes in flight. A pilot had stopped an engine because of unusual signals in the cockpit. Later, he found out the signals came from a passenger playing with an electronic game.

Maybe laws about pollution will someday have to include electronic pollution!

Remote Access Communication Systems

How can terminals such as the point-of-sale terminals send their data to a central computer? How does a person working at home on a terminal send work to the office? The answer is a pathway called a **communication channel**. Such channels include telegraph lines, communication satellites, and laser beams. The combined use of computers (data-processing equipment) and these channels is called telecommunications.

Businesses may use the satellite "pathways" for teleconferencing. Publications such as *The Wall Street Journal, U.S. News and World Report, Time, People,* and *Sports Illustrated* use satellite transmission to send text and photographs to regional printing stations. Businesses and banks use the telephone lines to link central computers to computers at branches. You can use the telephone channel with your home computer system, too.

Modems

Messages sent over telephone or telegraph lines are in the "wave" or analog form. They cannot be understood by digital computers.

Figure 4-21. *A telephone can be used with a modem to send messages from computer to computer.*

Anyone sending or receiving such messages must have a **modem**. A modem will change digital pulses into waves (<u>MO</u>dulate) to be sent over the lines. It will change waves back to digital pulses (<u>DEM</u>odulate) to be received by a computer. It can also slow down or speed up the rate of transmission. <u>MO</u>dulate plus <u>DEM</u>odulate shortens to the word modem.

Modem A device that changes digital impulses to wave forms and back again.

A modem used with a telephone and a microcomputer can hook into **networks or electronic bulletin boards** (see Figure 4-21). Some modems have a place for the handset of the telephone to rest. Others can be connected to the wall jack of the telephone lines. Usually, an extra plug-in device and special software programs are necessary to make the modem work with a computer. Once the equipment is in place, the user simply dials the number to which another computer is connected. The modem takes care of the rest.

Electronic bulletin board An electronic clearinghouse where messages may be posted or received through a computer.

Networks

With the use of a computer terminal and a telephone modem, a computer turns into a library or a network for communicating with other people. For instance, a subscription to an on-line (direct connection to a computer) service will buy video versions of newspapers, stock market reports, movie reviews, and a host of other information.

Two commercial networks are The Source and CompuServe, Inc. CompuServe offers an on-line encyclopedia called Grolier's

Academic American Encyclopedia. It also offers news, sports, and weather. A popular feature supplied by some networks is the electronic bulletin board. Users can exchange or post messages through this service. Perhaps one reason why the electronic bulletin boards are so popular is because people can communicate from a terminal instead of face-to-face. Many people are shy.

Someday, nearly everyone will have access to electronic libraries. Who knows what other possibilities computer power will bring.

 LEARNING CHECK 4-3

1. The pathway over which data travel from remote terminals is called _____.

2. How does a modem work?

3. TRUE   FALSE   A service by which users can post or exchange news is an electronic bulletin board.

1. a communication channel   2. changes digital language into wave language and back again   3. TRUE

Perspective   Once data were entered into computers by punched cards and tape. The methods were slow and often inaccurate. Today, the keyboards, graphics tablet, mouse, joystick, and even the voice make it easier to enter data and use computers.

But a device is available—for a mere $100, depending on which computer you own—that will enable you to control a computer with your facial muscles. Sounds crazy? The package is Relax, by SYNAPSE.

Relax is a hardware and software package in one. It has an electromyograph (EMG) that checks internal electrical impulses. The package also has a headband and an audio cassette tape with sounds of the ocean, birds, and music. You use muscle tension to control certain games. The games you can play include Pong, Breakout, and Space Invaders.

Devices such as Relax are just-for-fun versions of input methods that are being explored by scientists. These devices are ways that computers are being made easier to use.

ISSUE/ELECTRONIC BULLETIN BOARDS OPEN TO SEARCHES?

Suppose someone posted a notice on your school bulletin board giving a computer system access code for a major business such as Sears, Roebuck, and Co. What if several students copied the code to get into the Sears computer system? Before school authorities could remove the notice, it was gone.

Who's responsible for the notice on the bulletin board? The school? Could the police raid the school because such a notice appeared?

A situation occurred with a Pacific Bell telephone credit card number and two Sprint access codes. The codes appeared on an electronic bulletin board system (BBS). The BBS owner, Tom Tcimpidis of Los Angeles, found out about the notice only when police presented a search warrant. By that time, the message was gone from the system. The person who posted it had given it a built-in expiration data of just a few days. Was Tom Tcimpidis responsible for the appearance of the notice? The police thought so. They seized his computer equipment as evidence. Although lawyers doubt that the case will hold up in court, it presents problems for sysops (system operators).

Tcimpidis' lawyer, Chuck Lindner, states that this case is like someone placing illegal messages on a grocery store bulletin board. Is the grocery store responsible for notices about illegal activities, credit card numbers, or telephone codes on their bulletin boards? One BBS user said that a grocery store would have to have a bulletin board three feet high and 660 feet long (longer than two football fields end-to-end) to store all the messages that most BBSs hold. A bulletin board that size would hold thousands of messages on three-by-five cards. He suggested that anyone seeing an illegal message should tell the sysop immediately.

Now sysops watch their bulletin boards more carefully, check for illegal messages more frequently, and even forbid use of terms like *underground*, *hacker*, and *pirate* on their systems.

BBSs are meant for computer users to trade tips about computer hardware and software and to write notes to their computer "penpals." But some people have begun to think twice about starting a BBS. In Southern California, according to one sysop, "problem messages" have increased ten times. A spokesperson for Pacific Bell suggested that sysops build in a delay system for messages. They should read the messages and approve them before placing them on the BBS. Sysops object. They believe that would be like reading other people's mail.

Tcimpidis' BBS is not the only one that has been used for pirating purposes. Are all electronic bulletin boards open to raids? Is the sysop responsible? Will illegal activity discourage the use of a very helpful and popular tool? Future court cases will decide the answers to these questions.

SUMMARY POINTS

- A bus describes the wires and cables that connect the components of a computer.

- Secondary storage is located outside the main computer. Some kinds of secondary storage are magnetic tape, magnetic disks, cartridges, and laser disks.

- Magnetic tape provides storage that is sequentially accessed. An item is found by searching through all the items in the order in which they appear on the tape.

- Magnetic disks are directly accessed. The read/write head of the computer finds an item by its place on the disk, not by the order in which it appears.

- To communicate with the computer, an input or output device is needed. Input devices include the keyboard and visual display terminal, punched cards, key-to-tape or key-to-disk devices, and devices that "read" data at their sources. Special input devices include joysticks, mice, light pens, touch-sensitive screens and pads, and graphics tablets. Some computers also have voice-recognition systems. The user inputs data by speaking.

- Source-data automation is the term used for the collection and preparation of data in computer-readable form when and where the event or transaction takes place.

- Some source data are entered into the computer by devices that read marks, characters, magnetic ink, and codes that "understand" speaking. Much source data are entered into a central computer from remote terminals.

- Output devices include cathode ray tubes (CRTs), which display output on a screen. Printers produce paper copy in letter-quality or dot-matrix type. Plotters print graphic displays as well as characters. Computer output microfilm devices produce microfilm and microfiche directly from the computer.

- Data travel to central computers from remote terminals by way of communication channels. The channels include telephone and telegraph lines, satellite communication, and laser beams.

- Modems allow computers to communicate with each other. Digital language is changed to a form that will travel over communication channels. It is then changed back to digital language upon arrival.

- Networks provide information services to be accessed directly through home computers or office computer systems.

- Electronic bulletin boards provide a way for people to communicate with other computer users.

CHAPTER TEST

Vocabulary

Match the term from the numbered column with the description from the lettered column that best fits the term.

1. Dumb terminals

a. In direct communication with the computer.

2. Cursor

b. A device that changes the impulses sent over communication channels to signals the computer can understand or to signals that will travel over the channels.

3. Modem

c. The term given to all of the wires and cables that connect the components of the computer.

4. Direct-access storage

d. An electronic clearinghouse where messages may be posted or received through a computer.

5. Source-data automation

e. The use of special equipment to capture data in computer-readable form when and where an event takes place.

6. Bus

f. Terminals that cannot be programmed but that can be used to enter data into a computer.

7. Online

g. Storage that is located outside the main computer or CPU.

8. Sequential-access storage	h.	Secondary storage from which data must be read one after another in a fixed order until the needed data are located.
9. Electronic bulletin board	I.	A mark or notation on the display screen that shows where the next character a user types will appear.
10. Secondary storage	J.	A method of storing data so they can be retrieved in any order without reading through all the other data in order.

Questions

1. Describe how magnetic tape or disks work in their respective drives.
2. Why are disks a form of direct-access storage?
3. How are laser disks better than magnetic disks?
4. Which input/output devices do you know about?
5. How are punched cards used today?
6. Describe some common methods of source-data automation.
7. What do the joystick, mouse, and other special input devices allow you to do?
8. Describe four kinds of output from computers.
9. What kinds of communication channels are there?
10. What does a modem allow you to do with your microcomputer?
11. How does a network help your computer serve you better?

DISCUSSION QUESTIONS

1. Source-data automation affects us through use in retail stores and restaurants. Discuss ways source-data automation is used in your community.
2. There are many types of printers on the market. What factors would you consider if you were buying a printer?
3. If you have a microcomputer at your school, what type of specialized input and output devices would you most like to use with the computer? Why?

ACTIVITIES

1. Visit stores in a local shopping area and make a list of the types of source-data automation devices that you see in use.
2. Visit a computer store and compare the hard copy produced by different types of printers. What differences did you notice among the printers as to the quality of the hard copy?
3. As a class, make a list of the items you would like to include in an electronic bulletin board if your class operated the board.

Chapter 5

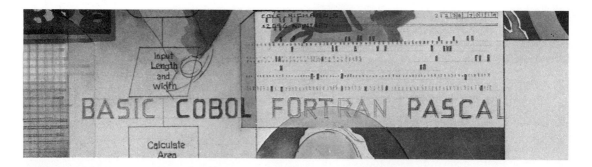

Programming and Its Languages

Learning Objectives

After reading this chapter, you should be able to:

1. Distinguish between application and systems programs and to learn about the operating system.

2. List differences among machine language, assembly language, and high-level languages.

3. Name five of the well-known high-level languages and their features.

Introduction

Even with smaller, faster, and more efficient computer hardware, the computer cannot perform until it has instructions. These instructions are called programs. Programmers use programming languages to write the instructions.

Some programs direct the computer to perform its own operations. These programs are **systems programs**. Other programs help the user to solve problems or perform tasks. They are **application programs**.

Systems program A program that coordinates the operation of computer circuitry.

Systems Programs

Systems programs directly affect the operation of the computer. They help the computer system to run quickly and efficiently by coordinating the operation of computer circuitry.

In early computer systems, human operators watched over computer operations. They decided the order that programs were run and prepared input and output devices needed by a program. As the processing speeds of the CPUs increased, the speed of the human operators stayed the same. Delays and errors caused by human operators became a serious problem. The CPU was often idle.

In the 1960s, operating systems were designed to overcome this problem. An **operating system** is a set of systems programs that allows a computer to manage its own operations and run at its own speed. It coordinates the computer's activities so that all the parts of the computer will be run smoothly.

Systems programs are often stored on secondary storage media. Programs are called into primary storage as needed. Primary storage may not contain the entire operating system at once.

Since computers vary in primary storage capacity, in the number of instructions they can perform, and in the methods used to code and store data, systems programs also vary among

Application program A program designed to meet a particular user need.

Operating system A set of systems programs that permit a computer to manage itself.

The hottest sounds in pop and rock are music and sound effects created with electronic synthesizers. You don't just plunk on a keyboard or strum a few strings anymore; you play with knobs and extra wires to get new sounds. The synthesizer bends sound waves to create brand-new sounds, many you would not normally hear in nature.

A number of today's popular groups have created hit songs with electronic gadgetry. But one musician has been playing with electronics since the early 1970s. He is soul star Stevie Wonder. He used the clavinet, an electric harpsichord with a hammering sound, to record his 1972 single, "Superstition." Later he graduated to a custom-built digital synthesizer called the Melodeon. This machine helped create a cacophony of jungle and bird noises for his 1979 album, *The Secret Life of Plants.*

Stevie Wonder has used many electronic instruments since then: the Fairlight, the Emulator, and the German-made PPG Wave 2.2. Songs like "It's Growing" and "Broken Glass" depend on the special sound effects of the PPG keyboard and a drum machine called the LinnDrum.

Since Wonder is blind, he uses two new systems to help him compose without relying on other people for help. The two machines are the Kurzweil Reading Machine (KRM) and the Versabraille. The KRM scans printed pages, interprets the words, and speaks them out loud. The Versabraille is a lap-sized computer that uses braille, a system of writing patterns of raised dots to represent letters. When Wonder gets all his electronic instruments, his computer, and these two systems linked up, he'll have true flexibility in creating the music in his mind.

Supervisor program The major program of an operating system.

computers. An operating system that will work with one type of computer will not work on another.

The **supervisor program** (also called monitor or executive), is the major program of the operating system. It manages the activities of all other parts of the operating system. When the computer is first turned on, the supervisor program is the first program to be moved into primary storage from secondary storage. The supervisor schedules the order of input and output operations. It also sends messages to the computer operator if an error occurs or if the computer needs more direction.

The operating system also manages the jobs, or specific work, the computer is to do. It manages input and output. When data are to be put in a special order or transferred from tape to disk or to printer, a special operating system program oversees the process.

The operating system also translates any other computer language into machine language. Remember that the computer only understands ons and offs, or 1s and 0s. For it to use an

English-like program, such as those written in BASIC or Logo languages (discussed later in this chapter), it must have a **language translation program**. Three types of language translation programs are the **compiler**, the **interpreter**, and the **assembler**. A compiler translates an entire program into machine code at once for later execution, while an interpreter changes the instructions one at a time as the program is run. The interpreter is usually found on smaller computer systems, such as microcomputers. It usually supports an interactive process (the process in which the user "talks" to the computer during program execution). The interpreter process is time-consuming. On the other hand, the compiler works well when large programs need to be run many times. Since the program is already translated and in main memory, the translation does not need to be repeated.

An assembler translates assembly language (discussed later in this chapter) into machine language. Assembler programs depend on the design of each computer.

Application Programs

While systems programs help the computer to function better, application programs help the user. Application programs are the programs that the user needs to do a specific job on the computer. In your school, for example, an application program may average and print your grades. Any software used for computer-assisted instruction (CAI) to help students with spelling or to imitate a science experiment are application programs. Schools have payrolls and other expenses, so these applications may be computerized.

In businesses, application programs figure out payroll, do the accounting for income and expenses, and provide reports for managers. CAD/CAM (computer-aided design and manufacturing) is an application program. At home, you may play games or use the computer to keep track of money. The programs to do these jobs are application programs.

To write either systems or application programs, the programmer must have a language to use. The next section discusses several programming languages.

Language translation program The instructions that translate English-like programs into machine-executable code.

Compiler A program that translates program statements into machine language all at once.

Interpreter A program that translates program statements one instruction at a time.

Assembler The translation program for changing assembly language to machine language.

 LEARNING CHECK 5-1

1. Programs that permit the computer to control its own operations are called what?
2. The supervisor program of the operating system is also called the _____ or _____ program.

3. A compiler _____.

    a. translates instructions one at a time

    b. translates only assembly language into machine language

    c. translates a whole program at once

    d. translates machine language into compiler language

4. Programs that help the user perform a specific job are _____ programs.

Programming Languages

Each programming language has different goals. One language may suit the needs of business processing, while another may use the computer's calculating abilities for complex scientific equations. Many allow users to "talk" with the computer while the program is running and permit batch processing, too.

Machine Language

Machine language is the language of the computer, the only language it knows and acts upon. Because the computer can run it directly, programs written in machine language work very fast. High-level languages must be changed into machine language by the translation program before the computer will understand what is said. Remember that machine language is written in 1s and 0s. Coding a program in this binary form is very time-consuming. It is easy to make mistakes in machine language.

What one brand of computer will understand in machine language, another will not. Programmers must know how the machine works internally to write machine instructions. They must tell the computer exactly what to do and when. The computer will not know when an instruction is wrong or that it needs more direction to carry out a command. Making a simple change in a program, such as inserting a new instruction, may require many other changes to the program besides that single change. It's like building a house—putting a window in your bedroom after the house is already built is not so easy. Other changes may be necessary.

Assembly language A symbolic programming language that uses abbreviations.

Mnemonics A symbolic name or memory aid.

Assembly Language

Assembly language overcomes some of the problems of machine language. Programmers use abbreviations, or **mnemonics**, to

78

ADAM	GPSS	LOTIS	PROLOG
AESOP	GRAF	MAD	SIMSCRIPT
BASEBALL	ICES	MAP	SNOBOL
CLIP	IDS	MATHLAB	SPRINT
COGO	IT	NELIA	STROBES
DIALOG	JOSS	OCAL	TRAC
DYANA	JOVIAL	OPS	TRANDIR
FACT	LISP 2	PAT	TREE
FLAP	LOLITA	PENCIL	UNCOL
FORMAC	LOGO	PILOT	UNICODE

Figure 5-1. *This list shows the variety of colorful names given to programming languages.*

name the machine operations. For instance, L may mean "load" and C may mean "compare." An assembler program in the language translator of the operating system changes the assembly language into machine code.

Yet assembly language has its drawbacks. The programs can be very long, even thousands of lines long. The mnemonic codes may differ among the various kinds of computers. Programmers must still know how each machine works.

High-Level Languages

High-level languages are more English-like than machine or assembly language. Since programmers do not have to worry about the internal workings of the computer, programs are shorter. While one assembly language instruction usually equals one machine language instruction, one high-level language instruction may correspond to a half dozen or more machine instructions. Also, the programs are easier to change. Just one statement may be all that is needed to make the change.

Some common high-level languages are FORTRAN, COBOL, BASIC, Pascal, Logo, and PILOT (see Figure 5-1).

FORTRAN **Fortran**, short for FORmula TRANslator, is the oldest high-level programming language. When FORTRAN was developed in the 1950s, computers were used mainly by engineers, scientists, and mathematicians. FORTRAN served the needs for quickly solving long and complex arithmetic calculations.

FORTRAN is not well-suited for building large data files or printing documents. It does not often serve business uses.

Computer languages are as varied as the languages of the world. We all know that in Europe, people speak such languages as German, French, Spanish, and Italian, and that in China, people speak many versions of Chinese. Well, computer programmers speak many languages, too. Some of these languages are the common ones: FORTRAN, COBOL, Logo, Pascal. But what about JOVIAL? Or LISP? Or even SMALLTALK?

JOVIAL, far from being funny, is a language created by Jules Schwartz to write air defense software. It stands for Jules' Own Version of the International Algebraic Language.

LISP is not what you do when you've knocked out a front tooth. It is a very high-level language used to write programs dealing with artificial intelligence, which we'll talk about in chapter 9.

SNOBOL? It was invented at Bell Telephone Laboratories. SNOBOL often is used in handling language—editing text, for example.

SMALLTALK is not something you do at parties, but a language that will help you use a mouse. (Remember? The device that allows you to move a cursor on the screen.) This language supports visual work on the computer.

See how many other languages for computers you can find.

COBOL COmmon Business-Oriented Language; a programming language used mainly for business applications.

COBOL Short for COmmon Business-Oriented Language, **COBOL** fits its name. It is used chiefly for business applications. It can handle large amounts of input and output. COBOL does not perform many of the complex figures used in FORTRAN programs. Large files of data can be handled easily in COBOL.

COBOL is a popular language for businesses and government. It is a standardized language, which means that COBOL programs written for one kind of computer will run with only minor changes on another computer.

BASIC Beginners' All-purpose Symbolic Instruction Code; a programming language used for interactive problem solving.

BASIC **BASIC** stands for Beginners' All-purpose Symbolic Instruction Code. It was meant to be an easy-to-learn language for beginning programmers, but many businesses and colleges now use it for business applications, too. BASIC is often used with microcomputers in homes. It is well-suited for interactive processing. The user can communicate with the computer in a question-and-answer style while a program is being run. It is less structured than most other languages (see Figure 5-2).

Pascal A structured programming language named after Blaise Pascal and used to teach programming concepts.

Pascal **Pascal**, named after Blaise Pascal who invented the first mechanical adding machine, was designed to teach programming concepts to students. It is popular for business and scientific uses. Many microcomputer manufacturers offer Pascal for their machines.

Figure 5-2. *Students use BASIC to communicate with the computer.*

Logo   **Logo** means "to reason" in Greek. In school, it is often used with students in the early grades (see Figure 5-3). Logo's graphics and simplicity make learning geometry and computer programming fun for students. Yet Logo can be used for very complex mathematical ideas.

With Logo, you control a "turtle," an object that moves around on the screen. The Logo programs make the turtle follow a path. Lines form as the turtle moves and pictures are drawn. As students use Logo, they learn how to think logically.

Logo A language that allows the user to program by defining new commands and creating graphics.

PILOT   Your teacher may use **PILOT** to make tests and teaching programs for use with the computer. PILOT stands for Programmed Inquiry, Learning, Or Teaching.

Many PILOT program lines begin with a code letter or two that tell the computer what to do with the rest of the line. For instance,

Figure 5-3. *Texas Instruments was the first computer manufacturer to make the children's programming language, Logo, available to consumers.*

in the program command "T: Name a large city in Ohio," the T tells the computer to type, or display on the screen, the message "Name a large city in Ohio." "M" stands for match, so a teacher can program "M: Akron, Cincinnati, Cleveland, Columbus, Dayton." "A" means accept answer, so a student types in an answer. If a student answers any one of those cities, the answer is correct. The command "TY" (type yes) tells the computer to type a reward message, "Very good," if there is a match. What do you think the command "TN" might mean?

LEARNING CHECK 5-2

1. What is the language that only the computer can understand?

2. Assembly language makes use of symbols, abbreviations, or _____.

3. One difference between computer language and high-level languages is that high-level languages _____.
    a. require an assembler
    b. are used by the government
    c. are more English-like
    d. require more knowledge of the computer's internal design

4. One good language for a student in the early grades might be _____.

1. machine language 2. mnemonics 3. c 4. Logo

Out of the 1960s came the Beatles, "flower children," miniskirts, the Civil Rights Movement . . . and BASIC.

BASIC was developed in the mid-1960s at Dartmouth College by Professors John G. Kemeny and Thomas E. Kurtz. BASIC stands for Beginners' All-purpose Symbolic Instruction Code. At first, it was used in large computer settings where one or more BASIC users could communicate with the computer during processing.

With the increasing popularity of minicomputers and microcomputers, manufacturers offered BASIC as a simple but effective language. A standard BASIC is accepted, but each manufacturer has changed the language to suit the equipment.

Many BASICs exist. Some of them are BASIC-80, S-BASIC, extended BASIC, Business BASIC, BASIC-Plus, minimal BASIC, U-BASIC, MBASIC, CBASIC, Power BASIC, Tiny BASIC, and Infinite BASIC.

Now you have some BASIC knowledge.

Perspective   *Many computer languages and portions of languages exist besides the six mentioned here. You may have heard of Ada, FORTH, C, SNOBOL, LISP—the list goes on and on. These languages let you, the user, learn to make a computer do what you want. Even though you may have to follow certain rules to write any one of these languages (just as you do when you write an essay in English), you still are commanding the computer.*

Language researchers are working on natural language patterns. In these patterns, you will be able to speak to the computer in commands and questions just as you would to a human. You could say into a microphone, "I want a list of all of my baseball cards that were printed before 1960."

Of course, the things you ask for will have to be in your personal files or a commercial data base. A computer won't be able to get something out of nothing. But natural language will take us into an even more user-friendly method of computing.

ISSUE/BASIC, PASCAL, OR LOGO?

Public schools for grades kindergarten through 12 usually teach one of three languages: Logo, BASIC, or Pascal.

Students who study Logo can learn enough about the language to begin programming right away. Beginning Logo programmers are caught in the excitement of seeing graphics on the screen. Their stress vanishes. Logo gives students a feeling of control over the computer. Logo also teaches good programming habits. The change from programming in Logo to programming in Pascal is much easier because of the likenesses in program structure.

Although many teachers

agree that Logo is a good beginning language for younger students, they disagree about the choice between BASIC and Pascal. BASIC has been "the language" of microcomputers. BASIC is fairly easy to learn. It is English-like. Beginners do not have to learn many commands before learning to program.

But many types of BASIC do not encourage structured programming. Teachers find that BASIC does not produce the excitement of learning to program that Logo does. Since the Logo taught in the early grades seems to lead naturally to the programming style of Pascal, Pascal more often is taught in high schools.

Pascal was chosen for the computer science advanced placement (AP) exam, first given in May 1984. The AP exams allow high school students to earn some college credit for their work in such subjects as English, history, calculus, and music. Since the computer science AP exam has been added, high schoolers have even more reason to learn Pascal.

Because so many colleges are teaching Pascal as the first programming language, high schools do not have much choice. An executive with the College Entrance Examination Board (CEEB) said, "It would be dreadful if what [students] were doing in high school had no relation to what followed in college."

On the other hand, most educators are better equipped to teach BASIC. The placing of Pascal on the AP exams may create a group of computer "haves" and "have-nots"—those students who do or do not learn Pascal simply because their schools teach it or do not teach it. Also, the content of one test will dictate whole courses of study of high schools and perhaps decide education paths of many students.

Perhaps everyone should be safe and learn both BASIC and Pascal! Then, for sure, the popularly taught language in colleges will be something else, such as FORTH!

SUMMARY POINTS

- Programs that direct the computer to do its own operations by managing the computer's circuitry are called systems programs. Programs that help the user to solve problems are application programs.

- Operating systems are groups of systems programs with certain functions. Some of these include controlling input/output activity, changing programs into machine language, calling up stored programs when needed, and doing work such as sorting data into a particular order.

- Machine language and assembly language are written for a certain type of computer. They are very hard to write. The computer must be told everything, with no details left out.

- High-level languages are easier to understand because they are more English-like.

- Both assembly language and high-level languages must be changed into machine language before the computer can understand the program. Assembly language is translated by an assembler; high-level languages are changed by either a compiler or an interpreter. A compiler translates a whole program at once, while an interpreter translates one instruction at a time.

- Some high-level languages are COBOL, FORTRAN, BASIC, Pascal, Logo, and PILOT.

Vocabulary

Match the term from the numbered column with the best description from the lettered column.

1. Application program

a. A translation program used by small computer systems to evaluate and translate program statements as the program is run, one instruction at a time.

2. Compiler

b. A collection of programs that permits a computer to manage itself and avoid idle CPU time.

3. Mnemonics

c. A symbolic programming language that uses abbreviations rather than 0s and 1s.

4. Interpreter

d. A popular programming language in business and government.

5. Assembly language

e. A program written to coordinate the operation of computer circuitry and to help the computer run quickly and efficiently.

6. Logo

f. A program designed to meet a particular user need.

7. Supervisor program

g. A popular programming language for students.

8. Operating system

h. Symbolic names or memory aids used in assembly language and in high-level computer languages.

9. COBOL

i. The major component of an operating system; it coordinates the activities of all other parts of the operating system.

10. Systems program

j. A translator program for a high-level language, such as FORTRAN, that changes the statements into machine code all at once.

Questions

1. What is the purpose of a systems program?

2. List four functions the operating system performs.

3. Give two alternate names for the supervisor program in an operating system.

4. List one advantage and one disadvantage of machine language.

5. Why is it still difficult to use assembly language, even though it has its advantages over machine language?

6. Choose two high-level programming languages and explain the differences between the two.

DISCUSSION QUESTIONS

1. To you, which language seems an attractive high-level language to learn? Why?

2. Discuss how a programmer might choose which programming language to use.

3. Discuss how an operating system improved computer operations. How could a natural language improve computer operations?

ACTIVITIES

1. Ask a parent, friend, or relative to get a copy of a computer program from work. Find out what language it uses and why that language was chosen. See if you can learn a few programming symbols or statements in that language.

2. PL/I is a computer language derived from FORTRAN and COBOL. Use library resources to find out more about it and why it was designed. Write a paragraph to read to the class.

3. Go to a computer store. Find out what systems programs are available and what is involved in coordinating a systems program with a particular computer. Do certain computers have to be changed in any way to accept, for instance, MicroSoft BASIC?

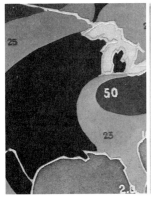 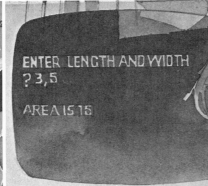 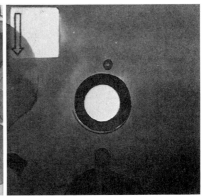

Software and Its Uses

Learning Objectives

After reading this chapter, you should be able to:

1. Describe some functions common to many software packages.

2. Name the functions that a word-processing package performs and list some uses for word processing.

3. Name the features and uses of graphics software.

4. Define a data base and list some ways data are stored.

5. Define spreadsheet software and explain how it handles data.

Introduction

What if you owned a computer but had no software? You could ask the same question about cars or televisions. What if you owned a car, but had no gasoline for it? What if you had a television, but could pick up no stations? You would be very limited in what you could do without the gasoline, the stations, or the software.

Computers are handy gadgets to own, but without software, they are just expensive paperweights. This chapter describes four types of software: word-processing programs, graphics software, data base software, and spreadsheets. The next section introduces software by discussing features common to many software packages.

General Features of Software Packages

Software that is hard to use can be almost as frustrating as no software at all. In the past, a person had to know how a computer worked to use the software. Many commands had to be memorized. Many steps were needed to make the computer perform one function. And many operations could not even be done.

Today's software is easier to use. Some features that help people use software are the menu, the window, special input devices, better documentation, and easier correction of mistakes.

Menu A list of choices from which the user can pick the needed operation.

A **menu** is a list of choices that appears on the display screen. The user can choose the item or data file needed. A menu on a graphics package might ask whether you want to paint, enter text, or choose your brush. Menus are easy to use because the user simply points to an option.

Some menus are displayed in pull-down **windows**. The windows are boxes that overlap data already displayed on a screen. These windows are pulled down from a bar of choices across the top of the screen. If "File" is pulled down, the choices may include Open, Edit, Save, Quit, or some other such command.

What kind of gimmick is this? You say this game will improve my science and reading skills? It will make me want to learn? You can't fool me. An educational game is still school.

Well, all right. I'll try it.

What's the game? It's *Space Shuttle: A Journey into Space*, by Activision. It dares players to fly a shuttle mission to repair a satellite spinning out of orbit 210 miles above Earth.

Students learn about the physics of space flight. What's more, they learn to read better. The game uses technical terms and detailed instructions. If students don't read well, they can't play. And they do want to play—especially at San Jose (California) Steinbeck Middle School. They want to play before school, after school—whenever they can.

Students must pass certain levels of training before they can fly a "real mission." They learn that one mistake can wipe out a flight! After 30 minutes of playing, one group aborted their flight because they forgot to put down their landing gear!

Even if only part of a class completes a mission, the other students become more curious about space flights. Maybe some of them will actually fly a mission someday.

Another type of window allows the user to choose part of a display that is too large to fit on the screen. The user can move the window so that it frames just part of the display. Some windows enlarge a section of a screen display. If the user is drawing a picture, for instance, a window is used to choose a small section of the picture. The picture portion is enlarged. The user adds details to the enlarged portion, and then returns it to its normal size.

Input devices other than the keyboard allow users to command the computer with a touch or a click. Users can pick options from menus by pointing with a light pen or by moving a mouse or joystick and clicking a button. Light pens can be used to draw on the screen, too. Touch tablets provide an easy way to enter drawings. Voice input allows users simply to talk to the computer. (See chapter 4 for details about input devices.)

Although some hardware and software are simple enough that you can sit down and begin working with little preparation, most users need written direction. User's guides containing instructions for using hardware and software accompany computer products. In addition, some software packages will direct users through instructions on the screen. Manufacturers of computer products know that clear documentation is important. They hire writers who can explain things clearly to even the beginning computer user.

Typing errors or misplaced data must be changed. Windows and menus, as well as easy cursor movement, make error handling easier. Many corrections can be made simply by backspacing and typing over the error.

Many software packages offer the features just listed. Each package also has features unique to the type of job to be performed.

Word-Processing Packages

The writer picks up a fresh, unused sheet of paper. After a few words are written, a mistake is made. Rather than erase it, the writer wads up the paper and tosses it aside. If the writer throws away a sheet after each mistake, no writing will get done.

Now writers can be messy and still produce a neat final copy—with little wasted paper, too. By using word-processing packages, our writer can scribble, cross out, add, scramble, and experiment with words without worrying about neatness. All the changes are made before anything appears on paper! When the product is finished, it slides neatly out of the printer.

Features

Word processing consists of four basic functions: writing, editing, formatting, and printing. Words appear on a screen during the first processes (the soft copy) and on paper during the printing process (the hard copy).

While writing, the user sees words in 24 to 25 lines per screen. Some monitors and software display only 40 characters or columns per line. Others show 80. After the 24 to 25 lines appear on the screen, the screen scrolls, or moves up, to display more lines.

Automatic word wrap A word-processing feature that lets users continue typing without pressing **RETURN**.

If more characters are typed on a line than the screen allows, **automatic word wrap** occurs. This feature permits you to keep typing without hitting the RETURN key at the end of a line, as you would on a typewriter. If a word is too long to fit on the line, the entire word shifts to the next line. For example, the final word on a line may be "keyboard," but only the "ke" will fit on the line. The "ke" moves to the next line when "y" is typed. Very few packages split a word, with "ke" appearing at the end of the line and "yboard" in the new line. Some word-processing software divides and types a hyphen in a word that is too long to fit at the end of a line.

Word processors also allow you to erase, insert, move, or search text. These are editing functions. Some packages display editing functions in menus. Others require pressing a series of keys.

Changing typing errors, awkward sentences, or paragraph order is a large part of the writing process. The easiest way to erase mistakes on most word processors is to backspace. Some-times sentences or parts of paragraphs need to be changed. Most word processors allow you to get rid of larger parts of text by using **block functions**. You block the amount to be erased and push a button (perhaps the RETURN key). The words are deleted from the screen.

A safety feature provides for second thoughts. If you wish you had kept the words, most software permits you to undo the deletion. But there is one catch: you must enter an UNDO com-mand before you do anything else.

Block functions also allow moving portions of the text. After choosing the part to be moved, you press certain keys, and the portion reappears at a new place. Sometimes this is called "cut and paste."

If you want to add a paragraph, sentence, or word to explain an idea better, move the cursor to the proper place and type the new words.

Search and replace is another editing function. If you are writ-ing a report about butterflies and see that you wrote "larve" instead of "larvae" (probably many times), use search and replace. Tell it to hunt for all instances of "larve." In a local search and replace, the cursor jumps to each place and you type the correct word. In a global search and replace, you tell the com-puter to search for each "larve" and replace it automatically. Either way, every misspelled word will be found and correc-ted.

If your spelling is poor, spelling checker packages are avail-able. A spelling checker amounts to a dictionary stored in the software. Many systems allow you to add words to the dic-tionary. If you use many technical terms or names that do not appear in a 20,000-word dictionary, you can add them to make your spelling checker fit your needs.

Some word-processing software permits **boilerplating**, which means placing the same sentence or paragraph in several documents. Boilerplating also allows you to fill in blanks on iden-tical forms to avoid retyping the forms many times. Boilerplating is a way to send out form letters without using a copying machine and typed-in greetings and addresses. The form letter looks like it was typed especially for each person.

When you have entered all of the text, it is time to prepare it for printing. In **formatting**, you add page numbers, define margins, set line spacing and the number of lines per page, or merge two or more documents. Perhaps some words need to be boldfaced (printed darker), underlined, or centered. Most word processing packages include these functions. Your printer should be matched to your computer and software so that it will print everything you request—boldface, underlining, margins, and so forth.

Block function A word-processing feature that allows users to choose text to save, delete, copy, or move.

Search and replace A word-processing function to locate words or phrases throughout the text.

Boilerplating A word-processing function that allows using the same text in different docu-ments.

Formatting Pre-paration of text for printing.

Uses

At home, you could use word processing to write reports, letters, or your first novel. At school, the teacher may ask students to write essays or reports using computers and word-processing software. Some teachers find that students who use computers make more and better revisions in essays or reports.

In the work place, word-processing software is used to write letters, brochures, reports, legal papers, and other documents. One of the most widespread business uses is in publishing. Many newspapers, magazines, and books are produced electronically from start to finish. Writers enter the text at computer terminals. Editors review the work at their terminals. Then, at other terminals, designers lay out entire pages at once. They choose type style, size, and column width. The text is placed at the proper place on the page. Titles or headlines are written. Some computer systems even print the pages electronically.

LEARNING CHECK 6-1

1. A list of choices displayed on a computer screen is called a _____.
   a. menu
   b. ledger
   c. window
   d. software package

2. The feature that allows you to choose portions of a large display to work on is called a(n) _____.

3. Which of the following is not one of the chief functions of word processing?
   a. writing
   b. editing
   c. blocking
   d. printing

4. The search and replace function permits you to do what?

5. The function by which you fill in blanks in identical documents or use portions of a document over and over in other documents is called _____.

1. a 2. window 3. c 4. find and correct errors 5. boilerplating

Graphics Packages

Early graphics software did well to produce simple bar graphs and funny little people made of squares. Today's graphics software and hardware is so advanced that sometimes it is hard to tell if a picture was produced by computer or trick photography.

Figure 6-1. *Computer Graphics*

Computer graphics appear in ads, logos, and sports broadcasts on television. A commercial for a cold medicine shows tiny time pills spilling out of a capsule. That cascading effect was produced with computer graphics. The NBC Nightly News logo is a product of computer graphics. Baseball fans see the baseball diamond spin and flip, zoom toward the viewers, or fade away to a tiny dot. Then, a single shot of a first baseman throwing the baseball to second resolves into colored squares.

Filmmakers use computers, too. The Cray supercomputer produced the lifelike scenes in some of the recent space adventure movies. Many animated movies are produced with computers.

Let us first look at the more common features of graphics packages and then at the many uses of the software.

Features

Much graphics software lists options on menus. The choices include shapes (squares, circles, rectangles), line widths (also called brush widths), and colors (see Figure 6-1). Textures can be added to parts of the picture. A portion of a drawing can be enlarged to add details, and then shrunk again. Figures can be repeated or overlapped, rotated or flipped. Software producers are even working on packages that will help the user draw three-dimensional (3-D) art with a personal computer.

Some graphics software may require certain input and output devices. Perhaps a light pen, mouse, joystick, or graphics tablet is needed to use the graphics package. Some graphics created in animated form can be stored on videotape. Some must be printed

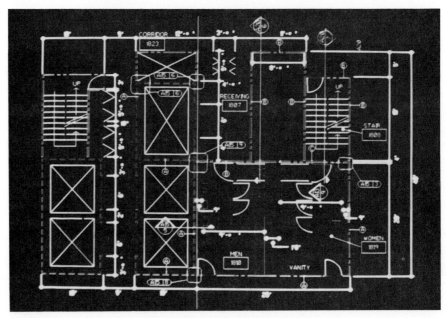

Figure 6-2. *Architectural Floor Plan by Computer.*

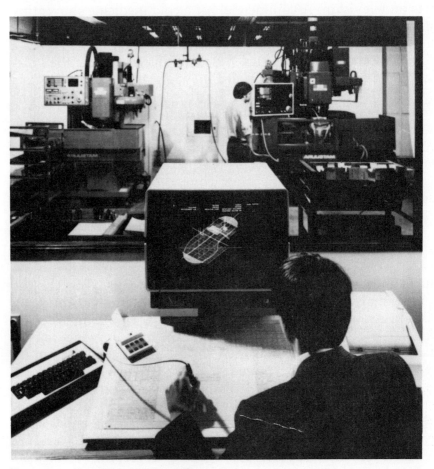

Figure 6-3. *Shoe Mold Design on Computer*

Figure 6-4. *Computers help astronomers to study planetary orbits.*

with plotters—the output devices with colored pens that "draw" the design.

The number of **pixels** in the screen limits the smoothness and reality of the final picture. The greater the number of pixels, the smoother and clearer the picture. On TV sets attached to micro-computers, the **resolution** is poor because the number of pixels is small—only about 300,000. For example, a circle is obviously made up of tiny squares. But many computer graphics artists use video monitors and software that achieve a resolution of 9 million pixels. The output almost looks like a photo.

Pixels Picture elements. When a pixel is addressed, a square dot lights up on the screen.

Resolution Clarity, detail of a picture.

Uses

Architects use graphics software to design and test structures and building materials (see Figure 6-2). Shoe manufacturers use CAD/CAM to design and test running shoes (see Figure 6-3). Scientists use graphics to map the earth's surface or to study the

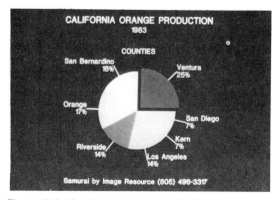
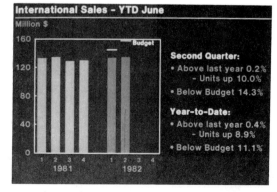

Figure 6-5. *Business trends can be shown in pie charts or bar graphs.*

People have been inventing new uses for computers faster than you can say "user-friendly." One recent idea puts a wrinkle in time.

Artist Nancy Burson of New York City uses a computer to create a picture of how a young person will look in 5 years, 20 years, or even 25 years. With her system, it takes just a few minutes to add decades to a face.

Burson owns a company called Face Systems, Inc., that markets her computer programs. Her portraits are of two kinds. One is a model of an aged face. The other is a mixture of the features of several faces. She has created elderly images of Brooke Shields, John Travolta, and Princess Diana for *People* magazine. One of her face mixtures was "Nuclear Powers"—a blend of the faces of world leaders, including Ronald Reagan and Margaret Thatcher.

Burson hopes that her system can be used for more practical purposes. One use aids in the search for missing people. Dee Scofield was 12 years old when she disappeared from an Ocala, Florida, shopping center. If she is alive, she would be 21 years old. Burson "drew" a portrait of how Dee would look to help in an ongoing search for the woman.

Burson also hopes plastic surgeons will use her programs. Surgeons could show patients how they would look with a thinner nose, a stronger chin, or fewer wrinkles.

orbits of the planets (see Figure 6-4). Business people use graphics software and microcomputers to draw pie charts, bar graphs, and line graphs that show profits, losses, income, and expenses (see Figure 6-5).

Using graphics software can be as simple as choosing options from a file of predrawn pictures—sometimes called clip art. Or it can be as complex as controlling each single pixel on the screen. More advanced graphics systems are used in computer-aided design (CAD) in industry or in entertainment for television viewers and moviegoers. But software for personal computers can produce a wide range of graphics effects, too..

For graphics at home, you can buy packages that help you create cartoons and video games. A cartoon movie package may give a choice of predrawn figures or allow you to draw your own. Each drawing in an animated sequence is called a frame. After a set of sequenced frames are drawn, they can be played back in a short motion picture.

Some packages are designed to let you create your own video game. Depending on the package, you can draw maze games, pinball games, racing contests, and even the "shoot-'em-up" kind, complete with explosions and sound effects.

One thing to remember when choosing graphics software is

that some packages require programming skills and others require special input devices, such as joysticks, mice, graphics tablets, or light pens. You will want to be sure you have all the equipment needed for the graphics package you choose.

 LEARNING CHECK 6-2

1. Pictures with greater smoothness and clarity can be produced when the monitor and software provide more _____.
  a. circles
  b. pixels
  c. rotation
  d. line width

2. Name two options in graphics software.

3. What is one input device that people can use to draw?

4. Business people might use graphics software to produce _____.
  a. pie charts, graphics tablets, and line graphs
  b. pie charts, bar graphs, and line graphs
  c. movies, squares, and bars
  d. bar graphs, line graphs, and options

5. TRUE   FALSE   Graphics software never requires special computer hardware.

1. b 2. texture, brush width 3. graphics tablet 4. b 5. FALSE

Data Bases

Software can act as a filing cabinet. A simple type of data management software is the **file handler**. File handlers copy standard filing methods. Material is filed by topic, and data can appear in several files. You must know which file the data are in to be able to access it.

A **data base manager** is software that allows users to enter thousands of records and then search through these records many different ways. The data are written compactly in a common format. Many data bases can be leased or purchased by large companies. Other data bases are available in software for personal computers.

Why use a data base? One major object of a data base is to avoid unnecessary repeating of data (**data redundancy**). Another main goal of a data base is to permit users to access the data with many kinds of questions. Take the data kept by your school as an example. Your principal's office may hold files on student names, addresses, parents, class schedule, teachers, and attendance. Your guidance counselor's office may hold files repeating the same data, along with grades and standard test scores. The health

File handler Data management software that imitates standard filing procedures.

Data base manager Data management software that builds a data base to access by many different questions.

Data redundancy Unneeded repetition of data.

office's files contain the names, addresses, parents, and health records of the students. This system follows the traditional filing methods.

In a data base, all the data would be kept in a central location. The principal, guidance counselor, and nurse could access those files for information they need. The guidance counselor could ask for the names of students who will graduate with academic honors. The principal could request the names of parents whose sons and daughters play in the school band.

Suppose a new type of data were needed (for instance, the students who had already had measles vaccinations). The new data could be added to the data base without entering again the students' names, addresses, and parents.

It is easy to update data bases because the data can be accessed directly. As you recall, direct access means the computer can go directly to the required data and pull them out. (This is opposed to sequential access, in which the computer must search through data in the order they appear on the storage media.) Updating is also easier because only one location of data must be changed. A new address is entered only once, rather than in the principal's files, again in the guidance counselor's files, and a third time in the health office's files.

Pharmacists use data bases for drug information to help patients use medications wisely. Law enforcement officers use data bases to find missing people or stolen cars. Scientists use data bases to map oil and gas reserves.

Data bases are expensive, especially for larger computer systems. But many organizations and personal computer owners see that data bases are an efficient and easy way to store and locate information.

Spreadsheets

Years ago, business people counted stock with marks on clay tablets and paid for goods with ivory or spices. As time went on, money and business became more complex. Business people learned to use math to plan for each year. Ledgers and journals were designed to keep track of profits and losses.

Soon business people learned to use spreadsheets to predict profits, losses, income, and expenses. Spreadsheets are green sheets of paper printed with a grid. The columns and rows form spaces called **cells**.

Today, these spreadsheets can be viewed on personal computer screens. The first popular spreadsheet was VisiCalc (the VISIble CALCulator), in the 1970s. Since then, many vendors have produced their own versions of spreadsheet software.

A spreadsheet is a model. It helps a business person see an overall picture of how the business is doing and how it should be doing. The business person can pinpoint areas that need changing.

The idea of an **electronic spreadsheet** is that the spreadsheet appears on a CRT screen. The same cells are formed by columns and rows as on a paper spreadsheet. The cells are filled with numbers that reflect sales, costs, taxes, wages, profits, and losses. The advantage is that it is easy to change the numbers. Changes in one group of numbers may affect another group of numbers. The computer calculates the changes, and instantly the new numbers appear on the screen.

Electronic spreadsheet A computerized grid for financial study. The user can see results of certain actions.

Electronic spreadsheets are good for asking "What if" questions.

"What if local taxes increase by 0.5 percent?"

"What if each salesman sells $100 more of our product per month?"

"What if we decide to build a new warehouse?"

With spreadsheet software, the computer instantly adjusts other numbers affected by the change in the "What if" questions. Most electronic spreadsheets also compute averages and adjust for inflation. These packages do in seconds what it would take an accountant several hours or days to do.

Evaluating Software

Recently there has been a large increase in prewritten software packages. The rising cost of writing software and the popularity of microcomputers have led to this increase.

If microcomputer users did not buy packaged software, they would have to write their own programs or hire programmers to do the job. Neither choice is likely for most microcomputer users. Packaged software, therefore, is a way for users to expand their computer use at a fair price.

But how do you choose software?

One question to ask is "How much time do I wish to spend learning how to use the software?" If you want to use the software within a half hour, you should look for software that is user-friendly. But a more complex package might do more jobs. If you do not mind spending several days learning how to use a package, then you might buy the complex package.

Another question to ask is, "What do I want the software to do?" If you have tried a friend's word-processing software and liked the spelling checker, you may be unhappy if the software you buy will not check your spelling. If speed is important, you will not like software that takes a long time to perform a job.

You should also ask friends how they like their software. If they get tired of a package quickly or find out that it lacks some features, you may be disappointed, too. On the other hand, some software requires patience—something a friend may lack and you may have. Be sure you understand why a friend dislikes a software package.

Read reviews in computer and software magazines. They will describe good points and bad points about software packages. Some stores allow you to try software before you buy. Find out more about trying before buying a package.

LEARNING CHECK 6-3

1. What are the two types of data management software?

2. Unnecessary repetition of data is called data _____.

3. A data base allows the user to _____.
   a. access data by asking many different questions
   b. ask many different questions by typing in the questions
   c. file the same information under many topics
   d. file data in an electronic spreadsheet

4. Spreadsheets are good tools to use for answering _____ questions.

5. TRUE   FALSE   Electronic spreadsheets are available only for large computer systems.

1. file handlers, data base managers 2. redundancy 3. a 4. "What if" 5. FALSE

Perspective   *Computers can do little without software. Each time a new use for computers is invented, someone must write programs to tell the computer what to do.*

In the future, computer memory may become large and microcomputers may become more powerful. But software must keep up the pace that hardware has set. In the next chapter, we see how software helps us at work. Chapter 9 explains how software is affected by ethics and crime and discusses the software of artificial intelligence and programming for homes of the future.

ISSUE/IS IT OKAY TO COPY SOMEONE ELSE'S SOFTWARE?

People photocopy pages from books. They videotape TV shows and record cassette tape copies of favorite albums. Why shouldn't they copy a disk or two of a favorite computer program? Sure, anyone who makes thousands of copies to sell for profit is a software pirate and should be punished. But one or two copies for friends? Why, copying is a way of life!

Yet many people in the computer industry—including young programmers—say much money is lost by illegal copying. The software authors and publishers invest huge amounts of time and effort to produce good programs. They want to make a profit. Any copying really means money has been "stolen" from the developers of software. It also means hard work has been stolen.

Some people who copy software say that TV viewers videotape copyrighted shows. The United States Supreme Court's "Betamax decision" made that kind of copying legal. Shouldn't the same kind of ruling apply to software? There are clear differences between videotaping a TV show and copying a piece of software. Home taping of television shows does not affect the market value of the show. Copying software does affect the profits that publishers and authors receive for producing a program.

Other people say that software prices are too high. They object to being called pirates because they insist they are not selling any programs to make a profit. They only want to *save* money. Some schools have even copied software

to "save money." After all, a blank disk costs perhaps $2.50 to $3, and software can cost from $20 to several hundred dollars. However, software companies say they have raised their prices to make up for profits lost because of illegal copying. This creates a cycle of price raising and illegal copying.

Another excuse given for copying disks is that people do not want to spend money for a program that might turn out to be useless. Most computer magazines review software so a buyer will know about a program before he or she buys it. Besides, friends tell each other which products they like. So the excuse is just that—an excuse.

Software companies have tried to protect disks against copying with special disk formats. This prevents software buyers from making a backup copy in case something happens to the copy-protected disk. But many computer users have been able to "crack" copy-protected disks. Software even exists to make copying easy.

One company, Penguin Software, believes customers should be able to copy their own disks. They removed protection codes from application and graphics software. But they asked people not to make copies

for friends. They sold more disks than before that action. Maybe pirates don't bother companies who are willing to take the chance of being copied. Penguin's games are still copy-protected, but they are also priced inexpensively. The prices discourage people from copying and encourage people to buy, the company's president said.

Another company, Infocom, has tried to fight piracy by making its user's manual and packaging attractive. The company has made the packages part of the games, as in the elaborate packages for *Suspended, Planetfall,* and *Deadline.* Infocom hopes people will want to own the package as much as they want the floppy disk.

Most of the current legal cases about copyrights concern the "big-time pirates" who copy thousands of disks to sell for profit. Yet even the seemingly innocent copying for friends can eat into the profits for software authors. Sometimes piracy causes programmers to stop writing certain kinds of programs. Is piracy a harmless act? Or is it stealing? Is it a crime, much like stealing a book from a bookstore, stealing answers to an exam, or stealing an album from a record store?

SUMMARY POINTS

- Computers need software to be able to perform tasks.

- Most software offers at least one of the following: menus, windows, special input devices, documentation, or error correction features.

- Word processing software allows the user to enter text, correct mistakes, format the output, and print the results. This software is useful for writing letters, reports, or memos.

- One feature of word processing is automatic word wrap. Word processors also allow erasing, inserting, moving, or searching within the text. Block functions and search-and-replace functions help do these jobs.

- Offices, homes, and businesses, such as publishing, use word-processing powers.

- Computer graphics are seen on television ads, program logos, and animated movies.

- The greater the number of pixels, the higher the resolution and the clearer the picture.

- Graphics options include color, texture, line widths, shapes, repetition, overlapping, rotation, or reversal of figures.

- Data management software includes file handlers and data base managers. File handlers file data in traditional filing cabinet methods. Data base managers handle data in a data base. Data appear once and are easily accessed by many different questions.

- Electronic spreadsheets are used for financial study. They copy a real situation and make changes in all related figures when a change is made in the "What if" question.

CHAPTER TEST

Vocabulary

Match the term from the numbered column with the best definition from the lettered column.

1. Format	**a.**	Something that data bases help to avoid.	
2. Menu	**b.**	A feature of computers that permits you to bypass the **RETURN** key at the end of each line.	
3. Block function	**c.**	A term for using identical text in a series of letters, now achieved by some word-processing software.	
4. Automatic word wrap	**d.**	A list of choices.	
5. Grid	**e.**	Clarity; detail of a picture.	
6. File handler	**f.**	A function of word-processing software that might involve a search and replace.	
7. Redundancy	**g.**	A way to edit text in word processing.	
8. Edit	**h.**	A type of data management software.	
9. Boilerplate	**i.**	What appears on an electronic spreadsheet.	
10. Resolution	**j.**	To plan computer text for printing; a word-processing function.	

Questions

1. Explain menu and window. How do these features help users?
2. Describe at least four operations you could perform with a word processing package that you could not do on a typewriter.
3. What jobs can be done with block functions?
4. What is meant by "search and replace"? Explain two ways it might be done.
5. Boilerplating is something you do during formatting. Describe two ways to "boilerplate."
6. How does the publishing business use word-processing software or hardware?
7. Why are some computer-made pictures smoother and clearer than others?
8. List six things you might be able to do with computer graphics software.
9. Contrast a file handler and a data base manager.
10. What are two goals of using data base software?
11. If you were a business person, what very important feature of electronic spreadsheets would you use?

DISCUSSION QUESTIONS

1. Discuss whether a word-processing package might help you improve your writing ability. What features would you like? What features do you like about using pen or pencil and paper?
2. Make a chart of the number of birthdays in each month for all the students in your class. Now use computer graphics software to design a bar graph that tells the same information.
3. Could a spreadsheet help your household with a budget? Describe how you might use it and what categories you might include for the columns and rows of figures.

ACTIVITIES

1. Use any word-processing package for this assignment. Find out how this particular package does automatic word wrap. Learn how to use the block functions, search and replace, and formatting. Is there a way to protect yourself against deleting material that you might wish later you had kept?
2. This assignment involves watching television. Pick a sports cast or a time when many half-hour shows follow each other. Write a log for two or three hours of viewing time. Record any commercial or program logo that you think might have been created by computer graphics. What features did you recognize from reading this chapter? Write them down after each example that you recorded.
3. Find out from your school how records are kept. How are the files managed? Is a data base manager used?

Chapter 7

Computers and the Workplace

Learning Objectives

After reading this chapter, you should be able to:

1. Define CAD and CAM.

2. Explain some uses of robots in industry.

3. Describe at least three ways computers are used in science and medicine.

4. Explain how graphics software is used with computers in sports and the arts.

5. Define CAI.

6. Outline some specific ways computers are used for individual classroom learning and special-needs students.

7. List some ways computers are used in automated offices and in service industries.

8. Describe five ways the federal government uses computers.

Introduction

Computer use in the workplace consists of an alphabet soup of processes—UPC, POS, CAI, CAD, CAM, NDT, CAT, MPHT. You name the initials and someone can probably match them with the name of a computerized process. New uses for computers are being found every day. It is almost impossible to function in a job without working with a computer.

Industry

Manufacturing involves shipping the right product to the right place at the right time in the right amount. Computers handle the scheduling of materials, machinery, and labor to reach this goal. They also help in the design, building, and testing of products.

CAD/CAM

One of the fastest growing uses of computers in industry is **computer-aided design (CAD)**. It is sometimes called CADD for computer-aided design and drafting (see Figure 7-1). CAD allows an engineer to design and draft a product by computer. The computer model also detects the strengths and weaknesses of a product before the first sample is ever built.

CAD is often paired with **CAM, computer-aided manufacturing**. CAM simulates, or models, the manufacturing process. This

Computer-aided design (CAD) The use of a computer to design, draft, and test a product.

Computer-aided manufacturing (CAM) The use of a computer to simulate or monitor the steps of a manufacturing process.

Figure 7-1. *CAD/CAM locates where robots will spot weld body sections.*

helps engineers spot and correct problems before the manufacturing really takes place. CAM also checks the actual manufacturing process (see Figure 7-2).

CAD/CAM saves time and money for firms. It enabled Ford Motor Company to design a light, efficient engine for its Escort and Lynx cars in record time. It helped McDonnell Douglas make fewer mistakes in shaping tubes for its F-18 fighter planes. Nike has used a CAD system to design the pebbling on the soles of athletic shoes.

Nondestructive Testing

Nondestructive testing (NDT) Testing done by electronic means to avoid breaking, cutting, or tearing apart the product.

What happens when something goes wrong with a product? It is possible to poke inside an engine or machinery part without having to tear it apart. **Nondestructive testing (NDT)** uses x-rays, sound waves, or lasers along with microcomputers. With NDT, engineers can see inside aircraft engines, gas pipelines, or nuclear reactors to check for weaknesses. NDT distinguishes between dangerous flaws and harmless nicks.

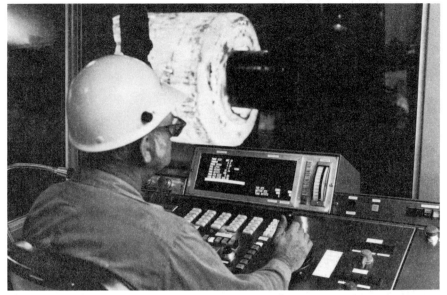

Figure 7-2. *At Bethlehem Steel, the steel rolling operation is watched from this computerized control center.*

Robots

Science fiction writer Isaac Asimov has written many stories about robots. He also has written a robot code of ethics, telling what a robot should and should not do. Since robots appear often in science fiction stories, you might think they are still to be invented. But robots are part of today's technology.

Production of industrial robots began in the 1960s. Yet it was not until the 1970s that industry began to accept robots as a way to lower costs of manufacturing. Even today, United States industries lag in the use of robots. Japan has been the world leader in both the production and use of robots.

Figure 7-3. *Robots paint cars.*

Figure 7-4. *Robots perform repetitious jobs on an automobile assembly line.*

Robots do risky jobs in factories (see Figure 7-3). They handle unsafe chemicals, very hot materials, and explosives. They perform jobs such as welding bolts onto cars (see Figure 7-4). The auto industry uses robots instead of humans to paint cars because of the strong paint fumes. Robot arms have also been used in space travel to hold and rotate cameras outside the spacecraft.

Robots save money for factories by doing two or three shifts of work that would take extra workers to perform. Factory owners like robots because they do not receive benefits and do not get sick.

But robots can be problems. A surge of electricity can give a robot an extra jolt of energy, so it loses control for a while. Maybe the computer program that controls its actions develops a fault. Perhaps an employee walks into the path of a robot while it is working. Property damage and physical injury can result. Factories need to develop safety rules for the workers who work near robots.

Robots are used more often in places other than factories. Coal mining companies are expected to "employ" robots in the mines by the 1990s. Robots also might clean the floors of public buildings and the outside windows of multistory buildings.

Science and Medicine

Computers help scientists and doctors do their jobs faster and more accurately. Before computers, these professionals depended on pencil and paper and checking and rechecking to come up with results. Now computers solve math problems and make predictions in seconds. They detect factors that might lie too deep for humans to see. These functions free scientists to spend more time on ideas instead of paperwork.

Those number-crunching computers have crunched their way into the potato chip industry. Last year Americans munched over $2.5 billion worth of chips. But still they seek that perfect chip. Some munchers want a crunchier chip. But a thicker slice of potato requires a longer frying time. This results in a chip with all the crunch of a plastic credit card! One company, Frito-Lay, put a computer to work on the problem.

Frito-Lay engineers began with the design of the Ruffles ridged chip. Then the engineers fed a computer with many wave patterns. The computer compared the Ruffles wave pattern with the desired qualities of a new chip and pronounced the answer: shift the bottom wave slightly, so the up-slope is thicker than the down-slope. The new chip is the "super dip chip."

But what's a crunchy chip if it has no flavor? Frito-Lay's computer technology gave the chip the correct blend of baked and fried potato flavors. The new chip, the O'Grady, may not be the deluxe chip, but it's one step closer in the quest for the perfect crunch.

Some scientists used computers to study Mount St. Helens. The 1980 eruption of Mount St. Helens drew a team of U.S. Geological Survey scientists to study the volcano. Meters placed inside the crater sent data to a computer every ten minutes.

With the help of computers, experts can also judge the best sites for drilling oil and check the earth for insects, forests, and pollution. They plan for environmental crises such as chemical spills or problems at nuclear power plants.

In hospitals, computers keep records, monitor patients, schedule events, order supplies, bill patients, and pay employees. Hospitals such as the Mayo Clinic in Minnesota use computers to ask patients about their medical histories.

Computers help doctors diagnose illnesses, too. Two types of computer-assisted diagnosis are multiphasic health testing (MPHT) and computerized tomography (CT or CAT) scanning.

When a patient goes to a center that does MPHT, a family medical history is completed. Then tests are run—chest x-ray, blood tests, pain tests, and so forth. A computer compares the test results and medical history with normal standards. The center's doctor adds comments. The patient then discusses the final results with the family doctor. This type of testing can help to prevent health problems, too.

A major advance in health care has been computerized tomography (CT or CAT) scanning (see Figure 7-5). X-rays and computers together give quick and correct diagnoses. This system is one of several noninvasive methods used to find problems in the heart, blood vessels, brain, and other soft tissues of the body.

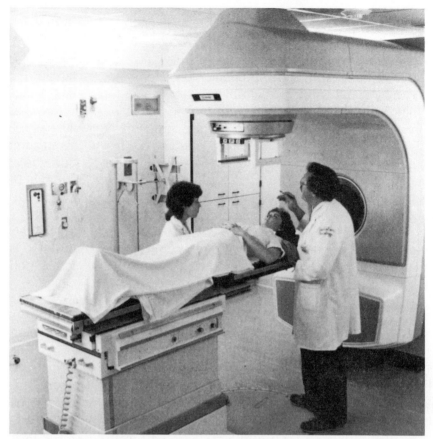

Figure 7-5. *Computerized elements aid this patient's treatment.*

Noninvasive means a doctor does not have to perform surgery or put chemicals into the body to find a problem.

Very ill patients in hospital intensive care or coronary units can be monitored by computers. The computers collect data about heart rate, temperature, and blood pressure. They sound alarms if anything goes wrong. Nurses watch monitors for as many as eight patients at once and can act quickly if the alarm sounds.

The Hospital for Special Surgery in New York City uses CAD/CAM to design and produce new bones to replace human bones. The artificial bones take the place of defective ones, such as broken knee joints or hip bones. Once, a patient would wait for 12 weeks and pay as much as $4,500 for a knee joint. CAD/CAM can produce the artificial knee for less than $3,000 in only two weeks.

LEARNING CHECK 7-1

1. What does CAD stand for?

2. A hospital can use CAD/CAM to design and build new _____.

3. How can NDT be helpful?

4. What kind of job would today's robot not do?
   a. painting cars
   b. welding bolts
   c. planning and designing
   d. handling hot materials

5. TRUE FALSE Robots might be used to work in mines in the future.

Entertainment

Even in sports, television, and movies, computers have made their impact. Computers offer graphics, sound, editing, word processing, and data-handling powers to the people that produce entertainment.

Sports

The field of sports—baseball, tennis, or football, for instance—often uses computers to figure statistics. Computers determine batting averages and runs batted in. Computers judge how a player performs on grass or artificial turf. They help prepare football game plans, monitor college players, and store current statistics on pros all over the nation.

Computers can also be used to judge how well athletes' bodies use oxygen and how strong their muscles are (see Figure 7-6). The tests help athletes who practice endurance sports, such as bike racing and long-distance running. One test measures how much oxygen an athlete uses while riding a stationary bicycle or running on a treadmill. If more oxygen is being used than should be, the athlete is given a training program to improve aerobic fitness.

With the use of high-speed cameras, computers can study gaits, or running forms. In some sports, such as race walking, correct form is crucial. Once the film is made, a computer produces a cartoon likeness of the athlete so that problems can be detected. Then the racer can correct his or her running form.

Even the scheduling of athletic events is handled by computers. Each baseball season, for example, the baseball leagues play 2,106 games. Not only does each game have to be scheduled for the right day, but also the right hour and turf. The Baltimore Orioles, as an example, must play out of town during the Preakness horse race.

Will too much zapping of purple invaders flashing across a video screen cause the players to become too aggressive? The writers of *Killer T-Cell* hope so. *Killer T-Cell* is played by cancer patient "warriors" at M.D. Anderson Hospital and Tumor Institute, Houston, Texas. The game helps kids understand and even battle their cancers.

Across the video screen race the fast-dividing cancer cells. A player moves a T-lymphocyte figure. This figure is one of two kinds of white blood cells that defend the body against viruses and bacteria. The patient makes the "T-Cell" attack the cancer cells. If the orange tumor cells spread too fast, the player can zap them with a dose of electronic "chemotherapy." This action costs the

player points. It is a reminder that chemotherapy can produce bad side effects.

The game makes cancer patients think that their bodies can fight the cancers with success. And many times it helps! Perhaps *Killer T-Cell* will lead to video games for winning battles against other serious illnesses.

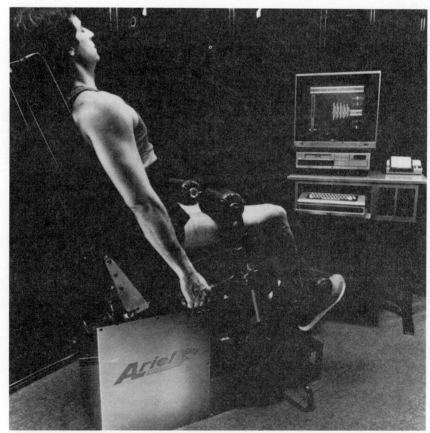

Figure 7-6. *An athlete's strength is measured as he strains against a resistance device.*

Olympic champion Carl Lewis had some high-tech help to get extra distance on his long jump. The help came from the Elite Athlete biomechanics program run by Dr. James Hay of the University of Iowa. The program focused on making the most of the laws of motion through greater acceleration, the angle of take-off, and the longer, more uniform stride length.

Carl's style in the long jump was videotaped, then rolled frame by frame. Using a special stylus, Dr. Hay marked different points in the images. A computer used that data to create a stick figure performing the same jump. Carl's coach, Tom Tellez, was then able to analyze the jump in detail. He discovered that Carl was hesitating as he approached the jump line. With training, Carl overcame his hesitation and improved his stride. The length of his jumps then increased.

Arts

We saw how artists can use computer graphics in the chapter on software. Film producers and photographers also use computers. Animated films once required many artists to draw the many frames to produce smooth cartoon motion. Now artists draw a basic set of pictures to outline the motion, and the computer does the rest.

For some movies, the entire background is drawn on computer. Then the actors are filmed against a plain background. The two films are combined to produce one scene of the movie. All sorts of fantasy lands can be made using this method.

Commercial and fine arts designers create drawings, charts, graphs, cartoons, and museum-quality "paintings" with computers.

Computers can mimic sounds of musical instruments and sound effects, such as chirping crickets, sirens, auto crashes, footsteps, and breaking glass. Computer-produced sound may decrease the cost of producing ads and theme songs. During ads like those for Dr Pepper, Club Med, and Kentucky Fried Chicken and opening themes for TV shows, you will hear computer-produced music.

Some musicians edit their recordings with computers. The late John Lennon used computer editing during the recording of his last album, *Double Fantasy*. After rejecting take after take, he agreed to let a computer pull the best portions of each take and join them.

Fiction and nonfiction writers use word processing packages to write their text. Many writers for films and TV shows write

Figure 7-7. *A teacher helps students use microcomputers.*

their scripts on microcomputers, too. They type their material into the computer on a keyboard and see the words displayed on a screen, making changes in the text easy. The scripts for shows can go through seven or more drafts. Word processing ends the need for retyping.

Education

A popular question in the past ten years has been, "Will the computer replace the teacher?" The answer is "No."

But computers will help teachers with their work. Computers become private tutors for students who need extra help or who learn very fast. Like films and television, computer technology brings the outside world to the classroom. Computers can even link several schools in a learning network.

Included in this section on education are computer-assisted instruction, computers for special-needs students and networks.

Computer-Assisted Instruction

Computer-assisted instruction (CAI) The use of a computer to instruct or drill students.

Computers were first used in classrooms in the 1960s. These electronic machines were dedicated learning machines. They drilled students on state capitals and multiplication facts.

Computer-assisted instruction (CAI) is still used for teaching by drilling. Teachers know the advantages of using a computer

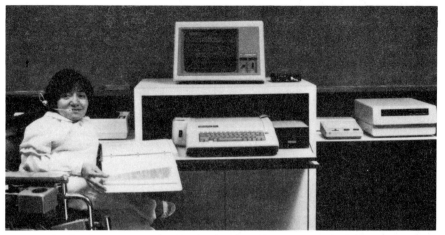

Figure 7-8. *A voice can operate this Apple microcomputer.*

for drills. Students learn at their own pace and get instant feedback. Students who need repeated drills find this patient teacher very helpful.

CAI has been expanded to teach new things and allow students to copy real-world events. Students learn to observe, measure, predict, and experiment. They use thinking skills rather than memory skills (see Figure 7-7).

Computers for Special-Needs Students

Computers help students who are handicapped, too. Some children have few language skills. Others are blind or deaf. Still others cannot use their muscles well.

The Infant Program at the Exceptional Children's Foundation based in Los Angeles, California, uses computers to help children learn to speak and write. At Roadrunner Elementary School in Phoenix, Arizona, students who need help in reading and writing use computers to build their skills.

Some computers will talk back to students. Others have special devices to help physically handicapped students. These students may not have the muscle skills to use a keyboard. They may work with computers by speaking into a recording machine, touching pictures on a special pad, or using a joystick or mouse (see Figure 7-8).

Videodisks and Networks

Besides programming and CAI, some schools allow students to access information utilities and use videodisk technology. Special equipment is needed. The tools include modems, communications software, phone lines, and videodisk players.

Utilities like CompuServe and The Source provide a range of services from electronic mail to on-line encyclopedias and additional CAI software. Students will be able to access sources that are not found in local libraries. Many sources are current.

Using utilities allows students to learn new computer skills. They learn how to sign on, download and upload items, and locate data.

Once the communications system is set up, schools can link with other schools. Students can send games, newsletters, and student-written programs to each other.

Using telecommunications can help students in remote schools expand their world. Videodisks are another technology that brings the outside world to school with motion and sound. Current news can be shown, as well as footage from old newscasts. Actors prepare videodisks to bring history to life. Students can watch colonists preparing for the Revolutionary War or the Wright Brothers trying out their first airplane.

Unlike films, videodisk technology permits students to answer questions, ask questions, and choose the "shows" they want to see. Like other CAI programs, videodisk lessons let students advance at their own rate and interact with a patient "teacher."

LEARNING CHECK 7-2

1. Computers can help check on how well an athlete's body uses _____.

2. Graphics artists would be least apt to use computers to _____.
   a. create animated pictures
   b. edit recordings
   c. produce a TV ad
   d. merge photographed film with computer-generated movies

3. Two new computer-aided technologies may help bring the world to remote schools. Judging from this chapter, what do you think they are?

4. Two input or output devices that might help handicapped students use computers are _____ and _____.

5. CAI stands for _____.

1. oxygen 2. b 3. telecommunications, videodisk technology 4. joysticks, mice, graphics tablets, recording machines 5. computer-assisted instruction

Business

Automated Offices

Offices are becoming automated. This means that data processing, communications, reporting, and other functions are computerized (see Figure 7-9).

Figure 7-9. *This office information system combines word and data processing along with a company-wide communications network.*

Word processing is an automated activity that greatly reduces paperwork. Letters, memos, reports, and original manuscripts can be written on word processors. Many copies can be made, but the text can also be stored for later use. A typical system consists of computer, keyboard, disk drives, CRT, off-line storage, and printers.

Word processing is only one of the many ways computers are used in offices. Electronic mail, teleconferencing, and information retrieval are commmon. Currently used for communications within a business, **electronic mail** may someday replace most regular mail. Commercial electronic mail services are offered by GTE Telenet (Telemail), among others. Messages are sent at high speed through special computer hardware.

Electronic mail
Messages sent at high speeds by telecommunication equipment.

Figure 7-10. *Teleconferencing.*

Teleconference A
meeting conducted
from two or more
locations over com-
munication lines.

Meetings can be held by computer, too (see Figure 7-10). To do this, offices need television-like devices so employees can watch and hear the other speakers. Although **teleconferencing** saves time and travel expenses, it is expensive. It also makes executives aware of small things like messy hair and crooked ties!

People in offices make decisions. They need information to make good decisions. Automated office computer systems allow the workers to access data through computers. Authorized users get information almost instantly. They can decide what action to take without waiting.

Offices may be linked to a central computer by a local network. This linking of equipment allows many users to access the data and use computer power.

Computers in Service Industries

Banks handle huge amounts of paper and figures daily. Checks, loan records, deposits, savings clubs, and investment plans must be processed daily. The balances of all accounts must be kept up to date. To do the job well, every bank across the country uses computers.

One of the newest advances in banking is the 24-hour banking service. A computer-controlled machine permits customers to do their banking day or night. The bank customer places a plastic card in a slot and selects a transaction by pushing a series of buttons. Many banks have the machines in the outside walls of the bank buildings. The machines are also in supermarkets, airports, and shopping malls.

Many banks also provide automated transaction service. Customers can have paychecks placed directly into their checking accounts by employers. The accounts are accessed regularly and automatically to pay utility and credit card bills and transfer funds to savings accounts.

Retail stores, especially groceries and large chain stores, record sales and inventory through point-of-sale (POS) terminals. The POS terminal acts as a cash register and also records sales and updates inventory (the quantity of goods on hand). Hand-held wands or scanning windows read product and manufacturer data printed in bar codes or characters on the packages. Some systems can even check a customer's credit.

Airlines and travel agencies consult CRTs to check flight schedules, make reservations, and confirm flights. Airlines keep track of arrivals, departures, empty seats, meals, baggage, fuel, weather, upkeep, and miles flown. Even the pilots make use of computer sytems to fly the plane and land at the correct time on the correct runway.

Figure 7-11. *Strategic Air Command Headquarters.*

Computers are used in many other ways. Hotels and hospitals use networks of computer and telecommunication hardware to plan their schedules. Restaurants and insurance agencies acquire computers to keep records.

As the cost of computer equipment decreases, more and more small businesses will be able to use computers. Much software for microcomputers can be bought at reasonable costs. Lawyers, physicians, landlords, and owners of small shops use computers to perform record-keeping, word-processing, and accounting chores. Soon computers will be as common as typewriters and adding machines in every aspect of business.

Government

The federal government is the largest user of computers in the United States. This fact is not surprising: many government agencies collect, process, and store data about people. The government uses computers in much the same way as do businesses. The government has many other uses for computers, too.

Tax Collecting

Every person living in the United States who earns more than a certain amount of money must report to the federal government for tax purposes. Businesses also file yearly tax returns to report their earnings. Each year, the Internal Revenue Service (IRS) receives millions of tax returns. The IRS uses computers to check the returns and record the data. The data are placed in huge data bases.

Figure 7-12. *Police officials use computers to keep track of arrest records, finger-print files, and crime occurrences.*

The IRS also audits selected returns. Computers select tax returns for this checking process.

Military Planning

Every branch of the armed forces is involved in military planning and decision-making. High-ranking officials use information obtained by computer. A network of 20 satellites sends data to computer centers from all over the world. The North America Air Defense Command, near Colorado Springs, Colorado, keeps a huge computer system to locate or update data at a moment's notice. The computer can spot rockets and missiles within seconds after they are launched (see Figure 7-11). The computer can signal and perform the proper actions in case of attack.

Military planners use computers to simulate wars. Commanders practice making decisions based on the lifelike events that the computer presents.

Environmental Planning

The Department of Health and Human Services uses computers to predict and control the effects of industrial waste in our country's rivers and streams. Computers check the amounts of chemicals and oxygen in the water to check how safe the water is.

The Environmental Protection Agency finds out the causes and effects of air pollution. The computer-produced information is vital in urging stronger pollution control laws.

Weather Forecasting

Huge computers process data about air pressure, wind speed, humidity, temperature, and so forth. The processed data help forecasters predict the weather.

The data are collected from weather stations, satellites, and other devices throughout the world. The data are processed by computers at the National Weather Service in Maryland. Without computers, processing would take so long that the weather conditions would happen before the forecast was ready.

Law Enforcing

The FBI (Federal Bureau of Investigation) and the CIA (Central Intelligence Agency) use computer systems to store data, outline their plans, and track criminals. One FBI system, the National Crime Information Center, uses a national network of computers to keep track of data. A centrally located data bank is open to police stations through computers in each state (see Figure 7-12). This system allows local police to get information about stolen property, criminals, and criminal records from all over the country.

 LEARNING CHECK 7-3

1. A word processing system is least apt to include _____.
   a. a printer
   b. word-processing software
   c. POS terminals
   d. CRT

2. In an automated office, a computer system may provide all of the following except

_____.
   a. electronic mail
   b. information retrieval
   c. local networks
   d. 24-hour teller machine

3. The Internal Revenue Service will probably keep all of its records in a _____.
   a. word processor
   b. data base
   c. file handler
   d. spreadsheet

4. Computers help the branches of the armed forces to _____ war.

5. The Department of Health and Human Services and the Environmental Protection Agency use computers to find the causes of _____ and plan measures to correct the problems.

1. c 2. d 3. b 4. simulate 5. pollution

Perspective As computer use increases, more people will use computers in jobs. Schools will offer courses about computers. They will teach computer use in English, math, science, and vocational classes, too. Students will learn about simulation and data bases at school.

But many current uses of computers may become outdated. Much computer hardware will no longer be useful. The computer field changes very fast. People will need to update their knowledge about computers.

How will computers in the work place change by the time you graduate from high school?

ISSUE/DO COMPUTERS KNOW TOO MUCH?

Computers know a great deal about you and your family. Well, they don't really "know" anything, but they provide access to huge data bases.

And who see these data? If clever teenagers can break into computer systems, so can criminals. So could an employer, a landlord, or a credit bureau. So can many government agencies.

The largest data bases are held by the federal government. If a person has served in the armed forces, had a physical or mental disability, committed a crime, or completed an income tax return, data have been entered into these data bases.

And how does one find out information from such a system? Simple. A number is entered in the system. It is a number we all have. It is the social security number. There are two problems with using the social security number as the sole key to computer data. First, if the person mistypes a social security number, information is retrieved about the wrong person. Second, the information about one person can be obtained from many different computer systems with only one key.

A recent debate arose over the use of the social security number as a key. Under the name Project Match, the Department of Health and Human Services (HHS) is trying to find federal workers who illegally receive welfare from the state. Three other federal agencies are working with HHS to find these people.

The project works simply. Social Security numbers from the HHS computer list of people who receive welfare are compared with social security numbers in the other three computers. When a "match" is found, the person is checked out.

When data are removed from one file to be checked against another, the right to privacy is violated. Yet time is saved by this system, and offenders are found.

The Privacy Act of 1974 helps protect against misuse of information by the government. But few laws exist to guard against invasion of privacy unless you work for the federal government.

Many files and data bases exist in businesses, schools, and colleges. Types of data include exam scores, results of physical and psychological tests, personal references, and disciplinary actions. Three main concerns people have about these files are release of data to the wrong people, data that are not needed for a certain situation, and incorrect data. People should be able to say who sees data, what data are collected, and how data are corrected.

Will we have control over data bases? Or are data bases already too large for us to control them?

SUMMARY POINTS

- New uses for computers are found every day.

- Industry uses computers in computer-aided design and manufacturing. These processes help companies test products, machinery, and manufacturing on a trial basis.

- Nondestructive testing allows engineers to test items without tearing them apart.

- Robots are being used in dangerous and boring jobs. Japan is the leading builder and user of robots.

- Scientists and doctors can use computers to do work that takes a lot of time, so they can use their own time better.

- Doctors and nurses use computers to diagnose illnesses, test patients, monitor patients, and build joints.

- The field of sports uses computers to compile statistics, keep records on pros and on potential players, schedule events, and judge athletic performance.

- Computers help people produce pictures, films, music, and novels.

- CAI (computer-assisted instruction) is only one area of computer use in schools. Computers used with videodisks and with telecommunications bring the outside world to schools. Computers also help special-needs students to learn.

- Offices can be automated when they make use of word-processing packages, electronic mail systems, teleconferencing, and information retrieval. Even small businesses can afford computing power today.

- The federal government uses computers in tax collecting, military planning, environmental planning, weather forecasting, and law enforcement.

CHAPTER TEST

Vocabulary

Match the process with a business or job that would most likely use that process. Several answers are possible. In addition, several processes may have more than one job or business that fits. Be sure you can explain the reasons for your choices!

Process	Job or Business
1. CAD	**a.** Doctor
2. CAM	**b.** Teacher
3. Teleconferencing	**c.** Engineer
4. CAI	**d.** Home owner
5. Word processing	**e.** Robot
6. NDT	**f.** Business executive
7. 24-hour banking	**g.** Scientist
8. Electronic mail	**h.** Secretary
9. Welding	**i.** Student
10. CAT scan	**j.** Writer

Questions

1. Explain how CAD can be used with CAM for a more efficient manufacturing process.
2. Judging from your reading, describe how nondestructive testing could save money for an oil company that needs to inspect pipelines.
3. Name three jobs that robots do or will do in industries.
4. List four ways that doctors, hospitals, or nurses use computers.
5. List five ways that computers have changed sports.
6. How might a filmmaker use computers?
7. How has CAI changed over the years? How does it help the teacher and the student?
8. Name four ways that computers have made offices more efficient.
9. Tell how the government uses computers in tax collecting.
10. Tell how the government uses computers in military planning.
11. Explain how computers can be used in environmental planning.

DISCUSSION QUESTIONS

1. Pick your favorite sport and discuss how the computer can be used to help the sport and its athletes.

2. What do you feel computers should be used for? Why? Discuss these questions in class or write a paragraph about them.

3. Discuss the computers you have seen outside of home and school. What are these computers used for?

ACTIVITIES

1. Locate three pictures of computers working in industry. Use any magazine or book. How is each of the computers in these pictures used? Do you think the computer helps the industry?

2. Ask someone you know that works whether or not the computer has helped their work. Write a summary of one or two paragraphs of what you learn from them.

3. Form groups of three or four people and discuss how a computer can be used in your school to help the students. Each group should share their ideas with the class.

Chapter 8

Careers and Computers

Learning Objectives

After reading this chapter, you should be able to:

1. Explain some trends of computer use in traditional jobs.

2. Name and describe several jobs that involve working with computer hardware.

3. Name and describe several jobs that involve working with computer software.

4. Name three careers that form support for the computer industry and explain the job duties.

Introduction

Computers have played a great role in our society. The impact of computers can be seen in almost every job. Most people depend on computers for some aspect of their work. Some employees do not use computers directly. However, their paychecks may be figured and printed by computers or their bills and bank account balances may be recorded by computers.

This chapter describes the jobs that have been created since computer use became widespread. It also talks about how computer use has affected other kinds of jobs.

Computer Use in Traditional Jobs

Teachers at all levels of school see the need to teach about computers. People now employed and those planning for jobs are finding that they need some experience with computers. This section discusses how many traditional jobs are affected by computer use.

Secretaries once took notes on steno pads, typed on slow manual typewriters, and copied materials on messy mimeograph machines. Today their jobs are streamlined with computer tools. They must be able to use word processors, run printers, and use many kinds of computerized files (see Figure 8-1).

Retail clerks often use computers. Many cash registers are point-of-sale terminals with code readers such as Universal Product Code scanners or hand-held wand readers (see Figure 8-2). The clerks also must know how to check credit ratings through computerized telecommunication lines.

Factory workers must know how to use computers. As industry keeps pace with new technology, new machines are controlled by computer. Although some factory jobs will still be done by people, often workers will find their duties changed. They will not perform the manufacturing jobs directly. They will monitor

Figure 8-1. *Secretaries use computer equipment in their jobs.*

machines that do the work. An assembly-line worker may see that the next worker on the line is not a person, but a robot doing a boring and unsafe job. A machinist must know how to use the hardware and software that shapes or cuts a part to exact measurements. Other factory workers must be able to check robots and manufacturing processes by computer.

Across the country, computers aid police officers in their jobs. Data about stolen vehicles, known criminals, missing people, fingerprints, driving convictions, and drug offenses are kept in huge data banks by federal and state law agencies. Sometimes, city and county officers have access to these files and create their own local files as well. Some officers are even able to get information from data banks through equipment in their police cars. The speed with which information can be received can shorten the time spent on each case.

Travel agents use computers to request travel costs, reserve hotel rooms, and find out about featured events in cities and foreign countries. Reservations for travel by airplane, train, or bus are often made through computer terminals. Pilots and air traffic controllers use computers to get information that is vital to the flight of aircraft. Most train traffic is governed by computer, too.

Many persons use computers in jobs outside the computer industry. Many more people will make, design, operate, or program computers. Around the country, young people are eager to take courses in computer science to prepare for these jobs. Other people who have been displaced by automation in factories and offices may be retrained for computer jobs. The rest of this chapter looks at computer-related jobs and their outlook.

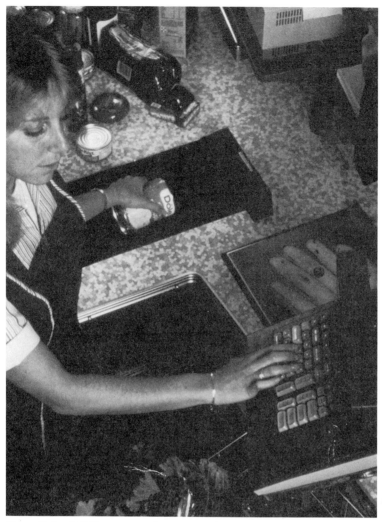

Figure 8-2. *A UPC scanner at a grocery store.*

Careers in Computer Hardware

Computer hardware must be designed, built, serviced, and operated. The people who do these jobs are engineers, technicians, manufacturers, assemblers, and operators. Persons with graduate degrees or high school diplomas may find jobs working with computer hardware.

Engineers and Technicians

Computer engineers usually have college degrees in electrical, mechanical, or electronics engineering. They also may have studied computer science. They help research and design computer systems. Electronics engineers may redesign old equipment or plan new hardware that uses the most recent technology. Mechanical engineers draft the machines needed to produce the

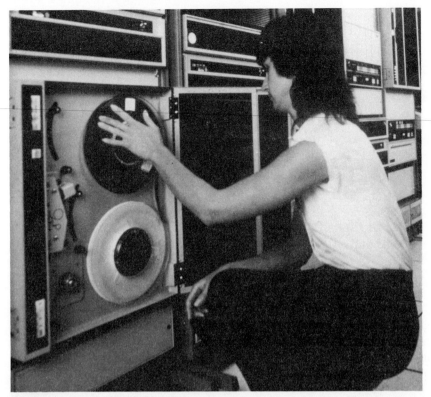

Figure 8-3. *A computer operator must load and unload tape drives and monitor the system during processing.*

new computer hardware. Electrical engineers design the circuitry connecting the parts of a computer and the circuits of the chips themselves. Computer hardware needs to be housed in some type of "package." Some engineers work only on designing the plastic or metal casings for the equipment.

The job outlook for engineers is good. In fact, engineers may be in short supply by the 1990s.

Technician The person who installs, maintains, and repairs computer equipment.

As with any equipment, computer systems must be installed, maintained, and repaired. The **technicians/field engineers** do these jobs. Some technicians are trained to spot computer problems before any damage is done.

Technicians may work for a maker of one brand of computers or may be hired to service all of a company's hardware. Some technicians set up their own service business. Most have two or three years of training in electrical or electronics engineering from colleges or technical schools. This area is expected to provide many jobs before 1990.

Computer operator A person who sets up machines and files needed to run a program and monitors the run for problems.

Operators

Computer operators direct and check the computer equipment. They set up equipment for each job the computer will do, mount or dismount the tapes or disks needed, and check the operation of the computer during its work (see Figure 8-3). They must be prepared to take action if a system "crashes," a user is performing an unauthorized activity, or a terminal breaks down. They handle any upkeep that does not need a technician's services.

Operators need training provided by a company or a technical or vocational school. Some companies will hire only operators who can work with a certain brand of computer system. As computer systems increase in large and small businesses, the job outlook for operators is good.

Manufacturers

Persons working in the manufacture of computer hardware include assemblers, machinists, and inspectors. Assemblers put together the computer parts. Machinists control the machinery that produces the parts. The job of running tests to be sure each part works the way it should belongs to the inspectors.

Training for most jobs in manufacturing is usually provided by the company, although many machinists and inspectors may have attended vocational or technical schools. Jobs in manufacturing may decrease in the future. Robots more often are doing the assembling jobs. In addition, many computer parts are being imported.

 LEARNING CHECK 8-1

1. Which of the following might not explain why factory workers need to know about computers?
   a. Factory workers may lose their jobs to robots.
   b. Factory workers may monitor machines by computer.
   c. Factory workers may have new responsibilities.
   d. Factory workers may buy robots.

2. Judging from material in other chapters, which input or output device do you think travel agents would be most apt to use?
   a. joystick
   b. graphics tablet
   c. CRT
   d. 24-hour teller

3. What job involves the installation and upkeep of computers?

4. The person who prepares the computer equipment for each job is the _____.

1. d 2. c 3. technician, or field engineer 4. computer operator

Figure 8-4. *This data entry operator is preparing shipping invoices.*

Careers in Computer Software

Some people write programs, arrange computer files, and compile and collect data. Although they need some knowledge about how hardware works, their main focus is on the software.

Data-Entry Operators

A **data-entry operator's** job involves putting data into the form needed for computer processing. In the past, this usually involved keypunching data onto cards. Although punched cards are still used for turn-around documents (such as bills) and other purposes, data entry on key-to-tape or key-to-disk devices is more common (see Figure 8-4).

The concept of word processing has provided yet another data-entry job: the word-processing operator. Although secretaries often do word processing, they have other duties as well. Word-processing operators, on the other hand, are hired for the sole purpose of doing word processing.

Data-entry jobs require typing or keying skills. Usually a high school diploma is sufficient for these jobs. Many data-entry operators have also attended technical or vocational schools. Companies also train data-entry operators on the equipment they will be using.

As data-entry methods such as voice input and optical scanners become more common, the need for data-entry operators will decrease.

Figure 8-5. *This data processing librarian gets magnetic tapes from the storage library for processing jobs.*

Librarians

When a company has volumes of data on tapes, disks, cards, microfilm, or other storage media, it houses them in a computer library. The data are kept as records or are used at a later date.

A **librarian** is responsible for managing—classifying, cataloging, and maintaining—the media (see Figure 8-5). The librarian may move back-up files to other storage sites, clean out old files, and oversee the cleaning of magnetic tapes and disks. One very important part of the librarian's job is to check that only authorized persons have access to the material.

A high school diploma and some knowledge of data-processing concepts is usually required for this job.

Librarian The person who catalogs and maintains computer files and programs that are on storage devices.

Programmers

Programmers fall into two groups—**systems programmers** and **application programmers**. A third group is **maintenance programmers**, but application programmers often do the work associated with program maintenance.

Systems programmers write the programs that tell the computer how to operate itself and its peripherals. Systems programmers must be very familiar with the design of the hardware they will be working with. The ability to write programs in assembly language and machine language is needed. A degree in computer science is often required.

Application programmers write the programs that serve the end users—payroll, inventory, simulation, games, education, financial organization (see Figure 8-6). They must have good

Systems programmer A person who writes programs that control a system's operations.

Application programmer A programmer who writes instructions to solve a specific problem.

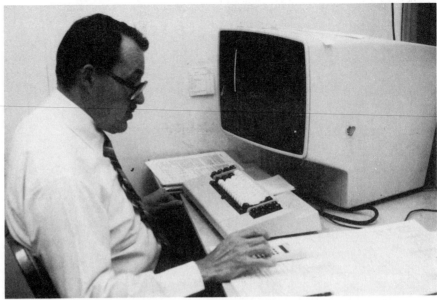

Figure 8-6. *A programmer works in a computer center at Hilheim, West Germany. The opportunities for skilled programmers are truly international.*

command of programming languages such as COBOL, FORTH, BASIC, Pascal, APL, and FORTRAN.

Many application programmers need background in the area for which they are programming. Programmers who write software for use in science must know about math. They may also study a science such as physics, biology, or genetics. A programmer who writes software for business use must have a background in accounting or finance.

The programming languages application programmers know must fit the field. For example, COBOL is a business-oriented language, and FORTRAN is used in scientific programs.

Programs may need updating when a company changes some of its operations. In addition, some programs may have never been debugged. Programmers who perform these duties are maintenance programmers. But the application programmers often do the maintenance programming.

Data-Base Analysts

A **data-base analyst** designs, tests, and puts into practice the data structures used in an organization. The analyst plans and manages the use of data within the system. Part of the data-base analyst's job is to help the user see relationships among the data and to remove copies of data. The analyst defines the way the data will be grouped, suggests changes, and designs new data-base systems.

Data-base analysts need a college degree with a background in computer science, data-base management systems, and business data processing. They must know about both programming and systems operation.

 LEARNING CHECK 8-2

1. The person who keys in data about invoices, bills, inventory, or other transactions is the _____.

2. A librarian's duties involve _____.
   a. preparing computer equipment for the next job
   b. monitoring who has access to computer hardware
   c. moving back-up copies to another site
   d. preparing invoices for data entry

3. Programmers fall into three groups: application, maintenance, and _____ programmers.

4. The programmers who often perform the job of maintenance programming are the _____ programmers.
   a. systems
   b. application
   c. data-entry
   d. analyst

5. Application programmers may have to know something about _____.
   a. the field for which they are programming
   b. the computer operators
   c. the computer manufacturing process
   d. the back-up storage site

1. data-entry operator 2. c 3. systems 4. b 5. a

Management and Administration

Like any department in business or industry, computer departments need managers or administrators. Two typical managers are the **management information system (MIS) manager** and the **data-base administrator (DBA)**. In the past, these managers have been promoted from positions as programmers, systems analysts, or data-base analysts. For today's complex systems, special study is often needed.

The MIS manager controls the physical and human resources of the department so that the company's goals are met. The MIS manager must know about data-processing methods and about the hardware and software used by the firm. Since MIS managers

Management information system (MIS) manager The person who organizes the resources of a company to meet its goals.

Data-base administrator (DBA) A management-level position responsible for controlling all the data resources of a company.

When the Mortensen twins, Keith and Craig, first saw a computer, they were not impressed. Then they tried graphics with an Apple II computer and the Apple graphics tablet. They liked graphics so well that they started a graphics business, Mortensen Computer Graphics, Inc.

The 18-year-old California boys have been draw-ing since they were in grade school. In the eighth grade, they used their school's computer for the first time. As their talents grew, they produced graphics for a computer store to demonstrate Apple computers. Later, Apple hired them to create graph-ics for ads.

Today, Apple is just one of the twins' clients. The Mortensens have created graphics and programming for software companies such as Applied Software Technology and Cham-bered Nautilus Software.

The next time you see Apple graphics in com-puter stores, ads, or com-puter fairs, you might be looking at art produced by Mortensen Computer Graphics, Inc.

work more with people than with machines, they must have leadership skills.

A college degree is required. Studies should include business administration and management information systems. At least two years experience as a manager in another area is helpful.

Data-base administrators control the data resources used in an organization. The job consists of designing the data base(s) and making sure the data base(s) is accurate and complete. Data-base administrators also must design plans to ensure data security and data-base back-up and recovery. They often help analysts, pro-grammers, and system users access the data bases. So they must be able to communicate well with many kinds of people.

The demand for DBAs is strong. Persons who plan this career should obtain a college degree. Studies should focus on computer science, data-base management system design, and business data processing.

Support Personnel

Many others help workers and managers use computer systems. The systems analysts help companies design and acquire their data-processing systems. Technical writers contribute by writing manuals, books, and articles that help users understand the sys-tems. Instructors train employees, students, or hobbyists who want to know more about computers.

Figure 8-7. *A systems analyst must consider the needs of users like the ones here when designing a computer system for a corporation.*

Systems Analysts

Systems analysts must be prepared to work chiefly with people rather than machines (see Figure 8-7). They must be prepared to question employees and managers. They must know how to research a subject. Why? They are the people who design information systems so that the user's information needs are met.

Systems analyst A person who studies, designs, and puts into use computer systems.

An important step in the work of an analyst is to meet with the users and find out what is currently going on in a company. The systems analyst may have to judge hardware and work with programmers to design a system.

Besides holding a college degree with a focus on information systems, analysts must be able to communicate clearly with users at all levels of computer experience.

Technical Writers

Computer hardware and software includes user's guides, technical manuals, and other documentation. This material explains how to use, repair, or understand computers and software. **Technical writers** prepare the documents. They must be able to put their ideas in order and explain the material clearly.

Technical writer A person who writes technical material in a form that is easy to understand.

Some technical writers become editors. They review what other writers have written to check its accuracy.

A technical writing job usually requires a college degree with a major in English. The technical writer should also have a background in the chosen field. That field may be computer science, electronics, software development, or some other technical field.

Teachers often travel by dog sled in the Yukon-Koyukuk School District in Alaska. Some students live very far away from a regular school. This year, each teacher will carry an Apple personal computer tucked under the furs and blankets on the dog sled.

The teachers visit students in small villages once a month. They bring lessons and study aids. But one visit isn't enough. The computers will help the isolated students to learn faster.

A major problem arose when temperatures were below freezing and snow lay deep on the ground. How do you protect the computers? Special cases were built to keep the machines dry and warmer. These cases also protected the computers from the dust and smoke of wood-burning stoves in the students' homes.

Now students in remote areas of Alaska can study the high-tech way!

Sales and Marketing People

Just as in any other business, the computer industry needs people who will sell the products. Personal computer stores have opened all over the country. The salespeople who work in these stores must know the equipment so they can answer most questions buyers might have. Salespeople may also work for large or small computer manufacturers, software developers, or service firms. Although some employers may demand a college education, others depend on the sales abilities of the people they hire.

On the other hand, people who work in marketing probably will have taken some college courses in business, marketing, or advertising. They must know how to present products so that stores will want to carry the brand name and so that companies will want to buy the systems. They must know the best qualities of the computers they are selling.

Instructors

Normally when we think of instructors, we think of schools. Many schools and colleges list courses in computer literacy and computer science. Some technical schools and colleges offer night classes for the beginning computer student. Many public schools provide computer education as part of another subject such as math, English, or science.

All need teachers who can clearly explain computers and programming. The ability to communicate and motivate students is vital.

Figure 8-8. *Training programs require teachers who are able to communicate clearly with the users of new systems.*

Most of us picture teachers in these typical school settings. Yet many companies hire people who will train employees to use new or upgraded computer systems (see Figure 8-8). These teachers must be able to relate to employees who might hesitate to use new or strange equipment.

People who work with computers find out that they must keep up to date about new equipment and ideas. They can do this by reading computer magazines, enrolling in night classes, and going to seminars. Talking with people in other areas of computing also can help.

The computer field changes so rapidly that today's knowledge may be outdated yesterday!

LEARNING CHECK 8-3

1. MIS stands for_____.
2. Systems analysts often work with _____ as well as computers.
3. Technical writers must have all but one of the following skills. Which is it?
   a. ability to explain material clearly
   b. ability to organize their thoughts
   c. knowledge of the subject they are writing about
   d. ability to repair computers
4. Some computer teachers do not teach in schools. Instead they teach employees in a company to use computers. Why would they need to do this?

5. List two ways people who have computer jobs can upgrade their knowledge about computers.

Perspective   *Since the computer industry is young and rapidly changing, anyone who wants to work in the field must be prepared to change rapidly, too. New jobs will evolve and old jobs will fade out. Jobs for data-entry operators may no longer exist when voice-input systems are perfected. Languages that translate plain English into machine languages may replace programmers. As robotics becomes widespread, more technicians will be needed to work with the robots. Microcomputers will also become more powerful. Then larger systems may not be needed—and neither will the skills be needed to run them.*

Just imagine! In the 1940s, people were needed to rewire and pull switches to prepare computers for each job. In the 1950s and 1960s, punched card technology was used. Keypunchers punched millions of IBM cards. Programmers fell over stacks of the cards they threw out when they tested and debugged programs. In the 1970s, word processing inched its way into the business world, only to speed into the 1980s, creating a whole new job market for data-entry operators. In the 1990s, we may work at home through telecommunications. By the turn of the century, we may be able to operate computers just by sending our thoughts to the computer. Well, maybe a bit farfetched. But who knows? Is nothing impossible? Just read the material about biochips and artificial intelligence in the next chapter.

ISSUE/BUT CAN YOU TYPE?

In the past, typing has been linked with secretaries. Many male executives wouldn't have been caught typing anything.

Computers are changing the image of typing. Of course, you do not call it typing anymore—it's keyboarding. Secretaries receive new respect for their skills with computers. And executives are learning to keyboard so that they can use a computer.

Students at Lyons Township High School in the Chicago area are building keyboarding skills. The last two weeks of typing classes are spent with hands-on experience on microcomputers.

Some teachers are training students as early as second grade. With laminated paper keyboards, the teachers explain the proper fingers to use on the proper keys. By this method, students learn good keyboarding habits early.

When students cannot type well, they may shy away from microcomputers. Their clumsiness at the keyboard gets in the way of entering data and writing programs. Hunt-and-peck just doesn't fit in the high-tech world of computers!

Knowing how to type helps a high school grad-uate get a job, too. Nurses, postal maintenance work-ers, airport baggage checkers, machinists, tool and dye makers, and exec-utives are learning key-boarding so they can use the computers on the job more effectively.

What do you say? Should you take a key-boarding class? Look at it this way—would you show off a clumsy hunt-and-peck style?

SUMMARY POINTS

- Workers at all levels of business and industry may need to know something about computers. Computers will be used in many jobs outside the computer industry.

- Some careers—engineering, manufacturing, repairing, operating—involve working with the computer hardware.

- Other careers—data entry, library work, programming, data-base preparation—mean working with computer software.

- Managers in computer-related work include the data-base administrator and the management information systems manager. Both involve using the company's resources to their fullest.

- Other related jobs support the computer industry. Persons may work as systems analysts, technical writers, sales and marketing people, and teachers.

CHAPTER TEST

Vocabulary

Match the term from the numbered column with the best definition from the lettered column.

1. Technical writer
2. Application programmer
3. Systems analyst
4. Technician
5. Librarian
6. Systems programmer
7. Computer operator
8. DBA

a. Catalogs and maintains computer files and programs already on storage media

b. Prepares user's manuals so that other people can understand the material

c. Installs, maintains, and repairs computer equipment

d. Sets up computer equipment for a run

e. Writes programs for such jobs as billing and payroll

f. Is responsible for control of all the data resources of a company

g. Works with users and programmers to analyze, design, and implement a system

h. Writes the programs that help a computer operate itself and its peripherals

Questions

1. Name four ways computers are changing the way people work in factories, stores, offices, and government.
2. Write a job description for one career working with computer hardware.
3. What duties does the data-processing librarian have?
4. Describe the duties of the systems programmer and contrast them with the duties of the application programmer.
5. Name one quality essential to the systems analyst. Why?
6. What does a technical writer do?
7. Tell how instructors can help a company.

DISCUSSION QUESTIONS

1. Describe some problems that may occur with employees when a company installs a new computer system or upgrades an old system. What kinds of things would help lessen those problems?
2. Discuss the importance of upgrading computer skills and knowledge.
3. Discuss the kinds of jobs that might be associated with the increased use of robots.

ACTIVITIES

1. Through your parents or some other adult, find out about a computer-related career listed in this chapter. Find out what the job duties are. Compare them with those listed in this chapter. Are some jobs combined in smaller companies? Are some jobs even more specialized in larger companies?
2. Write a short user's guide that explains how to begin using a particular computer program for the computer at school. You may choose any program. Be sure that the user could turn on the machine, load the disk, and begin the program without help from you. Try it out on a student who has had no computer experience.
3. Prepare a chart that shows the differences and likenesses of the jobs of a librarian of a computer library and a librarian of a book library (school or public).

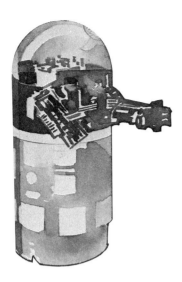

Chapter 9

Ethical Issues and Computers of Tomorrow

Learning Objectives

After reading this chapter, you should be able to:

1. Cite several problems that have been created by the use of computers.

2. Discuss the major points of the Fair Credit Reporting Act of 1970 and the Privacy Act of 1974.

3. Explain how the development of artificial intelligence and new chip technology will affect computers in the future.

4. Describe how computers are used in homes with respect to telecommuting, home control, and personal robots.

Introduction

The impact of computers on our lives becomes stronger every day. This chapter examines some ways computers are creating problems in our lives and some ways the government is dealing with these problems through legislation. Advances in artificial intelligence and chip technology are also described. Discussions of the present and future effects of computers on telecommuting, home control, and personal robots conclude the chapter.

Privacy, Security, and Ethics

Despite all the ways computers help our society, they have created some problems in privacy, security, and ethics. In this section we discuss some of the problems created by the growing use of computers in all areas of our lives. We also discuss legislation designed to help protect people from the effects of these problems.

Problem Areas

Most of us have some aspect of our lives we would rather keep private. Yet we can see the need for others to have information. Doctors need accurate medical histories of their patients. Banks need financial information to issue credit cards or lend money. The government may need private information about persons applying for secret service jobs. As data about us are collected and computerized, the potential for abuse becomes greater. People are, or should be, wary of three kinds of abuse: 1) information being collected without their knowledge; 2) wrong information that cannot be corrected; 3) information that is used for purposes other than the original ones.

Many people fear that personal information will be collected and used without their knowledge. Widespread use of mailing lists is one example. Through some transaction in the past, you may have placed yourself on a company's mailing list. Perhaps you order some sporting goods from a mail order company. Later, that company sells its mailing list to other companies. A detail about yourself has been interpreted to mean that you have special interests and that you may be a potential customer for other companies. Correct or incorrect, that data has been collected and passed around without your knowledge.

Another area of concern is the problem of disclosure. Just think how many files of information might have been collected on a single person. Any person who has attended school has medical records, psychological and scholastic test scores, grades, and teachers' comments stored in school files. A person who has served in the armed forces has a mass of data stored in government computers. Anyone who has received credit cards, other kinds of credit, or government help will have data about themselves stored in files somewhere. Employers keep work and absence records, medical information, and personal remarks about employees. With so many files in so many locations, the potential for incorrect or outdated information is great.

Some people have been denied credit or jobs because data in a computer file were incorrect or issued under the wrong name. How can you find out whether data collected about yourself are correct? Can you have the data changed easily? You should have the right of disclosure—the right to see and challenge the contents of your files.

A third problem involves data collected for one purpose and used for other purposes. For example, the federal government keeps some of the largest data banks. Files include data on people who receive aid, who pay federal income taxes, who have traveled to foreign countries, who own boats . . . the list goes on and on. These data, plus data gathered by private organizations, are accessed by using the social security number. People fear the data may be used by the wrong people for the wrong reasons—perhaps to deny jobs or secretly to monitor their actions.

Another problem area that involves computers is security. Most security problems are caused by accidents. They occur when data are omitted or destroyed by mistake. Problems also arise when events occur like fire, natural disasters, and computer crime.

Security in many computer systems is designed to prevent simple errors by humans or machines. For example, sometimes data entered into a computer system are erased or never processed. Other times the data may be sent to the wrong remote terminal. Hard copy has disappeared when the wrong person picked up the output from a printer. Sometimes data or equipment are destroyed accidentally when someone has pushed the wrong button.

Fires can destroy equipment, and water used to put out fires will damage computers. Earthquakes and floods can ruin entire computer centers. Protecting computer systems against natural disasters like these is a major concern for many companies.

Computer crime worries companies, too. Vandals can destroy both hardware and software. Software can be stolen or copied without permission. More people are using home computers for illegal purposes, too. One example is the illegal transfer of electronic funds. Many of these crimes are not detected. Millions of dollars are lost every year from crimes that are never discovered.

Ethics Rules or
standards to guide
personal conduct.

Computer **ethics** present another problem area. Computers have become an important part of our lives within a rather short period of time. For this reason, no standard code of ethical behavior guides their use. Problems such as illegal copying of software and improper access to and use of data grow daily. Employees are using company-owned computers for personal tasks at the expense of the company. Workers copy disks to use at home. Data entry people peek into files they should not be reading. Guidelines to help resolve these problems are needed.

Legislation

As computers have grown in popularity, a need has been created for legislation to help control some of the problems discussed earlier. Two of the most important federal laws are the Fair Credit Reporting Act of 1970 and the Privacy Act of 1974.

The Fair Credit Reporting Act of 1970 is one of the first major efforts to protect the privacy of individuals. Before 1970, people had little protection against false information and often could not see their own credit files. The purpose of the Fair Credit act is to help people protect themselves against errors in credit information used by credit-reporting agencies. The act gives people the right to know what data an agency keeps filed about them. People may challenge the contents of a file. Changes must be made when appropriate. Outdated information must be removed from a file.

This act also restricts use of the data contained in the files. Only people with valid court orders or written permission from the consumer can have access to the files. Also, the data must be used for a valid purpose. Investigating a loan application or transacting a business deal are examples of valid uses of credit information.

The Privacy Act of 1974 was passed to limit the information practices of the federal government. The act restricts the government's use of personal data. Data collected for one purpose

You need a house key to unlock your house and go inside. A car key will unlock your car and help you start it and drive off. Why not use an electronic key to help you "open" a computer system and start working?

Some major companies require computer users to type a secret password and code so the computer will recognize those people as legitimate users. However, some people are careless with passwords and codes. They copy them on paper and leave the paper lying around where anybody can see the secret codes. Now DataKey, Inc., in Minneapolis, Minnesota, has developed an electronic key. The plastic key has an integrated circuit imbedded in it.

Businesses can use these keys with their computer systems to ensure that only the right people use the computers. Anyone trying to use the computer system without the keys will be refused access. Software companies can store segments of computer programs on the keys. The aim is to block pirating of expensive software. A program cannot be used without the portions stored on the keys. Hotels can also use these plastic keys for room security. The hotel personnel can change the lock codes on the room locks and the keys each time a room is vacated. This prevents a guest from using a copy of the room key to come back later and rob the new occupants of the room.

cannot be used for another purpose without the consent of the individual. For example, the IRS cannot routinely use data collected by the Social Security Administration. The act also allows people access to personal data stored in data bases. Errors in the data collected must be changed. Another provision states that agencies must safeguard the contents of files and data bases. Federal employees who violate the confidentiality provision are subject to a $5,000 fine. However, the act has been criticized because it applies only to employees of the federal government.

 LEARNING CHECK 9-1

1. Name three areas in which computers have created some unique problems.
2. TRUE FALSE Because computers have become an important part of our lives within a rather short time, no standard code of ethics guides their use.
3. The Privacy Act of 1974 has been criticized because it applies only to employees of the _____.

1. privacy, security, and ethics 2. TRUE 3. federal government

Artificial Intelligence

Chapter 8 discussed the many computer-related jobs. Perhaps the most exciting jobs of all involve research. Right now, scientists are studying ways to increase the speed of computers, decrease the size of computers, experiment with biochips, improve the actions of robots, and develop artificial intelligence.

Artificial intelligence (AI), thinking as humans do, is a term that Dr. John McCarthy used in 1956 when he started official meetings about the subject. McCarthy also designed the computer programming language LISP. LISP stands for LISt Processing and is used in exploring AI.

Today, AI programs (sometimes called expert systems) contain vast amounts of data and will respond to questions that ask them to evaluate data. Some AI programs help doctors. They contain data about many diseases and symptoms. One medical system is CADUCEUS. CADUCEUS contains data about 600 diseases and 2,500 symptoms. The doctor feeds the patient's symptoms to the computer and the computer responds with a list of diseases the patient might have. This helps the doctor decide on a diagnosis and treatment.

Another application of AI involves using computers to read books, newspapers, journals, and magazines and prepare summaries of the material. AI can also help geologists find the best places to drill oil wells.

As artificial intelligence becomes more advanced, scientists hope to make computers that can think on their own. Intelligence programs might solve experiments in physics or suggest courses of action in legal cases. Scientists are also trying to program computers to read a person's handwriting and to interpret a wider range of spoken language. Such programs could sort the mail or help blind people.

Chip Technology

A new material called **gallium arsenide** may replace the silicon in computer chips. Chips made with gallium arsenide already achieve speeds up to five times quicker than the fastest silicon computer chips. This new chip is now being used in military systems. The chip could also be used in television antennas. Since the chip yields strong signals, much smaller antennas are possible.

But the newest idea in chip development is the biochip. These **biochips** might be made from living material, such as protein molecules, and would need oxygen just as other life forms do. They would have ten million times the power of today's most advanced computers. Since these chips would be made from a living material, they could repair and reproduce themselves. A computer with the power of today's largest mainframe computer would be only the size of a bacterium if it were made with

Artificial intelligence The ability of computers to think like humans.

Gallium arsenide A substance that may replace silicon in computer chips.

Biochips Tiny computer circuits that, in theory, will be grown from living material.

molecules. Imagine! You'd have to use a microscope to see one!

One use of biochips may be to give sight to the blind. A biochip could be placed in a person's brain and then connected to a visual sensor to help the blind see. These very tiny computers could also be placed in human blood to monitor it and fight any disease found.

 LEARNING CHECK 9-2

1. The ability of computers to think as humans do is known as _____.

2. Gallium arsenide is a new material that may someday be used _____.
   a. for telecommunication lines
   b. to replace silicon in chips
   c. for growing chips
   d. to create artificial intelligence

3. What is the name for computer chips that may someday be made from living matter?

1. artificial intelligence 2. b 3. biochips

Computers in Our Homes

The Electronic Cottage

"Telecommuting from a Flexiplace" is the title of a *Time* magazine article about working at home instead of going to the office. Using a computer hookup and telephone lines between work and home, the worker can write any reports on the computer and then transfer them to a main computer at the office (see Figure 9-1). Of course, some kinds of work must be done at the office. But some salespersons, writers, and typists can work from their homes easily. **Telecommuting** helps people who are disabled, who live far away from the office, who must travel, and who do not need daily meetings with other workers. Jack M. Nilles, director of interdisciplinary programs at the University of Southern California, predicts that by 1990, 15 to 20 percent of American workers will be working from their homes. They will be working from "electronic cottages," a term coined to describe telecommuting.

Telecommuting
Linking computers between offices and homes to allow employees to work at home.

The Computer-Controlled Home

Will the home of the future be run by a computer? Will everyone have a robot butler or housekeeper? At one time, this seemed unreal. Today, computer magazines advertise computers for the home. What can computers do to manage a household? Some sys-

Figure 9-1. *Telecommuter*

tems can sense when a person enters or leaves a room. The lights are run by computers so that electricity is not wasted when someone leaves a room. Other systems manage thermostats, fans, doors, and windows to control the temperature. There are computer systems that secure a home against intruders. And personal robots can serve a can of soda pop, greet guests, and sweep the carpet.

Your home may already have tiny computers of which you are not aware. Microprocessors are often used inside appliances such as sewing machines, microwave ovens, stereos, and televisions. These microprocessors have only one job. They control the appliance. You cannot remove a microprocessor from a sewing machine and expect it to make your TV work.

A recent product is a screening system that hooks onto a telephone. It hangs up on any unwanted calls. A call is answered before the phone even rings. An electronic female voice chip asks the caller for his or her phone number. If the number is accepted, the call is completed and the phone rings. The caller's number is displayed on a tiny digital screen, so you know who is calling. If the caller has a number not in your system (for example, an obscene caller or someone calling the wrong number) the phone will never ring.

A very common dedicated computer in the home is the video game machine. Most people use systems similar to those built by Atari and Intellivision with joysticks and regular TV sets. Recently, add-on equipment has been designed to turn video game

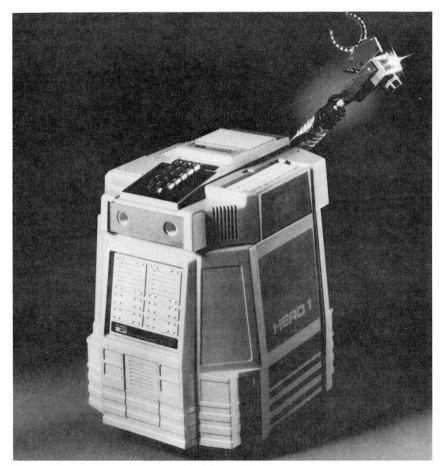

Figure 9-2. *HERO I can be assembled from a kit.*

machines into general-purpose computers. Then families can run word processors and financial packages, too.

Personal Robots

Today's personal robot is little more than a toy or pet. Much as you would like it to cut the grass, wash the dishes, or do the laundry, it cannot. However, it can become a computer teacher for children. Many of these robots are run by a joystick. One such robot is HERO I (see Figure 9-2). HERO is the two-foot-high robot built by Heathkit. Its name stands for Heath Educational RObot. HERO can be bought already assembled or as a kit.

Two other robots that help children learn to program computers are TOPO and B.O.B. (Brains On Board). These robots were designed by Androbot, Inc. By giving directions through a computer, children are able to make these robots move (see Figure 9-3).

Another good use of robots is to help quadriplegic patients. A patient who has little or no use of arms or legs can command a robot to do helpful things. In a rehabilitation center at the

Freely moving robots already have enough problems! They really cannot see where they are going. Since they "see" only width and height, they find it difficult to move around in a three-dimensional world without bumping into things.

But let's add one more problem. How do robots move out of a closed room? Imagine the possibilities. They could just forge ahead—perhaps through the wall. They could sound an alarm to call a human for help. But Hans Moravec, a professor at the Robotics Institute in Pittsburgh, wants his robot, Pluto, to be able to open the door by itself. Robot researcher Karen Hensley designed a "hand" for Pluto to grip and turn the doorknob.

To build a "hand" for Pluto, Hensley used a gripper found in a janitorial catalog. Janitors use the gripper on the end of a long pole to change light bulbs on high ceilings. Pluto will now use the gripper to get into and out of closed rooms.

Veterans Administration Hospital in Palo Alto, California, a quadriplegic meets a robot. The robot will fetch and carry, bring drinks, or hold a book for the patient. Perhaps one day robots will help quadriplegics the way seeing-eye dogs help the blind.

Robots are still limited in what they can do. Many problems must be solved. One problem is that robots must be able to move around freely and to see objects. Right now, robots "see" by cameras. They see only width and height. Unlike humans, they cannot judge depth.

Robots also must receive very exact orders to function. They cannot think. To be truly useful, robots must be taught to think. Artificial intelligence will be used to solve this problem.

Ways to Learn about Computers

Students do not have to wait until school starts to begin learning about computers. Even without a computer in their own home, students can learn about computers.

Many computer magazines are available. Some are written for junior high school and high school students. Others are written for computer hobbyists. Still others are written for families to enjoy. Even if the student does not own a computer, the magazines offer product reviews, stories about how people use computers, and ideas about the future of computers.

If schools do not offer computer classes, the YMCA or other community groups often list computer courses. Students may be able to earn badges in computer science through Boy Scout, Girl

Figure 9-3. *TOPO and B.O.B.*

Scout, and 4-H clubs. Classes are focused on beginning, intermediate, or advanced computer users. Often, computers are provided by the group offering the course.

A recent idea in computer education is the neighborhood computer center. Parents in a three- or four-block area will earn money through garage sales, bake sales, and raffles to buy enough computers to start a center. The center may be located in a rented building or in someone's garage. People in the neighborhood use the computers on a sign-up basis or on a group basis.

Local libraries have books and magazines about computers, too. Some libraries set up special computer rooms so that library card holders can use a computer for an hour or two at a time.

Students who do have computers at home can join computer clubs. Sometimes the clubs are meant for users of certain brands of computers. Other clubs help people who want to learn more about telecommunications, electronic bulletin boards, and information utilities.

As microcomputers become more powerful and less expensive, computing power should be available for almost anyone who needs it—at home, at school, or in the neighborhood.

LEARNING CHECK 9-3

1. Working at home on a terminal connected to a main computer at an office is called
_____.

2. Name three types of home appliances often controlled by microprocessors.

3. Two robots that help children learn to program computers are _____ and _____.

4. List three ways that students can learn about computers outside of school.

1. telecommuting 2. microwave ovens, sewing machines, and stereos 3. TOPO, B.O.B. 4. computer magazines, neighborhood computer centers, computer clubs

---

Perspective   *No one knows how to make a machine think like a human. We really do not know how natural intelligence works. To make a machine think logically, we have to program it to do so. But if the yet-to-be-developed biochips are combined with artificial intelligence, many things may become possible.*

Already computers do wonderful things. Computers can save time, make boring jobs easier, do unsafe jobs, help with medical diagnoses, and explore outer space. But the instructions and programs still come from people. People still determine how computers will be used. And people will have to be much smarter before they can build a completely intelligent machine.

ISSUE/COMPUTERS OR JOBS?

Two million manufacturing jobs were affected by robots, optical scanners, microchips, and other electronic devices during 1980-1982. With unemployment problems continuing throughout the 1980s, loss of jobs due to robots has become an issue. Even high school students wonder whether they will be able to find jobs when they graduate. Will robots do away with good-paying jobs?

A top AFL/CIO official fears that we will become a country of engineers and floor sweepers. Union officials and workers wonder whether jobs will create two groups of people—those with college education and high-paying jobs and those working in low-paying service jobs.

Yet manufacturers say they must become even more automated. They need to reduce costs, increase efficiency, and improve the quality of products. The weaving industry sets one example. Air-jet looms have been introduced. These automated looms produce three times more fabric than the older shuttle looms. The fabric produced by air-jet looms is a better quality fabric, too. But fewer workers are needed when air-jet looms are installed.

Factory owners invest in industrial robots because it is cheaper to buy and maintain robots than to pay workers. Although the range of $5,000 to

154

$125,000 sounds expensive, the average industrial robot costs the factory about $4.80 an hour. The average worker costs $15 per hour. Workers in many countries receive from less than $1 to $5 per hour in wages. Comparing these numbers shows the kinds of costs our industries are facing.

Looking at a company's point of view, managers see inexpensive foreign-made products cutting into their profits. They see automation as one answer to this problem. For instance, in the automotive industry, almost 50 percent of the factory jobs have been replaced by robotics. The steel industry has faltered because steel from the automated factories in Japan is cheaper. So steel manufacturers are turning to automation, too.

To workers, however, using robots may seem heartless. Robots do not have refrigerators to fill or rent to pay. Workers may agree that robots are more effective at certain jobs. But they do not like the trade-off. American industries seem to be getting back on their feet by putting workers out of jobs. With no jobs, how can people afford to buy the products that industries produce?

There are no easy answers. Industries must be able to compete to provide any jobs at all. Workers need the jobs to provide for families and feel productive. Although many jobs will be created in the electronics and software fields, all the people seeking jobs will not find employment there. Some workers can be retrained and relocated, but not all will be so fortunate. The solution lies in being able to help both groups without hurting either.

SUMMARY POINTS

- Computerized data about people can be abused in three possible ways. Information can be collected without their knowledge; information may be wrong; and information may be used for purposes other than originally intended.

- The security of a computer system can be threatened by fires, natural disasters, and accidents.

- Computer crime causes problems for many companies. Vandals can destroy costly hardware and software. Software can also be copied without permission.

- No standard code of ethics has been designed for computer use.

- The Fair Credit Reporting Act of 1970 gives people the right to know what credit data are kept on file about them. It also restricts the use of data contained in the files.

- The Privacy Act of 1974 restricts the use of personal data gathered by federal government agencies.

- Artificial intelligence (AI) means thinking as humans do. AI is used to answer questions based on vast amounts of data stored in a computer system.

- New computer chips made using gallium arsenide can achieve speeds up to five times faster than the fastest chips made of silicon.

- Biochips, made from some type of living matter, may have ten million times the power of today's most advanced computers and may be able to repair and reproduce themselves.

- Telecommuting lets employees work at home by using a computer hookup and phone lines to connect work and home.

- Microprocessors are tiny computers. Sometimes they are placed inside appliances to do only one job—control the appliance.

- Today's personal robots are used to teach children.

- Before robots can be used to perform more human-like actions, they must be able to see width, height, and depth. They must also be taught how to think.

CHAPTER TEST

Vocabulary

Match the number of the term from the column on the left with the best definition from the column on the right.

1. Ethics
2. Biochips
3. Telecommuting
4. Gallium arsenide
5. Artificial intelligence

a. The ability of computers to think like humans.
b. A substance that may replace silicon in computer chips.
c. Tiny computer circuits that may be grown from living material; still in the design stage.
d. Rules or standards that are used to guide conduct.
e. Computer hookups between offices and homes that allow employees to work at home.

Questions

1. As data about people are collected and computerized, people fear three kinds of abuse. Name the three kinds of abuse.
2. What federal law restricts ways in which federal agencies can use personal data collected about people?
3. In what area of computer development is Dr. John McCarthy considered a leader?
4. How could a biochip be used to help a blind person see?
5. What is an electronic cottage?
6. What can computers do to help manage a household?
7. What is a neighborhood computer center?

DISCUSSION QUESTIONS

1. Discuss what the world might be like with artificial intelligence. What effects would this have on you? Would this be good or bad?
2. Discuss whether robots will ever be used in homes. What would they do?
3. Discuss how you would feel if the computer ever invaded your privacy. Should computers be banned because of it? Why?

ACTIVITIES

1. Locate a magazine article about computers and either security or privacy. What are the important points in the article? Discuss the article in class or write a paragraph about it.

2. Pick a partner and think of seven ways the computer has made your lives easier. Next, think of seven more ways the computer will be able to help you in the future. Discuss these ideas in class.

3. Write a science fiction story about a problem caused by artificial intelligence.

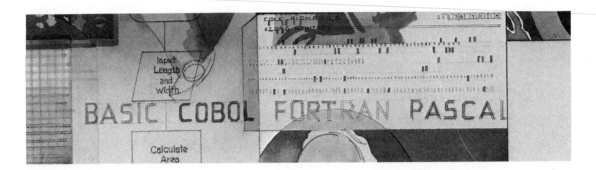

Chapter 10

BASIC Programming and Problem Solving

Learning Objectives

After reading this chapter, you should be able to:

1. Explain the logical (step-by-step) thinking needed for computer problem solving.

2. Define a problem in terms of the output, input, and processing required.

3. Explain the different logic patterns and when each one should be used.

4. Write a pseudocode.

5. List the different flowchart symbols and draw a simple flowchart.

Introduction

People often solve problems without thinking through every step of the process. Computers do not have this ability. As a result, solving a problem with a computer requires planning. All the steps needed to solve the problem must be identified and put in order before the program can be written. This helps to ensure that the program will produce the expected output. Documenting a program is also an important part of programming.

Solving Problems with a Computer

Computer programs lead computers step-by-step to solve a problem. Each program instruction must be written exactly so the computer can read and understand it. A programmer must follow five steps to decide what instructions are needed to solve a problem:

1. Define the problem.
2. Design a solution.
3. Write the program.
4. Enter, debug, and test the program.
5. Document the program.

Defining the problem and designing a solution are critical steps in developing a good program. They should be completed no matter which programming language is used.

Figure 10-1. *Summer Camp*

Defining the Problem

Before a solution can be found, the problem must be completely defined and understood. First, you should decide what output is needed and how you want it to look. The output is the information expected when the problem is solved. Then the input needed to get the desired output can be determined. You will also need to

Figure 10-2. *Summer Camp*

Figure 10-3. *Summer Camp*

decide what must be done to the input to get the correct output. This is called processing. Examples of processing might be printing your name on the computer screen or figuring the total dollar amount needed for a camping trip. The printed name and the dollar amount needed are the desired outputs (see Figure 10-1).

Before any output can be produced, input is needed. You should study the output requirements to decide what inputs will be needed to produce that output. In the example of printing a name, the desired name would have to be entered before it could be printed. To figure out how much one week at summer camp will cost, inputs would be the costs of items needed to attend camp (see Figure 10-2).

Once the inputs are defined, you must decide what processing is needed to turn the inputs into the desired output. In the first example mentioned, in which a name is printed, the only processing required is to change the input into a printable form. However, in the example of the week at camp, a math operation is needed to produce the correct dollar amount. The cost of each item must be added to get the correct output (see Figure 10-3). Only after this processing has been done can the correct output be given.

This method of defining a problem through the desired output and required inputs and processing can be used for any problem-solving task whether it is computer-related or not. Once the problem has been defined, a solution can be designed.

1. What are the five steps in computer problem solving?

2. The _____ represents the information desired when the problem is solved.

3. Why should the output requirements be studied?

4. _____ is needed to transform the inputs into the desired output.

4. processing

necessary to get the output can be determined.

document the program. 2. output 3. By studying what output is needed, the inputs and processing

1. define the problem; design a solution; write the program; enter, debug, and test the program; and

Designing a Solution

Designing a solution to the problem is a complex step in problem solving. Each part of the problem—output, input, and processing—must be broken down into detailed steps. If you miss a step, you cannot assume that the computer will make up for your error. A computer cannot do any thinking on its own. It must be instructed every step of the way. What this means is that the programmer must be able to outline the solution in distinct logical steps.

What steps do you take to make a phone call? Although you may not think about each step when making a phone call, each is part of the process.

SIMPLE SEQUENCE

Instructions for baking a cake:

1. Turn oven on.
2. Get mixer out.
3. Grease and flour pans.
4. Combine mix, eggs, and water.
5. Beat mixture.
6. Pour mixture into pans.
7. Put pans in oven.
8. Bake until done.
9. Remove pans from oven.
10. Cool cakes.
11. Take cakes out of pans.
12. Frost cake.

Figure 10-4. *Simple Sequence Pattern*

Which one do I want?
If I only have 20¢, then I can buy the chewing gum.
If I have 30¢, then I can either buy the chewing gum or the candy bar.
If I have 50¢, then I can buy the cookies, the gum, the candy bar, or both the gum and the candy bar.

Figure 10-5. *Selection Pattern*

- Find a phone.
- If no phone is available, forget the call.
- If phone is found, find the phone number.
- If phone number is not found, forget the call.
- If phone number is found, pick up the receiver.
- Listen for dial tone.
- If no dial tone, the phone is broken; forget the call.
- If dial tone is heard, dial phone number in order given.
- Listen for ringing or busy signal.
- If busy, hang up and try later.
- If ringing, wait for someone to answer.
- If no answer, hang up the phone and try later.
- If answered, begin conversation unless it is a wrong number.
- If wrong number, start over or talk to a stranger.
- Hang up the phone when conversation is over.

This is an example of how a process can be broken into logical steps. These logical steps must be defined for every computer program. If any step is left out or is out of sequence, the program will not produce the desired results.

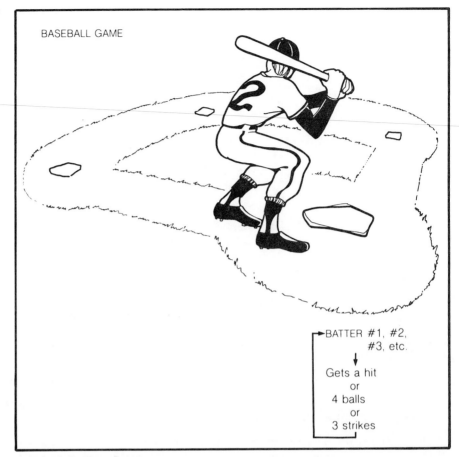

BASEBALL GAME

→ BATTER #1, #2,
#3, etc.

↓

Gets a hit
or
4 balls
or
3 strikes

Figure 10-6. *Loop Pattern*

Simple sequence pattern Program logic in which statements follow each other in sequence and are executed that way.

Selection pattern Program logic that includes a test to determine which of two paths is taken.

Loop pattern Program logic that repeats a group of instructions.

Branch pattern Program logic that is used to skip certain instructions.

Execute To perform.

Logic Patterns   A solution design can include any of four logic patterns. The **simple sequence pattern** (see Figure 10-4) completes each step in order until the problem is solved. It is a widely used logic pattern and is followed automatically by the computer.

In the **selection pattern**, a choice between two or more alternatives is made (see Figure 10-5). The computer compares two items and chooses a response based on the result of the comparison. The **loop pattern** refers to the repetition of any group of steps. Instead of rewriting a group of steps, the program loops back to an earlier step and repeats the same sequence of steps over, but usually with new data (see Figure 10-6). The **branch** pattern occurs when certain steps are skipped and are not **executed** or performed (see Figure 10-7). The branch pattern is usually used with the loop or selection patterns.

In BASIC, branching occurs when a GOTO statement is used in a program. The GOTO tells the computer to "go to" another line. For example, if the program was on line 20 when the computer read GOTO 80, it would skip down to line 80. In that way, the computer would "branch around" or skip lines 30 through 70.

WHEN IT IS THE BOTTOM OF THE NINTH INNING AND HOME TEAM IS WINNING,
HOME TEAM DOESN'T GET TO BAT. (SKIP TO END OF GAME)

Is it bottom of 9th inning
and home team is ahead?
If YES, GOTO end of game
If NO, batter up
   Batter 1
   Batter 2
   ●
   ●
   ●
End of game

(Home Team Does Not Bat)

Figure 10-7. *Branch Pattern*

LEARNING CHECK 10-2

1. Designing a solution involves breaking the problem into distinct, logical _____.

2. Which logic pattern completes each step in order until the problem is solved?

3. The _____ logic pattern is used to make a decision between two or more alternatives.

4. Which logic pattern should be used if the same sequence of steps is repeated over and over again?

5. When a GOTO statement is used in a BASIC program, which logic pattern is being followed and what is really happening?

1. steps 2. simple sequence pattern 3. selection 4. loop logic pattern 5. The branch logic pattern is being followed. The GOTO statement tells the computer to go to another line, skipping over all the lines in between.

Pseudocode One way to describe a solution to a problem is to write a **pseudocode**. Pseudocode is a written description of the processing steps performed in a program. The listing of the steps followed to make a phone call would be similar to pseudocode for a computer program.

Pseudocode A written description of the processing steps to be per formed in a program.

The pseudocode for keeping score at a tennis match could look like this:

- If server misses first serve, nothing happens.
- If server misses second serve, opponent scores.
- If server's first or second serve is good and opponent misses return, server scores.
- If opponent returns ball and server misses, opponent scores.
- Server continues to serve ball until either player wins game.
- Next game, opponent becomes server.

There are no special rules for writing a pseudocode. Pseudocode allows the programmer to focus on the actual processing steps without worrying about the rules of the programming language. Think of writing pseudocode as being similar to writing an outline or rough draft for a term paper.

Flowchart A diagram composed of symbols representing the processing steps of a program.

Flowcharts Another aid in designing a problem solution is a **flowchart**, sometimes called a **block diagram** or a **logic diagram**. A flowchart uses symbols to stand for the logic patterns and processing steps to be run. These symbols are arranged in the same general logical order as the program instructions appear. The flowchart helps in writing the actual program because the sequence and contents of the processing steps have already been thought out.

The following standard flowchart symbols are commonly used by programmers.

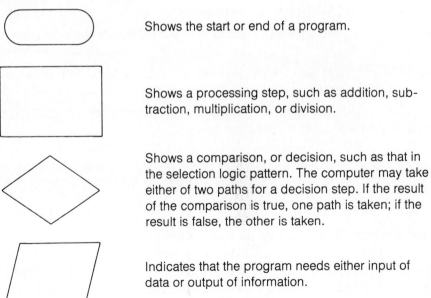

Shows the start or end of a program.

Shows a processing step, such as addition, subtraction, multiplication, or division.

Shows a comparison, or decision, such as that in the selection logic pattern. The computer may take either of two paths for a decision step. If the result of the comparison is true, one path is taken; if the result is false, the other is taken.

Indicates that the program needs either input of data or output of information.

These symbols are connected by lines with arrows showing the direction of flow. The direction of flow should be down the page or clockwise.

A flowchart is used to outline only the general logic of a problem. Therefore, a single flowcharting symbol may correspond to more than one program statement because programs are very detailed. For example, consider the following problem. Input two numbers (X and Y) into the computer and perform the operation (X + Y) ÷ 2. If the result is even, draw a circle. If the result is odd, draw a square. The flowchart outlining the logic might be:

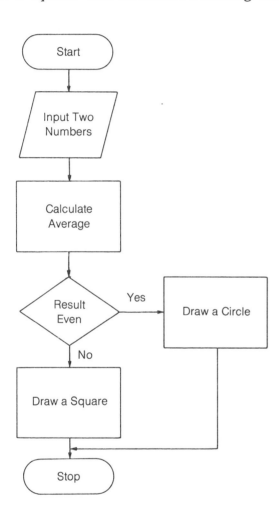

The flowchart shows only the general logic needed to solve the problem.

The example in Figure 10-8 shows a flowchart and pseudocode for a program that reads a name and then prints that name on the computer screen.

Each symbol of the flowchart matches one line of the pseudocode. The first statement of the pseudocode is represented on the flowchart by a ⬭, showing the beginning of the program. The second statement calls for the name to be inputted and is rep-

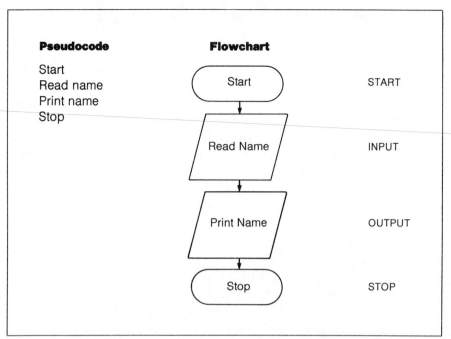

Pseudocode

Start
Read name
Print name
Stop

Flowchart

Figure 10-8. *Pseudocode and Flowchart of a Simple Sequence Logic Pattern*

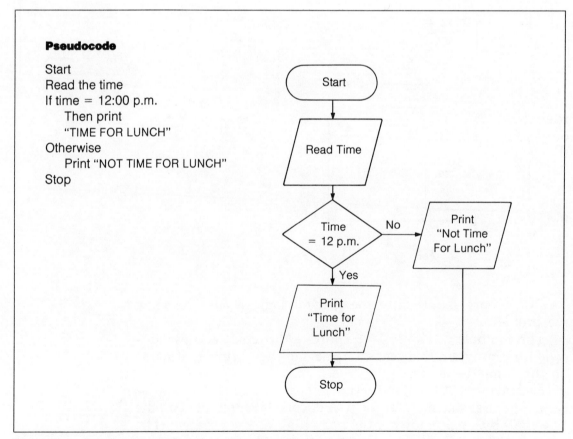

Pseudocode

Start
Read the time
If time = 12:00 p.m.
    Then print
    "TIME FOR LUNCH"
Otherwise
    Print "NOT TIME FOR LUNCH"
Stop

Figure 10-9. *Pseudocode and Flowchart of the Selection Logic Pattern*

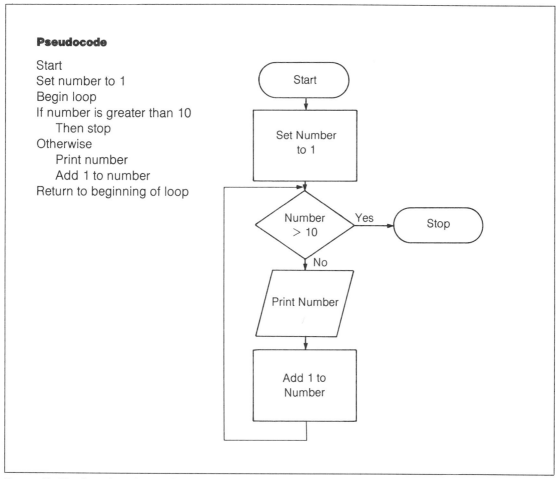

Pseudocode

Start
Set number to 1
Begin loop
If number is greater than 10
 Then stop
Otherwise
 Print number
 Add 1 to number
Return to beginning of loop

Figure 10-10. *Pseudocode and Flowchart of the Loop Logic Pattern*

resented by the ▢ symbol. This symbol is again used to show output, the printing of the name. Finally, the ⬭ symbol shows the end of the program.

The next example (in Figure 10-9) shows how the decision symbol is used in a flowchart. This program prints a message that tells whether or not it's time to eat lunch depending on the time of day.

The ⬭ and ▢ symbols are used in the same manner as in the prior example. The ◇ symbol shows the decision of what message to print. If the time equals 12:00 p.m., then the "Time for Lunch" message is printed. This is shown by the "yes" arrow pointing down. If the time does not equal 12:00 p.m., then the "Not Time for Lunch" message is printed, shown by the "no" arrow pointing to the right. The ⬭ symbol is used to show the program's end.

In the final example (in Figure 10-10), a loop is used in a flowchart. This program prints the numbers one through ten in order.

The program begins with a $\ominus$ symbol. The next symbol, $\square$, stands for the processing step of setting the beginning number equal to one. So that the program will know when to stop, the $\diamondsuit$ symbol is used to check whether the number is greater than ten. If so, it is time to stop the program $\ominus$. If not, the number is printed, shown by the $\square$ symbol.

The next step is to add one to the number. After this, the number must be checked again to see whether it is greater than ten. Since this step has already been shown on the flowchart, a line can simply be drawn to the desired step rather than drawing the symbol a second time. A loop has now been made. The same steps will be run until the number is greater than ten. Then the program will end.

These are not the only flowcharting symbols that can be used, but they provide a good base for making simple flowcharts to help write a program. At this time, you may not see the merit of flowcharting simple problems such as the ones just shown. But flowcharts can be valuable tools for choosing and understanding the logic needed to solve complex problems.

LEARNING CHECK 10-3

1. A written description of the processing steps to be done in a program is called

_____.

2. A(n) _____ uses different symbols to stand for the different logic patterns and processing steps of a program.

3. The $\ominus$ symbol represents the _____ or _____ of a program.

4. Which symbol would be used to represent a processing step, such as addition, subtraction, multiplication, or division?

5. What does the $\diamondsuit$ symbol represent?

6. The _____ symbol indicates that either input or output is required.

Writing the Program

The third step in the programming process—writing the program—is easier if the solution has been carefully designed in the second step. Producing the correct output is not the only standard for a good program. More than one solution can give the correct output, but one program can be better than another. Every program should have the following qualities:

1. A program should be easy to read and understand by everyone who uses it.

2. A program should be sound. It should always produce the correct output.

3. A program should work under all conditions. If data are entered that are not realistic, the program should be able to test it and alert the user that the data don't meet certain conditions. For example, a program that asks for the age of a person should test the data for illogical ages. The program should not process ages entered such as −30 or 986.

Testing and Debugging the Program

The fourth step in the programming process includes typing the program into the computer, **debugging** it, and testing the program. Debugging a program means to find and correct any errors in it. These processes are discussed in Chapter 14.

Debug To locate and correct program errors.

Documenting the Program

The final step in the programming process involves writing, or documenting, all work that has been done. **Documentation** is the written information about the various aspects of the program. The names used to identify data and the logic followed should be included. Documentation should also include a definition of the problem and a description of the inputs, outputs, and processing used in the program.

Documentation The written explanation of the program and its logic.

Additional documentation may include copies of all flowcharts and pseudocodes, the final program, and the results of any test samples tried.

You might wonder why documentation is needed. A short, simple program is often self-explanatory. But longer, more complex programs can be very confusing without good documentation.

Suppose you wrote a long program in February and it ran smoothly. In June you decided to update the program but you have forgotten details about the program.

When you print out the program, you discover that you did not document, or explain, the program. You realize you do not remember what the data names mean, how the logic of the program is designed, or how each part of the program is to work. You will have to spend a lot of time deciding what is done in each statement.

What if someone else wanted to use your undocumented program? Much time can be saved by good documentation.

Although documenting the program is listed as the last step in program development, it should be included with all stages of the process. Programmmers can include statements in a program that explain variables and the purpose of program segments. In the end, good documentation can save time, money, and problems.

Cross an Apple with a bunch of creative, bilingual kids and what do you get? Urban Adventure, of course! In Hartford, Connecticut, some 175 bilingual children in grades 3 through 6 benefit from the project, funded by money from the Apple Education Foundation and a federal program called Encendiendo Una Llama (Lighting a Flame). The goal of Urban Adventure is to let players explore the educational resources of the city (museums, parks, and government buildings) and to help develop language skills. Students are creating the games to explore the city. Since most of the students are Hispanic, they improve language abilities in both English and Spanish.

For the first adventure game, students first explored the Hartford Public Library. Then they created their game using a graphics tablet and light pen. They wrote both Spanish and English versions of the game. This was accomplished with the Mountain Computer Super-Talker, which changes the sound waves of a voice into digital signals to store on a computer disk. The game not only teaches other students about the library; it also teaches correct pronunciations in Spanish and English so the player can build language skills. The bilingual students are "lighting a flame" for many other bilingual students to follow through the maze of languages.

LEARNING CHECK 10-4

1. What qualities should every program have?

2. Finding and correcting errors in a program is called _____.

3. TRUE   FALSE   Documentation of a program should be done when the programmer has extra time, but it is not very important.

4. Including statements in a program that explain variables or the purpose of certain program segments is part of _____.

1. easy to read and understand, sound, work under all conditions 2. debugging 3. FALSE 4. documentation

---

COMPREHENSIVE PROGRAMMING PROBLEM

The discussion of this problem and its solution is designed to give you a better idea of how the problem-solving process works. All four logic patterns are used to solve the problem and create a solution design. An example of the pseudocode and flowchart used to define the solution are provided.

Problem

A group of your friends likes to play the video game *Star Shooter*. They want to have a contest to see who the best players in the group are. The group wants to give titles to the best, middle, and worst players based on an average score of three games played. The scores and title names are as follows:

Score	Title name
0 - 99,999	Junior Star Shooter
100,000 - 199,999	Star Shooter
200,000 - and above	Super Star Shooter

Your friends have asked you to write a program to determine the average score for each player and to print the player's name, average score, and title to hang on their *Star Shooter* Clubhouse wall.

Write the pseudocode and a flowchart to input the player's name and three scores and to output the player's name, average score, and title. Be sure to mark the end of the data so that the computer will be able to tell when all of the data have been input.

Discussion

The first step in writing a program is to define the problem. The desired output and the inputs and processing needed to get the output must be determined. The desired output for this problem is a player's name, the average score for three games, and the title name given based on the average score. To get this output, the player's name and the three scores must be input. The player's name does not need any processing since it remains the same throughout the problem. However, processing is required to get one average score from the three individual scores. This average score is then used to decide what title name the player should receive.

The next step is to design a solution. This requires that the input, output, and processing be broken into detailed steps for the computer. The pseudocode and flowchart help show the logical steps of the problem and the breakdown of the details.

The pseudocode and flowchart begin with the word "Start." Since the number of names to be entered is not known, the program must test the data to show when the end of the input data has been reached. A loop pattern is used to repeat the input process until the end has been reached. After each set of data is input, a selection pattern is used to decide whether the input is a data item or the end of the data. If the input is a data item, the entire process is run to get an output. If the end of the data is reached, the computer is told to skip all the processing steps and go to the end of the program. This is done with a branch pattern.

The next step is to process the data to get the desired output. The only processing needed is to change the three scores for each player into one average score. Adding the three scores together and dividing by three gives the average score for a player. After the average score is calculated, the player's skill level must be decided. A selection pattern is a good way to do this.

First, check to see whether the player is a Junior Star Shooter by comparing the average score with the number 100,000. If the average score is less than 100,000, the title is "Junior Star Shooter" and the name, average score, and title are output. The computer then returns to the input process (the beginning of the loop) and the next set of data is read. If the average score is greater than or equal to 100,000, the process continues.

Next, the computer must check to see whether the player is a Star Shooter by comparing the average score with the number 200,000. If the average score is less than 200,000, the title is

"Star Shooter," and the player's name, average score, and title are output. The computer then returns to the input process.

If the average score is greater than or equal to 200,000, the player is a Super Star Shooter and the player's name, average score, and title are output. The computer then returns to the input process.

The pseudocode could look like this:

Pseudocode

Start
Begin loop
If no other names, then stop
Input player name and three scores
Add scores and divide by three
> If average score < 100,000, then output player name, average score, and title "Junior Star Shooter." Get next name.
> Return to beginning of loop

> If average score < 200,000, then output player name, average score, and title "Star Shooter." Get next name.
> Return to beginning of loop

> Average score must be ≥ 200,000, so output player name, average score, and title "Super Star Shooter." Get next name.
> Return to beginning of loop

The flowchart, using the correct symbols and flow design, is as follows:

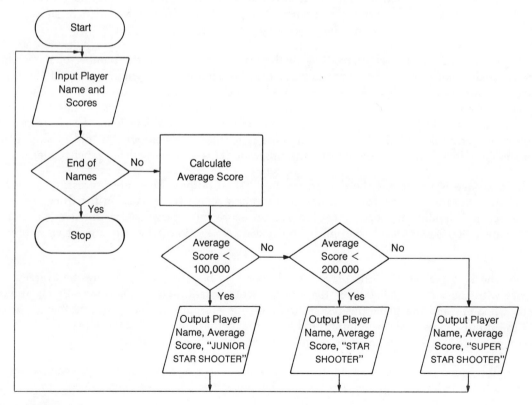

To be sure you understand the pseudocode and flowchart, use the following data to produce the same output as shown below. Pretend that you're the computer and follow the steps exactly as given.

	Game 1	Game 2	Game 3
John	215,000	202,000	213,000
Rick	60,000	100,000	80,000
Susan	101,000	150,000	130,000

After completing the program, you should have the following output:

John	210,000	Super Star Shooter
Rick	80,000	Junior Star Shooter
Susan	127,000	Star Shooter

Did you get the same output? If not, go through the steps again until you do.

SUMMARY POINTS

- The five steps to computer problem solving are define the problem; design a solution; write the program; enter, debug, and test the program; and document the program.

- When defining a problem, first the desired output must be decided upon. From this, the necessary input and processing can be determined.

- To design a solution, you should develop a list of step-by-step procedures.

- The four basic logic patterns are simple sequence, selection, loop, and branch.

- Pseudocode is a written description of the processing steps to be performed in a program.

- A flowchart is a programming aid composed of symbols that represent the different logic patterns and processing steps of a program.

- ⬭ represents the start or end of a program; ▭ represents a process step; ◇ represents a comparison or decision; and ▱ represents either input or output.

- Good documentation of a program is very important. It should be part of all stages of program development.

CHAPTER TEST

Vocabulary

Match the term from the numbered column on the left with the description from the lettered column on the right that best fits the term.

1. Debug

    a. A written description of the processing steps to be performed in program.

2. Execute

    b. Program logic that includes a test; depending on the results of the test, one of two paths is taken.

3.	Flowchart	c.	To find and correct errors in the program.
4.	Selection pattern	d.	Program logic that repeats a group of instructions.
5.	Output	e.	To perform.
6.	Document	f.	A diagram made of symbols representing the processing steps of a program.
7.	Loop pattern	g.	The information expected after a problem has been solved.
8.	Pseudocode	h.	To make written descriptions of the program and its logic.

Questions

1. The problem should be defined in terms of input, processing and _____.
   a. output
   b. programs
   c. pseudocode

2. The computer can automatically figure out the specific steps of a solution without being told.
   a. TRUE
   b. FALSE

3. Which of the following symbols indicates that the program requires either input or output?
   a. ⬭
   b. ▢
   c. ▱

4. Which of the following symbols represents the start or stop of a program?
   a. ⬭
   b. ◇
   c. ▭

5. Which of the following symbols represents a decision or test in a program?
   a. ▢
   b. ◇
   c. ▱

6. Which of the following symbols represents a processing step such as addition or subtraction?
   a. ▢
   b. ◇
   c. ▱

Provide the correct symbols to complete the following flowchart, which shows the processing steps to figure out how much money you will receive for babysitting a certain number of hours in a week.

7.   Start

8.   Enter
   Number of
   Hours

9.   Enter
Wage
Rate

10.   Multiply
Hours ×
Rate

11.   Print
Amount
To be
Received

12.   Stop

13. The above flowchart uses a loop pattern.

  a. TRUE
  b. FALSE

14. Which step in the programming process should be done during all other stages of program development?

  a. defining the problem
  b. designing a solution
  c. documentation

15. Pseudocodes and flowcharts are used during which stage of program development?

  a. defining the problem
  b. designing a solution
  c. debugging the program

PROGRAMMING PROBLEMS

1. Develop simple flowcharts for the following short program using the symbols just discussed.

  a. This program will keep track of how many miles you ride on your bike each day. You may have six pieces of information as input:

  1. Distance to school in miles
  2. Number of trips to school per day
  3. Distance to a friend's house
  4. Number of trips to friend's house per day
  5. Distance to the video arcade
  6. Number of trips to video arcade per day

You will need to include a step that multiplies the number of miles to each place by the number of trips per day. The output should be the total miles traveled in a day.

  Draw a simple sequence flowchart using only the following symbols:

  b. Now draw a flowchart for the bike problem but use a loop pattern and the following symbols:

2. Mr. Moneybags, your next-door neighbor, has asked you to shovel his long driveway every time it snows this winter. He will pay you $4 an hour for every hour you work. If you can get his drive shoveled in three hours or less, he will give you a bonus of $3. Write the pseudocode and a flowchart, using the correct symbols, to input the number of hours you work each time you shovel. The output should be the amount of money Mr. Moneybags owes you for the day. Don't forget your bonus!

3. Write the pseudocode and flowchart, using the correct symbols, for a program that will tell fortunes. The user must choose a number to input, either a 1, 2, or 3. The computer will give the user a fortune based on the number that was chosen. If "1" is chosen, the computer prints "YOU WILL BE A DOCTOR." If "2" is chosen, the computer prints "YOU WILL BE A FAMOUS MOVIE STAR." If "3" is chosen, the computer prints "YOU WILL HAVE 13 CHILDREN." If none of the above numbers is chosen, the computer prints "YOU HAVE ENTERED A WRONG NUMBER, TRY AGAIN." The user must then input another number.

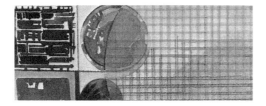

Using a Microcomputer

Learning Objectives

After reading this chapter, you should be able to:

1. Care for the computer and floppy disks.

2. Operate the disk drive.

3. Turn the computer on and off.

4. Use the keyboard to enter data and make changes.

5. Control scrolling on the terminal screen.

Introduction

If you have a pet such as a dog, cat, or fish, you already know that pets can be a lot of fun. And you also know they need care. The same is true of a computer. A computer can make some jobs easier and faster. It can also help you learn. But you can have fun when you're working on a computer if you use your imagination and are not afraid to try new things.

Just as you have to take care of a pet, you also have to take care of a computer. Computers are expensive machines, not toys, and you must know how to use them correctly. If you don't, the computer will not be useful for you.

This chapter shows you how to turn on the computer and how to use the keyboard. It also gives you advice about how to take care of the computer and the disks you will be using.

Instructions for four computers—the Apple II, IBM PC, Commodore 64, and TRS–80—are given in this chapter. If you have a computer model different than these, check with your teacher or the computer's user's manual for detailed instructions.

Computer Care

The key to keeping your computer in good working order is to use common sense when handling it. Spilling food or drinks on the keyboard can make the keys jam or stick, just as they would on an electric typewriter. Dust and dirt also can cause keyboard problems. Dust can carry electrical charges (static electricity) that will break the flow of current through the microprocessor.

While the computer is turned on, it is best not to move it or jolt it. This includes not jolting the table or desk the computer sits on. Remember to be just as careful around your classmates when they're using the computers. You may lose a friend or make an enemy if you cause a classmate's work to be destroyed because of your carelessness.

If you ever need to unplug any electrical cord around the computers, check to make sure it is not the cord to a computer some-

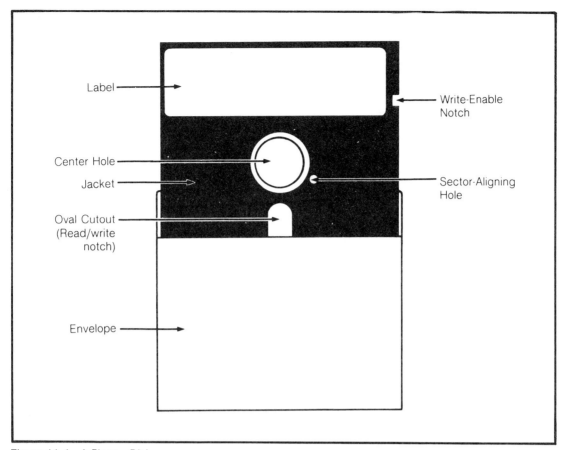

Figure 11-1. *A Floppy Disk*

one is using. When a computer loses its power supply, any data that have not been saved are erased.

As long as you treat your computer with care, it will be a useful tool for you to use now and for others to use in the future. Whenever the computer acts differently than usual, tell your teacher so that a repairperson can be called. Fixing problems before they get too serious will keep the computer running better and longer.

Disk Care

The **floppy disk**, also called **floppy diskette** or **flexible diskette**, is probably the most common type of external memory used with microcomputers. It is a small, flat piece of plastic with a hole in the center. Floppy disks are available in two standard sizes—8 inches and 5¼ inches in diameter. The microcomputers you will work with use the popular 5¼-inch diskette.

Flexible disks need special care. Because they are made of a plastic-like material and are flexible, they can be damaged quite

Floppy disk Low-cost external storage made of plastic and used with a disk drive.

easily. But if you follow certain rules, your disks will last a long time and won't cause you problems.

Disks should never be folded or bent. If they are, the read/write head of the disk drive may not be able to retrieve the data stored on them or write new data to them. Keep the disk in its paper envelope when not in use (see Figure 11-1). The envelope protects the disk from dirt, dust, and static that might damage the data on the disk.

Disks should always be stored vertically to prevent warping. They should be kept away from magnets and magnetic fields, which may erase the data stored on them. Do not lay your disk on top of the monitor or the disk drive, because both have magnetic fields.

Heat can damage flexible disks, so never put them near a heater or oven or on top of a television or stereo. It's a good idea to keep disks away from windows where the sun shines in strongly. Since automobiles can get very hot even on cool, sunny days, remember to take your disks out of the car.

The labels that come with the disks can be used to record what is stored on them so you don't forget. Always use a felt-tip marker to write on the label and press lightly. Pressing hard can leave dents on the disk's recording surface and can distort the data.

The final rule is never to touch the recording surface that shows through the oval cutout in the plastic disk jacket. If you do, dirt and oil from your fingers could distort the data.

 LEARNING CHECK 11-1

1. What might happen if a computer being used is jolted or moved?

2. Name the two most common sizes of floppy disks used with microcomputers.

3. TRUE   FALSE   A good place to keep your disks is on top of the television set.

4. What type of pen should you use to mark on the disk's label?

1. Data may be distorted or lost.   2. 8 inches and 5¼ inches in diameter   3. FALSE   4. felt-tip marker

---

Using the Disk Drive

Disk drive The device which rotates the floppy disk, reads data from, and writes data to the disk.

A **disk drive** is a device that holds a floppy disk. The disk drive rotates the disk just like a record player spins a record. It also reads data from the disk and writes data to the disk.

To open a disk drive door, lift the small door on the drive (see Figure 11-2). To insert a disk, hold the disk with your thumb on the label and remove it from its envelope (see Figure 11-3). Gently insert the disk into the slot of the drive. The oval cutout (read/

Opening the
Disk Drive Door

Figure 11-2. *Opening the Disk Drive Door*

write notch) goes in first, with the label up (see Figure 11-4). Do not bend or force the disk. When the disk is all the way inside, push the small door on the disk drive down until it clicks shut.

To remove a disk from a disk drive, be sure the small red disk drive light is off, open the drive door, gently pull out the disk, and return it to its envelope.

Turning On the Computer

The following instructions for turning on the computer assume that a disk drive is being used for external memory. Check with your teacher to determine what type of external memory you will

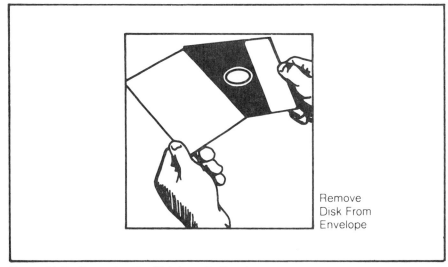

Remove
Disk From
Envelope

Figure 11-3. *Removing the Disk from Its Envelope*

Insert
Disk
Into Drive

Figure 11-4. *Inserting the Disk into the Drive*

be using. If you are not using floppy disks, check the computer's user's manual or ask your teacher for the proper instructions for your machine.

Apple II

The main computer and the monitor (television-like screen) have different power supplies. They must be turned on individually. Complete the following steps to start the Apple II and prepare it for use.

1. Turn the monitor on. Switches for most monitors are on the front, right-hand side of the monitor (see Figure 11-5). Be sure the brightness control is not turned all the way to dark. Otherwise, nothing will appear on the screen. Dark is usually all the way to the left, while bright is all the way to the right.

2. Insert the disk into Drive 1 and close the drive door.

3. Reach behind the left corner of the computer case and find the power switch with your left hand (see Figure 11-6). Turn your computer on.

The power indicator on the keyboard and the small light on the front of Drive 1 will light up. The disk drive will make whirring sounds as it reads the disk. After a few seconds, the sounds will stop, and the red light on the disk drive will go out. The monitor screen for the Apple II should now look like Figure 11-7. The computer is ready to use.

Figure 11-5. *Monitor*

Commodore 64

The main computer and the monitor (television-like screen) have different power supplies. They must be turned on individually. Complete the following steps to turn on the Commodore 64 and prepare it for use.

1. Turn on the display monitor by pushing the power switch down (see Figure 11-8). The power indicator light on the

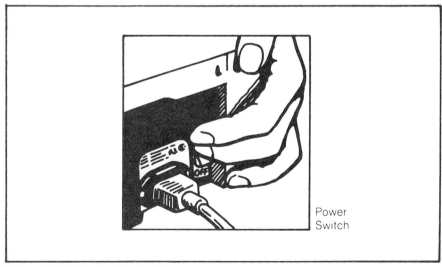

Power
Switch

Figure 11-6. *Turning On the Power*

```
                    APPLE II

        DOS VERSION 3.3 SAMPLE PROGRAMS


                 JANUARY 1, 1983


    COPYRIGHT APPLE COMPUTER,INC. 1980,1982
           BE SURE CAPS LOCK IS DOWN

    ]
```

Figure 11-7. *Opening Display—Apple II*

front of the monitor will light up. Always turn on the monitor *before* you turn on the computer.

2. Turn on the disk drive using the switch on the back of the drive. Always turn the disk drive on *before* you turn on the computer.

3. Be sure there are no disks in the disk drive before the computer is started. Otherwise, the information on the disk could be destroyed. Turn on the computer using the rocker switch on the right side of the keyboard. The message shown in Figure 11-8 should appear on the monitor after a few moments.

4. Insert the disk in the disk drive and close the door. The computer is now ready to use.

IBM PC

The main computer and the monitor (television-like screen) have different power supplies. They must be turned on individually. Complete the following steps to turn on the IBM PC and prepare it for use.

1. Turn or pull the ON switch of the monitor to the "on" position (see Figure 11-9). Be sure the brightness control is turned to the right.

2. Insert the disk into Drive 1 (the slot on the left) and close the disk drive door.

3. Push the red power switch, located at the back of the right side of the computer, to the "on" position (see Figure 11-10). There should be one short beep. After a few moments,

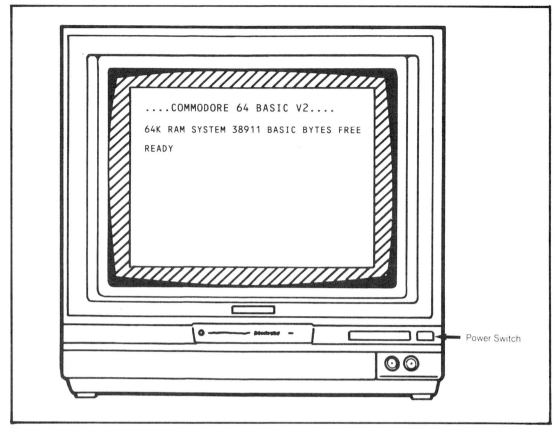

Figure 11-8. *Opening Display—Commodore 64*

the monitor screen should look similar to the one in Figure 11-11. The computer will ask you to input today's date and time. Press the ENTER key after you type the date and after you type the time. If you do not want to enter the date and time, press the ENTER key twice.

4. To use the BASIC programming language, type the letters BASICA and press the ENTER key.

TRS-80

Complete the following steps to turn on the TRS–80 computer using a floppy disk.

1. Be sure there are *no* disks in the disk drive before the computer is started. Otherwise, the information on the disk could be destroyed. Turn the power switch located under the front right corner of the computer to the "on" position (see Figure 11-12).

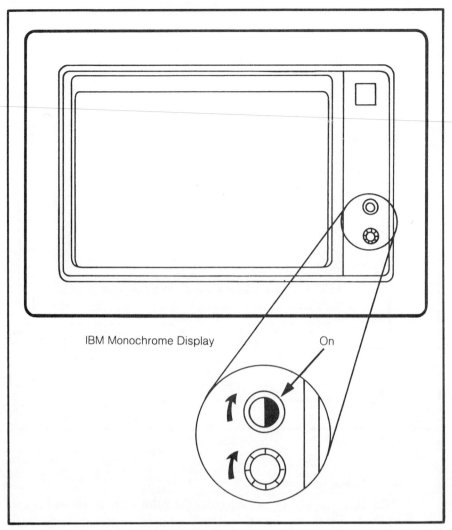

Figure 11-9. *IBM Monochrome Display*

2. Insert the disk in Drive 0 (see Figure 11-12), the bottom slot, and close the disk drive door.

3. Press the ⎡RESET⎤ button, located to the right of the numeric keypad on the keyboard (see Figure 11-12).

4. The computer will respond with a message similar to that in Figure 11-13. The computer will then ask you to enter the date in the form MM/DD/YY. Type in the correct date, for example, 04/21/84 for April 21, 1984, and press the ⎡ENTER⎤ key. It will then ask you for the time. You may simply press the ⎡ENTER⎤ key at the beginning of the line if you do not wish to enter the time. The computer will then display the message TRSDOS READY.

5. To use the BASIC programming language, type the word BASIC and hit the ⎡RETURN⎤ key.

Figure 11-10. *Turning on the IBM*

Figure 11-11. *Opening Display—IBM PC*

Figure 11-12. *TRS-80 Model III*

Using the Keyboard

Keyboard The part of the computer with the typing keys.

The **keyboard** of most computers is very similar to the keyboard of an ordinary electric typewriter. Most of the keys work in the same way—when depressed, characters appear on the monitor. The character will appear where the cursor is. However, most computers have certain keys that are special to that computer. The layout and usage of the keyboards for the four computers are discussed in this section.

Apple IIe

Since the Apple IIe is one of the most popular of the Apple family, the Apple IIe keyboard is discussed here (there are some differences among the keys for the other models). Figure 11-14 shows the layout of the Apple IIe keyboard. Most of the keys work the same as a regular typewriter. If you press any one of the regular keys and hold it down for more than one second, the character it makes is repeated. The RETURN key returns the carriage and enters the line of data just typed into the computer's memory. The SHIFT key changes small letters to capitals and the numerals to their corresponding special characters. The TAB key performs a tab similar to a typewriter. Tabs are usually set every eight characters.

If you make a mistake while typing a program, the following

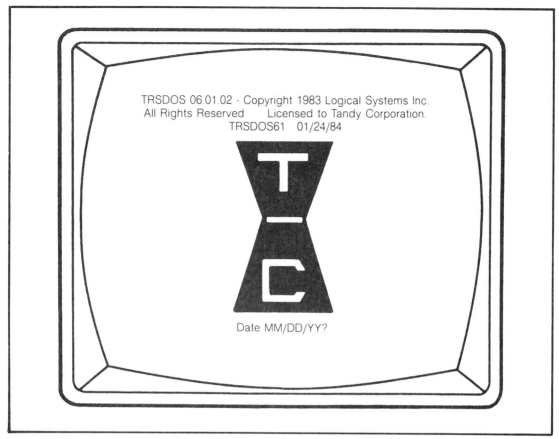

Figure 11-13. *Opening display—TRS-80 Model IV*

keys will help you correct it: ⬅ moves the cursor to the left of the screen and ➡ moves the cursor to the right. To move the cursor down, hit the ESC key and then press the ⬇ key. To move the cursor up, hit the ESC key and then press the ⬆ key. Using these keys, you can move the cursor to the exact character where the mistake begins. Then you can type the correction.

There are other special keys on the keyboard, but you do not need to understand them at this time. Some of these keys are introduced later in this book. Check the user's manual for more information on the other special keys not discussed.

Commodore 64

Figure 11-15 shows the layout of the Commodore 64 keyboard. Most of the keys work the same as those on a regular typewriter. Look at the keyboard to find the following keys and note their description as follows: RETURN performs a carriage return and enters the line of data just typed into the computer's memory. SHIFT changes small letters to capitals and the numerals to their

191

Figure 11-14. *Apple IIe Keyboard*

corresponding special characters. While in the graphics mode, the
SHIFT key displays the graphics character that appears on the
right-hand side of the front part of the character keys.

If you make a mistake while typing a program, two special
keys will help you correct it. ⇩CRSR⇧ lets you move the cursor up
or down the screen (for up press SHIFT at the same time).
⇐CRSR⇨ lets you move the cursor to the right or left (for left
press SHIFT at the same time). Once you have moved the cursor
to the beginning of the mistake, you can type the correction. In
this manner, you do not have to retype a complete line of text.
INST moves the cursor back one space and deletes the character
where the cursor was. If this key is shifted, it allows you to insert
information on a line where the cursor appears.

The four keys to the right of the keyboard are called program
function keys and are used by more advanced programmers. C=
is the Commodore key and allows you to move between text and
graphics (see the user's manual for more details).

There are other special keys on the keyboard, but you do not
need to know how to use them at this time. Some of these keys are
introduced later in this book. Check the user's manual for information on the other special keys not discussed.

IBM PC

Figure 11-16 shows the layout of the IBM PC keyboard. The keys
with single characters and the top row of keys with numbers and
symbols are used the same as the keys of a typewriter. The group
of keys on the left labeled F1 through F10 are called program
function keys. They have been programmed to perform special
system commands. Some of these are explained later in this
book.

System command
A command used
to communicate
with the operating
system of the
computer.

A system command is a command that tells the computer to do
something. Usually it tells the computer to do something with the
program, such as SAVE it, or RUN it.

Look at the keyboard to find the following keys and note
their description:

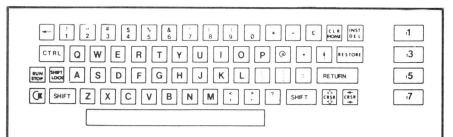

Figure 11-15. *Commodore 64 Keyboard*

TAB performs a tab similar to a typewriter; tabs are set every eight characters.

SHIFT changes small letters to capitals and numerals to their corresponding special characters.

BACKSPACE moves the cursor back one space and deletes the character just typed.

ENTER performs a carriage return and enters that line of data into the computer's memory.

If you make a mistake while typing a program, the following keys located on the right side of the keyboard may be used to correct it.

moves the cursor up the screen.

moves the cursor down the screen.

moves the cursor to the left.

moves the cursor to the right.

moves the cursor to the last character on that line.

deletes the character where the cursor appears and moves the rest of the text one space to the left.

inserts information where the cursor appears (press ⌶ key again to get out of INSERT mode).

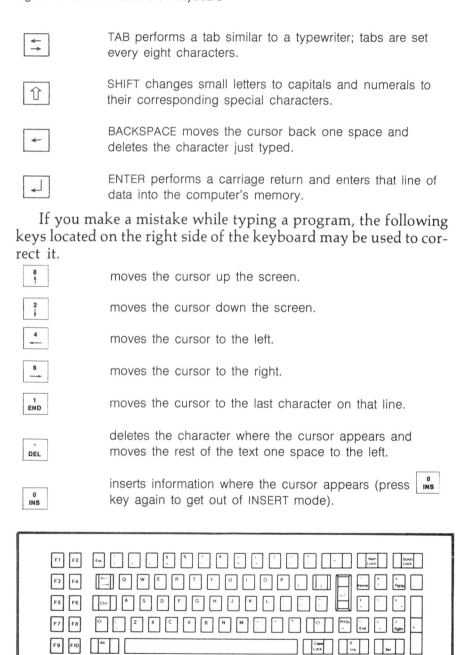

Figure 11-16. *IBM PC Keyboard*

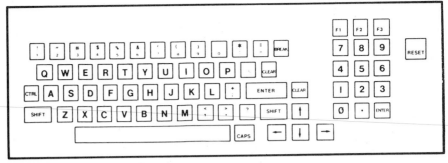

Figure 11-17. *TRS-80 Keyboard*

When the computer is first turned on, it is in the edit mode, and you can use the keys just discussed. If you want to use the numbers on the keys like a calculator, press LOCK. This numeric keypad mode is useful when inputting many numbers at a time. To get back into the edit mode, press LOCK again.

There are many other special keys on the keyboard, but you will not use them at this time. Some of these keys are discussed later in this book. Check the user's manual for more information on the other special keys not discussed.

TRS-80

Most of the keys on the TRS–80 work the same as those on a regular typewriter (see Figure 11-17). Locate the following keys on the keyboard:

ENTER — returns the carriage and enters that line of data into the computer's memory.

SHIFT — changes small letters to capitals and the numerals to their corresponding special characters.

→ — performs a tab similar to a typewriter; tabs are set every eight characters.

backspaces and erases the last character typed.

There are other special keys on the keyboard, but their use is not necessary to know at this time. Some of these keys will be introduced later in this book. Check the user's manual for more information on the other special keys not discussed.

Knowing Your Screen

Terminal screen A television-like screen used to display information.

Computer **terminal screens** are also called **visual display terminals** (VDTs) or **cathode-ray tubes** (CRTs). These names refer to the television-like screen that is used to display information while using the computer. Some home computers can be connected to a regular television. Terminal screens provide **soft-copy** output.

Numerous types and brands of terminal screens can be used with different home computers. Terminal screens come in different sizes. Most screens display 80 characters across and 24 lines down. However, the early Apple computers display only 40 characters across. Also, some terminal screens can display colors, while others display only black and white, or green and white.

Most terminal screens have a brightness knob to control the brightness of the output. This should be adjusted to a level that is comfortable for viewing.

When a program more than 24 lines long is displayed on the screen, the screen will begin to **scroll**. This means that the top line on the screen will disappear, all other lines will move up one line, and a new line will appear at the bottom of the screen. If the screen scrolls too fast, you may want to stop it so that information on the screen can be read. The commands that can be used to stop the scrolling of the screen are listed in Table 11-1.

Scroll The process of moving lines up and down on the terminal screen.

SCROLL CONTROL   Table 11-1

Computer	Scroll Stop/Start
Apple	CTRL-S (Hold down the **CTRL** key and the **S** key at the same time.)
TRS-80	SHIFT @ (Hold down the **SHIFT** key and the **@** key at the same time.)
Commodore 64	None (There are no scroll stop/start keys; however, pressing the **CTRL** key slows down the scroll to one line at a time.)
IBM PC	CTRL-NUMLOCK (Hold down the **CTRL** key and the **NUMLOCK** key at the same time.)

 LEARNING CHECK 11-2

1. What does the disk drive do?

2. TRUE FALSE Most computers let you move the cursor to mistakes in text after you've typed past them.

3. Computer terminal screens are also called _____ or _____.

4. Information being displayed on a terminal screen will _____ when there is more information than will fit on one screen.

3. video display terminals, cathode ray tubes   4. scroll
1. The disk drive rotates the disk so that data can be read from and written to it.   2. TRUE

SUMMARY POINTS

- The computer is not a toy. It should be handled with care.

- Floppy disks should be kept away from magnets, magnetic fields, and heat to prevent data from being destroyed.

- The oval cutout on a floppy disk should never be touched. If it is, the data stored on the disk may be damaged.

- The disk drive rotates the disk so that data can be read from it or written to it.

- The proper instructions for each machine must be followed when turning on the computer.

- The keyboard of most computers is very similar to that of an ordinary typewriter. Special keys and their uses should be studied for each computer.

- Computer terminal screens, also called video display terminals and cathode ray tubes, provide soft-copy output.

CHAPTER TEST

Vocabulary

Match the term from the numbered column with a description from the lettered column that best fits the term.

1. Floppy disk
2. System command
3. Keyboard
4. Envelope
5. Program function keys
6. Scrolling
7. Disk drive
8. Video display terminal

a. An instruction that tells the computer to do something.
b. A television-like screen used to display information.
c. Perform(s) special system commands.
d. The process of moving lines up and down on the terminal screen.
e. Protect(s) floppy disks.
f. The device that rotates a floppy disk and reads date from and writes data to it.
g. A low-cost form of external storage made of plastic and used with a disk drive.
h. The part of the computer containing the typing keys.

Questions

1. The computer is not a(n) _____.
   a. expensive machine
   b. machine that should be treated with care
   c. toy
2. Disks can be damaged by _____.
   a. disk drives
   b. bright light
   c. static

3. _____ commands tell the computer to do something such as SAVE a program.
   a. system
   b. function
   c. keyboard

4. The _____ of a disk should never be touched.
   a. label
   b. read/write notch
   c. center

5. A disk should be inserted into a disk drive with the _____ going in first.
   a. label
   b. read/write notch
   c. label on the read/write notch

6. The disk should be returned to its _____ after use.
   a. envelope
   b. disk drive
   c. CRT

7. The keyboard of most computers is very similar to a(n) _____.
   a. television
   b. calculator
   c. typewriter

8. A computer terminal screen is also called a _____.
   a. printer
   b. CRT (cathode ray tube)
   c. keyboard

9. A computer terminal screen produces _____ output.
   a. soft-copy
   b. hard-copy
   c. no

10. To see lines on the computer screen once the screen becomes full, the feature to use is the _____.
   a. disk drive
   b. revolve
   c. scroll

Chapter 12

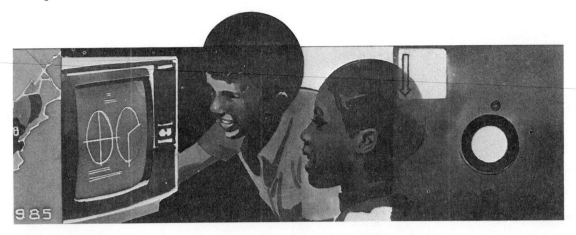

Using Constants and Variables

Learning Objectives

After reading this chapter, you should be able to:

1. Use line numbers in BASIC programming.
2. Use BASIC statements such as REM, LET, PRINT, and END.
3. Explain constants and variables.
4. Recognize reserved words that have special meaning to the computer.

Introduction

We've talked about computers and programming for eleven chapters. But learning is doing, right? Let's begin some hands-on computer experience using the BASIC programming language (Beginners' All-Purpose Symbolic Instruction Code).

The programming samples for the BASIC chapters were written for Apple II computers. Each program gives the differences for three other computers: the Commodore 64, IBM PC, and TRS-80. If you are using a different computer, check with your instructor or the computer's user's manual for detailed instructions.

Some Simple Commands

Figure 12-1 shows an example of the BASIC programs you will be writing. A BASIC program is a list of instructions written in the BASIC programming language that tells the computer what to do. Each instruction in the program contains a **line number** and a **BASIC statement**. The line number tells the computer the order in which statements are to be executed. The BASIC statement consists of a programming command, constants, variables, expressions, and/or documentation.

The programming samples in this chapter use several BASIC commands that will not be introduced until the next chapter. So that you can follow the computer's processing, you will need a brief explanation of these commands.

The REM statement documents the program, giving a brief comment of what the program or program segment will do. The LET statement assigns values to variables. The PRINT statement tells the computer to print or display something. The END statement signals the computer that the program is complete and processing should stop. Finally, the RUN command tells the computer to execute the program.

Computers accept only those BASIC statements that are written according to certain rules. Let's examine the rules for writing constants and variables.

Line number A natural number or zero that specifies the order in which statements should be executed.

BASIC statement The part of the instruction composed of a programming command, constants, variables, and formulas.

```
10    REM *** THIS PROGRAM WILL PRINT ***
20    REM *** A PERSON'S NAME AND AGE ***
30    LET N$ = "BONNIE STAHL"
40    LET AG = 14
50    PRINT "MY NAME IS ";N$
60    PRINT " I AM ";AG;" YEARS OLD"
999   END
```

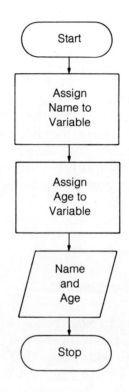

```
]RUN
MY NAME IS BONNIE STAHL
I AM 14 YEARS OLD
```

MICROCOMPUTER DIFFERENCES

IBM PC: Two spaces will apppear in the output
              between "M" and "14."
TRS-80: Same as for IBM
Commodore 64: Same as for IBM

Figure 12-1. *Name and Age Program*

```
]PRINT "HELLO"
HELLO

]PRINT "I AM 13 YEARS OLD"
I AM 13 YEARS OLD

]PRINT "HOW OLD ARE YOU?"
HOW OLD ARE YOU?
```

Figure 12-2. *Direct Mode Operation*

Line Numbers

Most microcomputers operate in two modes—**direct** (also called **immediate**) or **indirect**. In the direct mode, an instruction entered into the computer is executed right away when the RETURN key is pressed. No line numbers are needed in the direct mode. Figure 12-2 is an example of a session at the computer in direct mode. Statements entered in the direct mode are not saved for later use.

In the indirect mode, line numbers must be used with the programming statements. The instructions are not executed until the computer is told to do so by the programmer. These instructions can be saved for later use. Figure 12-3 contains the same instructions executed in Figure 12-2, now being executed in the indirect mode.

Line numbers specify the order in which statements are executed—from lowest to highest. However, program statements do not have to be typed in the order in which they are to be executed. Figure 12-4 shows how the computer follows the order of the line numbers, not the order in which the instructions were typed.

Direct (or immediate) mode The mode of operation in which statements are executed when the RETURN key is pressed.

Indirect mode The mode of operation in which statements are not executed until told to do so.

```
10    PRINT "HELLO"
20    PRINT "I AM 13 YEARS OLD"
30    PRINT "HOW OLD ARE YOU?"
99    END


]RUN
HELLO
I AM 13 YEARS OLD
HOW OLD ARE YOU?
```

Start

Print
Information

Stop

Figure 12-3. *Indirect Mode Operation*

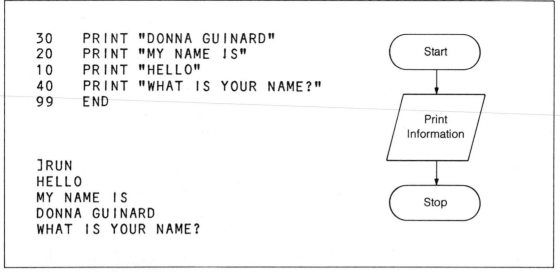

```
30    PRINT "DONNA GUINARD"
20    PRINT "MY NAME IS"
10    PRINT "HELLO"
40    PRINT "WHAT IS YOUR NAME?"
99    END


]RUN
HELLO
MY NAME IS
DONNA GUINARD
WHAT IS YOUR NAME?
```

Start

Print
Information

Stop

Figure 12-4. *Line Number Example*

A line number must be a natural number or zero. The highest number accepted varies for each microcomputer. The Apple II and Commodore 64 will accept any number between 0 and 63999. For the TRS-80 and IBM PC microcomputers, the range is 0 to 65529. No commas are included in a line number.

Line numbers do not have to be assigned in increments of one. Using increments of five or ten (as shown in the programming samples) makes it easier to insert new statements between existing lines without renumbering all the old statements. For exam-

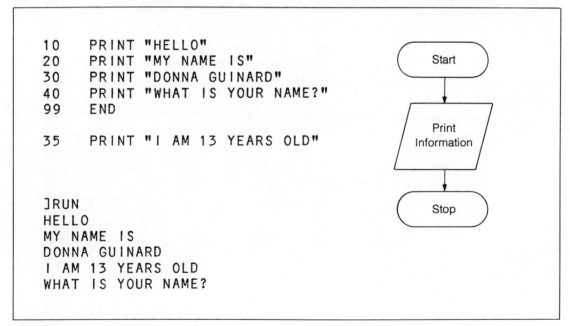

```
10    PRINT "HELLO"
20    PRINT "MY NAME IS"
30    PRINT "DONNA GUINARD"
40    PRINT "WHAT IS YOUR NAME?"
99    END

35    PRINT "I AM 13 YEARS OLD"


]RUN
HELLO
MY NAME IS
DONNA GUINARD
I AM 13 YEARS OLD
WHAT IS YOUR NAME?
```

Start

Print
Information

Stop

Figure 12-5. *Line Increment Example*

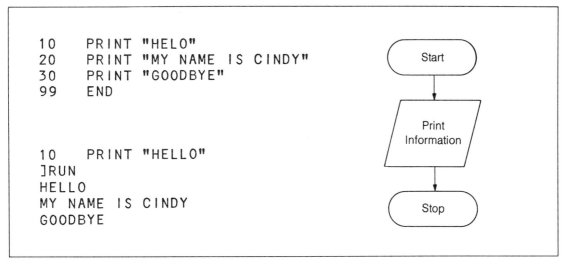

```
10    PRINT "HELO"
20    PRINT "MY NAME IS CINDY"
30    PRINT "GOODBYE"
99    END



10    PRINT "HELLO"
]RUN
HELLO
MY NAME IS CINDY
GOODBYE
```

Figure 12-6. *Program Change with Line Number Example*

ple, we could insert a new line ("I am 13 years old") between lines 30 and 40 by numbering the new statement 35. The new output is shown in Figure 12-5.

Another advantage of BASIC line numbers is that they allow changes to be made to the program. For example, if two lines are typed in with the same line number, the computer will accept the last one entered as the correct one. If you make a mistake in a statement, you can simply type in the same line number and the correct statement. Note in Figure 12-6 that the second line number 10 was executed, not the first one typed.

LEARNING CHECK 12-1

1. The following instructions will be executed in _____ mode.

```
PRINT "HELLO"
PRINT "GOODBYE"
```

2. What will the output look like for the following instructions?

```
30    PRINT "GOODBYE"
20    PRINT "HOW ARE YOU?"
10    PRINT "HELLO"
99    END
]RUN
```

3. What is wrong with the following set of instructions? How should they be written?

```
-10    PRINT "I LIVE IN NEW YORK"
 20    PRINT "WHERE DO YOU LIVE"
 10    PRINT "COME VISIT ME"
 99    END
```

4. What will the output look like for the following set of instructions?

```
10   PRINT "HELLO"
20   PRINT "WHAT YOUR NAME?"
99   END
20   PRINT "WHAT IS YOUR NAME?"
```

]RUN

Constants

Constant A value that does not change during a program's execution.

Constants are values that do not change during a program's execution. Consider the calculations needed to determine how much money you make while babysitting. If the per-hour wage remains the same while the number of hours spent babysitting changes, the per-hour amount would be a constant. There are two kinds of constants: numeric and character string.

Numeric Constants

A numeric constant is a number that does not change. Here are some rules to remember when using numbers in BASIC:

1. No commas can be used within numbers:

   3751.6 (valid)   7,892.8 (invalid)   612,000 (invalid)

2. If the number is negative, it must be preceded by a minus sign:

   –3.75 (valid)   82.59– (invalid)

3. If no sign is included, the number is assumed to be positive:

   2081 is the same as +2081

4. Fractions must be written as decimals.

Character string A group of alphanumeric data enclosed in quotation marks.

   2.75 (valid)   2 3/4 (invalid)

Character String Constants

Alphanumeric data Data comprised of letters, numbers, and/or special characters.

The other type of constant is the **character string**. Character strings consist of **alphanumeric data** enclosed in quotation marks. Alphanumeric data is a group of letters, numbers, and/or special

204

characters (such as $, @, ¢, and %). If a number is enclosed in quotation marks, it is considered to be a character string. Numbers used in character strings may contain commas. The following are examples of valid character strings:

"GEORGE"

"222-50-4003"

"209 CARR AVE."

"3 PENS @ 49¢ ea."

"20,000 LEAGUES UNDER THE SEA"

The PRINT statements in Figure 12-6 contain character string constants. These character strings do not change during the execution of a program.

 LEARNING CHECK 12-2

1. A value that does not change during a program's execution is called a(n) _____.

2. Commas *can/cannot* be used within numbers in BASIC.

3. Character strings must be enclosed in _____.

4. Identify each of the following as either a valid or invalid character string:
   a. "$2,801.49"
   b. "MY DOG IS A BEAGLE
   c. "HUCKLEBERRY FINN"
   d. 180 SCHOOL DAYS

1. constant 2. cannot 3. quotation marks 4. a. valid, b. invalid, c. valid, d. invalid

---

Variables

Many times you will want to change the values within BASIC statements. For example, a program may call for the names of all of the students in your class. Or it might call for the number of hours spent babysitting, which can change with each job. The values that can change either before or during execution of a program are called **variables**.

Each variable must be assigned a **variable name**. When a variable name is used, it is associated with a storage location in the computer's memory. When the program comes across a variable name, it directs the computer to the associated storage location where the value of the variable is stored.

Although the value of a variable can change throughout the program, it can have only one value at a time. Computer memory works something like mailboxes at the post office (see Figure 12-7).

Variable A value that can change either before or during program execution.

Variable name A name that identifies the value that can change either before or during program execution.

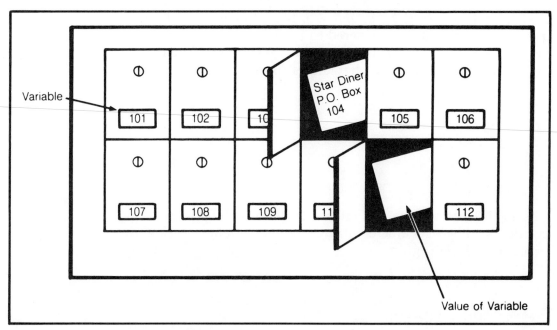

Figure 12-7. *Variables Are Like Mail Boxes*

The variable name is like the name on the envelope that is associated with an address (P.O. Box 104). The variable is the mail itself. The value of the variable is what's inside the envelope. The variable name points to the correct location in computer memory, just as the address on the envelope directs the postman to the correct mailbox. However, in a computer memory "box" there can only be one piece of "mail" at a time. Each time a new piece of data is put in the memory location, the old one is taken out.

There are two types of variables: numeric and string.

Numeric Variables

A numeric variable name represents a number that may change during execution of the program. In the babysitting example stated earlier, the number of hours spent babysitting each week may change. A variable name would be assigned to the hours value. A numeric variable name can be either one letter alone or one letter followed by one numeric digit or another letter. Most computers permit the use of more than two characters in a numeric variable name (see Table 12-1). Remember that only the first two characters are recognized by the Apple, TRS-80, and Commodore computers. For instance, if you assign two numeric variable names, such as *WEIGHT* and *WEATHER*, these computers will see them as the same name. The following examples show valid and invalid numeric variable names:

```
10    REM *** THIS PROGRAM COMPUTES THE ***
20    REM *** PAY RECEIVED FROM A WEEK ***
30    REM *** OF BABYSITTING ***
40    LET HR = 5.0
50    LET PA = 0.75 * HR
60    PRINT "TOTAL BABYSITTING PAY IS $";PA
70    END
```

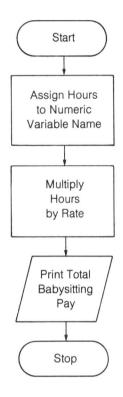

```
]RUN
TOTAL BABYSITTING PAY IS $3.75
```

MICROCOMPUTER DIFFERENCES
IBM PC: A space, saved for the negative sign, is printed printed between the $ and the value 3.75.
TRS-80: Same as for IBM
Commodore 64: Same as for IBM

Figure 12-8. *Babysitting Pay Program*

Microcomputer	Number of Unique Characters Recognized	Additional Characters Permitted
Apple	2	Yes
TRS-80	2	Yes
Commodore 64	2	Yes
IBM	40	Yes

Valid	Invalid and Why
X	33 (must begin with a letter)
B4	*C (must begin with a letter)
AC	6 (cannot be a single digit)

In Figure 12-8, line 40 assigns the value of 5 to the variable HR (5 hours were spent babysitting). Line 50 says that PA holds the result of the hours multiplied by the rate of pay.

String Variables

A string variable name represents a character string, such as a name, an address, or a Social Security number. The character string may contain letters, digits, and special characters (such as %, $, ¢, and so on). A string variable name is one alphabetic character followed by a dollar sign ($). The following example shows valid and invalid string variable names:

Valid	Invalid and Why
R$	8$ First character must be alphabetic
T$	$ No alphabetic character before $
Q$	T1 Last character must be $
M$	SV Last character must be $

Most computers permit the use of more characters in the variable name. However, all computers require that the first character be alphabetic and the last character be a $ (see Table 12-2). As with numeric variable names, even though the Apple, TRS-80, and Commodore computers allow more than two characters (plus $), only the first two characters in a string variable name are recognized. So, the string variable names *BASEBALL$* and *BASKETBALL$* are seen as the same name by the computer.

In Figure 12-9, line 40 allows the user to input his or her name. That name is stored at location N$. The value of N$ is then retrieved and printed in line 50.

```
10    REM *** THIS PROGRAM ACCEPTS A NAME ***
20    REM *** AND THEN PRINTS IT OUT ***
30    PRINT "WHAT IS YOUR NAME?"
40    INPUT N$
50    PRINT "YOUR NAME IS ";N$
60    END
```

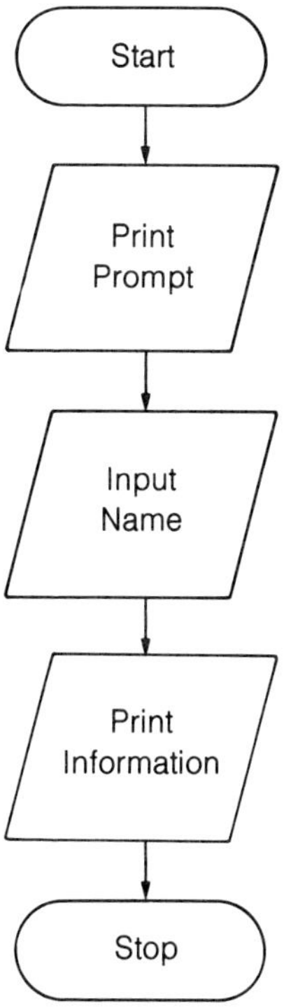

```
]RUN
WHAT IS YOUR NAME?
?CHRIS
YOUR NAME IS CHRIS
```

Figure 12-9. *Name Program Using String Variable*

STRING VARIABLE NAMES

Table 12-2

Microcomputer	Number of Unique Characters Recognized	Additional Characters Permitted
Apple	2(plus $)	Yes
TRS-80	2(plus $)	Yes
Commodore 64	2(plus $)	Yes
IBM PC	40(plus $)	Yes

When additional characters are used, the last character must be a dollar sign ($).

Reserved word A
word recognized by
the computer as
having special
meaning; cannot
be used as a vari-
able name.

Reserved Words

There are certain words that have special meaning to the computer. These words are called **reserved words**. They cannot be used as
variable names. Table 12-3 lists some of the commonly used
reserved words for the Apple II. Check your computer's user's
manual for additional reserved words or any differences in your
system. The appendix to this book contains additional reserved
words for the Apple II Plus, Apple IIe, and Apple IIc computers
plus reserved words for the Commodore, IBM PC and TRS-
80 computers.

SOME COMMONLY USED APPLESOFT RESERVED WORDS   Table 12-3

END	VLIN	DEF	RESUME	REM
FOR	HCOLOR=	POKE	RECALL	STOP
NEXT	PEEK	TO	STORE	PRINT
DATA	RIGHT$	AT	SPEED=	LIST
INPUT	HPLOT	STEP	LET	CLEAR
DEL	DRAW	NORMAL	GOTO	GET
DIM	XDRAW	STR$	RUN	NEW
READ	HTAB	MID$	IF	TAB(
GR	HOME	INVERSE	RESTORE	THEN
TEXT	ON	FLASH	CHR$	NOT
CALL	WAIT	COLOR=	&	AND
PLOT	LOAD	POP	GOSUB	OR
HLIN	SAVE	VTAB	RETURN	LEFT$

LEARNING CHECK 12-3

1. The contents of a(n) _____ can change during the execution of the program.

2. TRUE   FALSE   A variable can contain more than one value at a time.

3. Identify each of the following as either a valid or an invalid numeric variable name:
   a. SCORE
   b. TE$
   c. T2
   d. MS

4. Identify each of the following as either a valid or an invalid string variable name:
   a. CL$
   b. J$1
   c. $
   d. Q2

5. Words that have special meanings to the computer and cannot be used as variable names are called _____.

1. variable 2. FALSE 3. a. valid b. invalid c. valid d. valid 4. a. valid b. invalid c. invalid, d. invalid 5. reserved words

SUMMARY POINTS

- Line numbers are not used when operating a computer in the direct mode. However, line numbers must be used when operating in the indirect mode.

- A line number must be a natural number or zero. It specifies the order in which the statements are executed. Line numbers do not have to be in increments of one.

- A constant is a value that does not change during a program's execution.

- Character string constants are composed of alphanumeric data and are enclosed in quotation marks.

- A variable is a storage location that can hold different values; it is assigned a variable name.

- A numeric variable name can be either one letter alone or one letter followed by one numeric digit or another letter.

- A string variable name represents a character string and is one alphabetic character followed by a dollar sign ($).

CHAPTER TEST

Vocabulary

Match the term from the numbered column on the left with the best description from the lettered column on the right.

1. Constant

    a. A storage location that can hold different values during execution of the program.

2. Alphanumeric data

    b. An integer that specifies the order in which the statements are executed.

3. Variable

    c. Data comprised of letters, numbers, and/or special characters.

4. Reserved word

    d. A value that does not change during execution of the program.

5. Line number

    e. A mode of operation in which computer statements are executed as soon as the [RETURN] key is pressed.

6. Character string

    f. Identifies the storage location of a variable.

7. Variable name

    g. A word that has a special meaning to the computer and cannot be used as a variable name.

8. Direct mode

    h. A group of alphanumeric data enclosed in quotation marks.

Questions

1. The program on the following page is:
- **a.** valid
- **b.** invalid

```
1    PRINT "ON MY SUMMER VACATION"
2    PRINT "I WENT SWIMMING"
5    PRINT "AT THE SHORE"
9    END
```

2. Line numbers _____.

   a. must be in increments of one

   b. must be typed in the order in which they are to be executed

   c. must be natural numbers or zero

3. The output from the following program will be:

```
20    PRINT "AT BRANDYWINE JUNIOR HIGH SCHOOL"
 5    PRINT "I PLAY SOFTBALL"
10    PRINT "ON THE J.V. TEAM"
99    END
```

   a. AT BRANDYWINE JR. HIGH SCHOOL
       I PLAY SOFTBALL
       ON THE J.V. TEAM

   b. I PLAY SOFTBALL
       ON THE J.V. TEAM
       AT BRANDYWINE JUNIOR HIGH SCHOOL

   c. None of the above—there is an error in the program

4. The output from the following program will be:

```
10    PRINT "I HAVE 3 BROTHERS"
20    PRINT "AND 1 SISTER"
99    END
20    PRINT "AND 2 SISTERS"
```

   a. I HAVE 3 BROTHERS
       AND 2 SISTERS

   b. I HAVE 3 BROTHERS
       AND 1 SISTER

   c. None of the above—there is an error in the program

5. The output from the following program will be:

```
10    PRINT "FOR LUNCH"
-5    PRINT "I HAD"
 5    PRINT "A PEANUT BUTTER AND JELLY SANDWICH"
99    END
```

   a. FOR LUNCH
       I HAD
       A PEANUT BUTTER AND JELLY SANDWICH

   b. I HAD
       A PEANUT BUTTER AND JELLY SANDWICH
       FOR LUNCH

   c. None of the above—there is an error in the program.

6. The following is a(n) _____ numeric constant: 7,831

   a. valid

   b. invalid

7. The following is a(n) _____ numeric constant: 843.99

   a. valid

   b. invalid

8. The following is a(n) _____ numeric constant: "743"

   a. valid

   b. invalid

9. The following is a(n) _____ character string constant: "3133 Main St."

   a. valid

   b. invalid

10. The following is a(n) _____ character string constant: MARY

   a. valid

   b. invalid

11. Which of the following is an invalid numeric variable name?

   a. A

   b. C6

   c. C$

12. Which of the following is a valid numeric variable name?

   a. 4B

   b. XY

   c. D*

13. Which of the following is a valid string variable name?

   a. A$

   b. 3$

   c. NM

14. Which of the following is an invalid string variable name?

   a. X$

   b. D$

   c. *$

15. Most computers allow more than two characters to be used in variable names.

   a. TRUE

   b. FALSE

PROGRAMMING PROBLEMS

1. There are some mistakes in this program. Can you find them?

```
10    PRINT "TOTAL WEIGHT OF EVERYONE
30    PRINT "IN THIS ELEVATER IS"
```

```
40     LET WT = 7,350
50     PRINT WT$
30     PRINT "IN THIS ELEVATOR IS"
99     END
```

2. Find and correct the mistakes in this program.

```
10     LET N$ = SANDY
20     LET D& = "FRITZ"
30     PRINT "HELLO, MY NAME IS";N$
40     PRINT "I HAVE ONE DOG"
50     PRINT "MY DOG'S NAME IS";D$
-99    END
```

3. Using the following output as a guide, assign appropriate variable names to the underlined words, numbers, or character strings for use in a program that gives information about our Presidents. Follow the guidelines for variable name assignments stated in the chapter. (Assign numeric variable names to any numbers.)

ABE LINCOLN WAS THE 16th PRESIDENT OF THE UNITED STATES. HE WAS PRESIDENT FROM 1861 TO 1865, DURING THE CIVIL WAR. HE WAS MOST FAMOUS FOR FREEING THE SLAVES OF THE SOUTH. HIS TERM AS A PRESIDENT ENDED WHEN HE WAS SHOT BY JOHN WILKES BOOTH. HE WILL ALWAYS BE REMEMBERED AS HONEST ABE.

Chapter 13

Learning the Fundamentals

Learning Objectives

After reading this chapter, you should be able to:

1. Define and use the REM statement.

2. Define and use the LET statement.

3. Describe the order of operation in an arithmetic expression.

4. Use the PRINT statement to print variables, literals, expressions, and blank lines.

5. Define and use the END statement.

6. Use the following system commands: NEW, LIST, RUN, SAVE, CATALOG, LOAD, and HOME as well as the scroll.

Introduction

It is finally time for you to start writing some simple programs in the BASIC programming language. This chapter explains four BASIC commands (REM, LET, PRINT, and END) and the system commands you will need to run your programs. You should have fun with the hands-on exercises in this chapter. Just remember to treat your computer and disks with care!

BASIC Programming Statements

If you have ever performed in a play, you know that the actors and stage crew receive cues from the script. These cues may direct the players to "Enter right," "Dim lights," or "Sniffle as if ready to cry." Your computer should also receive cues. The cues are written into the BASIC programs. They tell the computer what to do with the constants and variables and other data that are entered. Some BASIC programming statements are REM, LET, PRINT, and END. Let's see how each statement cues the computer to perform some function within the program.

The REM Statement

REM (remark) **statements** document a program. They provide information for the programmer or anyone else reading the program but have no effect on how the program is executed. The computer saves these statements as part of the program but ignores them when the program is executed. The REM statements in Figure 13-1 explain the program and the variables used in the program.

The general format of the REM statement is:

line# REM comment

```
10     REM *** THIS PROGRAM WILL PRINT ***
20     REM *** A PERSON'S NAME AND ***
30     REM *** BIRTHDATE. ***
40     REM *** VARIABLES:  ***
50     REM *** N$ = NAME ***
60     REM *** B$ = BIRTHDATE ***
70     REM
80     LET N$ = "ROBIN HIGINGBOTTOM"
90     LET B$ = "7/24/66"
100    PRINT N$;" WAS BORN ";B$
999    END

]RUN
ROBIN HIGINGBOTTOM WAS BORN 7/24/66
```

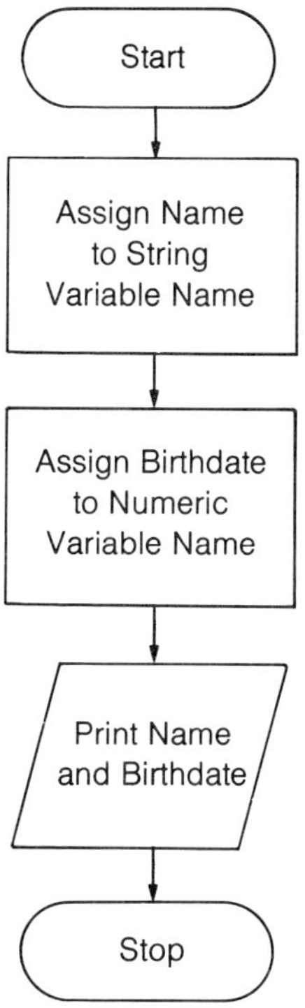

Start

Assign Name
to String
Variable Name

Assign Birthdate
to Numeric
Variable Name

Print Name
and Birthdate

Stop

Figure 13-1. *REM Statement Program*

The asterisks (*) used in Figure 13-1 are not necessary but set off the remarks from the other statements in the program. Lines 10-30 explain what the program does. Lines 40-60 explain what the variable names stand for. A REM statement can be used anywhere in a program to explain a portion of the program. It is a good idea to use REM statements to comment about the program so that anyone reading the program will understand it. Also, you will be able to recall what is being done in the program if changes to the program are required later.

It is possible to have a REM statement with no comment following it, such as in line 70 of Figure 13-1. In this case, the REM statement can be used to set off comments from other program statements. As stated earlier, the REM statement has no effect on how the program is executed.

The LET Statement

The **LET statement** allows the programmer to assign (give) values to variables. The general format of the LET statement is:

line# LET variable name = expression

Expression A constant, variable, or mathematical formula.

The **expression** may be an arithmetic formula, another variable, or a constant. The following are examples of expressions:

Statement		Expression	Type
10	LET X = 10	10	Numeric constant
20	LET T = 4 + 5	4 + 5	Arithmetic formula
30	LET P = T	T	Numeric variable
40	LET N$ = "BOB"	"BOB"	Character string constant
50	LET A$ = B$	B$	String variable
60	LET S = 10 - X	10 - X	Arithmetic formula containing a numeric variable

The value or calculated result of the expression on the right side of the equal sign is assigned to the variable on the left side. When BASIC assigns a value to a variable on the left side of the equation, it really is putting that value in a storage location in memory represented by that variable name. Since a storage location can only be represented by a variable name, only a variable can appear on the left side of the equation.

The following examples show how LET statements are executed by the computer.

LET Statement		Computer Execution
10	LET X = 1	The numeric value 1 is assigned to the variable name called X.
40	LET C = A + B	The values of A and B are added together and assigned to C.
85	LET N$ = "JOHN HENRY"	LET assigns the value JOHN HENRY to the string variable name N$.
100	LET M = M + 1	1 is added to the current value of M and the result is assigned to M. This result replaces whatever was in M previously.

```
200    LET A = (10 + J + 0.5)
           / (M * 4)
```
The arithmetic expression to the right of the equal sign is evaluated and assigned to location A.

Arithmetic Expressions   In BASIC, arithmetic expressions can contain constants, numeric variables, and arithmetic operators. The arithmetic operators that can be used are shown in Table 13-1.

ARITHMETIC OPERATORS   Table 13-1

BASIC Arithmetic Operation Symbol	Operation	Arithmetic Example	BASIC Arithmetic Expression
+	Addition	A + B	A + B
−	Subtraction	A − B	A − B
*	Multiplication	A × B	A * B
/	Division	A ÷ B	A / B
∧	Exponentiation	A^B	A ∧ B

```
MICROCOMPUTER DIFFERENCES
SYMBOL FOR EXPONENTIATION

IBM PC: ∧
TRS-80: [ SHIFT ]  and  [ ; ]
Commodore 64:
```

These examples are valid expressions in LET statements:

```
10     LET M = 5 + 4
20     LET T = N1 + N2 + N3 + N4
30     LET J = A - B
40     LET X = 3 * C
50     LET Y = (P * D) * C
60     LET Q = N ^ 5
70     LET C = 6.4 + P / X
```

In an addition operation, such as

```
10     LET X = A + B
```

the value in the memory location identified by the variable A is added to the value in the memory location identified by the variable B. The result is then placed in the memory location identified by the variable X. If A equals 5 and B equals 3, the computer would add 5 to 3 and place the result, 8, into the variable X. The values at A and B are not changed by this operation. Only the value at X is changed. Whatever value was at location X is replaced by the new value.

In a subtraction operation, such as

```
20     LET Z = D - C
```

the same steps occur except that the value stored in C is subtracted from the value stored in D, with the result stored at Z.

The multiplication operator (*) is used to multiply two values. For example:

```
30     LET X = A * B
```

multiplies the value in A by the value in B and places the product in the memory location identified by X. Once again, the values at A and B are not changed by the multiplication operator. Suppose the following values were assigned to the variables listed:

```
A = 3
B = 2
X = 1
```

After the multiplication operation is performed (A * B), the variables now represent the following values:

```
A = 3
B = 2
X = 6
```

The values A and B remained the same, but the old value of X was replaced by the new value (3 * 2 = 6).

The division operator (/) is used to divide two values. For example:

```
40     LET X =   A / B
```

divides the value in A by the value in B and places the result in the location X.

The result of an arithmetic operation can be used in other calculations, for example:

```
20     LET X = A + B

30     LET Z = X * 3
```

The value of X in line 30 will equal the sum of the addition operation performed in line 20. If the value of A equals 2 and the value of B equals 4, the final value of X will equal 6 and the final value of Z will equal 18:

```
X = 2 + 4
Z = 6 * 3
```

The last arithmetic operation is **exponentiation**, or raising a number to a power. For example, X^3 is the same as $X * X * X$. In the statement

```
20    LET Y = X ^ 3
```

X would be cubed ($X * X * X$). The result would be stored at location Y.

Exponentiation
Raising a number
to a power.

Priority of Operations   When more than one operation is to be performed in an arithmetic expression, the computer follows a priority, or order, of operations. Any expressions enclosed in parentheses receive first, or top, priority. Comparisons receive the lowest priority. Other operations fall in the order as shown below:

Priority	Operation
First	Parentheses
Second	Exponentiation
Third	Multiplication or division
Fourth	Addition or subtraction
Fifth	Equal to, greater than, or less than

Operations with high priority are performed before operations with lower priority. If more than one operation is to be performed at the same level, for example:

```
3 * 4 / 6
```

the computer evaluates them from left to right. In this example, the 3 would be multiplied by 4, then the result, 12, would be divided by 6. The answer is 2.

Here are examples of these priority rules:

Expression	Computer Evaluation
Expression 1 2 * 5 + 1	
First: 2 * 5 = 10	Multiplication has a higher priority than addition, so it is done first.
Second: 10 + 1 = 11	Then the addition is done.
Expression 2 2 * (5 + 1) First: (5 + 1) = 6	In this case, the addition must be done first, because it is enclosed in parentheses.
Second: 2 * 6 = 12	The result is multiplied by 2. Compare this result with the result in Expression 1.
Expression 3 2 ∧ 3 / 4 − 2 First: 2 ∧ 3 = 8	The priority order tells the computer to start with exponentiation.

Second: 8 / 4 = 2   Next is division.

Third: 2 − 2 = 0   Last, the subtraction is done.

Expression 4
4 * 5 + 2 / 5 * 15
First: 4 * 5 = 20   There are three operations at the same level: *, /,
                           and *. They are performed in order from left to
                           right.

Second: 2 / 5 = 0.4
Third: 0.4 * 15 = 6
Fourth: 20 + 6 = 26   Last, the addition is done.

Expression 5
4 * 6 / (2 ∧ 3)
First: (2 ∧ 3) = 8   The exponentiation is done first, because it is
                           enclosed in parentheses.

Second: 4 * 6 = 24   Next, the priority order tells the computer to do
                           the multiplication.

Third: 24 / 8 = 3   Last, the division is done.

Character Strings   The LET statement also can be used to assign a character string value to a string variable name. A character string is composed of alphanumeric data enclosed in quotation marks. For example:

```
10    LET T$ = "TOTAL SALES"
20    LET X$ = T$
```

In line 10, the value "TOTAL SALES" is assigned to the string variable name T$. In line 20, the string value located at T$ is assigned to the string variable name X$.

The following examples show valid and invalid LET statements involving character strings.

Valid		Invalid and Why
20	LET N$ = "BOB"	20 LET N = "BOB" (a character string must be assigned to a string variable name)
30	LET P$ = QS	30 LET P$= 3 * QQ (a string variable cannot be part of an arithmetic expression)
40	LET A$ = "HELLO"	LET A$ = HELLO (a character string must be enclosed in quotation marks)

Figure 13-2 calculates an average daily lunch bill and shows several uses of the LET statement. The LET statement in line 30 assigns the total amount spent on lunches for a week to the

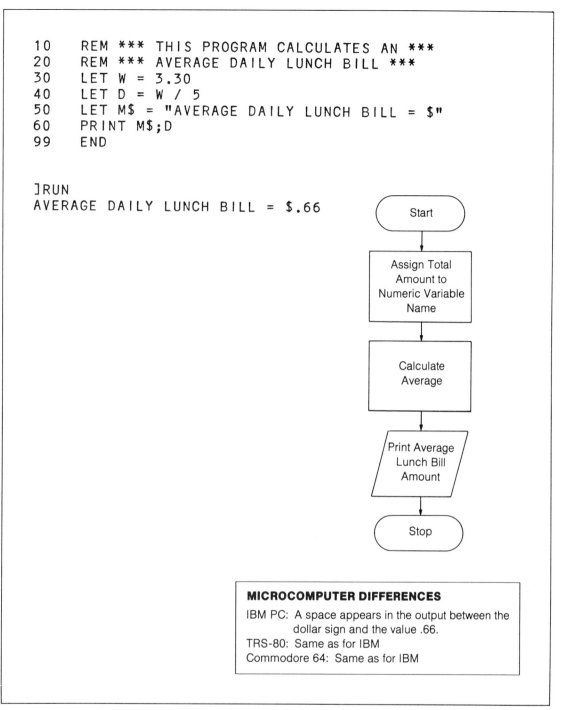

```
10    REM *** THIS PROGRAM CALCULATES AN ***
20    REM *** AVERAGE DAILY LUNCH BILL ***
30    LET W = 3.30
40    LET D = W / 5
50    LET M$ = "AVERAGE DAILY LUNCH BILL = $"
60    PRINT M$;D
99    END


]RUN
AVERAGE DAILY LUNCH BILL = $.66
```

Start

Assign Total
Amount to
Numeric Variable
Name

Calculate
Average

Print Average
Lunch Bill
Amount

Stop

MICROCOMPUTER DIFFERENCES

IBM PC: A space appears in the output between the
dollar sign and the value .66.
TRS-80: Same as for IBM
Commodore 64: Same as for IBM

Figure 13-2. *LET Statement Program*

numeric variable name W. Line 40 calculates the daily average by
dividing the weekly total, W, by 5 (the number of school days in a
week). The LET statement in line 50 assigns a character string to
the string variable name M$. The character string and the results
of the calculation are printed by line 60.

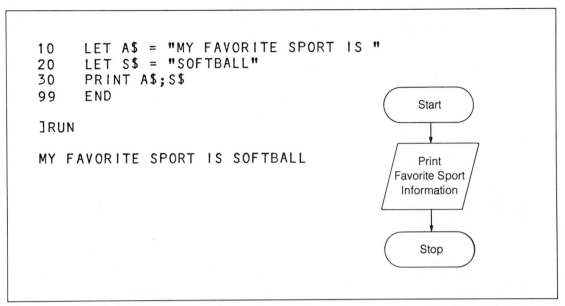

```
10    LET A$ = "MY FAVORITE SPORT IS "
20    LET S$ = "SOFTBALL"
30    PRINT A$;S$
99    END

]RUN

MY FAVORITE SPORT IS SOFTBALL
```

Start

Print
Favorite Sport
Information

Stop

Figure 13-3. *Sports Program*

Before you actually begin writing short programs, there are a few points you will need to remember. When you use a character string in either a PRINT or a LET statement, you must consider how you want it to be spaced. The computer will print exactly what you tell it to print. So you must remember to put spaces within the quotation marks if they are needed when the output is printed. For example, carefully look at the program in Figure 13-3.

In line 10 a space was left within the quotation mark, after the word "IS". The reason was so that there would be a space between the words "IS" and "SOFTBALL" when the two character strings were printed.

Refer back to Figure 13-2. In line 50, no space was left after the dollar sign in the character string. That was because the programmer wanted the dollar sign to be printed right next to the .66.

It is also important to include a space after the line number and after the BASIC commands, such as REM, PRINT, LET, and so on.

 LEARNING CHECK 13-1

1. TRUE   FALSE   REM statements are ignored when a program is executed.

2. Assign variable names to the variables *teacher's name*, *class*, and *number of students* (a numeric variable) that are to be used in a program. Then write REM statements to include in the program describing each variable name. (Be sure to include line numbers.)

3. Which of the following is not a valid statement? Why?

   a. LET 5 + 4 = M

   b. LET X = 3 * 2

   c. LET Z = A ∧ 2

4. Which of the following is not a valid statement? Why?

   a. LET N$ = "STEVE"

   b. LET A$ = B$

   c. LET Z$ = P$ * 5

5. Following the priority of operations, the result of this arithmetic expression is:

1 + 2 * 6 / 3

   a. 4.33

   b. 5

   c. 6

1. TRUE 2. 10 REM *** T = TEACHER'S NAME; 20 REM *** C$ = CLASS; 30 REM *** ST = NUMBER OF STUDENTS; Any string variable name can be used for teacher's name and class. Any numeric variable name can be used for number of students. 3. a. Only a variable can appear on the left side of the equation. 4. c. A string variable cannot be part of an arithmetic expression. 5. b

---

HANDS-ON EXERCISE 13-1

NOW TRY THIS ⟹ Type NEW, hit the RETURN key (from now on shown as [RETURN])
and type in the following program:

```
10    REM *** A PROGRAM FOR MATHEMATICS ***
20    LET A = 6
30    LET B = 3 + 1
40    LET C = (A * B) / (A * 2)
50    LET D$ = "THE ANSWER IS "
60    PRINT D$;C
99    END
```

Now type RUN [RETURN] on a new line. Do not assign a line number to RUN. This tells
the computer to execute the program. Look at the output to see if it is as follows:

```
]RUN
THE ANSWER IS 2
```

If it is not, there may have been a mistake in typing the program. Type LIST [RETURN]
and the computer will list the program again.

    Check to see where the error was. Retype the line that had an error. The computer will
substitute the new line for the old one. Type RUN [RETURN]. The output should now be
correct. If it is not, repeat the LIST process again. Be sure you understand why the
answer is 2.

Now retype line 40 to read

```
40    LET C = A * B / A * 2
```

and RUN the program. Taking out the parentheses will change the order of the arithmetic operations, thus changing the value of C to 8.

Now change line 20 to read

```
20    LET A = 3 + 3
```

and RUN the program. The output is still 8 since 3 + 3 places the same value (6) in location A.

The PRINT Statement

Format To arrange the design of output.

The **PRINT statement** is used to print or display the results of computer processing. It also permits **formatting**, or arranging, of output. The general format of the PRINT statement is:

$$\text{line\# PRINT} \begin{cases} \text{Variables} \\ \text{Literals} \\ \text{Arithmetic expressions} \\ \text{Combination of the above} \end{cases}$$

PRINT statements can take several forms, depending on the output being printed. The following sections give some examples.

Printing the Values of Variables Using the word PRINT followed by a variable name tells the computer to print the value of the variable. In this example:

```
10    LET X = 5
20    PRINT X
```

the computer will display the variable 5. Several variable names, separated by commas, can be listed after the word PRINT:

```
30    PRINT X, Y$, Z
```

The computer will print the value of each variable listed.

Printing has no effect on the contents of storage. The PRINT statement simply causes the computer to read and print the value that is stored.

Printing Literals A **literal** is an expression consisting of alphabetic, numeric, or special characters, or a combination of all three, whose value does not change during the execution of a program. The value is not stored in a memory location. It is simply printed as shown.

A character string literal is a group of letters, numbers, or special characters enclosed in quotation marks (''). Whatever is inside the quotation marks is printed exactly as it is. For example:

```
10    PRINT "ARE YOU LISTENING?"
```

would appear on the output page as

```
ARE YOU LISTENING?
```

The quotation marks do not appear; they simply tell the computer that a character string is to be printed.

To print column headings, put each heading in quotation marks and separate each group by a comma. The comma instructs the printer to skip to the next print zone (more on this in chapter 15). In the example:

```
30    PRINT "NAME", "AGE", "PHONE"
```

the character strings are printed out exactly as typed except that the quotation marks do not appear and the groups are spread apart:

```
NAME           AGE         PHONE
```

Numeric literals do not have to be enclosed in quotation marks to be printed. For example, the statement

```
20    PRINT 108
```

will print the following:

```
108
```

Printing the Values of Expressions The computer also prints the values of arithmetic expressions:

```
10    LET X = 4
20    LET Y = 3
30    PRINT X * Y / 6
```

Literal An expression consisting of alphabetic, numeric, or special characters whose value does not change during execution.

First, the computer evaluates the expression according to the rules of priority. However, instead of assigning the result to a variable name, the result is simply printed out as follows:

2

Printing Blank Lines A PRINT statement with nothing typed after it will provide a blank line of output. To skip more than one line, simply include more than one PRINT statement:

```
 90     PRINT
100     PRINT
```

The END Statement

Typing END after a line number signals to the computer that your program is complete and processing should stop. The general format of the END statement is:

line# END

Programmers usually type the highest number a computer will recognize before the END statement. This practice reminds them to include the END statement and helps make sure that it is positioned properly.

 LEARNING CHECK 13-2

1. Which of the following PRINT statements should be used to print the value of the variable N$?

   a. PRINT VAR N$

   b. PRINT N$

   c. PRINT: N$

2. A _____ literal must be enclosed in quotation marks in a PRINT statement.

3. TRUE   FALSE   Only one variable can be printed per PRINT statement.

4. Which of the following PRINT statements should be used to print a blank line?

   a. PRINT BLANK

   b. PRINT "SPACE"

   c. PRINT

5. The _____ statement indicates the last statement of the program.

1. b 2. character string 3. FALSE 4. c 5. END

NOW TRY THIS ⟹ Type NEW ⎡**RETURN**⎤ and type in the following program:

```
10    REM *** A PROGRAM ABOUT JIM ***
20    LET A$ = "FISH"
30    LET N = 3 * 5
40    PRINT "JIM'S FAVORITE ANIMAL IS A ";A$
50    PRINT
60    PRINT "JIM HAS ";N;" ";A$
99    END
```

Now type RUN ⎡**RETURN**⎤ on a new line. The correct output is:

```
]RUN
JIM'S FAVORITE ANIMAL IS A FISH

JIM HAS 15 FISH
```

If your program did not produce this output, there may have been a mistake in typing the program. Type LIST ⎡**RETURN**⎤ and the computer will list the program again.

Check to see where the error is. Retype the line correctly. The computer will substitute the new line for the old one. Type RUN ⎡**RETURN**⎤. The output should be correct. If it is not, repeat the LIST process again.

Now change line 20 by retyping it as follows:

```
20    LET A$ = FISH
```

and RUN the program.

You can see that removing the quotation marks from the character variable will produce an error message. Retype line 20 with the quotation marks.

Type 50 to remove the extra blank line between the printed output. RUN the program to check this.

Retype line 60 as

```
60    PRINT "JIM HAS "; 15; " "; A$
```

and RUN the program. Note that the 15 is printed as it appears.

Now retype line 60 as

```
60    PRINT "JIM HAS "; 10 + 5; " "; A$
```

and RUN the program. Note that the expression 10 + 5 is first evaluated and then the result is printed.

System Commands

If you have a dog, you have probably taught it to sit, roll over, heel, and stay. The well-trained dog will obey your commands automatically—most of the time. The well-trained computer obeys certain commands, too. Among the commands are NEW, LIST, RUN, SAVE, CATALOG, LOAD, and HOME. These commands are **system commands** because they are used to communicate with the operating system of the computer.

System command
A command used to communicate with the operating system of the computer.

You have already used NEW, LIST, and RUN with your hands-on exercises in BASIC. You saw that these commands did not require line numbers. System commands are usually immediate-mode commands. As soon as the RETURN or ENTER key is pressed, they are executed. Table 13-1 lists the formats of the commands for the four microcomputers discussed throughout the book. However, the detailed discussion that follows is for the Apple microcomputer.

SYSTEM COMMANDS   Table 13-1

System Commands	Apple	Commodore 64	TRS-80	IBM PC
List program statements	LIST	LIST	LIST	LIST
List selected program statements	LIST LINE#-LINE#	LIST LINE#-LINE#	LIST LINE#-LINE#	LIST LINE#-LINE#
Execute a program	RUN	RUN	RUN	RUN
Store program on disk	SAVE name	SAVE "name",8	SAVE "name"	SAVE "name"
Retrieve program from disk	LOAD name or RUN name	LOAD "name",8	LOAD "name"	LOAD "name"
Erase active memory	NEW	NEW	NEW	NEW
Display files on disk	CATALOG	LOAD "$",8 LIST	DIR	FILES
Clear the screen	HOME	SHIFT and HOME	CLS	CLS

NEW

Before typing a program on the computer, you should make sure there is no other program in active memory (a work area in RAM). The NEW command tells the computer you are starting a new program. The computer will erase any program currently in active memory. No line number is used and nothing follows the command.

Type:

```
NEW
```

and press RETURN every time you begin a new program.

LIST

After typing a long program, you may want to check the finished product. Type:

LIST

and press RETURN to see the program statements displayed on the screen. If you have a very short program, LIST can display the whole program on the video screen. However, if the program has more lines than the screen does, the top part of the program will scroll off the screen, and only the last part of the program will remain on the screen. On most computers, portions of your program can be displayed by naming the lines to be listed. For example, LIST 250-400 will display only lines 250 through 400.

RUN

The RUN command executes a program once it has been typed. Type:

RUN

and then press RETURN. Your program will be executed immediately. If there are no errors in the program, the desired output will be displayed. Chapter 14 discusses methods of finding and correcting errors.

SAVE

After many lines of program statements have been typed, they should be saved so that they will not be lost when the computer is turned off. Then the program can be used again without typing it again. To save a program, the program must be copied from active memory to an auxiliary storage medium, such as disk. The SAVE command does this for you. The format of the SAVE command is as follows:

SAVE
or
SAVE filename

with RETURN being pressed afterwards.

Apple—The filename can be 1 to 30 characters long including blanks. It must begin with a letter but the following may be any character except a comma.

Commodore 64—The filename can be up to eight characters long.

TRS-80—Filename/ext—the filename can be one to eight characters long. It must begin with a letter, but the following characters can be any digit (0-9) or letter (A-Z). The ext (extension) is optional. It must begin with a letter and can be followed by up to two letters or digits.

IBM PC—Filename/ext—the filename must be one to eight characters long. The extension must be no more than three characters. Only the following characters may be used in the filename and extension:

A – Z

0 – 9

$, &, #, @, !, %, ', (,), –

Figure 13-4. *Rules Governing Filenames*

The "SAVE filename" command saves the program under a specific filename. This name should be different than any other programs saved on the disk so that it is uniquely identified. The name must follow the rules governing filenames (see Figure 13-4). The SAVE command with no name specified saves the program under its previously assigned name.

CATALOG

In case you forget what name you have assigned to a program, or you just want to know what files have been saved on the disk, you can summon a catalog to list the file names saved on the disk. The format of the CATALOG command is:

CATALOG

followed by the RETURN key.

LOAD

If you want to execute or change a program that is already saved on a disk, the program must be retrieved from the disk and placed in active memory. The LOAD command erases any data currently in active memory and loads the desired program into active memory, where it can then be listed, changed, or run. The format of the LOAD command is:

LOAD filename

followed by the RETURN key. The filename entered is the unique name assigned to the desired program when it was saved.

HOME

The HOME command clears the display screen and positions the cursor at the upper left-hand corner of the screen. It does not have any effect on the contents of active memory. The format of the HOME command is:

HOME

followed by RETURN .

LEARNING CHECK 13-3

1. The _____ command tells the computer to erase any program currently in active memory.

2. The _____ command is used to display the program statements on the video screen.

3. The _____ command is used to execute a program after it has been typed.

4. The _____ command tells the computer to copy the program currently in active memory to an auxiliary storage medium.

5. The _____ command tells the computer to retrieve a file from an auxiliary storage medium and place it in active memory.

1. NEW 2. LIST 3. RUN 4. SAVE 5. LOAD

HANDS-ON EXERCISE 13-3

NOW TRY THIS ⟹ Type NEW RETURN and type in the following program, using your own name and age:

```
10    REM *** A PROGRAM ABOUT JODY ***
20    LET N$ = "JODY"
30    LET AG = 13
40    PRINT N$;" IS ";AG;" YEARS OLD"
99    END
```

Now type RUN RETURN on a new line. After the computer has executed the program, save the program on the external storage device. To do this, use the SAVE statement, beginning on a new line. (Do not assign a line number to it, but remember to give your program a filename.)

```
10    REM *** THIS PROGRAM COMPUTES THE NUMBER ***
20    REM *** OF GALLONS OF GAS NEEDED TO TAKE ***
30    REM *** A TRIP AND THE COST OF THE GAS.  ***
40    REM *** VARIABLES USED: ***
50    REM *** DI = MILES TRAVELED ***
60    REM *** MG = MILES PER GALLON ***
70    REM *** GL = GALLONS OF GAS NEEDED FOR TRIP ***
80    REM *** PR = PRICE OF GAS PER GALLON ***
90    REM *** CS = COST OF GAS FOR TRIP ***
100   REM
110   LET DI = 310
120   LET MG = 25
130   LET GL = DI / MG
140   LET PR = 1.19
150   LET CS = GL * PR
160   REM *** PRINT HEADINGS AND OUTPUT ***
170   PRINT "GALLONS ", "COST"
180   PRINT
190   PRINT GL,"$";CS
999   END
```

Figure 13-5. *Gasoline Amount and Cost Program*

Now type CATALOG [**RETURN**] to list the files saved on the storage device. The new file just saved should be listed in the catalog. Use the LOAD statement to reload the program into active memory. Type LIST [**RETURN**] and the program will be listed on the screen, ready to be edited or executed again.

Type HOME [**RETURN**] to clear the screen.

COMPREHENSIVE PROGRAMMING PROBLEM

This program is useful for travelers planning a trip by car. It tells the traveler how many gallons of gas are needed and how much the gas will cost for the trip. The input needed for this program is the number of miles to be traveled, the car's mileage per gallon of gas, and the cost per gallon of gas.

The traveler wishes to drive 310 miles, the car gets 25 miles per gallon, and the current price of gas is $1.19 per gallon. Assume the program has been written and is ready to be typed into the computer. An auxiliary storage device is to be used. Insert the disk, turn on the computer, and wait for the cursor to appear. Type NEW and hit the RETURN key. Then type HOME and hit the RETURN key. When the cursor appears again, it should appear in the upper left-hand corner of the screen. The program can then be typed into the computer's active memory. The program is shown in Figure 13-5.

```
]RUN
GALLONS                    COST

12.4                       $14.756
```

```
MICROCOMPUTER DIFFERENCES
IBM PC:  A space is printed between the $ and the
         value 14.756. There is also a space before
         12.4.
Commodore 64:  Same as IBM
TRS-80:  Same as IBM
```

Figure 13-6. *Output of Gasoline Amount and Cost Program*

The REM statements tell what is to be computed and define the variables. These statements would help future users of the program understand what is being done. The REM statement in line 100 separates the documentation of the program from the statements the computer actually executes.

Lines 110 and 120 place the values on the right into the variables DI and MG. To compute the number of gallons of gas needed, the computer divides the distance traveled by the miles per gallon the car gets and stores the result in the variable GL in line 130.

The price of gas is stored in the variable PR in line 140. Then the cost of the gas is computed in line 150 by multiplying the gallons of gas needed (GL) by the price per gallon of gas (PR). Line 150 stores the result in the variable CS.

Line 160 is called an "embedded" remark statement since it comes in the middle of the program. It tells the program user that the next statements are output-related. Line 170 prints the headings for the output so it is in a readable chart. Line 180 prints a blank line between the headings and the final computed output. Line 190 prints out the computed answer: the number of gallons needed and the cost of gas for the traveler's trip.

The END statement is given a high number, 999, to make sure it is the last statement read by the computer.

If you want to see the entire program again, type LIST . If no corrections are needed, you are ready to execute the program. Type RUN and hit RETURN . The program is then executed and the output is printed as shown in Figure 13-6.

Since this is the desired output, the program is correct and should be saved for future use. Type SAVE filename and RETURN . Name the file anything that has not already been used as a filename. When you wish to use the program again, type LOAD filename RETURN , and LIST RETURN . The program will be loaded into active memory and displayed on the screen.

SUMMARY POINTS

- REM statements are used to document a program; they are not executed by the computer.

- The purpose of the LET statement is to assign values to variables. The computer first evaluates the expression on the right side of the equal sign and then assigns that result to the variable name on the left side of the equal sign.

- Arithmetic expressions are evaluated according to the following priority of operations: 1) operations in parentheses; 2) exponentiation; 3) multiplication and division; and 4) addition and subtraction. Multiple operations at the same level are evaluated from left to right.

- The PRINT statement is used to print or display the results of processing.

- The END statement signals the computer that processing should stop.

- The NEW, LIST, RUN, SAVE, CATALOG, LOAD, and HOME commands are system commands used to manipulate a BASIC program. They are executed as soon as the RETURN key is pressed.

CHAPTER TEST

Vocabulary

Match the term from the numbered column on the left with the best description from the lettered column on the right.

1. Expression
2. Document
3. Literal
4. Immediate mode
5. System command
6. Exponentiation
7. Priority of operations
8. Formatting

a. To provide written information explaining various aspects of a program.

b. Raising a number to a power.

c. A constant, variable, or mathematical formula.

d. A command used to communicate with the computer's operating system.

e. An expression consisting of alphabetic, numeric, or special characters whose values do not change during the execution of a program.

f. Arranging computer output in a certain order.

g. When the computer performs arithmetic calculations in a given order.

h. The method of computer operation whereby statements are executed as soon as they are typed.

Questions

1. Which of the following is true of the REM statement?
    a. It alters the execution of a program.
    b. It is used to document a program.
    c. It is not saved as part of a program.

2. Which of the following is an invalid REM statement?
    a. `40 REM WAGE PROGRAM`
    b. `REM ***WAGE PROGRAM***`
    c. `40 REM`

3. The _____ statement allows the programmer to assign values to variables.

  a. END
  b. LET
  c. ASSIGN

4. What is the expression in the following statement?

LET X = 10 – Z

  a. LET
  b. X
  c. 10 – Z

5. Which of the following is an invalid statement?

  a. 40   LET A$ = B$
  b. 40   LET X = X + 1
  c. 40   LET 4 + 5 = A

6. Which of the following is a valid statement?

  a. 50   LET "DONNA" = N$
  b. 50   LET Q = "HELLO"
  c. 50   LET Y = A + B

7. What is the value of D after the following statement is executed?

20   LET D = (3 + 5) / 4 * 2

  a. 4
  b. 1
  c. 5.2

8. What is the value of X after the following statement is executed?

100   LET X = 8 / 2 + 5 * 2 ^ 2

  a. 104
  b. 24
  c. 36

9. What is the value of R after the following program segment is executed?

40   LET A = 6
50   LET B = A + 6
60   LET C = A + B
70   LET R = A + C / A * B

  a. 42
  b. 48
  c. $\frac{24}{70}$

10. What is the value of Z after the following program segment is executed?

60   LET X = 2 ^ 3
70   LET Y = X / 2
80   LET Z = X – 2 + 12 / 2

  a. 0
  b. 12
  c. 9

11. Which of the following is an invalid statement?

  a. 80   LET X = 5
  b. 80   LET X$ = "5"
  c. 80   LET X$ = 5

12. Which of the following is a valid statement?

  a. 60   LET M$ = HENRY
  b. 60   LET M$ = "HAROLD"
  c. 60   LET M = "HARRY"

13. Which of the following is a valid statement?

  a. 40   LET T$ = S$ + 1
  b. 40   LET X$ = A$
  c. 40   LET R$ = X

Use the following variables and their assigned values for questions 14-16.

```
X = 24
N$ = "MARY"
A = 7
H$ = "HELLO"
```

14. What will be printed by the following statement?

```
30    PRINT H$, A
```

  a. HELLO   7
  b. H$, A
  c. MARY   A

15. What will be printed by the following statement?

```
50    PRINT X, "N$"
```

  a. 24   N$
  b. 24   MARY
  c. X   MARY

16. What will be printed by the following statement?

```
70    PRINT "A", A, X
```

  a. "A"   7   24
  b. 7   7   24
  c. A   7   24

17. What will be printed by the following statement?

```
90    PRINT 3 * 5 * 2
```

  a. nothing—invalid statement
  b. 30
  c. 3 * 5 * 2

18. What will be printed by the following statement?

```
20    PRINT 107
```

  a. 107
  b. "107"
  c. nothing—invalid statement

19. _____ commands are used to communicate with the operating system.

   a. operating

   b. system

   c. BASIC

20. The _____ command tells the computer to erase any programs currently in active memory.

   a. NEW

   b. ERA

   c. HOME

21. The LIST command can only be used to list an entire program, not program segments.

   a. TRUE

   b. FALSE

22. When a program is to be executed, the _____ command is used.

   a. EXE

   b. DIR

   c. RUN

23. The _____ command is used on the Apple to copy a program from active memory to an auxiliary storage device.

   a. SAVE

   b. RENEW

   c. EXE

24. The _____ command is used on the Apple to display the list of files saved on a disk.

   a. LOAD

   b. CATALOG

   c. HOME

25. The _____ command is used on the Apple to retrieve a program from auxiliary storage and place it in active memory.

   a. NEW

   b. LOAD

   c. RET

PROGRAMMING PROBLEMS

1. Write a program that will average three exam scores for Julie Wells' final grade score in her math class. Julie received a 90 on her first exam, an 89 on her second exam, and an 82 on her third exam. The output should put Julie's name and score in table form with headings. A sample of the output is:

Student Name	Ave. Score
JULIE WELLS	87

Use REM statements to document the program.

2. Write a program that will convert a temperature from Fahrenheit to Celsius and print the results as "x degrees Fahrenheit is y degrees Celsius." The equation for converting Fahrenheit to Celsius is $C° = 5/9 * (F° - 32)$.

   Use REM statements to document the program. Use your own input.

3. Write a program that will add the cost of the items Bob bought on his shopping trip. Then add the state sales tax of 5% of the subtotal to give Bob his total bill. He bought a comb that cost 59¢, a comic book that cost 40¢, and two E.T. buttons for 45¢ each. The output should tell Bob how much he owes. Try to do the arithmetic calculations in one LET statement. (Remember 5% = .05)

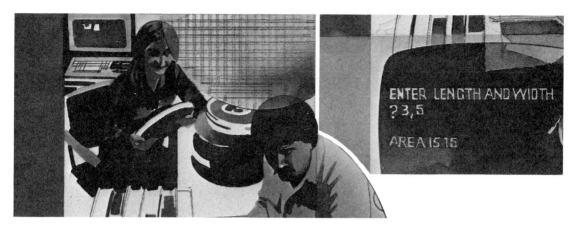

Testing the Program

Learning Objectives

After reading this chapter, you should be able to:

1. Describe the different types of errors that can occur.

2. List the methods of locating errors.

3. Explain how to stop a program during its execution.

4. Name some common error messages provided by the computer.

5. List ways to correct errors.

Introduction

Bug An error in a
program.

Because computers cannot think for themselves, the programs
that tell the computer what to do must be very precise. They must
follow the spelling and punctuation rules of the programming
language exactly. If the program is not written correctly, an error
will occur. Errors in programs are called **bugs**. The process of
finding and getting rid of the bugs is called "debugging." The
amount of time spent on debugging depends on the quality of the
program. A newly written program rarely runs successfully the
first time. In fact, one third to one half of a programmer's time is
spent debugging.

This chapter describes the different types of errors that may
occur and shows you how to prevent, locate, and correct programming errors.

Types of Errors

Four types of errors may occur during the programming process:
typographic, syntax, logic, and system-related.

Typographic Errors

Typographic error
An error resulting
from mistyping
characters.

Typographic errors occur when characters are mistyped into the
computer. Usually, these errors are recognized as syntax errors by
the computer. Typographic errors are usually the easiest to find
and can be avoided by checking your typing carefully. Two common typographic errors occur when a lower-case l is typed instead of the digit 1, and when the letter O is typed instead of the
digit 0 in a number.

Syntax Errors

Syntax error An
error that occurs
when the program-
mer fails to follow
rules of the lan-
guage used.

A **syntax error** occurs when the programmer fails to follow the
grammatical rules of the BASIC language. Perhaps a key word (a

BASIC statement, such as LET or PRINT) is misspelled, punctuation is incorrect, or parentheses are mismatched.

Some examples of syntax errors and an explanation of each error are:

20	LT X = A + B	LET is misspelled
30	LET Y = (1 + 2)5 * 3	Missing arithmetic operator after the second parenthesis
40	PRINT X Y "HELLO"	Punctuation missing between items
50	LET A = (5*3+(4-2)	Missing right parenthesis
60	LET T, = 55	Improper punctuation after T

Luckily, the computer will find these errors for you and print an error message along with the line number where the error occurred.

Logic Errors

A **logic error** occurs when the program does not process the data the way you expected. This can happen when the programmer has not studied the problem in detail, when a typographic error has been made that does not produce a syntax error, or when the programmer has not thoroughly checked the program logic. For example, if a programmer entered 10 LET P = H + R to compute an employee's pay (hours worked ✕ pay rate), the computer

Logic error An error resulting from incorrect thinking patterns in developing the program.

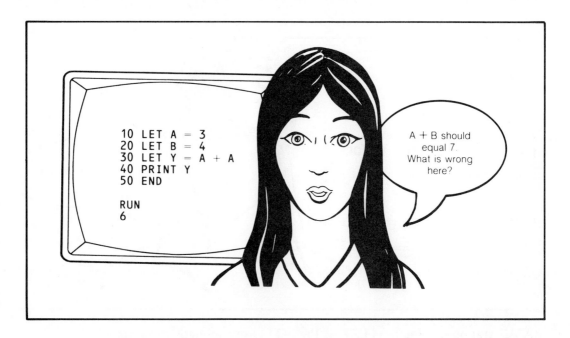

would figure a value for P. However, this value would be incorrect. A multiplication operation should have been done instead of addition. But the computer did not know that there was anything wrong! And the only way the programmer would know that there was an error would be either to check the program statements carefully or to compare the computer result with an answer figured by hand.

Because logic errors can be so well-hidden, they are the most difficult type of error to find. You should not put blind faith in the computer output. You should always check the computer-calculated results and run enough test data to be sure the program is working as planned.

System Errors

System error An error that involves the computer equipment.

A **system error** involves a problem with the hardware of the system, such as the printer or disk drive. A system error can occur if the diskette is bent or warped, or if you try to print something when the paper is stuck in the printer. An error message will usually appear on the screen that describes the type of error. If this happens, ask your teacher or the person in charge for help.

 LEARNING CHECK 14-1

1. An error in a program is called a(n) _____.

2. The process of locating and getting rid of errors in a program is called _____.

3. a. A(n) _____ error occurs when the programmer fails to follow the grammatical rules of the BASIC language.

b. A(n) _____ error occurs when the program does not process the data in the desired manner.

c. A(n) _____ error occurs when characters are mistyped into the computer.

d. A(n) _____ error occurs when there is a problem with the computer hardware.

1. bug 2. debugging 3. a. syntax error b. logic error c. typographic error d. system error

---

Locating Errors

Some programming errors are easier to spot than others. Careful proofreading of each program statement helps to prevent typographic and syntax errors. This can be done as the statements are typed or after the entire program is typed. Be sure to check every word and punctuation mark. One wrong letter can increase the amount of debugging time.

Although the computer will find any syntax errors and output an error message (see Common Error Messages section), it is still very important to proofread your typing carefully. All error messages should be read to decide where and why the error happened. If you want the computer to print the value of T but accidentally type 90 PRINT S, a syntax error will not occur. Instead an incorrect value will be output. At that point, you might spend much time studying the calculation for the value of T and think that there is a problem with the calculations. However, a careful comparison of the typed program with a flowchart or pseudocode would uncover the error.

Desk-checking

Desk-checking can also help find logic errors. When desk-checking, you pretend to be the computer, read each instruction, and imagine how the computer would process the data items. If items are processed incorrectly, you should discover the error and be able to correct it before it causes further problems.

Desk-checking A method used to mentally trace the correctness of processing logic.

Testing the Program

Once all the syntax errors are corrected and the program has been desk-checked for logic errors, you are ready to test the program.

To test a program, run the program with test or sample data. This test data should be like the actual data that will be used in the program. For example, if real numbers are used in the program, be sure to include some in the test data. Several different sets of data should be used to ensure that the correct output is produced. To check for accuracy, carefully compare the output with manually figured results.

In the programs you have seen so far, the use of test data does not make much sense because the data used is actually written into the program. However, in the next chapter, the statements for inputting different data values are introduced. At that time, it will be important to begin using sample data to test the accuracy of your programs.

Other Tools

Sometimes an error occurs and you have a difficult time locating the error. Perhaps you have overlooked a simple typographic error or misunderstood the actual logic of the program. When this happens, it can be very helpful to insert PRINT statements throughout the program. PRINT statements print the contents of variables at different points during the execution of the program. This helps to pinpoint the problem and assists in the debugging process. By comparing the computer-made results with results figured by hand after each major calculation, it will be easier to determine which statement has the error.

LEARNING CHECK 14-2

1. Explain what you would do to make sure your program is free of typographic and syntax errors.

2. What is the purpose of testing a program using sample data?

3. How can PRINT statements be used to detect errors?

HANDS-ON EXERCISE 14-1

NOW TRY THIS ⟹ Type NEW `RETURN` and the following program:

```
10   REM   ***CHECKING FOR INPUT ERRORS***
20   REM   ***THIS PROGRAM CHECKS FOR CORRECT ENTRY OF MONTH***
30   PRINT "ENTER YOUR BIRTHDAY."
40   PRINT "USE NUMBERS TO NAME"
50   PRINT "THE MONTH, DAY, AND YEAR IN THAT ORDER."
60   INPUT MO,DA,YR
70   IF MO < 1 OR MO > 12 THEN 100
80   PRINT "MY BIRTHDAY IS ";MO;"-";DA;"-";YR;"."
90   STOP
100   REM   ***ERROR MESSAGE***
110   PRINT "BIRTH MONTH IS INVALID.  PLEASE REENTER."
120   GOTO 30
130   END
```

Now RUN the program and input your birthday. The printout should be correct. RUN the program again and input 27,6,70. The error message is printed because the 27th month does not exist; the data is invalid. Try inputting the birthdays of your family members. Change line 50 to read "My sister's birthday ..." or "My grandmother's birthday ..." to match the birth date you are using.

Stopping a Program During Execution

There may be occasions when you want to stop the execution of a program. Perhaps an **infinite loop** has occurred. A loop is a logic pattern in which the computer repeatedly executes a series of statements as long as certain conditions are met. An infinite loop is a loop within a program that has no ending point; it will loop forever (more on infinite loops in chapter 17). You also might want to stop execution of a program when a long list of items is printed and you realize that the output is incorrect. Instead of

Infinite loop An error in which the computer repeats a step over and over.

waiting for the entire incorrect list to be printed, you can stop the program. Table 14-1 shows the commands that will stop the execution of a program for the four microcomputers.

STOPPING THE EXECUTION OF A PROGRAM   Table 14-1

Microcomputer	Command
Apple*	`CTRL` + `C`
	or
	`CTRL` + `RESET`
Commodore 64	`RUN STOP`
TRS-80	`BREAK`
IBM PC*	`CTRL` + `Break`

*These two keys must be pressed at the same time.

Common Error Messages

Some of the more common error messages and their causes are listed in Table 14-2. The messages may differ slightly for each computer. These and other error messages can be found in each computer's user's manual. Read the error message carefully when an error occurs so that you can locate the error quickly.

Message	Explanation
DISK FULL	Too many files on disk
DIVISION BY ZERO	Division by zero attempted
END OF DATA	A READ was attempted with no data in a DATA statement
FILE NOT FOUND	File misspelled or not on disk
I/O ERROR	Drive door open or disk not initialized
SYNTAX ERROR	A missing or extra parenthesis, misspelled keywords, and so on
TYPE MISMATCH	Number used in place of string, or vice versa

Correcting Errors

Once the errors in a program are located, they must be corrected before the program will execute properly. Different editing methods can be used to correct mistakes in a program.

Before RETURN Has Been Pressed

Correcting mistakes is easiest before a line has been entered in computer memory (before the RETURN key has been pressed). Suppose LOST is typed in a statement instead of LIST. If the error is noticed before the RETURN key is pressed, the computer's cursor can be moved back to the O in LOST by pressing the [←] key (on the IBM, Apple, or TRS-80), or the [INST DEL] key(on the Commodore 64). Then LIST can be typed correctly. It is a good idea to proofread your typing at the end of each line before you press the RETURN key. Then errors can be found and corrected quickly and easily.

After RETURN Has Been Pressed

If you notice an error in a line after the RETURN key has been pressed, there are two methods that can be used to correct the error. First, the entire line can be retyped with the correct information. Remember that if duplicate line numbers are typed, the computer uses the last one typed. Lines can be deleted from a program by typing only the line number of the statement to be deleted and then pressing the RETURN key, such as:

When the computer reads this, it takes line 90 out of the program.

The second way to correct errors after the RETURN key has been pressed is to use the screen or line editor. The TRS-80 uses a line editor. The Apple and Commodore use screen editors, and the IBM PC uses both.

To use the **screen editor**, list by line numbers the section of the program containing the error. Then move the cursor to the position of the error—usually by pressing the four arrow keys that move the cursor up, down, left, or right. The incorrect characters can then be typed over or deleted, or new characters can be inserted between existing characters. Because each computer has its own specific procedures for screen editing, you should check the user's manual for your particular computer.

The **line editor** works on individual lines. The user names the line containing the error and uses commands such as REPLACE, INSERT, and DELETE instead of moving the cursor to the error. Check the user's manual for more details on the line editor.

LEARNING CHECK 14-3

1. A(n) _____ loop is a loop within a program that has no stopping point.

2. Error messages *are/are not* very useful.

3. It is easiest to correct mistakes *before/after* the RETURN key has been pressed.

4. Assume you are typing a program when you notice an error in a line at the beginning of the program. You have already pressed the RETURN key. What are the two ways you can use to correct the line?

1. infinite 2. are 3. before 4. retype entire line; use screen editor or line editor to move cursor to mistake

---

COMPREHENSIVE PROGRAMMING PROBLEM

The program in Figure 14-1 was hurriedly written one Monday morning. As you can tell, it needs to be debugged before it can be run on the computer. This program is supposed to figure how many hours a person should plan on working from graduation until the time he or she retires. To help set up the original problem, it was decided that a person would begin work at the age of 18 and retire at the age of 65. Two weeks of vacation and eight days for holidays were to be taken throughout each year. The average number of hours spent working each day would be eight hours.

The output for the program should be:

    I HOPE I LIKE MY JOB BECAUSE I WILL WORK
    ??? HOURS AT IT.

The question marks stand for the total number of hours a person works in a lifetime.

```
10     REN *** THIS PROGRAM ESTIMATES HOW MANY HOURS A PERSON ***
20     REN *** WILL WORK DURING HIS OR HER LIFETIME. ***
30     REN ***      VARIABLE LIST ***
40     REN
50     REN ***   YR = YEARS TO WORK
60     REN ***    V = WEEKS OF THE YEAR MINUS VACATION TIME
70     REN ***    D = WORKING DAYS OF THE YEAR
80     REN ***    W = DAYS OF THE YEAR MINUS HOLIDAYS
90     REN ***    H = HOURS TO WORK FOR A YEAR
100    REN ***    T = TOTAL HOURS OF A LIFETIME SPENT WORKING
110    REN ***
120    REN ***  CALCULATING THE NUMBER OF YEARS TO WORK ***
130    LET YR = 65 + 18
140    PRINT *** CALCULATING THE NUMBER OF DAYS PER YEAR TO WORK ***
150    LET V = 52 - 2
260    LET V * 5 = D
170    LET W = D - 8
180    REN *** CALCULATING THE HOURS PER YEAR TO WORK ***
190    REM W * 6 = H
200    REN *** CALCULATING THE TOTAL HOURS TO WORK IN A LIFETIME ***
220    PRINT "I HOPE I LIKE MY JOB BECAUSE I WILL WORK ';
       T;" HOURS AT IT."
230    STOP
```

Figure 14-1. *Comprehensive Programming Problem*

To desk-check this program, we would begin at line 10 and see that the REM statement had been mistyped in the first 12 lines. Therefore, the N in REN needs to be changed to an M. The REM statements are used to explain or comment about the program, so each line must also be read for content.

The contents of the REM statements appear to be fine, so continue with line 130. Grammatically the line is correct, but what is it we are trying to figure? (The number of years to work.) There is a logic mistake in line 130. This figure would lead to a drastic error in the final total because an additional 36 years would be figured into the variable YR. Line 130 should read:

130   LET YR = 65 - 18

Line 140 uses the wrong command for a comment line. The PRINT command should be replaced by the REM command.

Line 150 begins to figure the number of working days per year. This line correctly calculates V, which is 52 weeks minus the 2 weeks for vacation time. Line 260 should be line 160. This number was keyed in wrong. Also, the V * 5 is on the wrong side of the equal sign. The variables D and V * 5 must be switched. Going back to the variable list at line 70 shows that D should equal the working days of the year. V (which equals 50) times 5 days per week will equal the days per year to work. Line 160 should read:

160   LET D = V * 5

Line 170 correctly figures the working days of the year minus holidays, then assigns that value to the variable name W. Line 180 has another typographic error in the REM command. Line 190 uses the REM command when the LET command should be used. Line 190 is similar to line 160 in that

```
 10    REM *** THIS PROGRAM ESTIMATES HOW MANY HOURS A PERSON ***
 20    REM *** WILL WORK IN A LIFETIME ***
 30    REM ***        VARIABLE LIST
 40    REM ***
 50    REM *** YR = YEARS TO WORK
 60    REM ***  V = WEEKS OF THE YEAR MINUS VACATION TIME
 70    REM ***  D = WORKING DAYS OF THE YEAR
 80    REM ***  W = DAYS OF THE YEAR MINUS HOLIDAYS
 90    REM ***  H = HOURS TO WORK FOR A YEAR
100    REM ***  T = TOTAL HOURS OF A LIFETIME SPENT WORKING
110    REM ***
120    REM *** CALCULATING THE NUMBER OF YEARS TO WORK ***
130    LET YR = 65 - 18
140    REM *** CALCULATING THE NUMBER OF DAYS PER YEAR TO WORK ***
150    LET V = 52 - 2
160    LET D = V * 5
170    LET W = D - 8
180    REM *** CALCULATING THE HOURS PER YEAR TO WORK ***
190    LET H + W * 8
200    REM *** CALCULATING THE TOTAL HOURS TO WORK IN A LIFETIME ***
210    LET T + YR * H
220    PRINT "I HOPE I LIKE MY JOB BECAUSE I WILL WORK"
225    PRINT T;" HOURS AT IT."
999    END


]RUN
I HOPE I LIKE MY JOB BECAUSE I WILL WORK
90992 HOURS AT IT.
```

Figure 14-2. *Corrected Comprehensive Programming Problem*

the variable H must be on the left side of the equal sign and W * 8 must be on the right side. H now equals the number of hours per year one would work minus vacation time and holidays. Line 190 should read:

```
190    LET H = W * 8
```

Line 200 should be REM, not REN. The statement that calculates the total number of hours is missing, so it must be added. The variable T should equal the total number of hours a person will work (years * hours). This statement should be:

```
210    LET T = YR * H
```

Leaving line 210 out would cause the output to be wrong. Can you explain what number would have appeared if this error had not been spotted? A zero would have appeared because the value of T would not have been calculated.

Line 220 tells the computer to print the output. All words to be printed must be in quotation marks, so the apostrophe after the word "WORK" should be changed to a quotation mark. Also, since T;" HOURS AT IT." will appear on a new line, a line number and a new PRINT statement must be used. Line 225 should read:

```
225    PRINT T;" HOURS AT IT."
```

Line 230 is the end of the program and should have the END command, not a STOP. It would also be wise to use 999 as the line number for this statement.

Now that the program has been desk-checked, it should be typed into the computer with the corrections as shown in Figure 14-2. After it is RUN, make sure there are no more syntax errors. Then the output should be checked against an answer figured by hand to make sure it is correct.

SUMMARY POINTS

- A bug is an error in a program; debugging is the process of locating and correcting those bugs.

- The four types of errors that may occur are typographic, syntax, logic, and system.

- Errors are by proofreading, desk-checking, testing the program, and inserting PRINT statements throughout the program.

- Error messages should be read carefully to assist in locating and correcting errors.

- Errors can be corrected before or after the RETURN key has been pressed. A screen or line editor can be used to correct errors after the RETURN key has been pressed.

CHAPTER TEST

Vocabulary

Match the term from the numbered column on the left with the best description from the lettered column on the right.

1.	Logic error	**a.**	An error in a program.
2.	Debugging	**b.**	The process of locating and correcting an error in a program.
3.	Syntax error	**c.**	An error relating to the hardware of the system.
4.	Desk-checking	**d.**	An error resulting from a character being mistyped.
5.	System error	**e.**	A method used to check for logic errors.
6.	Bug	**f.**	An error that occurs when the program does not process the data in the desired manner.
7.	Typographic error	**g.**	An error that occurs when the programmer fails to follow the "grammatical" rules of BASIC.
8.	Infinite loop	**h.**	An error in which the computer repeats a step over and over again.

Questions

1. A newly written program usually executes successfully the first time it is run.
   a. TRUE
   b. FALSE

2. The computer will find and print an error message for all _____ errors.
   a. repeated
   b. logic
   c. syntax

For questions 3-9, determine whether the statement has an error or not.

3. LET Z = 3+5
   a. correct
   b. error

4. PRNT X, Y, Z
   a. correct
   b. error

5. LET T = B
   a. correct
   b. error

6. LET T = 5 * (3 + 5)2
   a. correct
   b. error

7. PRINT N$, T, Q$
   a. correct
   b. error

8. LET N$,5,X
   a. correct
   b. error

9. PRINT X,"TIMES",Y
   a. correct
   b. error

10. A programmer should check computer-generated results because the output of the computer is not always correct.
   a. TRUE
   b. FALSE

11. Which of the following is not a good way to locate program errors?
   a. desk-checking
   b. proofreading
   c. blind faith

12. Once a program has begun execution, there is no way to stop that execution.
   a. TRUE
   b. FALSE

13. Errors can only be corrected after the RETURN key has been pressed.
   a. TRUE
   b. FALSE

14. One way to correct an error is to retype the entire line.

    a. TRUE

    b. FALSE

15. Which of the following commands would delete line 60?

    a. 60

    b. LET 60 = 0

    c. 60 DELETE

16. When a(n) _____ editor is used, the cursor is moved to the error for corrections to be made.

    a. line

    b. program

    c. screen

17. A(n) _____ editor works on individual lines and uses special editing commands.

    a. line

    b. program

    c. screen

18. Which of the following is an invalid statement?

    a. 40   PRINT

    b. 40   REM * PRINT THE SUBTOTAL *

    c. 40   CORRECT 60

PROGRAMMING PROBLEMS

1. The following program was written to find the area of a rectangle that is 11 inches long and 8 inches wide. Use the formula: width * length = area. The output should look like the following, only with the correct numbers inserted:

```
WIDTH = XX
LENGTH = XX
THE AREA IS XX
```

Debug this program so that it will give the accurate output in the proper format.

```
10    REM *** THIS PROGRAM CALCULATES THE AREA OF A RECTANGLE ***
20    REM ***  8 INCHES WIDE AND 11 INCHES LONG ***
30    REM ***
40    REM             VARIABLE LIST ***
50    REM ***   L = LENGTH OF THE RECTANGLE ***
60    REM ***   W = WIDTH OF THE RECTANGLE ***
70    REM ***   A = AREA OF THE RECTANGLE ***
80    LET L = 8
90    LET W = 11
100    LET A = L * L
110    PRINT "WIDTH" = ;W
120    PRINT "LENGTH = ";L
130    PRINT,
140    PRINT "THE AREA IS A"
END
```

2. The Goodies Company has just written a program to figure the number of cookies it can bake in each nine-hour day. But it seems that either the workers are loafing and eating most of the cookies, or the new program needs to be debugged. There are five bakers using four ovens each. Each oven produces 145 cookies in a batch. It takes 1½ hours to mix and bake a batch. The program runs but the actual number of cookies baked is nowhere near the number of cookies the computer says should be made every day. Calculate the correct number of cookies by hand and then debug the program.

```
10      REM *** THIS PROGRAM CALCULATES THE NUMBER OF COOKIES ***
20      REM *** THAT THE GOODIE COMPANY BAKES IN A DAY ***
30      REM ***
40      REM ***              VARIABLE LIST
50      REM *** C = THE NUMBER OF COOKIES EACH BAKER BAKES
60      REM *** O = THE NUMBER OF COOKIES EACH OVEN BAKES
70      REM *** TC = THE TOTAL COOKIES BAKED EACH BATCH
80      REM *** GT = THE GRAND TOTAL OF COOKIES BAKED EACH DAY
90      REM ***
100     REM *** CALCULATING THE NUMBER OF COOKIES BAKED IN EACH BATCH ***
110     LET C = 145 * 5
120     LET O = 145 * 4
130     LET TC = C * O
140     REM *** CALCULATING THE NUMBER OF COOKIES BAKED EACH 9 HOUR DAY ***
150     GT = TC * 9
160     PRINT GT;" COOKIES WERE BAKED TODAY"
170     END


]RUN
 3784500 COOKIES WERE BAKED TODAY
```

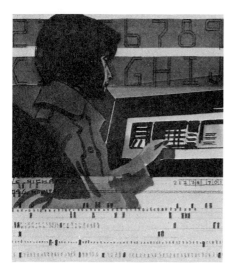

Chapter 15

Entering Data and Printing Results

Learning Objectives

After reading this chapter, you should be able to:

1. Enter data in programs using the INPUT statement.

2. Use the READ and DATA statements in a program when entering lists of data.

3. Format output in different ways.

Introduction

You will not always want to input data as constants using LET statements. There are other ways to enter data into a computer. Although the LET statement can be used to enter small amounts of data, the INPUT statement and the READ/DATA statements are more commonly used. The INPUT statement allows you to put data into the computer while the program is running. The program asks you for the data it needs. The READ/DATA statements are more efficient than the LET statement for working with large amounts of data or data that change often.

After entering data, you may want your output to look neat for easy reading. This chapter explains how to produce output with headings, columns, and correct spacing.

Input

INPUT statement A statement that allows the user to enter data while the program is running.

The **INPUT statement** lets you enter data at the keyboard while the program is running. It can be used for question-and-answer sessions. The computer displays the question and you type the answer.

The general format of the INPUT statement is:

line# INPUT variable list

For example:

```
90     INPUT X, Y, Z

100    INPUT N$,S$
```

These could also be combined into one line:

```
90     INPUT X,Y,Z,N$,S$
```

or they could be on separate lines:

```
 90     INPUT X
100     INPUT Y
110     INPUT Z
120     INPUT N$
130     INPUT S$
```

The variables listed in the INPUT statement may be string variables or numeric variables. The value entered at the keyboard will be assigned to the listed variable. For example, if a 5 were typed in response to INPUT X, X would now equal 5. When an INPUT statement contains multiple variables, the values typed will be assigned in the order in which they appear. For example, after line 40 is executed with the input as shown:

```
40      INPUT L,H,P$
]RUN
?20,40,APPLE
```

L will equal 20, H will equal 40, and P$ will equal "APPLE". When a value is entered for a character string variable, quotation marks are not required. Just be sure to match the type of data with that called for by the variable name.

INPUT statements are placed where data values are needed in a program. This is determined by the logic of the program. After the program has been keyed in and you type the execution command RUN, the computer starts to execute the program. Whenever the computer reaches an INPUT statement, it stops, prints a question mark at the terminal, and waits for the user to enter data. After typing in the data, press the RETURN key. The computer then assigns the data value to the variable indicated in the INPUT statement and continues processing.

More than one variable can be listed in the INPUT statement. You must then enter the same number of values in the right order. When not enough data values are entered, an error message is printed telling you there are not enough data. For example, when line 140 is executed with only one value, the result would look like this:

```
140     INPUT L,W,H
]RUN
? 28.5

??
```

MICROCOMPUTER DIFFERENCES
IBM PC: Error message appears: "?Redo from start"
TRS-80: Same as IBM PC
COMMODORE 64: Same as Apple

If the user knew what three entries to make, the output would look like this:

```
]RUN
? 28.5,25,10
```

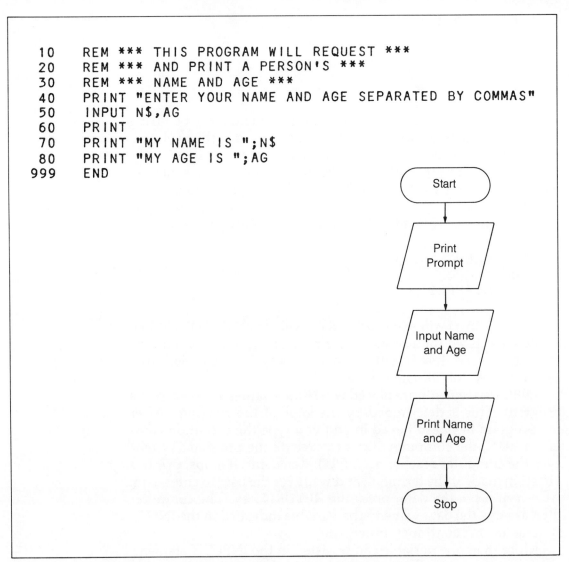

```
 10    REM *** THIS PROGRAM WILL REQUEST ***
 20    REM *** AND PRINT A PERSON'S ***
 30    REM *** NAME AND AGE ***
 40    PRINT "ENTER YOUR NAME AND AGE SEPARATED BY COMMAS"
 50    INPUT N$,AG
 60    PRINT
 70    PRINT "MY NAME IS ";N$
 80    PRINT "MY AGE IS ";AG
999    END
```

Figure 15-1. *Input Example*

The variable L would have the value 28.5, W would be assigned the value 25, and H would contain the value 10. As you can see, the INPUT statement offers a great deal of flexibility. Each time the program is run, new values can be entered without changing any program statements.

Prompts

Prompt A message printed out during computer program execution to tell the user to enter data.

For you to know what values the computer is requesting, a PRINT statement is usually placed right before the INPUT statement. This PRINT statement is called a **prompt**. Since the INPUT statement signals the need for data with only a question mark, the prompt is used to explain what data should be entered. Otherwise, when you see only a question mark requesting data, you may not know what data values are being asked for.

Figure 15-1 is a program with a prompt that prints a person's name and age. Lines 40 and 50 cause the program to be executed in a question-and-answer mode (also called **inquiry-and-response**, or **conversational mode**). When the program is executed, line 40 causes the computer to print a message at the terminal that says, "ENTER YOUR NAME AND AGE SEPARATED BY COMMAS". A question mark appears to signal that data values are to be entered. You then type in your name, a comma, and your age and press the RETURN key to continue execution of the program.

Inquiry-and-response mode A question-and-answer mode in which the user interacts with the computer during a program run.

The output for the program in Figure 15-1 would appear as follows:

```
]RUN
ENTER YOUR NAME AND AGE SEPARATED BY COMMAS
? BECKY, 8
MY NAME IS BECKY
MY AGE IS 8
```

Most computers allow the prompt to be included within the INPUT statement, so that a separate PRINT statement is not needed. For example, the following line could be substituted for lines 40 and 50 in the preceding program:

```
40   INPUT "ENTER YOUR NAME AND AGE SEPARATED
        BY COMMAS"; N$,AG
```

When the program is run with this new line, no question mark appears immediately after the prompt:

```
]RUN
ENTER YOUR NAME AND AGE SEPARATED BY COMMASBECKY,8
MY NAME IS BECKY
MY AGE IS 8
```

LEARNING CHECK 15-1

1. The _____ statement allows the user to enter data at the terminal while the program is running.

2. TRUE   FALSE   The INPUT statement may contain multiple variable names.

3. TRUE   FALSE   All INPUT statements should appear at the very beginning of a program.

4. A printed explanation of what data the user should enter is called a _____.

5. Most computers do/do not permit the prompt to be included within the INPUT statement.

1. INPUT 2. TRUE 3. FALSE 4. prompt 5. do

NOW TRY THIS ⇨ Type NEW `RETURN` . Then type the following program and RUN it:

```
10  REM *** THIS PROGRAM INPUTS AND PRINTS ***
20  REM *** THE NAME AND ADDRESS OF A PERSON ***
30  PRINT "ENTER YOUR NAME AND ADDRESS SEPARATED BY COMMAS."
40  INPUT N$,A$
50  PRINT "MY NAME IS ";N$
60  PRINT "MY ADDRESS IS ";A$
99  END

]RUN
ENTER YOUR NAME AND ADDRESS SEPARATED BY COMMAS.
?CANDY,100 MAIN STREET
MY NAME IS CANDY
MY ADDRESS IS 100 MAIN STREET
```

Now change the program to read as above except:

```
]40  INPUT N$
]45  INPUT A$
]30  PRINT "ENTER YOUR NAME"
]44  PRINT "ENTER YOUR ADDRESS"
```

RUN the program with these changes. Note that the output is the same. Only the way of inputting the program is different.

```
]RUN
ENTER YOUR NAME
?CANDY
ENTER YOUR ADDRESS
?100 MAIN STREET
MY NAME IS CANDY
MY ADDRESS IS 100 MAIN STREET
```

READ/DATA Statements

READ/DATA statements
Statements that work together to enter data into a program.

The **READ** and **DATA statements** provide another way to enter data into a BASIC program. These two statements always work together. Values contained in the DATA statements are assigned to variables listed in the READ statements.

The general format of the READ and DATA statements is:

line# READ variable list
line# DATA value list

```
10     REM *** THIS PROGRAM CALCULATES THE ***
20     REM *** AMOUNT OWED BY CUSTOMERS ***
30     REM *** ON A PAPER ROUTE. ***
40     READ N$,D
50     READ R
60     LET T = R * D
70     PRINT N$,T
80     READ N$,D,R
90     LET T = R * D
100    PRINT N$,T
110    DATA MARY ZIGLER
120    DATA 20,.40
130    DATA JOHN GARRISON, 25
140    DATA .40
999    END

]RUN
MARY ZIGLER      8
JOHN GARRISON   10
```

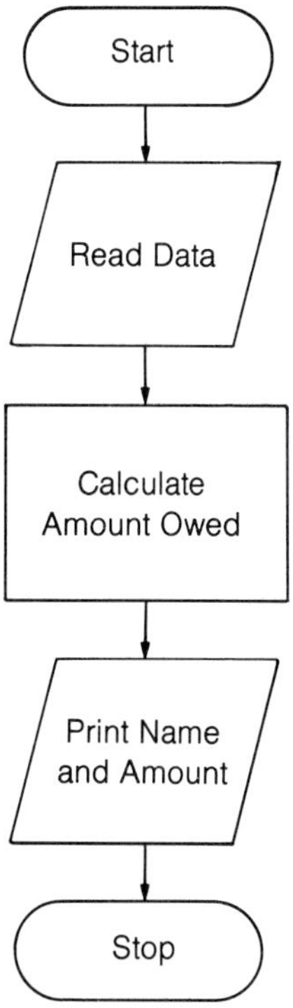

Figure 15-2. *READ/DATA Example*

Here are some examples of READ and DATA statements:

```
100    READ X,Y
200    READ N$,J$,Z
500    DATA 76,81,"JILL","PROGRAMMER"
510    DATA 1072
```

The READ and DATA statements do not allow the user to enter data at the terminal while the program is running. Instead, the READ statement tells the computer to search through the BASIC program until it finds the next DATA statement. The computer then assigns the data values listed in the DATA statement to the variables listed in the READ statement in order. Each READ statement causes as many values to be taken from the data list as there are variables in the READ variable list. There does not have to be one DATA statement for every READ statement, but there does have to be one DATA item for every READ variable. For example:

```
READ X,Y,Z
READ N$
DATA 10,20,30,"STEVEN"
```

could be used instead of:

```
READ X,Y,Z
READ N$
DATA 10,20,30
DATA "STEVEN"
```

The computer keeps track of what DATA items have been read. It assigns the next DATA value available to the next READ variable whether or not the data value begins a new DATA statement.

Figure 15-2 shows this process of assigning values from the data list to variables. Line 40 will read Mary Zigler and assign that value to N$. The value 20 will then be read and assigned to D. Line 50 instructs the computer to read the next available data item, .40, and assign it to the variable R. Line 80 once again tells the computer to read data items starting with John Garrison and to assign the values to the corresponding variables.

If a READ statement is attempted when no values are left in the data list, an error message is produced to show that the end of the data list has been reached.

READ statements, like INPUT statements, should appear wherever the logic of the program states the need for data. DATA statements, however, are not executable. They may be anywhere in the program. Although DATA statements may be anywhere in a program, it is common practice to group them together at either the beginning or the end of a program. This makes debugging easier. The BASIC interpreter or compiler simply takes all the data items in all the DATA statements and forms one combined data list. It puts the DATA statements in order from lowest line number to highest line number. Then it uses the data from left to right. For example, the following three program segments look different, but the data lists they produce are alike:

DATA statements			DATA list
10	DATA	"JIM",27	JIM
20	DATA	"JOANN",23	27
			JOANN
or			23
10	DATA	"JIM",27,"JOANN",23	JIM
			27
or			JOANN
			23
30	DATA	"JOANN"	JOANN
40	DATA	23	23
10	DATA	"JIM"	JIM
20	DATA	27	27

When two or more data values occupy one line, they must be separated by commas. But a comma may not be placed at the end of a data line. Character strings may or may not be enclosed in quotation marks in DATA statements. However, if the character strings are to contain leading or trailing blank spaces, commas, colons, and/or semicolons, they must be enclosed in quotation marks.

Comparison of the Three Methods of Data Entry

The LET, INPUT, and READ/DATA statements all can be used to enter data into a BASIC program. How do you decide which method is best to use? The answer depends on the particular program and data to be input. Here are some general guidelines.

1. When a small amount of data is to remain constant each time the program is run, the LET statement should be used. For example, when figuring peoples' wages, if the rate of pay does not change, the LET statement would be used to assign the value to the pay rate variable. The LET statement also is often used to assign a beginning value to a variable. This is called **initialization**. It is usually done when something is to be counted, such as in a loop.

   Initialization A process that assigns a beginning value to a variable with the LET statement.

2. The INPUT statement is used when a question-and-answer mode is desired. It is also a good method to use when data values are likely to change each time the program is executed. An INPUT statement might be used in an airline ticket reservation program—the information, such as date of flight, place of departure, and final destination, will change with each new reservation.

3. When many data values must be entered that will not change each time the program is run, READ/DATA statements are ideal. READ/DATA statements could be used in a program to print mailing labels for a magazine subscription. There is a large amount of data that does not change too much from month to month.

1. The values contained in the _____ statements are assigned to variables listed in the _____ statements.

2. There does/does not have to be one DATA statement for every READ statement.

3. TRUE FALSE Character strings must always be enclosed in quotation marks in DATA statements.

4. The _____ statement(s) is/are recommended for data entry when data values are likely to change each time the program is executed.

5. The _____ statement(s) is/are recommended for data entry when many data values are used that are not likely to change each time the program is executed.

1. DATA, READ 2. does not 3. FALSE 4. INPUT 5. READ/DATA

HANDS-ON EXERCISE 15-2

NOW TRY THIS ⇨ Type NEW RETURN and type the following program; then RUN the program.

```
10    REM *** THIS PROGRAM READS THE NAME ***
20    REM *** AND ADDRESS OF A PERSON ***
30    REM *** AND PRINTS IT ***
40    READ N$,A$
50    PRINT "MY NAME IS ";N$
60    PRINT "MY ADDRESS IS ";A$
70    DATA CANDY,100 MAIN STREET
99    END

]RUN
MY NAME IS CANDY
MY ADDRESS IS 100 MAIN STREET
```

Now change line 40 and add line 45 to read as follows:

```
40    READ N$
45    READ A$
```

RUN the program

```
]RUN
MY NAME IS CANDY
MY ADDRESS IS 100 MAIN STREET
```

Now change line 70 and add line 80 to read as follows and RUN the program.

```
70    DATA CANDY
80    DATA 100 MAIN STREET
]RUN
MY NAME IS CANDY
MY ADDRESS IS 100 MAIN STREET
```

Note that the output is the same, only the way of reading the data has changed.

Formatted Printing

The PRINT statement will display the results of processing. You may want to produce output with everything placed in columns or in some other format. Commas, semicolons, and blank spaces can be used to produce the desired output format.

Print Zones and Commas

The number of characters that can be printed on a line varies with the computer brand. Table 15-1 presents the formatting differences among the four computers.

COMPUTER DISPLAY CHARACTERISTICS Table 15-1

Computer	Screen Width (Characters)	Screen Height (Lines)	Number of Print Zones	Zone Width	Space for Sign?	Space Following Number?
Apple	40/80*	24	2-1/2	16	No	No
TRS-80	64/32*	16	4/2*	16	Yes	Yes
Commodore 64	40/80*	24	4	10	Yes	Yes
IBM PC	40/80*	25	3/5*	14	Yes	Yes

*Slash indicates that both options are available to user.

The Apple computer screen consists of 40 characters per line. (If you are using an 80-column card with the Apple, check the user's manual for differences in the commands.) Each line is divided into 2½ print zones, each 16 characters wide. The beginning columns of the print zones are shown below:

Zone 1   **Zone 2**   **Zone 3**

Column 1   Column 17   Column 33

A comma separating data items in a PRINT statement instructs the computer to skip to the next print zone to begin printing the next item. Therefore, when the following program is executed:

```
10      READ C$,I$,P
20      PRINT C$,I$,P
30      DATA BLUE,SLACKS,7.99
99      END
```

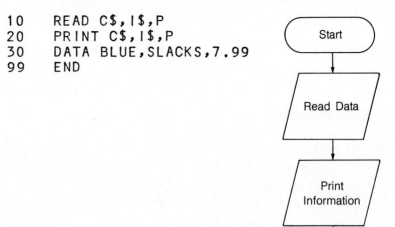

the output will appear as follows:

```
]RUN
BLUE              SLACKS              7.99
```
| Zone 1 | Zone 2 | Zone 3

The value in C$, which is BLUE, will be printed starting in column 1, the first print zone. The comma between C$ and I$ tells the computer to space over to the next zone, beginning in column 17, and to print the value contained in I$ (SLACKS). After SLACKS is printed, the comma again directs the computer to space over to the next zone, column 33, and print the value in P. Since the value in P, 7.99, is a positive number, most computers will leave a blank before the number for the sign printing the value in column 34. However, as noted in Table 15-1, the Apple computer does not leave a space before a positive number for the sign. Thus, the value is printed beginning in column 33.

With the Apple computer, the statement

```
10      PRINT -2;-1;0;1;2
```

would print:

```
-2-1012 (no space between numbers)
```

With the TRS-80, IBM PC, and Commodore 64 computers, the same statement would print:

```
-2 -1  0  1  2
```

leaving a space before the positive numbers and a space after all numbers.

The differences in spacing between the four computers have been noted in the Microcomputer Differences boxes in previous chapters. Now that you are aware of why the spacing is different, it will no longer be mentioned in the boxes. If you are using a TRS-80, IBM PC, or Commodore 64 computer, make sure you remember the spacing differences when formatting output.

If there are too many items listed in a PRINT statement for the number of print zones, the computer starts printing in the first zone of the next line. If the value to be printed is too wide for the print zone, the computer will print out the whole value, even though part of it goes into the next print zone. If this happens in the last print zone, the remaining portion of the value is printed on the next line. The comma then directs the printing to start in the following print zone. For example, note where the value of P (7.99) is printed below:

```
 10   LET P = 7.99
 20   PRINT "BLUE SLACKS ON SALE FOR", P
999 END

]RUN
BLUE SLACKS ON SALE FOR        7.99
```

| | | |
| Zone 1 | Zone 2 | Zone 3 |

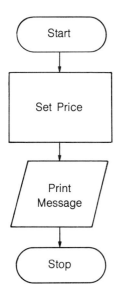

In the example on the following page, note how the last value is continued on the next line.

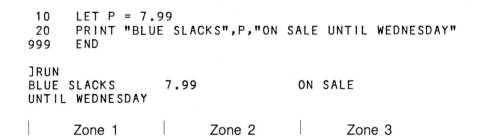

```
10    LET P = 7.99
20    PRINT "BLUE SLACKS",P,"ON SALE UNTIL WEDNESDAY"
999   END

]RUN
BLUE SLACKS        7.99              ON SALE
UNTIL WEDNESDAY
```

| | Zone 1 | | Zone 2 | | Zone 3 |

Skipping Print Zones   A print zone can be skipped with two different methods. The first one involves enclosing a space in quotation marks. This causes the entire zone to appear empty:

```
10    PRINT "ENGLISH"," ","A"
```

The second method (allowed on all four computers, but not on every computer) is to type two commas together:

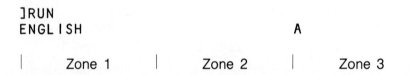

```
10    PRINT "ENGLISH",,"A"
```

Both of these methods cause ENGLISH to be printed in Zone 1, the second zone to be blank, and A to be printed in the third zone, as follows:

```
]RUN
ENGLISH                                A
```

| | Zone 1 | | Zone 2 | | Zone 3 |

Ending with a Comma   As mentioned earlier, output given by a PRINT statement normally begins in the first zone of a new line. However, if the previously executed PRINT statement ends with a comma, the output of the next PRINT statement starts in the next available print zone. For example, the following program:

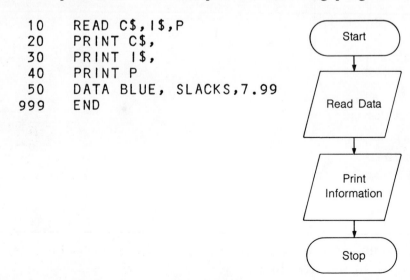

```
10    READ C$,I$,P
20    PRINT C$,
30    PRINT I$,
40    PRINT P
50    DATA BLUE, SLACKS,7.99
999   END
```

Start

Read Data

Print
Information

Stop

will produce the following output:

```
]RUN
BLUE            SLACKS          7.99
```

| Zone 1 | Zone 2 | Zone 3

Although separate PRINT statements were used, each value was printed on the same line in the next print zone be cause of the comma at the end of the PRINT statements.

LEARNING CHECK 15-3

1. A _____ separating data items in a PRINT statement instructs the computer to skip to the next print zone.

2. If the value to be printed is wider than the print zone, what will happen?

3. TRUE   FALSE   Two commas typed together in a PRINT statement will usually cause a print zone to be skipped.

4. Write a statement to include in a program that will print your first name in zone 1, your middle name in zone 2, and your last name in zone 3.

5. What will the output look like after the following statements are executed?

```
70    PRINT "BEING A WINNING GYMNAST",
80    PRINT "REQUIRES","MANY HOURS OF HARD WORK"
```

1. comma 2. The rest of the value will be printed continuing into the next print zone. 3. TRUE 4. 20 PRINT "FIRST NAME", "MIDDLE NAME", "LAST NAME" (Quotation marks around each name and commas separating them are the punctuation you must include.)
5. BEING A WINNING GYMNAST   REQUIRES
MANY HOURS OF HARD WORK (REQUIRES is printed in zone 3 because GYMNAST runs into zone 2.)

HANDS-ON EXERCISE 15-3

NOW TRY THIS ⇨ Type NEW [RETURN], and type the following program. Then RUN it.

```
10    REM *** THIS PROGRAM READS A CLASS ***
20    REM *** AND ITS MEETING TIME ***
30    REM
40    READ C$,T$
50    PRINT C$,T$
60    DATA MATH,10 O'CLOCK
99    END

]RUN
MATH            10 O'CLOCK
```

| Zone 1 | Zone 2 | Zone 3

Now change line 50 and add line 55 to read as follows:

```
50    PRINT C$,
55    PRINT T$
```

RUN the program and examine the output. It should be the same as above. Now, delete line 55 by typing 55 RETURN . Then change line 50 to skip a print zone before printing the time. It should be typed as follows:

```
]50    PRINT C$,,T$
```

RUN the program with this change. You will get the following output with the noted space between the class and the time of the class.

```
]RUN
MATH                                    10 O'CLOCK
  |      Zone 1        |     Zone 2     |     Zone 3
```

Semicolons

Using a semicolon instead of a comma to separate data items in a PRINT statement tells the computer to skip to the next column to print the next item—not the next print zone. This gives you greater flexibility in formatting the output. In the following examples, notice the difference in spacing when semicolons are used instead of commas.

Using commas:

```
10    PRINT 100,-200,300

]RUN
100                -200              300
  |      Zone 1        |     Zone 2     |     Zone 3
```

Using semicolons:

```
10    PRINT 100;-200;300

]RUN
100-200300
```

As stated earlier, most computers leave a space in front of a positive number for the sign and a space following each number. However, the Apple does not do this (see Table 15-1).

When semicolons are used with character strings, no spaces are inserted on any of the computers. For example:

```
50    PRINT "TOMMY";"WATSON"
```

will produce the following output:

```
]RUN
TOMMYWATSON
```

Since letters do not have signs, they are run together. The best way to avoid this problem is to enclose a space within the quotes (the symbol for one blank space is b̸):

```
50    PRINT "TOMMY ";"WATSON"

]RUN
TOMMY WATSON
```

When printing character strings after numbers, it may also be necessary to enclose a leading space within quotes (for the Apple), as follows:

```
50    PRINT 289;" WEST";" MAPLE";" STREET"

]RUN
289 WEST MAPLE STREET
```

If a semicolon is included as the last character of the PRINT statement, the output of the next PRINT statement will appear in the next available column. The output is not advanced to the next print zone or the next line. For example:

```
50    PRINT 289;
60    PRINT " WEST MAPLE STREET"
```

produces the following output:

```
]RUN
289 WEST MAPLE STREET
```

Line 50 causes 289 to be printed. The semicolon after this number keeps the printer on the same line. When line 60 is executed, WEST MAPLE STREET is printed in the next available column on the same line.

```
100     REM *** INVENTORY REPORT ***
105     REM
110     PRINT TAB(10);"INVENTORY REPORT"
115     PRINT
120     PRINT TAB(5);"ITEM";TAB(25);"QUANTITY"
125     PRINT
130     READ I$,Q
135     PRINT TAB(5);I$;TAB(25);Q
140     READ I$,Q
145     PRINT TAB(5);I$;TAB(25);Q
150     READ I$,Q
155     PRINT TAB(5);I$;TAB(25);Q
160     DATA PENCILS,1000,ERASERS,200,PAPER,500
999     END

]RUN

             INVENTORY REPORT

   ITEM                    QUANTITY

   PENCILS                 1000
   ERASERS                 200
   PAPER                   500
```

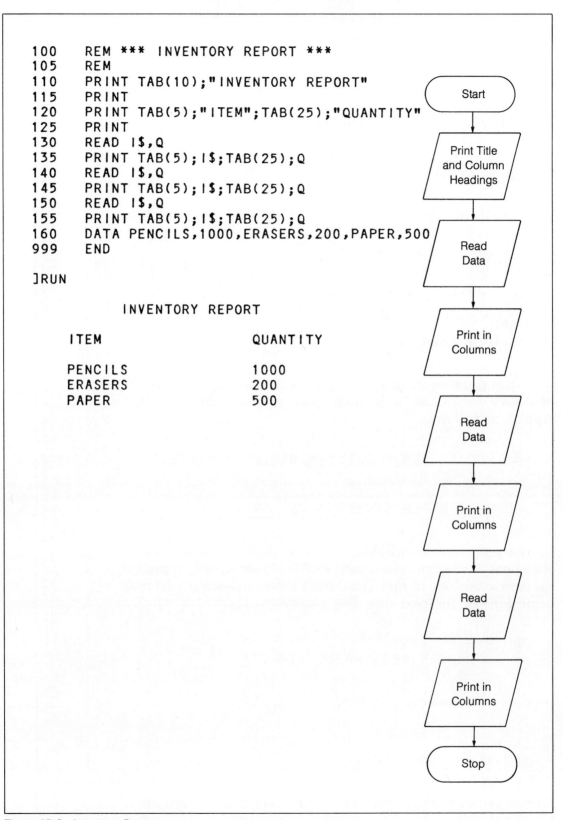

Figure 15-3. *Inventory Program*

The TAB Function

The comma causes the output to be printed according to predefined print zones. The semicolon causes them to start printing in the next position on the output line. Both are easy to use. Many reports are formatted this way. However, there are times when a different output format is desired.

The TAB function allows output to be printed in any column in an output line. This gives the programmer greater flexibility to format printed output.

The general format of the TAB function is:

```
line# TAB(expression)
```

The expression in parentheses may be a numeric constant, a variable, or an arithmetic expression. It tells the computer the column in which printing is to occur. The TAB function (as used in a PRINT statement) must appear right before the variable or literal to be printed. For example, the statement

```
60     PRINT TAB(10);A$;TAB(25);B
```

causes the printer to be spaced to column 10 (shown in parentheses) and to print the value stored in A$. The printer then spaces over to column 25, as indicated in the next parentheses, and prints the value in B. The program in Figure 15-3 illustrates the use of the TAB function.

Note that the semicolon is used as the punctuation mark with the TAB function. The semicolon separates the expression from the values to be printed. If commas were used instead, the printer would use the predefined print zones, and ignore the columns specified in parentheses. Be sure to use semicolons rather than commas in PRINT statements containing the TAB function.

It is also important to remember that when the TAB function is used, the printer cannot be backspaced. Once a column has been passed, the printer cannot go back to it. If more than one TAB function is used in a PRINT statement, the column numbers in parentheses must increase from left to right. For example:

Valid:
```
20     PRINT TAB(5);3;TAB(15);4;TAB(25);5

]RUN
3          4          5
```

Invalid:
```
20     PRINT TAB(25);5;TAB(15);4;TAB(5);3

]RUN
```

```
20   PRINT TAB(15);4;TAB(5);3;TAB(25);5

]RUN
              4   3     5
```

The first invalid example tells the computer to print the number 5 in column 25. The computer does this, but because the printer cannot backspace to column 15 and column 5, it prints the numbers four and three as it normally would, using semicolons.

The column number of the TAB function may be expressed as a numeric constant, a numeric variable, or a numeric expression. All previous examples have used numeric constants. The following are examples using the other two expressions:

```
10   LET Y = 25
15   LET X = 10
20   PRINT TAB(X);7;TAB(Y);"SUEANN"

]RUN
         7                SUEANN

100  LET Y = 20
105  LET X = 15
110  PRINT TAB(X - 5);7;TAB(Y + 5);"SUEANN"

]RUN
         7                SUEANN
```

Notice that both program segments give the same output, but the first one uses numeric variables and the second uses numeric expressions.

⟍ LEARNING CHECK 15-4

1. A _____ separating data items in a PRINT statement instructs the computer to begin printing in the next column.

2. The _____ function allows output to be printed in any column.

3. What would the output look like (on the Apple) after the following statements are executed?

```
110  READ P
120  PRINT "OUR TEAM SCORED ";P;" POINTS"
130  PRINT "ON FRIDAY NIGHT"
140  DATA 65, SCOTT, 63
```

4. In what column will PIZZA be printed (on the Apple) in the following example?

```
10   PRINT "QUANTITY";TAB(13);"ITEM";TAB(28);"PRICE"
20   READ Q, IT, P
30   PRINT Q;TAB(15);IT;TAB(30);P
40   DATA 3, PIZZA, 6.95
```

HANDS-ON EXERCISE 15-4

NOW TRY THIS ⟹ Type NEW `RETURN` , and then type the following program. RUN the program.

```
10   REM *** THIS PROGRAM READS A CLASS ***
20   REM *** AND ITS MEETING TIME ***
30   REM
40   READ C$,T$
50   PRINT C$;T$
60   DATA MATH,10 O'CLOCK
99   END

]RUN
MATH10 O'CLOCK
```

Now change line 50 to use the TAB function to space the output as below. Type RUN.

```
50   PRINT TAB(5);C$;TAB(17);T$

]RUN
     MATH            10 O'CLOCK
```

Now change line 50 to use both the TAB function and commas to space output. When the program is RUN, it produces the same output as before. Examine the output to make sure it does this.

```
50   PRINT TAB(5);C$,T$

]RUN
     MATH            10 O'CLOCK
```

COMPREHENSIVE PROGRAMMING PROBLEM

Mr. Kelly is an eighth-grade teacher who is having problems keeping his grade book up to date. He has to give out grades for the term next week and needs a report listing a student's name, identification number, and average grade for the course. The average grade is a score based on three exam scores. Mr. Kelly gave his secretary a list of the students' names and a format for the report. The following is a copy of the format for the output (data will be inserted for the Xs):

	STUDENT	FINAL
NAME	NUMBER	GRADE
XXXXXXXXX	XXXX	XX

Mr. Kelly's secretary wrote a program for the formatted output, using the test data for one student. The student was Jay Riggins. His three exam scores were 91, 86, and 96 for the term. Jay's identification number is 1806. The program is as follows:

```
10    REM *** THIS PROGRAM READS A STUDENT'S NAME ***
15    REM *** STUDENT ID NUMBER, AND 3 EXAM GRADES ***
20    REM *** AND PRINTS THE NAME, ID NUMBER, AND ***
25    REM *** FINAL GRADE FOR THE TERM. ***
30    REM *** VARIABLES: ***
35    REM *** N$ = NAME OF STUDENT ***
36    REM *** ID = IDENTIFICATION NUMBER OF STUDENT ***
37    REM *** G1 = GRADE OF FIRST EXAM ***
38    REM *** G2 = GRADE OF SECOND EXAM ***
39    REM *** G3 = GRADE OF THIRD EXAM ***
40    REM *** AV = AVERAGE GRADE OF ALL EXAMS ***
45    REM
50    REM *** READ DATA ITEMS ***
60    READ N$,ID,G1,G2,G3
70    LET AV = (G1 + G2 + G3) / 3
75    REM *** PRINT HEADINGS ***
80    PRINT " ","STUDENT","FINAL"
90    PRINT TAB(4);"NAME","NUMBER","GRADE
100   PRINT TAB(4);"_____","_____","_____"
110   PRINT
115   REM *** PRINT OUTPUT ***
120   PRINT N$," ";ID," ";AV
130   DATA JAY RIGGINS,1806,91,86,96
999   END
```

]RUN

	STUDENT	FINAL
NAME	NUMBER	GRADE
————	————————	—————
JAY RIGGINS	1806	91

Lines 10 to 50 are remark statements that define the problem and the variables. Line 60 reads the data from the DATA statement in line 130. Remember, the DATA statement does not have to follow the READ statement directly. Most often, it is placed at the end of the program.

Line 70 averages the three exam scores and stores the value in the variable AV. Lines 80 and 90 print the headings for the report. Since the words "student" and "final" are a line above "name," "number," and "grade," they are printed a line before them. Remember, each PRINT statement prints on a different line unless the line ends with a semicolon or comma to keep it on the same line.

Line 100 prints a continuous underline the length of each heading. This is done by depressing the underline character key four times for "NAME", seven times for "STUDENT NUMBER", and five times for "FINAL GRADE". Line 110 prints a blank line between the headings and the data.

Line 120 prints the data, centering it under the headings. The TAB function causes the computer to print the next character string variable, numeric variable, or constant in the column specified. For example, in line 90, the TAB statement moves the printer to column 4. The semicolon tells the computer to print "NAME" in the same column (column 4).

The comma moves the printer to the start of the next print zone, column 17, and prints "NUMBER". This format is used in all of the remaining PRINT statements. Remember, the blank space between quotes is used in line 80 to make the zone appear empty. It is used in line 120 to cause spaces to be printed before the output for the student number and the final grade.

Now go through all the PRINT statements to be sure you understand the corresponding output. The importance of a formatted print statement is to obtain output in readable form. A table such as the one created by Mr. Kelley's secretary is easy to read and to compare data items.

SUMMARY POINTS

- The INPUT statement allows the user to enter data at the computer while the program is running. It is used when a question-and-answer mode is needed.

- To inform the user what data are to be entered in response to the INPUT statement, a prompt may be included either in a separate PRINT statement, or within the INPUT statement.

- The READ and DATA statements must be used together. They provide another way to enter data into a BASIC program. They are generally used when many data values must be entered that will not change each time the program is run.

- A comma in a PRINT statement instructs the computer to skip to the next print zone to output information. A semicolon in a PRINT statement tells the computer to begin printing the next value in the next available column.

- The TAB function allows output to be printed in any column in an output line.

CHAPTER TEST

Vocabulary

Match the term from the numbered column on the left with the best description from the lettered column on the right.

1. Prompt
2. Initialize
3. READ statement
4. Inquiry-and-response mode
5. INPUT statement
6. Format

a. To control the way in which output will be printed.
b. To assign a beginning value to a variable.
c. A statement that tells the user that data should be entered.
d. Allows data to be entered to the computer while the program is running.
e. A mode in which the computer asks a question and the user enters a response.
f. A statement paired with the DATA statement to input data to the program.

Questions

1. What would be the value of T after the following computer session?
```
10     INPUT A$, X, T, N$
999    END
]RUN
? CAT, 10, 15, GEORGE
```
   a. 10
   b. 15
   c. GEORGE

2. What is the value of A$ after the above session?
   a. CAT
   b. 10
   c. GEORGE

3. Which is a correct response to the following program?
```
50     INPUT X,M$,G$,D
```
   a. SMART, 5, 10, DUMB
   b. 5, SMART, DUMB, 10
   c. 5, SMART, DUMB, DOG

4. A _____ is used to inform users what values are being requested in an INPUT statement.
   a. question mark
   b. DATA statement
   c. prompt

5. The _____ and _____ statements are always used together.
   a. READ/INPUT
   b. INPUT/DATA
   c. READ/DATA

6. There must be _____ DATA statement(s) for every READ statement.

   a. one
   b. two
   c. none of the above

7. There must be _____ DATA item(s) for every READ variable.

   a. one
   b. two
   c. none of the above

8. DATA statements must be located _____.

   a. at the top of the program
   b. anywhere in the program
   c. at the bottom of the program

9. Which of the following is the correct output for this statement (using the Apple)?

```
130    PRINT "A", "MARK", "GO"
```

   a. A   MARK   GO
   b. A MARK GO
   c. AMARKGO

10. Which of the following is the correct output for this program segment (using the Apple)?

```
70    LET N$ = "REBECCA ZIMMERMAN"
80    PRINT N$,"25"
```

   a. REBECCA ZIMMERMAN25
   b. REBECCA ZIMMERMA25
   c. REBECCA ZIMMERMAN   25

11. Which of the following is the correct output for this statement (using the Apple)?

```
60    PRINT "HI","MY","NAME","IS","MIKE"
```

   a. HI   MY   NAME
   b. HI   MY   NAME
       IS   MIKE
   c. HI MY NAME IS MIKE

12. Which of the following is *not* a method of skipping a print zone?

   a. PRINT A,,B
   b. PRINT A," ",B
   c. PRINT A,SKIP,B

13. Which of the following is the correct output for this program segment (using the Apple)?

```
20    LET A$ = "DOG"
30    LET B$ = "CAT"
40    LET E = 10
50    LET F = 15
60    PRINT A$,F,
70    PRINT B$,E
```

   a. DOG   15   CAT
       10
   b. DOG   15   CAT   10

c. DOG   15
     CAT   10

14. Which of the following is the correct output for this program segment (using the Apple)?

```
20     READ N$,X$,S$,A,B,C
30     PRINT S$,
40     PRINT A,B,
50     PRINT N$
60     PRINT X$,C
80     DATA ANNA,CHAIR,CAR,5,20,10
```

a. CAR
     5   20
     ANNA
     CHAIR   10
b. CAR   5   20
     ANNA
     CHAIR   10
c. CAR   5   20
     ANNA   CHAIR   10

15. Which of the following is the correct output for this statement?

```
100     PRINT "HELLO";"MISS";"MOLLY"
```

a. HELLO   MISS   MOLLY
b. HELLOMISSMOLLY
c. HELLO MISS MOLLY

16. Which of the following is the correct output for this program segment (using the Apple)?

```
120     LET A = -120

130     LET B = 55

140     LET N$ = "KAREN"

150     PRINT A;N$;B
```

a. -120KAREN55
b. -120 KAREN 55
c. -120   KAREN   55

17. Which of the following is the correct output for this program segment?

```
80     PRINT "IT IS SUMMER.";
90     PRINT "I'M GOING SWIMMING."
```

a. IT IS SUMMER
     I'M GOING SWIMMING
b. IT IS SUMMER. I'M GOING SWIMMING
c. IT IS SUMMER.I'M GOING SWIMMING.

18. In the following program segment, 20 will be printed in what column (using the Apple)?

```
30     LET X = 20
40     LET H$ = "HOURS"
50     PRINT TAB(10);H$;TAB(20);X
```

a. 20
b. 30
c. 31

19. Which of the following is an incorrect use of the TAB function?

   a. PRINT TAB(30);H$;TAB(10);X
   b. PRINT TAB(10−5);H$;TAB(20−5);X
   c. PRINT TAB(15);X;TAB(20);H$

20. Which of the following is an incorrect way to use the TAB function?

   Assume Y = 10.

   a. PRINT TAB(Y − 5);X;TAB(Y + 5);H$
   b. PRINT TAB(5),H$,TAB(20),X
   c. PRINT TAB(Y + 5);H$;TAB(Y + 15);X

PROGRAMMING PROBLEMS

1. Write a program that will report the temperature during certain times of the day at the airport. Use INPUT statements and prompts to enter data. The output should be in a table with the headings DATE, TIME and TEMP. The data should be centered under each heading. For test data, use the temperature of 45° for Monday, March 15 at 6:00 a.m.

2. Write a program for a farmer that will report sales, cost, and profit (sales minus cost) for this year's corn crop. The output should look like this:

ACRES	SALES	COST	PROFIT
XXX	$XXXXX	$XXXX	$XXXXX

This year's corn sales were $250 per acre, the farmer's costs were $60 per acre, and the farmer owns 100 acres. Use READ/DATA statements to enter data and the TAB function for the output.

3. Get-Well Drug Store is selling its inventory at 20 percent off the regular price. Write a program that lists an item, the regular price of the item, and the sale price of the item in three centered columns with underlined headings. The regular price of box candy is $5.95, the regular price of perfume is $8.95, and the regular price of shampoo is $3.65.

Chapter 16

Setting Up Conditions

Learning Objectives

After reading this chapter, you should be able to:

1. Explain and use the ON/GOTO and IF/THEN statements.

2. Prepare loops with trailer values or counters.

Introduction

So far, the programs you have studied follow the simple sequence logic patterns. In programs using simple sequence logic, the computer cannot select one path from several or make a yes/no decision. This chapter shows how to build into your program the selection, loop, and branch logic patterns discussed in chapter 10. The statements that direct these logic patterns are called **control statements**.

Some control statements are the GOTO statement, the IF/THEN statement, and the ON/GOTO statement.

Control statement
A statement that gives control to program statements out of sequence.

The GOTO Statement

Suppose you want to record the running times for the 100-yard dash for everyone in your gym class. You could use READ/DATA statements to make the computer read the data you give it. If you want the computer to print each student's name and running time, you must either run the program for every student or write the same instructions for every student. If you have 30 classmates, you would have to write 30 sets of READ/DATA and PRINT statements, or input the data and RUN the same program 30 times.

Let's try out this idea with a short program.

```
]LIST

10   REM  *** PRINT NAME, RUNNING TIME FOR
     100-YARD DASH ***
20   INPUT "WHAT IS YOUR NAME?";N$
30   INPUT "WHAT IS YOUR RUNNING TIME IN
     SECONDS?";RT
40   PRINT N$,RT
50   END


]RUN
WHAT IS YOUR NAME?JIM
WHAT IS YOUR RUNNING TIME IN SECONDS?12
JIM               12
```

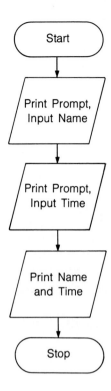

So far so good. But what happens when you want to record the running times for all 30 classmates? You must run the program 30 times.

Now let's try a program using READ/DATA statements.

```
10    REM *** PRINT NAME, RUNNING TIME IN 100-YARD DASH
20    READ N$,RT
30    PRINT N$,RT
40    DATA JIM,12,MARY, 13.5,JOE,14,SUSAN,12.5,BILL,11.5,
      STEVE,13,...
50    END
```

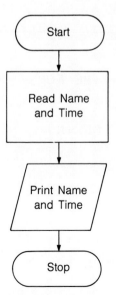

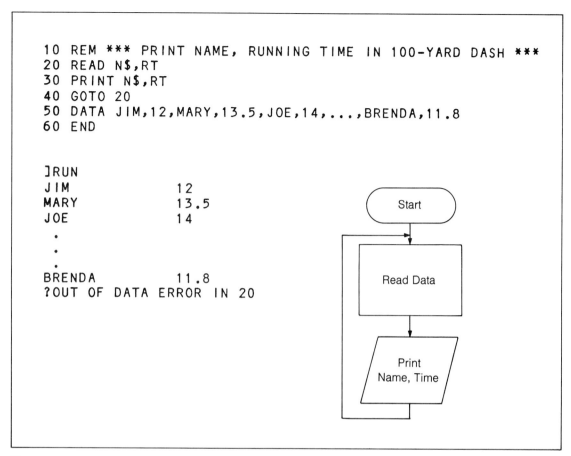

```
10 REM *** PRINT NAME, RUNNING TIME IN 100-YARD DASH ***
20 READ N$,RT
30 PRINT N$,RT
40 GOTO 20
50 DATA JIM,12,MARY,13.5,JOE,14,....,BRENDA,11.8
60 END


]RUN
JIM            12
MARY           13.5
JOE            14
  .
  .
  .
BRENDA         11.8
?OUT OF DATA ERROR IN 20
```

Figure 16-1. *100-Yard Dash Program Using GOTO*

But wait! This program will only print the first name and the first running time. So you must type in lines 20 and 30 for as many names and running times as you have classmates. Wouldn't it be easier to make a loop to repeat the instructions?

Three methods create a loop: the **GOTO statement** paired with a counter, the GOTO statement paired with a "dummy" value, and the FOR/NEXT process, which is discussed in chapter 17. The GOTO statement is often used with IF/THEN statements. Using GOTO alone will result in an ?OUT OF DATA ERROR message in a READ/DATA statement situation.

The GOTO statement directs the program to another line before or after the GOTO statement line:

```
400    GOTO 250
```

GOTO is like the GO TO JAIL move in Monopoly. If you land on a GO TO JAIL space or get a GO TO JAIL card, you are sent or transferred unconditionally to JAIL. The GOTO statement is also an **unconditional transfer**. Every time the computer sees GOTO, it moves execution to the line named in the GOTO statement.

GOTO statement A statement that unconditionally transfers program execution to a given line number.

Unconditional transfer A transfer of program control made every time a statement is met regardless of conditions.

```
10  REM *** PRINT NAME, RUNNING TIME IN 100-YARD DASH ***
20  LET X = 0
30  READ N$,RT
40  PRINT N$,RT
50  LET X = X + 1
60  IF X = 30 THEN 90
70  GOTO 30
80  DATA JIM,12,MARY,13.5,JOE,14,...,BRENDA,11.8
90  END
```

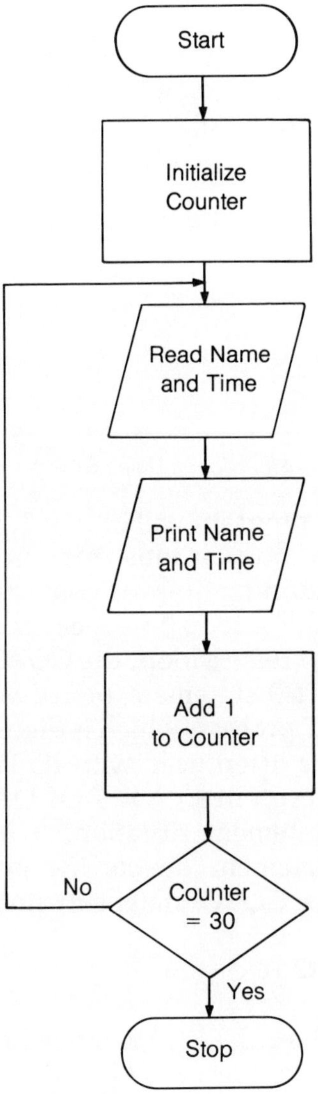

Figure 16-2. *100-Yard Dash Program Using GOTO and a Counter*

```
10  REM *** PRINT NAME, RUNNING TIME IN 100-YARD DASH ***
20  READ N$,RT
30  IF N$ = "WHO" THEN 70
40  PRINT N$,RT
50  GOTO 20
60  DATA JIM,12,MARY,13.5,JOE,14,...,WHO,1000
70  END
```

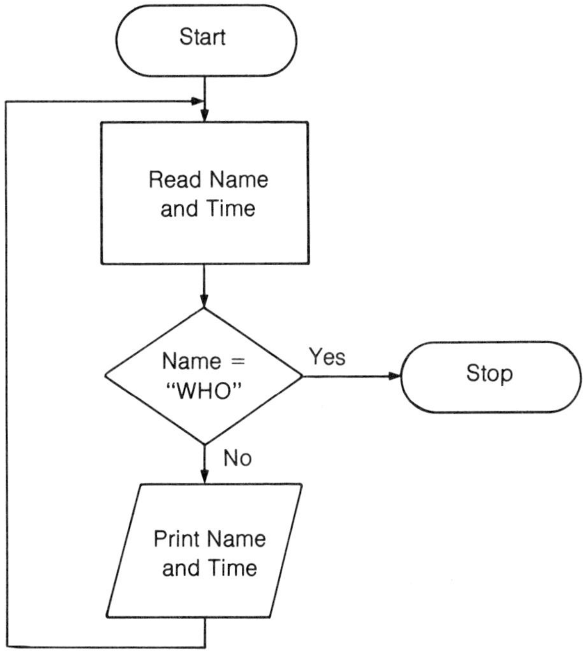

Figure 16-3. *100-Yard Dash Program Using Trailer Values.*

GOTO with a Counter

In Monopoly, you can get out of jail after missing three turns or by turning in a card that says, "Get Out of Jail Free." In a GOTO loop, you can get out of the loop by using a counter or a trailer value.

GOTO can be used in the 100-yard dash program (see Figure 16-1).

Look at the flowchart for this program. The arrows show the loop. No stop symbol is used. Running the program shows how the computer will print an ?OUT OF DATA ERROR message. But it is possible to control the number of times the loop is executed.

```
10 REM *** PRINT NAME, RUNNING TIME FOR 100-YARD DASH ***
20 PRINT "ENTER NAME, RUNNING TIME"
30 PRINT "TYPE'WHO,1000'TO END PROGRAM"
40 INPUT N$,RT
50 IF N$ = "WHO" THEN 90
60 PRINT N$,RT
70 PRINT
80 GOTO 20
90 END

]RUN
ENTER NAME, RUNNING TIME
TYPE 'WHO,1000' TO END PROGRAM
?JIM,12
JIM   12
ENTER NAME, RUNNING TIME
TYPE "WHO,1000" TO END PROGRAM
?WHO, 1000
```

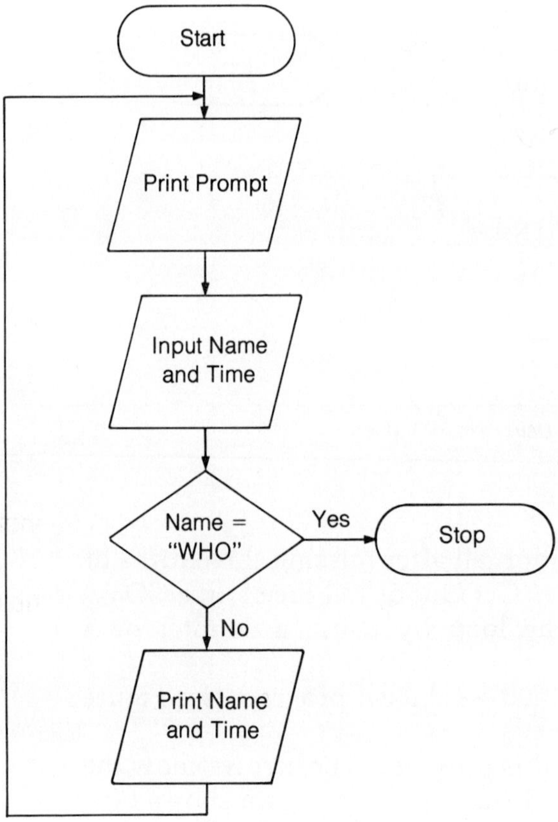

Figure 16-4. *100-Yard Dash Program Using Prompt and Trailer Value*

A **counter** will control the number of times a loop is executed so the error message will not appear. First, you initialize the counter (Let X = 0) to give it a beginning value. Then the counter must count the number of times through the loop. In LET X = X + 1, the counter adds 1 to X, and X gets a new value, 1. Then the value is tested in an IF/THEN statement: IF X = 30, THEN line number.

The 100-yard dash program in Figure 16-2 shows how a counter would work.

Counter A variable used to count the number of executions in a loop.

GOTO with a Trailer Value

A **trailer value** or "dummy" value can also be used to end a loop. The dummy value is placed as the last value in the DATA list. There must be as many dummy values as there are variables to be read. Remember to use dummy values that cannot be mistaken for real values in a program.

The 100-yard dash program can use a dummy value and an IF/THEN statement (see Figure 16-3).

In Figure 16-3, when the computer reads WHO,1000 it goes to line 70, as directed by line 30. Line 30 does not need to list more than one variable. But, as stated earlier, the dummy data do need to list data for all variables—in this example, the values for N$ and RT are WHO and 1000.

The dummy value can be typed into the program by using an input prompt (see Figure 16-4). In the 100-yard dash program, the prompt would ask for the student's name and running time. If there are no more names to input, the prompt would instruct the user to type "WHO,1000" to end the program. An IF/THEN statement provides the condition to end the loop.

Trailer value A dummy value added to the end of a data list to stop loop execution.

✎ LEARNING CHECK 16-1

1. A statement that will unconditionally transfer control of the program to another program line is the _____ statement.

2. To use a counter to control a loop, you must set a beginning value for the counter variable. This is called _____ the counter.

3. A false value that is used to end a program is called a _____ or _____ value.

1. GOTO 2. initializing 3. dummy, trailer

HANDS-ON EXERCISE 16-1

NOW TRY THIS ⇨ GOTO is tricky. Used improperly, it can send a program into an infinite loop—a loop that loops on and on until it reaches the highest value the computer can reach. This exercise will depend on your ability to use the panic buttons quickly. After you instruct the typed-in program to RUN, you must be ready to push the `CONTROL` and `c` keys together or the `CONTROL` and `RESET` keys together to stop the program.

Type and RUN this program:

```
10    LET K = 1
20    LET K = K + 1
30    LET L = K * K
40    PRINT K,L
50    GOTO 10
60    END
```

Did you stop the program? What values for K and L were printed? Were they the same for each loop? What went wrong? Line 50 directs the computer to line 10, which returns the value of K to 1. The same values will be printed over and over.

Now try this program:

```
10    LET K = 1
20    LET K = K + 1
30    LET L = K * K
40    PRINT K,L
50    GOTO 20
60    END
```

Again you had to stop the program from processing. What happened to the values of K and L this time? Yes, the computer assigned new and increasing values to K and L. What statement should be written to stop the looping? Where should it be placed?

Did you suggest a statement like this?

```
45    IF K = 10 THEN 60
```

If you did, you are beginning to understand looping! Line 45, an IF/THEN statement, breaks the loop. It sets a condition: If K equals 10, then end this loop. When the value of K reaches 10, line 45 directs the computer to end the processing.

In READ/DATA programs, GOTO has an easy way out of the loop. When the last data are used, the computer prints an ?OUT OF DATA message and processing stops. But as you learned in this HANDS-ON EXERCISE, other types of logic using GOTO statements must be handled very carefully!

The ON/GOTO Statement

GOTO can be combined with ON to provide choices, or a "menu," in your program. The program in Figure 16-5 asks you to pick a number that tells the computer how much money you have in your wallet. When you input a number, to be assigned to the variable name A, the GOTO portion of the ON/GOTO statement directs the computer to lines 70, 80, or 90, depending upon your answer. Then the computer will tell you where you can eat supper for two with the amount of money you have.

As you study the order of the lines, you see that the PRINT messages are in the same order as the money messages. Therefore, the eating places the computer suggests range from least expen-

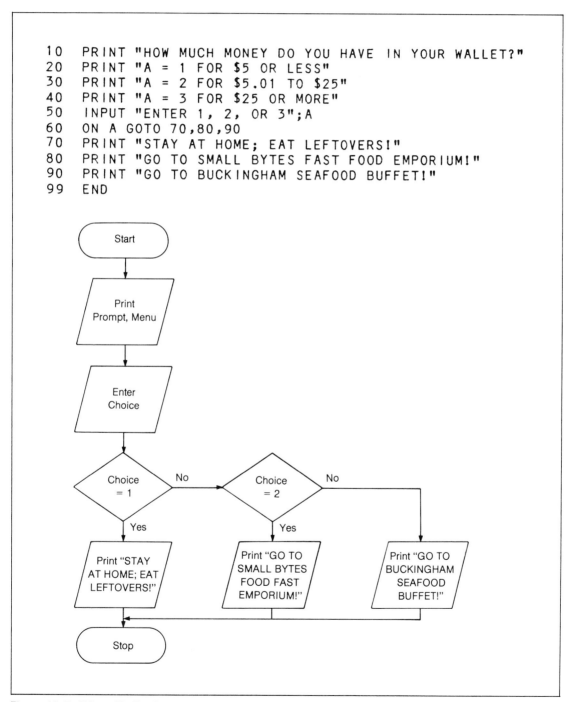

```
10   PRINT "HOW MUCH MONEY DO YOU HAVE IN YOUR WALLET?"
20   PRINT "A = 1 FOR $5 OR LESS"
30   PRINT "A = 2 FOR $5.01 TO $25"
40   PRINT "A = 3 FOR $25 OR MORE"
50   INPUT "ENTER 1, 2, OR 3";A
60   ON A GOTO 70,80,90
70   PRINT "STAY AT HOME; EAT LEFTOVERS!"
80   PRINT "GO TO SMALL BYTES FAST FOOD EMPORIUM!"
90   PRINT "GO TO BUCKINGHAM SEAFOOD BUFFET!"
99   END
```

Figure 16-5. *Where To Eat Program Using ON/GOTO*

**ON/GOTO state-
ment** A statement
that transfers pro-
gram execution to
one of several listed
line numbers.

sive to most expensive. ON/GOTO statements provide an interesting pattern for the flowcharts. You can see how the multiple
choices are looped.

The **ON/GOTO** is a conditional transfer statement. Any
mathematical expression can be evaluated to transfer control to
the appropriate statement. The general format of the ON/GOTO
statement is:

line# ON expression GOTO line#1, line#2,...line#n

If there is an arithmetic expression, it is always evaluated to an
integer. The line numbers following the GOTO statement must
identify lines in the program.

The ON/GOTO statement proceeds as follows:

1. If the value of the expression is one, control is transferred
   to the first line number indicated.

2. If the value of the expression is two, control is transferred
   to the second line number indicated.

   .
   .
   .

n. If the value of the expression is n, control is transferred to
   the nth line number indicated.

The following examples show how the ON/GOTO statement
works. When the expression evaluated is not an integer, as in the
second example, either the value is rounded or the digits to the
right of the decimal are ignored.

Statement		**Computer Expression**
30	ON N / 50 GOTO 90,100	IF N / 50 = 1, control goes to line 90 IF N / 50 = 2, control goes to line 100.
40	ON N / 3 GOTO 60,80,100	IF N = 7, then N/3 = 2.33. The decimal fraction (.33) is dropped and the result becomes the integer 2. Control passes to statement 80.

LEARNING CHECK 16-2

1. The _____ statement is used to transfer control to different line numbers depending
   on the evaluation of an expression.

2. To what line number will control be transferred in the following program segment?

   ```
   10    LET Y = 1
   20    ON Y + 1 GOTO 40,60,80
   ```

a. 40
b. 60
c. 80

3. If the following expression is rounded to the nearest integer, what line number will control be passed to?

```
30    LET X = 11
40    ON X / 3 GOTO 110,120,130,140
```

a. 110
b. 120
c. 130
d. 140

1. ON/GOTO 2. b 3. d (11/3 = 3.66, which rounds to 4)

The IF/THEN Statement

The GOTO statement always transfers control. By pairing an IF/ THEN statement with the GOTO statement, you can test a condition and exit from a GOTO loop. IF/THEN tests the value of a dummy piece of data or the value of a counter. But IF/THEN has other uses. It can compare values in relationships other than equality, such as less than or greater to.

A general format for IF/THEN is:

```
line#   IF condition THEN do this
400     IF test score = 98 THEN give 'A'
500     IF hungry THEN eat apple
600     IF bored THEN go jogging
```

IF/THEN statement
A statement that conditionally gives control to a named line number or request a certain task.

In many computer programs, IF/THEN directs the program to another line number.

```
100    IF X = Y + 1 THEN 230
```

IF/THEN also can tell the computer to do a special task, such as LET:

```
340  REM *** ADD $3.00 IF MAIL ORDER IS LESS THAN
     $25.00 ***
350 IF COST < 25.00 THEN LET SUM = COST + 3.00
```

or PRINT:

```
200    REM *** PRINT NAMES OF FRESHMEN ONLY **
210    IF YEAR$ = "FRESHMAN" THEN PRINT NAME$
```

In line 210, YEAR$ = "FRESHMAN" is the condition, and the equal sign is a relational symbol. Conditions may contain numeric

Relational symbol
A symbol that
shows the relation-
ship between two
items.

data or character string data. If the value on one side of a relational symbol is a character string, the value on the other side must also be a string. If the value on one side of a relational symbol is numeric, the value on the other side must also be numeric.

So far we have used the equal sign and less than sign as **relational symbols**. Other relationships can be shown with the signs listed in Table 16-1.

Relational Symbols   Table 16-1

Symbol	Meaning	Examples
$<$	is less than	$12 < 20$
		$A < B + C$
$<=$	is less than or equal to	$J <= K * L$
$>$	is greater than	"65 MPH" $>$ "55 MPH"
$>=$	is greater than or equal to	$A >= B$
$=$	is equal to	$X = T$ N\$ = "MICHAEL"
$<>$ or $><$	is not equal to	"APPLE" $<>$ "PEAR"

The program in Figure 16-6 uses both numeric and character string comparisons to search a school's records to find students eligible for honors on graduation day. The conditions tested are 1) whether the student is a senior (the character string condition) and 2) whether the student's grade point average shows that he or she is eligible for academic honors.

A flowchart shows IF/THEN with the decision symbol $\diamondsuit$.

Looping to Accumulate a Total

A loop reduces the number of program statements needed to perform a task. It provides a way to repeat steps without retyping them into the program. A loop also provides a method of accumulating, or adding up, numbers. For instance, the manager of a bakery wants a method of adding up a bill. As the cost of each item is rung up, it is added to the total figured to that point.

To accumulate totals using the loop method, the program must do three things:

1. Initialize the total to give it a beginning value.
2. Increase the total each time the loop is executed.
3. Print the total outside the loop.

```
10      REM *** GRADUATION PROGRAM ***
20      REM *** FOR HONORS STUDENTS. ***
30      REM *** VARIABLES: ***
40      REM *** N$ = NAME ***
50      REM *** CLASS$ = CLASS IN SCHOOL ***
60      REM *** GRADE = GRADE POINT AVERAGE ***
100     READ N$,CLASS$,GRADE
110     REM *** REJECT ALL BUT SENIORS ***
120     IF CLASS$ < > "SENIOR" THEN 170
130     REM *** REJECT ALL BELOW 3.5 ***
140     IF GRADE < 3.5 THEN 170
150     PRINT N$,"QUALIFIES"
160     GOTO 100
170     PRINT N$,"DOES NOT QUALIFY"
180     GOTO 100
190     DATA "SUE BARTELL","SENIOR",3.42
200     DATA "TOM DIX","JUNIOR",3.60
210     DATA "BOBBY SOOD","SENIOR",3.63
999     END

]RUN
SUE BARTELL         DOES NOT QUALIFY
TOM DIX             DOES NOT QUALIFY
BOBBY SOOD          QUALIFIES


?OUT OF DATA ERROR IN 100
```

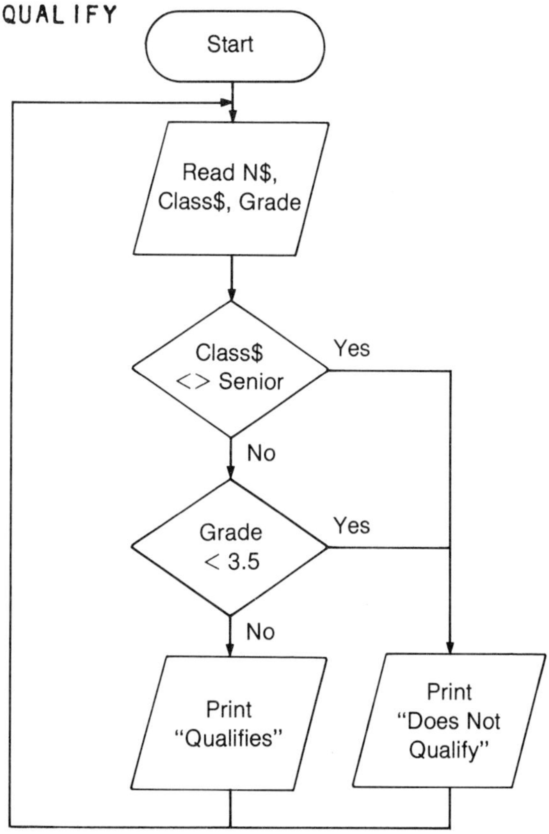

Figure 16-6. *Graduation Program*

```
100    REM *** BAKERY BILL ***
110    REM *** VARIABLES: ***
120    REM *** QTY = QUANTITY ***
130    REM *** PRICE = PRICE OF ITEM ***
140    REM *** GT = GRAND TOTAL ***
150    REM *** IT = ITEM TOTAL COST
160    REM *** INITIALIZE TOTAL ***
170    LET GT = 0
180    REM *** LOOP BEGINS HERE ***
190    PRINT "ENTER QTY,PRICE"
200    PRINT "(TYPE 0,0 TO QUIT)"
210    INPUT QTY,PRICE
220    REM *** TEST FOR LAST ITEM ***
230    IF QTY = 0 THEN 280
240    REM *** ACCUMULATE TOTAL ***
245    LET IT = QTY * PRICE
250    LET GT = GT + IT
255    PRINT
260    REM *** REPEAT LOOP ***
270    GOTO 190
280    PRINT
290    PRINT
300    PRINT "TOTAL COST IS $";GT
999    END

]RUN
ENTER QTY,PRICE
(TYPE 0,0 TO QUIT)
?3,.15

ENTER QTY,PRICE
(TYPE 0,0 TO QUIT)
?8,.20

ENTER QTY,PRICE
(TYPE 0,0 TO QUIT)
?6,.35

ENTER QTY,PRICE
(TYPE 0,0 TO QUIT)
?0,0

TOTAL COST IS $4.15
```

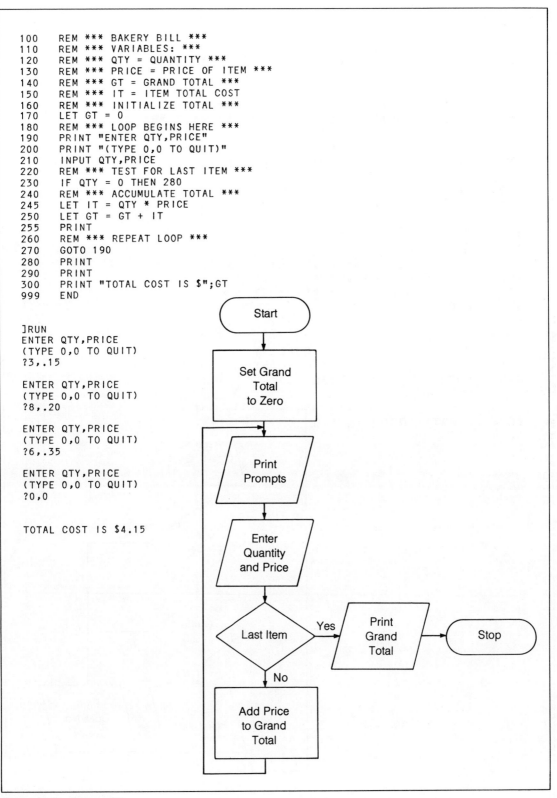

Figure 16-7. *Bakery Bill*

The program in Figure 16-7 shows how to figure the total bill for one customer's sale at the bakery. The program must first initialize the total with a beginning value.

```
160     REM *** INITIALIZE TOTAL ***
170     LET GT = 0
```

Then a prompt asks for a quantity and price, after which the item total cost is figured. In lines 245 and 250, the grand total is accumulated:

```
245     LET IT = QTY * PRICE
250     LET GT = GT + IT
```

Each time IT is added to GT, a new total is placed in the GT location. The first value of GT is zero. But if the first IT total is $4.50, GT takes on the value $4.50. The next time an IT total is figured, say $5.65, it is added to the current amount in GT, $4.50. Now GT equals $10.15 (4.50 + 5.65). The totaling continues until the user enters the dummy value, 0,0.

Printing the total must occur outside the loop. After the last execution of the loop, GT equals the total cost of the purchase. The program continues with line 280 until the END statement. A grand total is printed so the customer will know how much he or she owes the bakery.

```
280     PRINT
290     PRINT
300     PRINT "TOTAL COST IS $";GT
999     END
```

LEARNING CHECK 16-3

1. The IF/THEN statement forces the computer to perform a task if a certain _____ is met.

2. Before a program can accumulate a total amount, it must _____ it to give it a beginning value.

3. Identify each part of the following statement:

IF X = 10 THEN 240

      a   b

HANDS-ON EXERCISE 16-2

NOW TRY THIS ⇨ The IF/THEN and GOTO statements can help you write a quiz program. Type in the following quiz question asking for the number of states in the United States.

```
10      INPUT "HOW MANY STATES ARE IN THE U.S.?";S
20      IF S = 50 THEN GOTO 50
30      PRINT "NO, TRY AGAIN!"
40      GOTO 10
50      PRINT "THAT'S RIGHT!"
60      END
```

RUN the program. Did you give the correct answer? Now RUN it again and enter an incorrect number of states. What appeared on the screen?

You can follow this pattern for other quizzes, too. Try this multiplication quiz:

```
10      INPUT "MULTIPLY 45 BY 67.";ANSWER
20      LET P = 45 * 67
30      IF ANSWER = P THEN 60
40      PRINT "NO, TRY AGAIN!"
50      GOTO 10
60      PRINT "YOU'RE SMART!"
70      END
```

Write a computer quiz for some information you learned recently in school. What would you do if you wanted to include several questions in your quiz?

COMPREHENSIVE PROGRAMMING PROBLEM

The students at JFK Junior High School have just finished a four-week candy sale to raise money for new gym equipment. Now the principal, Ms. Warren, would like a list of the students who sold any boxes of candy and their grade. Since the students were competing for prizes based on the number of boxes sold, Ms. Warren would also like the prize each student earned to be listed.

The prizes were awarded as follows:

Boxes Sold	Prize
Less than 25	Bookmark
25-49	Calendar
50-99	Pen set
100 or more	Radio

Ms. Warren would also like to give special credit to the students who sold more than 100 boxes of candy by setting their names apart. The list will be posted on all school bulletin boards, so output should be orderly and easy to read.

```
10   REM *** THIS PROGRAM WILL PRINT A LIST OF ***
20   REM *** STUDENTS WHO PARTICIPATED IN THE SCHOOL CANDY SALE ***
30   REM *** AND WILL DETERMINE THE PRIZE THEY'LL RECEIVE ***
40   REM *** BASED ON NUMBER OF BOXES SOLD ***
50   REM
60   REM *** VARIABLES USED ***
70   REM      N$ = NAME OF STUDENT
80   REM      GR = GRADE
90   REM      BX = BOXES SOLD
100  REM
110  PRINT "GRADE","STUDENT","PRIZE"
120  PRINT "-----","-------","-----"
130  PRINT
140  PRINT
150  READ N$,GR,BX
155  IF N$ = "XXXXX" THEN 999
160  REM *** DETERMINING THE PRIZE EARNED ***
170  IF BX < 25 THEN 310
180  IF BX < 50 THEN 280
190  IF BX < 100 THEN 250
200  REM *** STUDENT SOLD OVER 100 OR MORE BOXES, AWARD RADIO ***
210  PRINT "***********************************************************"
220  PRINT TAB(3);GR,N$,"RADIO"
230  PRINT "***********************************************************"
240  GOTO 150
250  REM *** STUDENT SOLD 50-99 BOXES, AWARD PEN SET ***
260  PRINT TAB(3);GR,N$,"PEN SET"
270  GOTO 150
280  REM *** STUDENT SOLD 24-49 BOXES, AWARD CALENDAR ***
290  PRINT TAB(3);GR,N$,"CALENDAR"
300  GOTO 150
310  REM *** STUDENT SOLD LESS THAN 25 BOXES, AWARD BOOKMARK ***
320  PRINT TAB(3);GR,N$,"BOOKMARK"
330  GOTO 150
500  DATA A. BISBEE,8,19,C. FEEHAN,7,115,L. STEINMETZ,8,54,M. STUMP,8,76
510  DATA L. WOLF,9,23,R. RABB,7,20,R. THOMPSON,9,62,K. MCKEE,7,45
520  DATA S. MORAN,9,102,D. SMITH,8,32,XXXXX,0,0
999  END


]RUN
GRADE           STUDENT         PRIZE
-----           -------         -----


   8            A. BISBEE       BOOKMARK
********************************************************************
   7            C. FEEHAN       RADIO
********************************************************************
   8            L. STEINMETZ    PEN SET
   8            M. STUMP        PEN SET
   9            L. WOLF         BOOKMARK
   7            R. RABB         BOOKMARK
   9            R. THOMPSON     PEN SET
   7            K. MCKEE        CALENDAR
********************************************************************
   9            S. MORAN        RADIO
********************************************************************
   8            D. SMITH        CALENDAR
```

Figure 16-8. *Candy Sale Program*

The program and output for this problem are listed in Figure 16-8. The program uses IF/
THEN statements to send control to various program sections depending on the number of
boxes of candy sold by each student. GOTO statements are used to return control to the
beginning of the loop. Data are entered using READ/DATA statements.

Lines 10 to 90 are remark statements that explain the program and identify the variables used. Lines 110 and 120 print the headings for the list. The data for the students who sold candy are read in line 150. Line 155 tests for the end of data by using a trailer (dummy) value.

The IF/THEN statements in lines 170 to 190 test the number of boxes sold to determine to which line control should be sent. If the student sold less than 25 boxes, control is sent to line 310, a remark statement. Then line 320 prints the student's grade, name, and "BOOK-MARK", the prize awarded for selling less than 25 boxes. The GOTO statement in line 330 sends control back to the beginning of the loop, and the next set of data is read.

Similarly, if the student sold between 25 and 49 boxes, control goes to line 280, a REM statement, and then to line 290 which prints the student's grade, name, and "CALENDAR". Control goes to line 250 if the number of boxes sold is between 50 and 99.

If the computer goes through all three comparisons in lines 170 to 190 without having control transferred, then it knows the student sold 100 or more boxes. The next lines, 200 to 230, print the student's grade, name, and the top award, "RADIO", with stars on the lines before and after. The stars set apart the student's names, as Ms. Warren requested.

To make the final output neat and easy to read, print zones are used for each item—GRADE, STUDENT, and PRIZE. The student's grade is indented under the heading by using the TAB function.

SUMMARY POINTS

- The GOTO statement is an unconditional transfer statement because it always transfers control to another part of the program. It may instruct the computer to skip some program statements or branch around to repeat some statements.

- A trailer value will control the number of times a loop is executed. It is a dummy value that is placed at the end of a data list. When it is read, control is transferred outside the loop. It is paired with an IF/THEN statement.

- A counter counts the number of times a loop is executed. When a certain number is reached, control is transferred outside the loop. The counter is paired with an IF/THEN statement.

- The ON/GOTO statement transfers control to other statements in the program based on the result of a choice.

- The IF/THEN statement is used to test for a certain condition. If the condition exists, IF/THEN may direct the program to another line number or tell the computer to do a special task. If the condition does not exist, control transfers to the next statement in the program.

CHAPTER TEST

Vocabulary

Match the term from the numbered column with the description from the lettered column that best fits the term.

1. **Conditional transfer**   **a.** A numeric variable that is used to keep track of the number of times a loop is executed.

2. **Trailer value**   **b.** A type of statement that transfers control only when a certain condition exists.

3. **GOTO statement**   **c.** A statement that directs the flow of execution in a program to a given line number.

4. **Unconditional transfer**   **d.** A statement that gives control to a program statement out of sequence.

5. **Counter**   **e.** A dummy value used to signal the end of data and the need to transfer control outside the loop.

6. **Relational symbol**   **f.** A type of statement that always transfers control.

7. **Control statement**   **g.** A statement that gives control of the program to a specified line number or calls for a certain task only if some condition is true.

8. **IF/THEN statement**   **h.** Symbols such as =, >, and < that show how two items are related.

Questions

1. Which is an example of an unconditional transfer statement?
- **a.** 10 IF X = 2 THEN GOTO 40
- **b.** 10 IF X = 2 THEN LET Y = 4
- **c.** 10 GOTO 40

2. In the line, 100 IF X > 1 THEN 260, the condition is _____.
- **a.** 260
- **b.** X > 1
- **c.** IF X > 1 THEN

3. Which of the following is a valid IF/THEN statement?
- **a.** 10   IF X = "MONKEY" THEN 70
- **b.** 10   IF Y >= 2 THEN PRINT "END"
- **c.** 10   IF "C$" = CAT" THEN 100

4. Which is an example of a conditional statement?
- **a.** PRINT "IF X = 1 THEN LET Y = 2"
- **b.** GOTO 200
- **c.** IF X =1 THEN LET Y =2

Use this program segment for questions 5 to 7.

```
20    LET X = 0
30    READ K
40    IF K > 4 THEN 70
50    LET X = X + 1
60    GOTO 30
70    PRINT K
80    DATA 3, 2, 7, 4
99    END
```

5. How many times is line 30 executed?

    a. 1
    b. 2
    c. 3
    d. 4

6. What is the value of X at the end of the program?

    a. 0
    b. 1
    c. 2
    d. 3

7. What is the printed output?

    a. 3   2
    b. 7
    c. 3   2   7   4

8. The transfer statement that allows the program to judge one expression or variable and, based on its value, branch to one of several points in a program is the _____.

    a. IF/THEN statement
    b. ON/GOTO statement
    c. GOTO statement

9. In the following statement, when will "POSITIVE" be printed?

```
50    IF X > 0 THEN PRINT "POSITIVE"
```

    a. when the condition is true
    b. every time the line is executed
    c. when X is greater than 0
    d. both a and c

10. Which is a valid ON/GOTO statement?

    a. 40   ON X GOTO 70, 90, 100
    b. 70   IF X + 1 GOTO 80, 100, 120
    c. 10   ON A$ GOTO 30, 70, 90

11. What statement is used to test a trailer value in loop control?

    a. IF/THEN statement
    b. GOTO statement
    c. ON/GOTO statement

12. A dummy value that could safely be used for the price of a grocery item would be

_____.

    a. "XXX"
    b. 1.00
    c. 999.99

13. Which line number will control be passed to in the following? (Assume X = 3.)

```
90    ON X GOTO 20,50,100
```

    a. 20
    b. 50
    c. 100
    d. 3

14. Which of the following is not a control statement?

   a. READ/DATA
   b. ON/GOTO
   c. IF/THEN
   d. GOTO

15. What will be the result of the following program?

```
 10    LET X = 3
 20    LET X = X + 1
 30    PRINT X ^ 2, X ^ 5
 40    GOTO 10
999    END
```

   a. 16   2
   b. 8   20
   c. an infinite loop
   d. the loop will execute 10 times and then stop

PROGRAMMING PROBLEMS

1. Write a program that will input any two numbers and compare them in size, printing a message to tell whether the first is larger, smaller, or equal to the second. Write the program in a loop so it may be executed as many times as the user wishes. Use a trailer value of 00 to end the loop and the program.

2. Write a program that will go through a list of job applicants for newspaper carriers and print the names of those applicants who qualify for the job. To qualify, the applicant must be 14 years or older and live in the town of Cedar Ridge. The following is a list of applicants, their ages, and addresses:

Name	Age	City
Dan Jones	17	Smithville
Carla Ellett	13	Cedar Ridge
Charlie May	26	Cedar Ridge
Mike Daniels	21	Albany
Gina Johnson	14	Cedar Ridge

Use a loop counter and conditional transfer to end the loop.

Looping with FOR/NEXT

Learning Objectives

After reading this chapter, you should be able to:

1. Explain and use FOR/NEXT statements in your programs.

2. Draw flowcharts for the FOR/NEXT loops in your programs.

3. Explain nested FOR/NEXT loops.

Introduction

You have seen how to repeat steps in your programs without re-writing all of the instructions for each repetition. You have read about designing choices in your programs and skipping over program steps, depending upon the answers to the choices. The counters and "dummy" values that allow you to program these logic patterns can be performed in yet another way—using FOR/NEXT loops.

FOR/NEXT Statements

The **FOR/NEXT statements** work like counters. FOR/NEXT defines how many times a loop is executed.

Suppose you have a pile of shirts to iron. FOR/NEXT would work like this:

```
10 FOR SHIRTS = 1 to 15 STEP 1
20     GROAN
30     IRON SHIRT
40     HANG SHIRT ON HANGER IN CLOSET
50 NEXT SHIRT
60 SIT DOWN AND RELAX
```

FOR statement
The first statement in a FOR/NEXT loop; shows how many times to execute a loop.

NEXT statement
The last statement in a FOR/NEXT statement; counts the loop variable to continue execution.

The 1 to 15 defines how many times the loop is executed. For every shirt, you will do the steps in lines 20, 30, and 40—unless, of course, you give up.

The format of FOR/NEXT statements is:

line# FOR loop variable = initial value TO terminal value STEP step value

.

.

.

line# NEXT loop variable

Look at the shirt example again:

10 FOR	SHIRTS =	1	TO	15	STEP	1
	Loop Variable	Initial Value		Terminal Value	Step Value	

```
10   LET N = 1
20   IF N > 5 THEN 60
30   PRINT N, N * 2
40   LET N = N + 1
50   GOTO 20
60   PRINT "THAT'S ALL FOLKS!"
99   END

]RUN
1                    2
2                    4
3                    6
4                    8
5                    10
THAT'S ALL FOLKS!
```

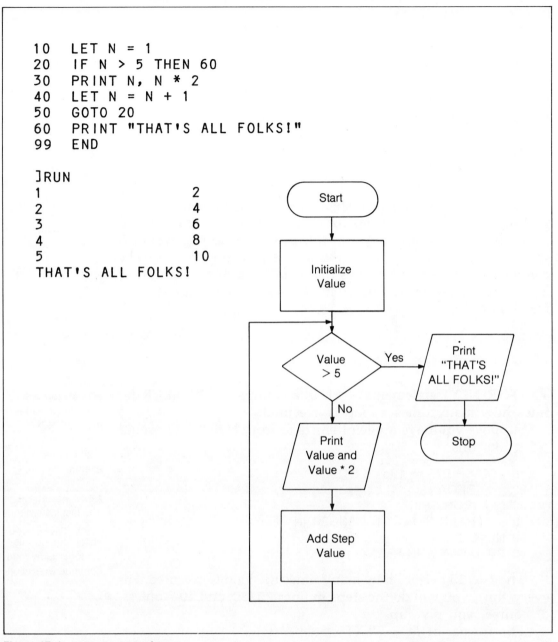

Figure 17-1. *IF/THEN, GOTO Loop*

Loop variable The variable in a FOR statement that sets how many times the loop is executed.

Initial value The beginning value of a loop control variable.

The FOR statement signals the beginning of the loop and tells the computer how many times to execute the loop. The **loop variable** (SHIRTS) serves as the loop counter and is set to an **initial value** (usually 1) in the FOR statement. This value is then tested against the **terminal value** (15). The counter will count from 1 shirt to 15 shirts. If the loop variable is less than or equal to the terminal value (15 in this example), the statements within the loop are executed. Until you iron the last shirt, number 15, you will groan, iron shirt, and hang it in the closet.

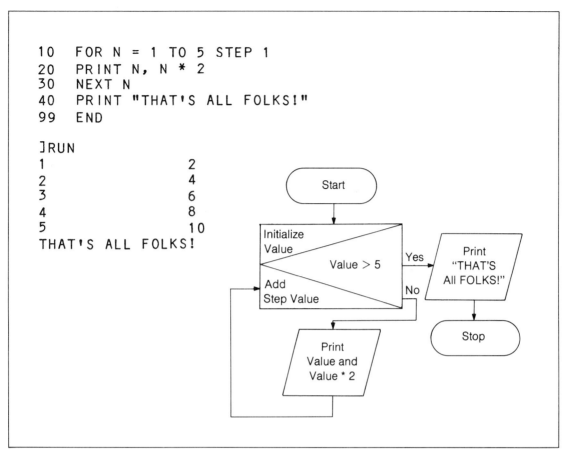

```
10    FOR N = 1 TO 5 STEP 1
20    PRINT N, N * 2
30    NEXT N
40    PRINT "THAT'S ALL FOLKS!"
99    END

]RUN
1                    2
2                    4
3                    6
4                    8
5                    10
THAT'S ALL FOLKS!
```

Figure 17-2. *FOR/NEXT Loop*

The initial, terminal, and step values may be constants, variables, expressions, or decimals, all of which must be numeric.

The NEXT statement marks the end of the loop. It tells the computer to add the specified **STEP value** to the loop variable and to test the new value of the loop variable against the terminal value. In the ironing example, the STEP value, 1, means that after finishing one shirt, iron the next shirt. If the step value had been 2, you would iron only every other shirt. At the NEXT statement, you would skip one shirt, then iron the next one. If the step value is 1, you do not need to write STEP 1 at the end of the FOR statement; the computer will automatically count by one.

The loop is executed until the loop variable is greater than the terminal value. For this example, if the loop variable is more than 15, you are finished ironing and can exit the loop. The first statement following the NEXT statement is then executed. In this case, SIT DOWN AND RELAX.

Figure 17-1 illustrates a loop using IF/THEN, GOTO, and LET statements. Figure 17-2 shows the same loop using FOR and NEXT statements.

Terminal value
The value at which a FOR/NEXT loop will stop execution.

STEP value The value by which the loop variable is counted when the FOR/NEXT loop is executed.

The program in Figure 17-2 is shorter and more concise. The FOR statement in line 10 sets the initial value of N at 1, the terminal value at 5, and the STEP value at 1. The initial value of N (1) is then compared with the terminal value (5). Since 1 is less than 5, the statement within the loop (line 20) is executed.

The NEXT statement (line 30) is then executed telling the computer to add the STEP value of 1 to N (1), and then compare the new value of the loop variable with the terminal value. The value of the loop variable is now 2. Since this is less than 5, control goes to the statement following the FOR statement and the loop is once again run. This pattern will continue until the value of N is greater than the terminal value. Therefore, when the value of N is 6, control will be sent to line 40. The remaining statements in the program will then be executed.

All of the loop information is contained in one statement. This makes the program easier to read, understand, and debug. Using FOR/NEXT loops also reduces the need for GOTO statements.

LEARNING CHECK 17-1

1. TRUE   FALSE   The NEXT and FOR statements are always used together.

2. The loop variable is set to its initial value in the _____ statement.

3. The statements within the loop are no longer executed when the value of the loop variable is _____ the terminal value.

4. The loop variable is counted when the _____ statement is executed.

5. When the value of the loop variable does not exceed the terminal value, control is transferred to the statement following the _____ statement.

1. TRUE 2. FOR 3. greater than 4. NEXT 5. FOR

HANDS-ON EXERCISE 17-1

NOW TRY THIS ⟹ Type NEW **RETURN** and type the following program which uses IF/THEN and GOTO statements for control:

```
10   REM *** PRINT STARS ***
20   LET X = 1
30   IF X > 10 THEN 99
40   PRINT "*";
50   LET X = X + 1
60   GOTO 30
99   END
```

RUN the program to see the results. There should be ten stars printed on one line. Now shorten this program by using a FOR/NEXT statement for control. Type NEW **RETURN** and the following new program:

```
10   REM *** PRINT STARS ***
20   FOR I = 1 TO 10
30   PRINT "*";
40   NEXT I
99   END
```

RUN this program. You should get the same output as before, and it only took four lines instead of six! Producing shorter programs is one advantage of using FOR/NEXT loops.

Flowchart of FOR/NEXT Statements

Figure 17-3a shows a standard flowchart for FOR/NEXT loops. A shorthand symbol for the FOR/NEXT loop is shown in Figure 17-3b. This symbol conveniently shows a loop, because the initial, terminal, and step values are all in one symbol.

In Figure 17-3b, the 1 in "N = 1" is the initial value. The 5 in "Is N > 5?" is the terminal value, and the 1 in "N = N + 1" is the step value. The "N = N + 1" represents the NEXT statement where the loop variable is counted and then tested against the terminal value. When the terminal value is less than or equal to N, the arrow shows a return to the beginning of the loop, "N = N + 1".

Processing Steps

Let's review the steps that the computer follows when it meets a FOR statement:

1. It sets the loop variable to the initial value.

2. It tests to see if the value of the initial loop variable is greater than the terminal value. (This may occur the first time the FOR statement is executed.)

3. If the value of the initial loop variable is not greater than the terminal value, the statements in the loop are executed.

4. If the value of the initial loop variable is greater than the terminal value, control is given to the statement immediately following the NEXT statement.

When the NEXT statement is encountered by the computer, the computer:

1. Adds the step value (given in the FOR statement) to the value of the loop variable.

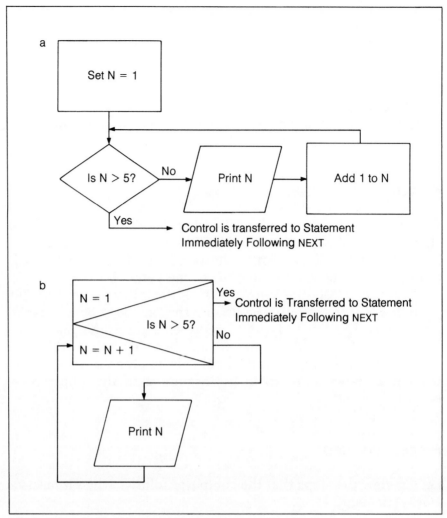

Figure 17-3. *Flowcharting FOR/NEXT Loops*

2. Compares the new value of the loop variable with the terminal value.

3. Gives control to the statement following the FOR statement if the value of the loop variable is not greater than the terminal value. Otherwise execution continues with the statement following the NEXT statement.

Rules for Using FOR/NEXT Statements

Certain rules govern the use of FOR/NEXT statements.

1. If no STEP value is given, the step is assumed to be +1. These two statements have the same meaning.

```
10  FOR A = 1 TO 10 STEP 1

10  FOR A = 1 TO 10
```

```
10   FOR I = 1 TO 4
20       READ N$, A
30       IF A < 10 THEN 50
40       PRINT N$
50   NEXT I
60   DATA "MARY KENNEDY",12,"TONYA SCHMIDT",5
70   DATA "DAVID SHORT",8,"TOM JONES",15
99   END

]RUN
MARY KENNEDY
TOM JONES
```

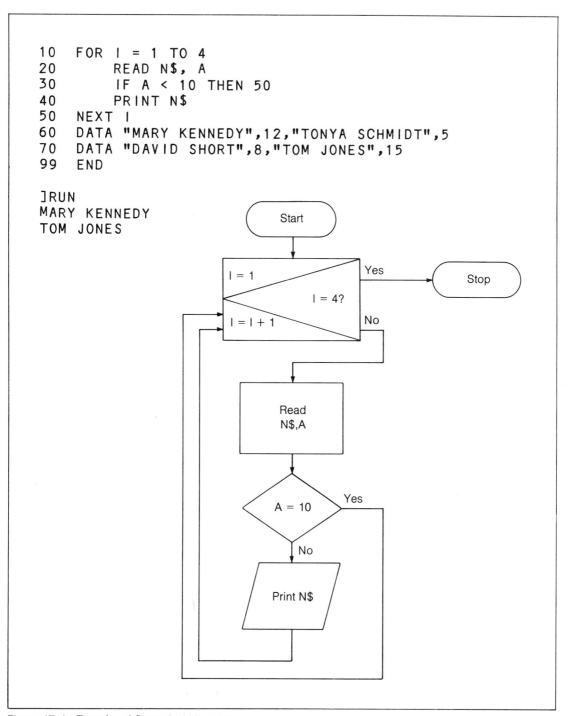

Figure 17-4. *Transfer of Control within a Loop*

2. The STEP value in a FOR statement should never be zero. The statement 50 FOR B = 1 to 20 STEP 0 would cause the loop variable to be the same after each execution of the loop. Then the loop would be run endlessly. This is known as an infinite loop.

3. You can send control from one statement to another within a loop. In Figure 17-4, an IF/THEN statement sends control to line 50 if A has a certain value. However, you cannot send control from within a loop directly to the FOR statement. If you want to continue the loop but bypass some other inner statement, give control to the NEXT statement.

4. The value of the loop variable should not be changed with a statement within the loop. The program below is invalid and will cause an infinite loop.

```
10    FOR X = 1 TO 10
20    LET X = X - 1
30    PRINT X
40    NEXT X
99    END
```

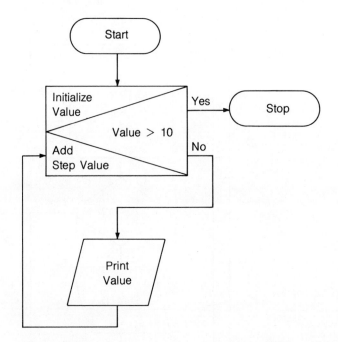

5. Each FOR statement must have a NEXT statement. The loop variable in the NEXT statement must be the same as that named in the FOR statement—FOR X...NEXT X, not FOR X...NEXT Y.

6. For easy-to-follow programming, a FOR/NEXT loop should have only one entry and one exit point. The entry point should be the first statement of the loop—the FOR statement. The exit should occur after the last statement of the loop—the NEXT statement.

7. There are times when it is desirable to use a negative step value. For example, Figure 17-5 illustrates a negative step value used to count backward from ten by twos.

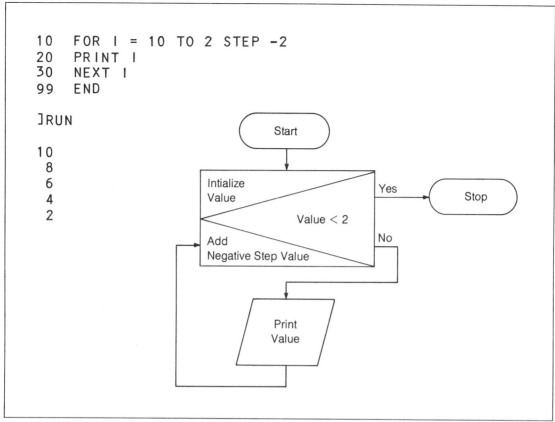

```
10   FOR I = 10 TO 2 STEP -2
20   PRINT I
30   NEXT I
99   END

]RUN

10
 8
 6
 4
 2
```

Figure 17-5. *Negative STEP Value*

The loop ends when the value of the loop variable, I, "exceeds" the specified terminal value, 2. With a negative step value, "exceeds" is used in a downward sense. The loop ends when I is smaller than the terminal value. The initial value of the loop variable should be greater than or equal to the terminal value when using a negative step value. For example,

Valid: FOR J = 10 TO 1 STEP -2
Invalid: FOR J = 1 TO 10 STEP -2

 LEARNING CHECK 17-2

1. The statements within a FOR/NEXT loop are executed if the value of the loop variable does/does not exceed the terminal value.

2. A step value of 0 will create a condition called a(n) _____.

3. TRUE FALSE The terminal value must be a numeric constant.

4. A FOR/NEXT loop should have _____ entry and exit point(s).

1. does not 2. infinite loop 3. FALSE 4. one

NOW TRY THIS ⇨ Type NEW [RETURN] and the following program segment:

```
10   REM *** ODD NUMBERS ***
20   FOR I = 1 TO 9 STEP 2
30   PRINT I
40   NEXT I
99   END
```

Now RUN the program. The odd numbers from 1 to 10 should be printed. If line 20 is changed to read:

```
20   FOR I = 9 TO 1 STEP -2
```

the numbers will appear from 10 to 1. Try making this change to see how it works.

Type NEW [RETURN] and a new program to print the even numbers between 1 and 10 as follows:

```
10   REM *** EVEN NUMBERS ***
20   FOR J = 2 TO 10 STEP 2
30   PRINT J
40   NEXT J
99   END
```

Now RUN the program. If you change line 20 to read:

```
20   FOR J = 10 TO 2 STEP -2
```

the numbers will appear from 10 to 1. Make this change and RUN the program.

Nested FOR/NEXT Loops

Nested loop FOR/NEXT loop inside another FOR/NEXT loop.

It is possible to have one FOR/NEXT loop located inside another FOR/NEXT loop. This is called a **nested loop** because one loop is completely nested within another. Imagine the baseball pitcher who is very sure he will strike out every batter in every inning! Each inning loop occurs within the larger loop of the game:

```
          ┌10   FOR INNING = 1 TO 9
           20       FOR BATTER = 1 TO 3 ┐
 outer     30         PRINT "STRIKE OUT" │ inner
 loop      40       NEXT BATTER ─────────┘ loop
           50   REM ***PITCHER'S TEAM BATS***
          └60   NEXT INNING
           99   END
```

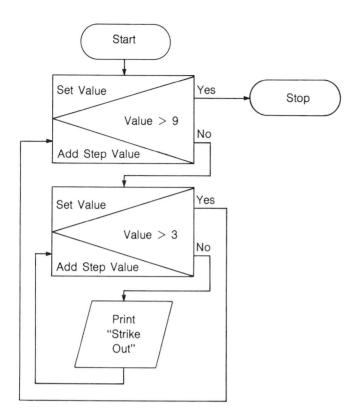

In the first inning, the inner loop (batter) will execute three times and the pitcher's team bats before control goes to the next inning. This inner loop will be repeated for nine innings—that is, the outer loop will execute nine times.

The inner loop is completely nested within the outer loop. Study the program below to see how the nested loops give the output shown.

```
        ┌10    FOR I = 1 TO 3
Outer   │20       FOR J = 1 TO 2┐  Inner
Loop    │30          PRINT I,J──┘  Loop
        │40       NEXT J
        └50    NEXT I
         99    END
```

Output
```
1,1
1,2
2,1
2,2
3,1
3,2
```

The outer loop will be executed three times, since I goes from 1 to 3. The inner loop will be run twice each time the outer loop is executed. Therefore, the inner loop will be run a total of six times (2 × 3).

I   J

First time through outer loop I = 1	{	1 1	1 2	First time through inner loop J = 1 Second time through inner loop J = 2
Second time through outer loop I = 2	{	2 2	1 2	Inner loop J = 1 Inner loop J = 2
Third time through outer loop I = 3	{	3 3	1 2	Inner loop J = 1 Inner loop J = 2

As many loops may be nested within one another as desired, but do not mix the FOR from one loop with the NEXT from another. Be sure one loop is totally inside the other. The nested loop below is invalid because the NEXT I statement of the outer loop is located inside the inner loop.

```
FOR I = 1 TO 10
    FOR J = 1 TO 5
        .
        .
        .
    NEXT I
NEXT J
```

Nested loops cannot be given the same loop variable:

```
FOR I = 1 TO 10
    FOR I = 1 TO 5
        .
        .
        .
    NEXT I
NEXT I
```

In this example, the value of the outer loop variable is changed every time the inner loop is executed. This breaks the rule for FOR/NEXT loops because the rule states that the value of the loop variable should not be changed by program statements within the loop.

Figure 17-6 shows a nested loop that draws rows of asterisks. The inner loop controls the number of columns to be printed, while the outer loop controls the number of rows to be printed.

The loop variable I (the rows) is first initialized to 1. Then execution of the inner loop begins. Line 30 tells the computer to print an asterisk. The semicolon instructs the computer to print the next output in the next column. So the next time the inner loop is executed, the asterisk will be printed on the same line immediately after the previous asterisk. When the inner loop has run five times, control will pass to line 50. This statement will not print anything but will instruct the computer to print the next

```
10    FOR I = 1 TO 5
20      FOR J = 1 TO 5
30        PRINT "*";
40      NEXT J
50      PRINT
60    NEXT I
99    END

]RUN

*****
*****
*****
*****
*****
```

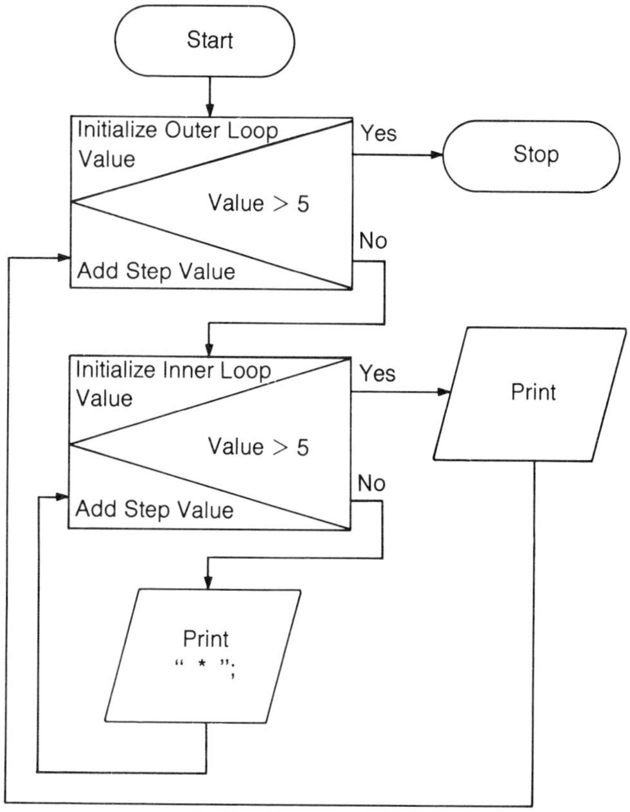

Figure 17-6. *Nested FOR/NEXT Loop*

output on the next line. After line 50 is executed, control returns to line 20. As long as I is less than or equal to 5, the inner loop will be repeated. Therefore, the outer loop controls the number of rows printed.

 LEARNING CHECK 17-3

1. A loop located within another loop is called a(n) _____.

2. The J loop in the following example will be executed _____ times.

```
10    FOR I = 1 TO 4
20       FOR J = 1 TO 2
30       PRINT I + J;
40       NEXT J
50    NEXT I
```

3. The output for the example in #2 above will be _____.

4. What is wrong with the following example?

```
10    FOR I = 1 TO 5
20       FOR J = 5 TO 1 STEP -1
30       PRINT I,J
40       NEXT I
50    NEXT J
```

5. The following example is a(n) valid/invalid nested loop.

```
10    FOR X = 3 TO 6
20       FOR X = 5 TO 10
30       PRINT X
40       NEXT X
50    NEXT X
```

HANDS-ON EXERCISE 17-3

NOW TRY THIS ⇨ Type NEW **RETURN** and the following program:

```
10    REM *** PRINTING SETS OF NUMBERS ***
20    FOR I = 1 TO 3
30       FOR J = 1 TO 2
40       PRINT I,J
50       NEXT J
60    NEXT I
99    END
```

RUN the program to get this output:

```
]RUN

1          1
1          2
2          1
2          2
3          1
3          2
```

Review the numbers listed to make sure you understand the FOR/NEXT looping process. Now type this new program to print colors:

```
10    REM *** PRINTING SETS OF COLORS ***
20    FOR I = 1 TO 3
30    PRINT "RED",
40       FOR J = 1 TO 2
50       PRINT "AND BLUE TOO"
60       NEXT J
70    NEXT I
99    END
```

If you understand the looping process, you should have an idea of the output before you run the program. After you have thought about the output and how it will look, RUN the program. You should get this output:

```
]RUN
RED                AND BLUE TOO
AND BLUE TOO
RED                AND BLUE TOO
AND BLUE TOO
RED                AND BLUE TOO
AND BLUE TOO
```

Were you right? If you were, you probably can explain nested FOR/NEXT loops. If you were wrong, make sure you study the process again.

COMPREHENSIVE PROGRAMMING PROBLEM

Mr. Sweetooth runs two donut shops in town. The donut shops sell donuts, sweet rolls, and coffee. Keeping track of monthly sales has become difficult since Mr. Sweetooth opened the second store. Now he would like to use a computer to do his monthly sales report. The programmer for Softsys, Inc. has offered to do Mr. Sweetooth's programming and has written a sample program. The program produces a report of how many dozens of donuts and sweet rolls each store sells as well as how many pounds of coffee they sell. The report also includes the total sales in dollars for the month.

The Eastside store sold 2,875 dozen donuts, 1,960 dozen sweet rolls, and 29 pounds of coffee during the month. The Westside store sold 2,650 dozen donuts, 1,230 dozen sweet rolls, and 35 pounds of coffee. Donuts sell for $2.40 a dozen, sweet rolls sell for $2.90 a dozen, and coffee sells for $.45 a cup, or about $15 per pound. Figure 17-7 shows the program for the report and the results.

The REM statements in lines 10 through 95 explain the purpose of the program and the variables used. A heading for the report is printed in lines 100 and 105.

The outer loop, which reads the name of the store and prints its heading, begins in line 130. The inner loop, beginning in line 180, reads each item name, the number sold, and its price

```
10   REM   *** THIS PROGRAM GENERATES A SALES REPORT ***
20   REM   *** FOR SWEETOOTH DONUT SHOP FOR ONE MONTH ***
30   REM   *** VARIABLES: ***
40   REM   *** S$ = STORE NAME ***
50   REM   *** I$ = ITEM NAME ***
60   REM   *** US = UNITS SOLD ***
70   REM   *** PR = PRICE PER UNIT ***
80   REM   *** TS = TOTAL SALES ***
90   REM   *** GT = GRAND TOTAL SALES ***
100  REM   *** PRINT HEADINGS FOR REPORT ***
110  PRINT "SWEETOOTH DONUT SHOPS"
120  PRINT "MONTHLY SALES REPORT"
130  PRINT
140  REM   *** READ SHOP ***
150  FOR I = 1 TO 2
160  READ S$
170  REM   *** PRINT HEADING FOR STORE ***
175  PRINT
180  PRINT S$;" STORE SALES REPORT"
190  PRINT
200  REM   *** READ ITEM,UNITS SOLD,PRICE PER UNIT ***
210  FOR J = 1 TO 3
220  READ I$,US,PR
230  REM   *** CALCULATE SALES ***
240  LET TS = US * PR
250  REM   *** PRINT RESULTS ***
260  PRINT I$,"$";TS
270  LET GT = GT + TS
280  NEXT J
290  NEXT I
300  REM   *** PRINT GRAND TOTAL ***
310  PRINT
320  PRINT "TOTAL SALES FOR THE MONTH ARE $";GT
330  DATA    WESTSIDE,DONUTS,2650,2.40
340  DATA    SWEET ROLLS,1230,2.90
350  DATA    COFFEE,35,15.00
360  DATA    EASTSIDE,DONUTS,2875,2.40
370  DATA    SWEET ROLLS,1960,2.90
380  DATA    COFFEE,29,15.00
999  END
```

```
]RUN
SWEETOOTH DONUT SHOPS
MONTHLY SALES REPORT




WESTSIDE STORE SALES REPORT

DONUTS          $6360
SWEET ROLLS     $3567
COFFEE          $525

EASTSIDE STORE SALES REPORT

DONUTS          $6900
SWEET ROLLS     $5684
COFFEE          $435

TOTAL SALES FOR THE MONTH ARE $23471
```

Figure 17-7. *Donut Shop Sales Program*

per unit. The loop then figures the sales dollars for the item and prints the results. Before the inner loop ends, it adds the total sales for each item to a grand total amount.

When all three items (donuts, sweet rolls, and coffee) have been read, the inner loop ends and control passes to the line following the NEXT J statement. This line, 250, is the NEXT I statement, which sends control back to the beginning of the outer loop. The entire process then repeats for the second store.

Finally, the total sales for all stores is printed in line 280. The report is finished and Mr. Sweetooth knows exactly how much sales were for donuts, sweet rolls, and coffee for each of his stores.

SUMMARY POINTS

- FOR and NEXT statements always appear together to create a loop. The FOR statement sets the loop variable, the terminal value, and the step value. The NEXT statement counts the loop variable, tests to see whether the value of the loop variable exceeds the terminal value, and transfers control to either the statement following the FOR statement or the statement following the NEXT statement.

- The processing steps of a FOR statement are: set initial value of the loop variable; test to see whether the value of the initial loop variable is greater than the terminal value; execute statements within the loop if the initial loop variable is not greater than the terminal value; and transfer control to the statement immediately following the NEXT statement if the value of the initial loop variable exceeds the terminal value.

- The processing steps of a NEXT statement are: add the step value to the value of the loop variable; test the value of the loop variable against the terminal value; and transfer control to the appropriate statement.

- A FOR/NEXT loop should have only one entry and one exit point.

- FOR/NEXT loops may be nested within one another. The nested loop must be totally contained within the outer loop and must use a different loop variable than the outer loop.

CHAPTER TEST

Vocabulary

Match the term from the numbered column on the left with the best description from the lettered column on the right.

1. Terminal value
   a. The value at which a loop variable starts.

2. Initial value
   b. A loop that is inside another loop.

3. Nested loop
   c. The statement that counts the loop variable and returns control to the beginning of the loop.

4. STEP value
   d. The value by which the loop variable is increased each time the loop is run.

5. NEXT statement

e. The statement that shows the number of times a loop should be executed.

6. FOR statement

f. The value at which a FOR/NEXT loop will stop executing.

Questions

1. The loop variable in a FOR/NEXT loop is set to a(n) _____.

    a. step value
    b. terminal value
    c. initial value

2. The step value is indicated in the _____ statement.

    a. FOR
    b. LOOP
    c. NEXT

3. The _____ statement marks the end of the loop.

    a. FOR
    b. LAST
    c. NEXT

4. The loop variable is counted in _____.

    a. the FOR statement
    b. a LET statement within the loop
    c. the NEXT statement

5. The initial, terminal, and step values may be _____.

    a. constants
    b. expressions
    c. both a and b

6. The value of the loop variable is tested against the _____ value.

    a. step
    b. terminal
    c. initial

7. The loop will no longer be executed once the value of the loop variable _____ the terminal value.

    a. is less than
    b. is greater than
    c. is equal to

8. When the loop ends, control is passed to _____.

    a. the NEXT statement
    b. the statement immediately following the NEXT statement
    c. a transfer line number stated in the FOR statement

9. If no step value is indicated in the FOR statement, the value is assumed to be _____.

    a. zero
    b. one
    c. an error

10. The step value can be

   a. positive

   b. negative

   c. both a and b

11. A step value of _____ is illegal.

   a. zero

   b. a negative value

   c. both a and b

12. A FOR/NEXT loop should have _____ entry and _____ exit point(s).

   a. one, one

   b. one, two

   c. two, one

13. A loop that is totally contained within another loop is called a(n) _____ loop.

   a. infinite

   b. nested

   c. outer

14. The outer loop of a nested loop will normally be executed more times than the inner loop.

   a. TRUE

   b. FALSE

Use the following program segment for questions 15 and 16.

```
10   FOR I = 1 TO 3
20      FOR J = 1 TO 5
30         PRINT J
40      NEXT J
50      PRINT I
60   NEXT I
```

15. How many times will the value of I be printed?

   a. 3

   b. 2

   c. 15

16. How many times will the value of J be printed?

   a. 4

   b. 5

   c. 15

17. Which of the statements is valid?

   a. FOR I = 1 TO 5 STEP 0

   b. FOR 2 = 10 TO 2 STEP −2

   c. FOR X = 10 TO 2 STEP −1

18. Which of the statements is valid? (Use A = 3 and B = 2)

   a. FOR J = 20 TO A STEP B

   b. FOR X = 10 TO B STEP 3

   c. FOR X = A TO A + B

19. Which of the statements is invalid? (Use D = 20)

    a. FOR X = 1 TO D STEP –3
    b. FOR X = 1 TO D – 5
    c. FOR X = 1 TO D STEP 30
    a. FOR X = 1 TO D STEP –3
    b. FOR X = 1 TO D – 5
    c. FOR X = 1 TO D STEP 3

20. The following program segment is:

    a. valid
    b. invalid

```
10    FOR X = 1 TO 5
20        FOR Y = 4 TO 1 STEP -1
30            PRINT Y
40        NEXT X
50        PRINT X
60    NEXT Y
```

PROGRAMMING PROBLEMS

1. Write a flowchart and a program to compute the average price of gasoline for a six-month period. The data is as follows:

Month	Price
Jan.	1.12
Feb.	1.20
Mar.	1.19
Apr.	1.14
May	1.19
June	1.21

Use a FOR/NEXT loop for the program and flowchart.

2. Write a program that will print the names of the players on a football team who gained more than 1,000 yards last season and the total yards gained by the *entire* team. Assume that this program will be run for several different teams. As a result, the number of players to be entered may change each time the program is run. Set up the FOR/NEXT loop to execute a variable number of times. The team statistics include the following data:

Player	Yards Gained
Bradshaw	200
Harris	1,495
Theisman	185
Dupree	1,596
Allen	1,980
Dorsett	1,000

The output should be formatted as follows:

PLAYERS GAINING OVER 1,000 YARDS

Player   **Yards Gained**

XXXXXX   XXXXX
XXXXXX   XXXXX

TOTAL YARDS GAINED THIS SEASON IS XXXXX.

Chapter **18**

Structuring with GOSUB

Learning Objectives

After reading this chapter, you should be able to:

1. Discuss the purpose and advantages of structured programming.
2. Explain how subroutines are used in programs.
3. Write a simple subroutine for a program using GOSUB, ON/GOSUB, RETURN, and STOP statements.

Introduction

High-level languages such as BASIC are very flexible. They also encourage programmers to write creative programs. But sometimes the logic behind a program gets lost in the programmer's creativity. For example, programs that have many branches can be very hard to follow, especially by persons other than the programmer.

Programmers can design programs that are easy to read, maintain, and change by using structured programming and subroutines. Both promote well-thought-out program logic and should be easy to follow and understand.

Structured Programming

Structured programming, developed in the mid 1960s, makes programs easier to maintain and change. Three of the four logic patterns are used for structured programming: simple sequence, selection, and loop.

By avoiding the branch logic pattern, structured programs are easier to understand and are more reliable. Also, the time a programmer spends writing programs can be reduced by following the rules of structured programming.

Structured programming involves three basic ideas: top-down design, module organization, and GOTO-less programming.

Structured programming A method of computer programming developed to make programs easier to maintain and change.

Top-Down Design

When using the top-down approach to design a program, a general solution to the problem is devised first. The solution is divided into major parts. Then each major task is broken into certain steps. Each step may need to be broken further into even more precise steps. In this manner, the programmer goes from the general to the specific, or from the top, down.

The use of this top-down approach helps to ensure the correctness of the overall logic of the program and therefore aids in producing reliable, logical programs.

Module Organization

Module A logical segment of a program that completes one function independently of other modules.

Because a large program is difficult to write, debug, and change, each major task of a program can be broken into specific steps. Each major task, or logical segment, is known as a **module**. It completes one function. Some of the specific tasks may also be broken into lower-level modules. The lowest level modules contain the greatest amount of detail.

A module should be independent of the other modules. It should be able to be tested for accuracy without considering the correctness of the other modules. With modules, testing and debugging the program are easier. The programs are also more reliable. If the program needs to be changed in the future, only the module related to the change must be modified, not the entire program.

Each module should have only one entry (beginning) and one exit (ending) point. Otherwise, the program will be very hard to understand, test, and debug. Use of the simple sequence, decision, and loop logic structures will help develop modules with one entry and one exit point.

GOTO-Less Programming

GOTO-less programming A structured programming method that avoids the branch structure (GOTO statement).

Because the branch structure (or GOTO statement) can produce programs that are hard to follow and understand, structured programming avoids GOTO statements. This is called **GOTO-less programming**. When the other three logic patterns are used properly, the use of the branch pattern can be reduced.

Some programming languages are better suited to structured programming than others. Standard BASIC is one language that does not lend itself to GOTO-less programming because it lacks some commands found in other languages. As a result, GOTO statements probably cannot be totally avoided in a complex BASIC program. However, using the loop and decision structures should reduce the number of GOTO statements in a program. With fewer GOTO statements, a program will be easier to understand, test, and debug.

 LEARNING CHECK 18-1

1. Which three logic patterns are used for structured programming?

2. Which structured programming approach calls for breaking the solution into parts and then breaking each part down further into specific steps?

3. In a structured program, modules should be _____ of each other.

Subroutines

One way to achieve structured programming is to use **sub-routines**. A subroutine is a sequence of statements, usually placed at the end of the main program. It performs a certain function and may be used in several different parts of the main program.

The GOSUB and RETURN statements will send control to the subroutine and then back to the main program after the subroutine has run.

Subroutine A set of statements placed outside the main lines of a program.

GOSUB

The **GOSUB statement** transfers control from the main program to a subroutine. The GOSUB format is:

    line# GOSUB line#

The line number following GOSUB names the first statement of the subroutine. GOSUB is similar to the unconditional GOTO statement. The difference is that the GOSUB statement makes the computer remember where to return after the subroutine has run.

The flowchart symbol for a subroutine is ☐ . It is placed in the main program flowchart where the subroutine is called for. Each subroutine should include a start, the input/output and processing steps, and a stop. The subroutine should have a descriptive name so the flowchart is easy to follow.

GOSUB statement Transfers control from the main program to a subroutine.

RETURN

The **RETURN statement** transfers control back to the main program after the subroutine is executed. RETURN follows this format:

    line# RETURN

No line number needs to follow RETURN, because the BASIC interpreter remembers to return to the statement immediately following the most recently run GOSUB statement.

RETURN statement Transfers control back to the main program after the subroutine has been run.

```
10   REM  *** THIS PROGRAM CONVERTS INCHES TO CENTIMETERS ***
20   INPUT "ENTER NUMBER OF MEASUREMENTS TO BE CHANGED ";M
30   PRINT
40   FOR L = 1 TO M
50   INPUT "ENTER NUMBER OF INCHES ";I
60   PRINT
70   GOSUB 200
80   PRINT "THERE ARE ";C;" CENTIMETERS IN ";I;" INCHES"
90   PRINT
100  NEXT L
110  STOP
200  REM  *** SUBROUTINE FOR CONVERSION ***
210  LET C = 2.54 * I
220  RETURN
999  END


]RUN
ENTER NUMBER OF MEASUREMENTS TO BE CHANGED 3

ENTER NUMBER OF INCHES 15

THERE ARE 38.1 CENTIMETERS IN 15 INCHES

ENTER NUMBER OF INCHES 7

THERE ARE 17.78 CENTIMETERS IN 7 INCHES

ENTER NUMBER OF INCHES 89

THERE ARE 226.06 CENTIMETERS IN 89 INCHES
```

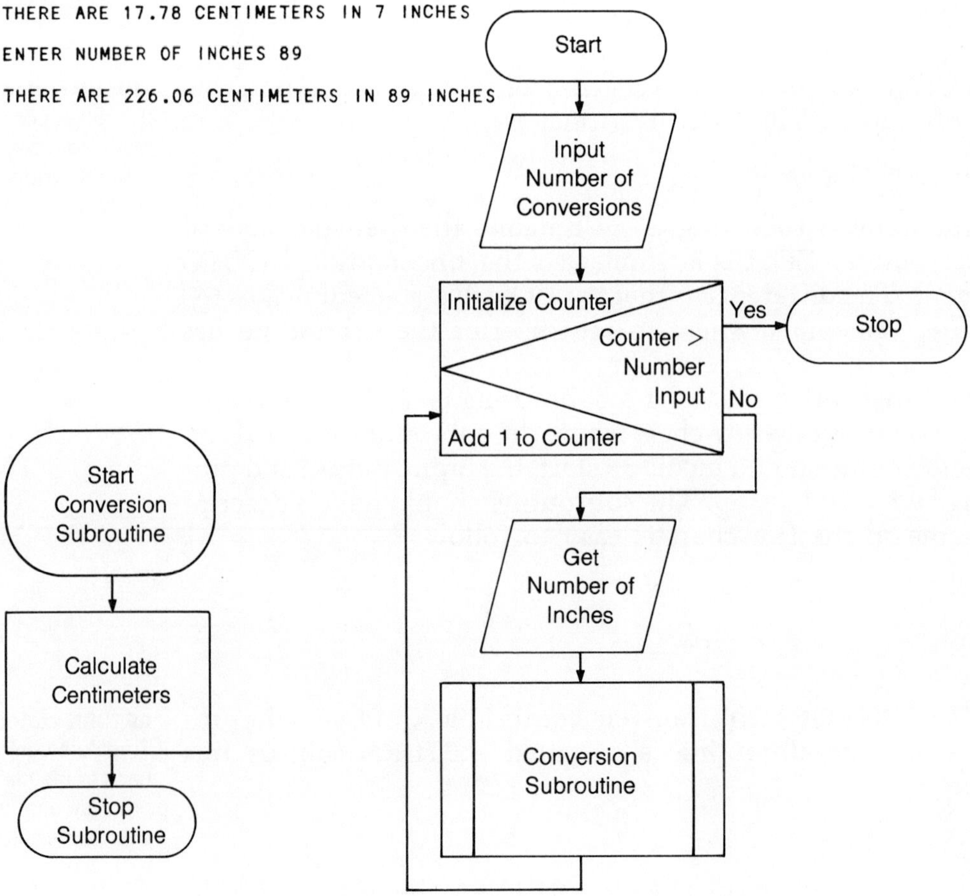

Figure 18-1. *Conversion Program using GOSUB.*

STOP

The **STOP statement** halts execution of the program. It is placed wherever a logical end to a program should occur. The general format of STOP is:

line# STOP

The STOP statement differs from the END statement in that STOP can appear as often as necessary in a program. However, the END statement can appear only once and must have the highest line number in the program. A good programming practice is to reserve the END statement for the very end of a program.

In a program with subroutines, the STOP statement is placed just before the start of the first subroutine. This stops the subroutine from being run when the computer comes to the logical end of the program.

Figure 18-1 uses a GOSUB statement in line 70 to branch to a subroutine. By using this GOSUB statement, line 210 does not have to be retyped each time inches are changed to centimeters. The RETURN statement in line 220 sends control back to the main program, to line 80. The STOP statement in line 110 makes sure the subroutine is not executed when the loop ends.

The beginning line number of the subroutine (line 200) is used in the GOSUB statement. The subroutine has been assigned a high line number so that it is easier to locate. Although subroutines may be placed anywhere in a program, they are usually placed at the end and given a large line number. This leaves room for statements to be added to the main program as needed. Also, it and makes reading and debugging the program easier.

ON/GOSUB

The ON/GOSUB statement allows conditional transfer to one of several subroutines. The general format of the ON/GOSUB statement is:

line# ON expression GOSUB line#1, line#2, line#3, ... line#n

The ON/GOSUB statement works in the same way as the ON/GOTO statement. The difference is that the transfer line numbers to which control is passed are the beginning line numbers of subroutines rather than lines in the main program. The line number to which control is passed depends on the evaluation of the expression. The arithmetic expression is always evaluated to an integer. For instance, if the expression evaluates to 2.8, the decimal is dropped so that the expression evaluates to 2. (Some systems round the number instead of dropping the fraction. In this case, 2.8 would evaluate to 3. Check your user's manual.)

```
100   REM      ***THIS PROGRAM WILL COMPUTE A STUDENT'S***
110   REM      ***LETTER GRADE FROM HIS/HER TOTAL POINTS AS***
120   REM      ***FOLLOWS:***
130   REM      ***
140   REM      ***500 - 599 = A***
150   REM      ***400 - 499 = B***
160   REM      ***300 - 399 = C***
170   REM      ***200 - 299 = D***
180   REM      ***0 - 199 = F***
190   REM      ***
200   REM      ***THE STUDENT'S NAME AND GRADE***
210   REM      ***WILL THEN BE PRINTED
220   REM      ***
230   REM      ***VARIABLES:***
240   REM      ***      N$ = NAME***
250   REM      ***      P  = POINTS***
260   REM      ***
270   PRINT "NAME","GRADE"
280   PRINT
290   READ N$,P
300   IF N$ = "XXXXX" THEN 999
310   ON P / 100 GOSUB 340,370,400,430,460
320   GOTO 290
330   STOP
340   REM      ***PRINT F***
350   PRINT N$," F"
360   RETURN
370   REM      ***PRINT D***
380   PRINT N$," D"
390   RETURN
400   REM      ***PRINT C***
410   PRINT N$," C"
420   RETURN
430   REM      ***PRINT B***
440   PRINT N$," B"
450   RETURN
460   REM      ***PRINT A***
470   PRINT N$," A"
480   RETURN
490   DATA   BOB JACKSON, 450
500   DATA   BRENDA MASTERS, 213
510   DATA   CHUCK VENTURA, 398
520   DATA   LYNN GREGOR, 580
530   DATA   XXXXX, 0
999   END
```

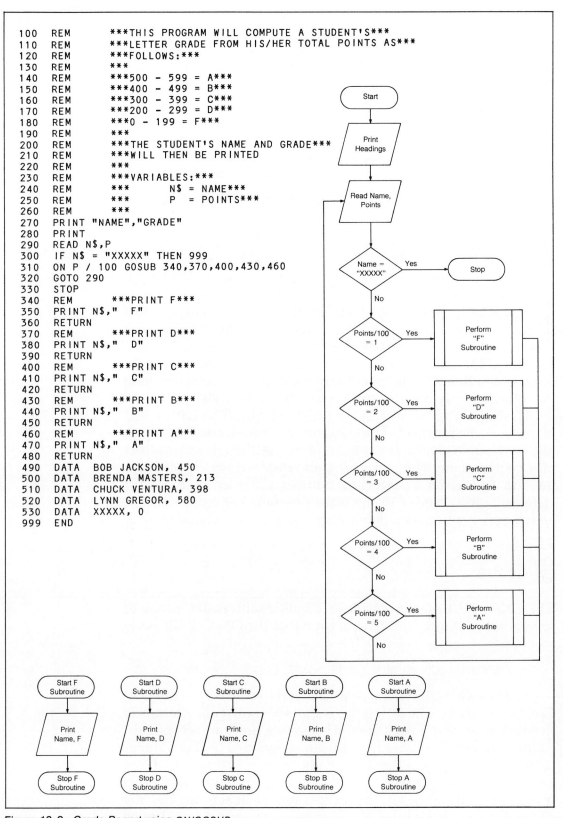

Figure 18-2. *Grade Report using ON/GOSUB.*

The general execution of ON/GOSUB proceeds as follows:

The general execution of ON/GOSUB proceeds as follows:

1. If the value of the expression is one, control is passed to the first subroutine line number listed.

2. If the value of the expression is two, control is passed to the second subroutine line number listed.

.

.

.

3. If the value of the expression is n, control is passed to the nth subroutine line number listed.

If the expression evaluates to zero or to a value greater than the number of transfer line numbers listed, execution of the program continues with the statement following the ON/GOSUB statement—no subroutine is run. If the value of the expression is less than zero or greater than 255, an error message will be produced.

The following example shows the operation of the ON/GOSUB statement:

```
40   ON X / 10 GOSUB 200,300,400
```

Computer execution is as follows:

If X/10 = 1, control is passed to the subroutine at line 200.
If X/10 = 2, control is passed to the subroutine at line 300.
If X/10 = 3, control is passed to the subroutine at line 400.

The last statement in each of these subroutines should be RETURN. When the computer executes the RETURN statement, control is passed back to the line immediately following the last ON/GOSUB statement executed.

The ON/GOSUB statement is shown in Figure 18-2. In this example, a student's letter grade is figured by dividing the student's total points by 100. The proper subroutine is then followed to print the student's name and letter grade. The RETURN statement in each subroutine passes control to line 290, the READ statement. The loop is repeated until the trailer value is read. Then the END statement is run.

 LEARNING CHECK 18-2

1. A set of statements that performs a certain function and may be used in several parts of the main program is a(n) _____.

2. The statement that will transfer control from the main program to a subroutine is the

_____.

3. The RETURN statement will transfer control from a subroutine to the statement _____ the most recently executed GOSUB statement.

4. The ON/GOSUB statement allows what type of transfer to subroutines?

HANDS-ON EXERCISE 18-1

NOW TRY THIS ⟹ Type NEW `RETURN` and the following main program and subroutine:

```
10   REM  *** SQUARES AND SQUARE ROOTS ***
20   LET N = 9
30   FOR I = 1 TO 2
40   GOSUB 200
50   PRINT "THE SQUARE OF ";N;" IS ";SQ
60   PRINT "THE SQUARE ROOT OF ";N;" IS ";SR
70   LET N = 4
80   NEXT I
90   STOP
200   REM  *** SUBROUTINE ***
210   LET SQ = N * N
220   LET SR = N ^ (1 / 2)
230   RETURN
999   END
```

```
┌─────────────────────────────────────────┐
│ MICROCOMPUTER DIFFERENCES                 │
│ IBM PC: No differences                    │
│ TRS-80: No differences                    │
│ Commodore 64: Line 220 should be          │
│ LET SR = N↑ (1/2)                         │
└─────────────────────────────────────────┘
```

RUN the program. The output should be as follows:

```
]RUN
THE SQUARE OF 9 IS 81
THE SQUARE ROOT OF 9 IS 3
THE SQUARE OF 4 IS 16
THE SQUARE ROOT OF 4 IS 2
```

Now change the subroutine to find the product N * 2 and to calculate the quotient N/2. The program should be:

```
10   REM  *** MULTIPLY AND DIVIDE BY 2 ***
20   LET N = 9
30   FOR I = 1 TO 2
```

```
40    GOSUB 200
50    PRINT N;" TIMES 2 IS ";PR
60    PRINT N;" DIVIDED BY 2 IS ";DI
70    LET N = 4
80    NEXT I
90    STOP
200   REM  *** SUBROUTINE ***
210   LET PR = N * 2
220   LET DI = N / 2
230   RETURN
999   END
```

RUN the program. The output should be:

```
]RUN
9 TIMES 2 IS 18
9 DIVIDED BY 2 IS 4.5
4 TIMES 2 IS 8
4 DIVIDED BY 2 IS 2
```

COMPREHENSIVE PROGRAMMING PROBLEM

The students at MacArthur Junior High School can choose two elective classes for the Fall term. One elective must be chosen from a group of three offered in the morning. The second elective must be one language chosen from a group of three offered in the afternoon.

The principal, Ms. Douglas, would like to have a program the students can use to choose their elective classes. The program should give the student a menu of morning elective classes and a menu of afternoon elective classes. A message telling the student to choose the number of the class he or she would like should also appear on the screen.

After the student picks the class, the program should print the name of the class, the teacher's name, the room number, and the meeting time. In this way, the principal's secretary will not be bothered by students asking who their teachers are or where and when the classes meet.

The classes for the Fall term are listed below with the teacher's name, room number, and class time.

Morning Electives

Class	Teacher	Room	Time
Art	Mr. Angelo	201	8:30
Computer Science	Mr. Rabb	220	9:30
Typing	Mrs. Phelps	142	9:30

```
10    REM   ***THIS PROGRAM WILL PRINT THE ROOM NUMBER***
20    REM   ***TIME, AND TEACHER FOR CLASS ELECTIVES***
30    REM   ***AT MACARTHUR JR. HIGH SCHOOL***
40    REM
45    PRINT "******************************************"
50    PRINT " ","MORNING ELECTIVES"
60    PRINT
70    PRINT "1.      ART"
80    PRINT "2.      COMPUTER SCIENCE"
90    PRINT "3.      TYPING"
95    PRINT "******************************************"
100   PRINT "PLEASE CHOOSE THE NUMBER FOR THE ONE"
110   PRINT "CLASS ELECTIVE YOU WOULD LIKE"
115   PRINT
120   INPUT X
130   IF X < 1 THEN 50
140   IF X > 3 THEN 50
150   ON X GOSUB 400,430,460
155   PRINT "******************************************"
160   PRINT " ","AFTERNOON ELECTIVES"
170   PRINT
180   PRINT "1.      FRENCH"
190   PRINT "2.      SPANISH"
200   PRINT "3.      GERMAN"
205   PRINT "******************************************"
210   PRINT "PLEASE CHOOSE THE NUMBER FOR THE ONE"
220   PRINT "CLASS ELECTIVE YOU WOULD LIKE"
225   PRINT
230   INPUT Y
240   IF Y < 1 THEN 160
250   IF Y > 3 THEN 160
260   ON Y GOSUB 500,530,560
390   STOP
400   REM   ***SUBROUTINE FOR ART CLASS***
410   PRINT "ART    MR. ANGELO    ROOM 201    8:30"
415   PRINT
420   RETURN
430   REM   ***SUBROUTINE FOR COMPUTER SCIENCE CLASS***
440   PRINT "COMPUTER SCIENCE    MR. RABB    ROOM 220    9:30"
445   PRINT
450   RETURN
460   REM   ***SUBROUTINE FOR TYPING CLASS***
470   PRINT "TYPING    MRS. PHELPS    ROOM 142    9:30"
475   PRINT
480   RETURN
500   REM   ***SUBROUTINE FOR FRENCH CLASS***
510   PRINT "FRENCH    MR.TRUDEAU    ROOM 212    12:30"
515   PRINT
520   RETURN
530   REM   ***SUBROUTINE FOR SPANISH CLASS***
540   PRINT "SPANISH    MS. GARCIA    ROOM 201    12:30"
545   PRINT
550   RETURN
560   REM   ***SUBROUTINE FOR GERMAN CLASS***
570   PRINT "GERMAN    MS. BRAUN    ROOM 222    1:30"
575   PRINT
580   RETURN
999   END
```

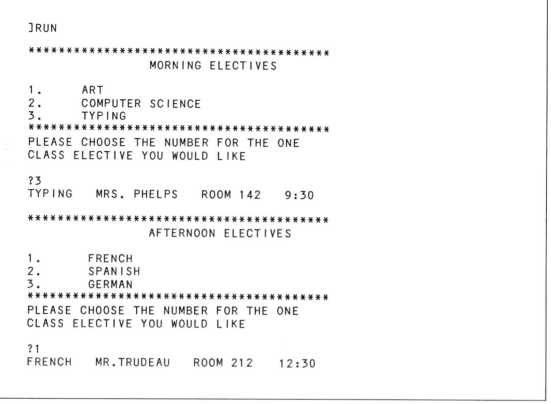

```
]RUN

*****************************************
                MORNING ELECTIVES

1.       ART
2.       COMPUTER SCIENCE
3.       TYPING
*****************************************
PLEASE CHOOSE THE NUMBER FOR THE ONE
CLASS ELECTIVE YOU WOULD LIKE

?3
TYPING    MRS. PHELPS    ROOM 142    9:30

*****************************************
                AFTERNOON ELECTIVES

1.       FRENCH
2.       SPANISH
3.       GERMAN
*****************************************
PLEASE CHOOSE THE NUMBER FOR THE ONE
CLASS ELECTIVE YOU WOULD LIKE

?1
FRENCH    MR.TRUDEAU    ROOM 212    12:30
```

Figure 18-3. *Class Electives Program*

Afternoon Electives

Class	Teacher	Room	Time
French	Mr. Trudeau	212	12:30
Spanish	Ms. Garcia	201	12:30
German	Ms. Braun	222	1:30

The program in Figure 18-3 shows the solution to Ms. Douglas' request. It uses subroutines to print the information for each class. Since the student can choose one class from each menu, the ON/GOSUB statement is an easy way to direct program control to the right subroutine.

The REM statements in lines 10 to 30 describe what the program will do. The menu for the morning electives is printed in lines 45 to 95. Then the message asking the student to select one class is printed in lines 100 and 110.

The IF/THEN statements in lines 130 and 140 test the number entered by the student to make sure it is one of the choices (1, 2, or 3). If the number is less than 1 or greater than 3, control goes back to line 50 and the menu is printed again.

If the number is 1, 2, or 3, the ON/GOSUB statement in line 150 sends control to the right subroutine. For example, if the number is 2, control passes to the second line number—430. The subroutine beginning in line 430 prints the information for computer science class: the teacher's name, Mr. Rabb; the meeting place, room 220; and the time, 9:30. A blank line is printed to separate the information from the next menu. The RETURN statement in line 450 sends control back to the statement immediately following the ON/GOSUB statement, line 155.

Lines 155 to 260 repeat the same steps for the afternoon electives. The menu and prompt are printed, the number is tested, and the ON/GOSUB statement sends control to the right subroutine. The STOP statement in line 390 prevents the subroutines from being run at the logical end of the program.

SUMMARY POINTS

- The logic patterns used in structured programming are simple sequence, selection, and loop.
- The advantages of structured programming are that programs are easier to understand, are more reliable, and save programmer writing time.
- The three basic concepts of structured programming are top-down design; module organization; and GOTO-less programming.
- The top-down approach calls for dividing a solution to a problem into major parts. Then each part is broken down further into specific steps.
- Module organization breaks a program into major tasks, called modules. Each module completes one function and is independent of the other modules.
- Each module should have only one entry and one exit point.
- GOTO-less programming avoids the branch pattern (GOTO statements) and makes programs easier to understand, test, and debug.
- Subroutines can be created using the GOSUB, RETURN, and STOP statements. The GOSUB statement transfers control to the subroutine. The RETURN statement transfers control back to the main program. The STOP statement halts execution of the program.

CHAPTER TEST

Vocabulary

Match the term from the numbered column with a description from the lettered column that best fits the term.

1. Structured programming

   a. A set of statements placed outside the main lines of a program.

2. RETURN statement

   b. A structured programming method that avoids the branch logic pattern.

3. Module

   c. Statement that transfers control from the main program to a subroutine.

4. GOTO-less programming

   d. Statement that halts execution of a program.

5. Subroutine

   e. A logical segment of a program that completes one function.

6. GOSUB statement   **f.** A method of structured programming in which the solution to a problem is designed from the general to the specific.

7. STOP statement   **g.** Statement that transfers control back to the main program after a subroutine has been executed.

8. Top-down design   **h.** A method of computer programming developed to make programs easier to maintain and change.

Questions

1. Structured programming and subroutines do not promote _____.
- **a.** programs that are easy to follow and understand
- **b.** well-thought out program logic
- **c.** the use of branches in program development

2. The logic patterns used in structured programming are _____.
- **a.** selection, simple sequence, and branch
- **b.** loop, simple sequence, and selection
- **c.** simple sequence, loop, and branch

3. The structured programming approach that allows the programmer to go from the general solution to more specific steps is _____.
- **a.** module organization
- **b.** top-down approach
- **c.** GOTO-less programming

4. The idea behind module organization is to develop programs so that _____.
- **a.** each module is dependent upon other modules
- **b.** each module completes many functions, thus having programs with few modules
- **c.** each module is independent of other modules so changes are easily made

5. Using the branch structure can make program logic _____.
- **a.** hard to follow
- **b.** easy to debug
- **c.** easy to follow

6. The BASIC programming language easily lends itself to GOTO-less programming.
- **a.** TRUE
- **b.** FALSE

7. The correct pair of commands to execute a subroutine is which of the following?
- **a.** GOTO and RETURN
- **b.** GOSUB and RETURN
- **c.** GOSUB and STOP

8. In the programming segment that follows, the RETURN statement returns control to which line of the main program?

```
110   GOSUB 300
120   INPUT N$,T1
      .
      .
      .
300   REM  ***SUBROUTINE FOR PRINTING MESSAGE***
310   PRINT
320   PRINT "YOU'VE PASSED THE TEST! CONGRATULATIONS!"
330   RETURN
```

a. line 110
b. line 120
c. line 300

9. The GOSUB statement is similar to the _____ statement.

a. ON/GOTO
b. conditional GOTO
c. unconditional GOTO

10. The ON/GOSUB statement is similar to the _____ statement.

a. ON/GOTO
b. GOSUB
c. unconditional GOTO

Use the following program segments for Questions 11 to 14. Assume that the computer system drops digits to the right of the decimal point when evaluating arithmetic expressions.

```
30    INPUT "NUMBER OF REVIEW QUESTIONS ";X
40    INPUT "NUMBER YOU ANSWERED CORRECTLY";Z
45    LET S = X/Z
50    IF S > 3 THEN  LET S = 3
60    ON S GOSUB 200,230,260
70    IF X < Z THEN 30
190   STOP
200   REM  ***SUBROUTINE--READY FOR TEST***
210   PRINT "YOU ARE READY FOR THE TEST."
220   RETURN
230   REM  ***SUBROUTINE--NOT READY FOR THE TEST***
240   PRINT "STUDY MATERIAL CAREFULLY BEFORE TAKING TEST."
250   RETURN
260   REM  ***SUBROUTINE--DO REVIEW QUESTIONS AGAIN***
270   PRINT "READ MATERIAL AND ANSWER REVIEW QUESTIONS AGAIN."
280   RETURN
```

11. Let $X = 12$ and $Z = 10$. To which line will control be passed when line 60 is executed?

a. line 70
b. line 200
c. line 230

12. Let $X = 30$ and $Z = 15$. To which line will control be passed when line 60 is executed?

a. line 200
b. line 230
c. line 260

13. Let $X = 10$ and $Z = 12$. To which line will control be passed when line 60 is executed?

a. line 70
b. line 190
c. line 200

14. To which line will control be passed after the subroutine starting in line 260 is executed?

a. line 50
b. line 60
c. line 70

15. The STOP statement is used to _____.

   a. signal the end of a subroutine

   b. send control back to the statement following the GOSUB statement

   c. prevent a subroutine from being run when the computer comes to the logical end of the program

---

PROGRAMMING PROBLEMS

1. Write a program that will give one of the eighth grade teachers, Mr. Jackson, a menu of the homework he has assigned for Monday. His students should be able to use the program to ask for the homework assignments for the classes they are in. Use the ON/GOSUB statement to print out the correct assignment after a class has been selected. Mr. Jackson's homework assignments are listed below.

Subject	Assignment
History	Read pp. 135-150. Review Questions 5-10.
Geography	Read chap. 4, chap. 4 Review Questions.
Science	Read pp. 65-86. Lab project #6.
Algebra	Read pp. 102-111. Problems 8-14.

2. Write a program that will input a request to add, subtract, multiply, or divide two numbers using subroutines. The operations should be listed in a menu. After the operation is chosen, the program should ask for the two numbers. Then the appropriate subroutine should do the figuring needed. Since a menu-type input is needed, use the ON/GOSUB statement.

RESERVED WORDS

Apple II Plus, Apple IIe, and Apple IIc

ABS	FOR	LEN	POS	SQR
AND	FRE	LET	PRINT	SPC(
ASC	GET	LIST	PR#	STEP
AT	GOSUB	LOG	READ	STOP
ATN	GOTO	LOMEN:	RECALL	STORE
CALL	GR	LOAD	REM	STR$
CHR$	HCOLOR=	MID$	RESUME	TAN
CLEAR	HGR	NEW	RESTORE	TO
COLOR	HGR2	NEXT	RETURN	TRACE
CONT	HIMEM:	NORMAL	RIGHT$	THEN
COS	HLIN	NOT	RND	TEXT
DATA	HOME	NOTRACE	ROT=	TAB(
DEF	HPLOT	ON	RUN	USR
DEL	HTAB	ONERR	SAVE	VAL
DIM	IF	OR	SCALE=	VLIN
DRAW	IN#	PEEK	SGN	VTAB
END	INPUT	POL	SCRN(	WAIT
EXP	INT	PLOT	SHLOAD	XDRAW
FLASH	INVERSE	POKE	SIN	
FN	LEFT$	POP	SPEED=	

Note: (= parentheses.
Note: The above reserved words are in addition to the Applesoft reserved words that are included in the text.

Commodore 64

ABS	EXP	LIST	PRINT#	STEP
AND	FOR	LOAD	READ	STOP
ASC	FRE	LOG	REM	STR$
ATN	GET	MID$	RESTORE	TAB(
CHR$	GET#	NEW	RETURN	TAN
CLOSE	GOSUB	NEXT	RIGHT$	THEN
CLR	GOTO	NOT	RND	TIME
CMD	IF	ON	RUN	TIME$
CONT	INPUT	OPEN	SAVE	TO
COS	INPUT#	OR	SGN	USR
DATA	INT	PEEK	SIN	VAL
DEF	LEFT$	POKE	SPC(	VERIFY
DIM	LEN	POS	SQR	WAIT
END	LET	PRINT	STATUS	

IBM PC

ABS	CVI	FOR	LOAD	ON KEY	REM	STRIG
ASC	CVD	FRE	LOC	ON PEN	RENUM	STRING$
ATN	CVS	GET	LOCATE	ON PLAY	RESET	SWAP
AUTO	DATA	GOSUB	LOG	ON STRIG	RESTORE	SYSTEM
BEEP	DATE$	GOTO	LPOS	ON TIMER	RESUME	TAB
CALL	DEF FN	HEX$	LPRINT	OPEN	RETURN	TAN
CDBL	DEF SEG	IF	LSET	OPTION BASE	RIGHT$	TIME$
CHAIN	DEF USR	INKEY$	MERGE	OUT	RMDIR	TIMER
CHR$	DELETE	INP	MID$	PAINT	RND	TRON
CHDIR	DIM	INPUT	MKDIR	PEEK	RSET	TROFF
CINT	DRAW	INPUT#	MKD$	PEN	RUN	USR
CIRCLE	EDIT	INPUT$	MKI$	PLAY	SAVE	VAL
CLEAR	END	INSTR	MKS$	PMAP	SCREEN	VARPTR
CLOSE	EOF	INT	MOTOR	POINT	SGN	VARPTR$
CLS	ERASE	KEY	NAME	POKE	SIN	VIEW
COLOR	ERR	KILL	NEW	POS	SOUND	WAIT
COM	ERL	LEFT$	NEXT	PRINT	SPACE$	WHILE
COMMON	ERROR	LEN	OCT$	PRINT#	SPC	WEND
CONT	EXP	LET	ON COM	PSET	SQR	WIDTH
COS	FIELD	LINE	ON ERROR	PUT	STICK	WINDOW
CSNG	FILES	LIST	ON-GOSUB	RANDOMIZE	STOP	WRITE
CSRLIN	FIX	LLIST	ON-GOTO	READ	STR$	WRITE#

TRS-80

ABS	DATA	EXP	LET	NEXT	RIGHT$	THEN
AND	DATE$	FIELD	LINE	NOT	RND	TIME$
ASC	DEF	FIX	LIST	OCT$	ROW	TO
ATN	DEFDBL	FN	LLIST	ON	RSET	TROFF
AUTO	DEFINT	FRE	LOAD	OPTION	RUN	TRON
CALL	DEFSNG	GET	LOC	OR	SAVE	USING
CDBL	DEFSTR	GOSUB	LOF	OUT	SGN	USR
CHAIN	DELETE	GOTO	LPOS	PEEK	SIN	VAL
CHR$	DIM	HEX$	LPRINT	POKE	SOUND	VARPTR
CLEAR	EDIT	IF	LSET	POS	SPACE$	WAIT
CLOSE	ELSE	IMP	MEM	PRINT	SPC	WEND
CLS	END	INKEY$	MERGE	PUT	SQR	WHILE
COMMON	EOF	INP	MID$	RANDOM	STEP	WRITE
CONT	EQV	INPUT	MKD$	READ	STOP	XOR
COS	ERASE	INSTR	MKI$	REM	STRING$	
CSNG	ERL	INT	MKS$	RENUM	STR$	
CUD	ERR	KILL	MOD	RESTORE	SYSTEM	
CVI	ERROR	LEFT$	NAME	RESUME	TAB	
CVS	ERRS$	LEN	NEW	RETURN	TAN	

KEYBOARDING

SECTION I   KEYBOARDING FUNDAMENTALS

Lesson 1   **Introduction to Keyboarding**

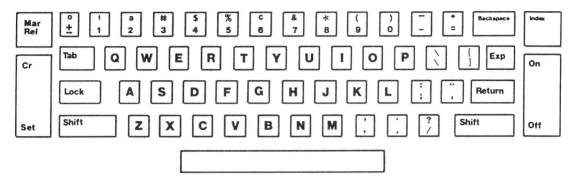

Why Learn Keyboarding Skills?

Keyboarding is an important job skill. Computers are used in all phases of the business world. Many jobs require that workers have typing skills in order to use computers.

Unlike typewriting, **keyboarding** focuses on working skills instead of those used for formatting.

Tips For Getting Ready

It is important to have good typing posture. Below are some general guidelines to follow:

1. Sit straight and lean slightly forward; feet should be apart and flat on the floor.

2. Center your body in front of the keyboard.

3. Relax your elbows and rest your fingers on the middle row of letter keys. Do *not* rest your wrists on the keyboard.

Keyboarding Overview

The most common keyboard layout is called the QWERTY layout. It gets its name from the six keys on the left-hand side of the first row of letter keys (see the highlighted area on the diagram on page A-4). This

standard **alphanumeric** (letters and numbers) keyboard is shown below. Not all computer keyboards are exactly the same. Note in the diagram that some of the keys are shaded. The characters or functions on these shaded keys may vary from keyboard to keyboard. Section II of this appendix shows these differences for six popular microcomputers: the Apple II Plus, Apple IIe, Commodore 64, IBM PC, and TRS-80 Models III and 4.

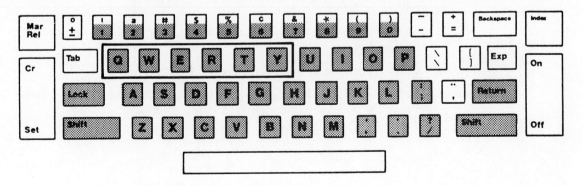

Proper keyboarding skills are necessary for you to work quickly and accurately. The following diagram shows the keys controlled by each finger. Each time new keys are introduced, this finger numbering system will be used to illustrate correct finger placement.

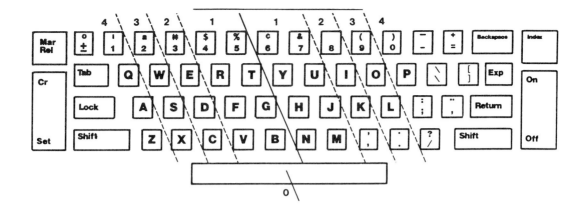

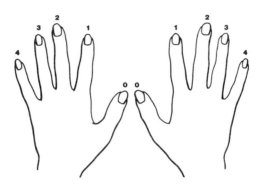

Lesson 2　　　**Getting Started**

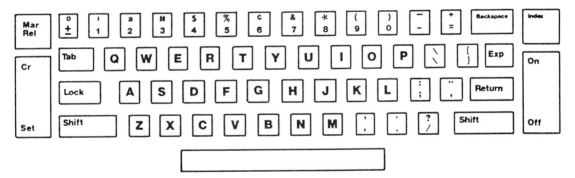

Introduction

To do the typing drills in this appendix, you will need to use a word-processing software package, such as the one that came with this book. The instructions with the software tell you how to use it.

New Keys

Before you begin typing, you will want to learn some basic keys—the space bar, the return key, and the shift and shift lock keys. The following diagram shows you the position of these keys.

The **space bar** is controlled by the right thumb. Rest your thumb on the space bar. When you press the space bar once, the cursor moves one space to the right. With some space bars you can move quickly across the screen by holding the space bar down. This is called repeating. Does your space bar repeat? The space bar is used to space words. Leave one space between words (unless you are typing columns or creating a design) and one space after a comma or a semicolon. Leave two spaces following a period, a question mark, an exlamation point, or a colon.

This example shows how many spaces come after a comma, a period, or a semicolon; these spaces all differ. Do you understand? Good! Continue.

The **return key** advances your work to the next line. It is on the right side of the keyboard. Your little finger controls this key (see the diagram above). Many return keys have a repeat feature.

The return key also allows you to space between lines of text. The return key can be pressed once to single space, twice to double space, and three times to triple space. The following examples show the difference among single-spaced, double-spaced, and triple-spaced text.

EX. 1: This is an example of single spacing. Single spacing is usually used for letters.

EX. 2: This is an example of double spacing. Double spacing is commonly used for manuscripts and reports.

EX 3: This is an example of triple spacing. Triple spacing is not often used. Sometimes you may use it between headings in a report.

For classroom drills, use double spacing unless you are told to do otherwise. Your teacher can tell you how to get double-spaced output on your computer.

Many computers have a wraparound feature. This means that as you reach the right-hand margin while typing, the next word is automatically placed at the beginning of the next line. When you keyboard on a computer, the return key will probably be used only to start typing on a new line. An example of this is starting a new paragraph. You will use the return key in the typing drills in this appendix.

On most machines, lowercase letters appear when you press a key. However, most computer programs use capital letters. To capitalize alphabetic characters, or to type special characters (*, $, @, and so on) on the top half of the numeric and other special character keys, use the **shift key**. The shift keys are in the bottom corners of the keyboard (see previous diagram). Your little fingers control these keys. Use the left shift when you want an uppercase character that is typed by your right hand. Use the right shift for characters typed with your left hand. To use the shift key, press it while you type the character to be capitalized. For example, hold the shift key and type the letter *a* for capital *A*. To type a *$*, press and hold the shift key, press the *4*, and then release the shift key.

If you have several uppercase letters in a row to type, press the **shift lock key**—located above the left-side shift key—until it clicks. This will allow you to type in uppercase characters. To change back to lowercase characters, press either shift key.

Many computer keyboards have a **caps** or a **caps lock key** rather than a shift lock key. However, this key works *only* with letters. To type special characters, the shift key must still be used. See Section II of this appendix for the location of the caps lock key for your specific computer. To change back to lowercase characters, press CAPS or CAPS LOCK again.

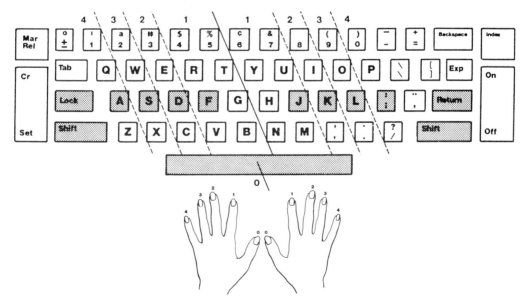

Home Row Key Finger Placement

Home Row Keys

Now you are ready to begin typing. The A, S, D, F, J, K, L, and ; keys are known as the **home row keys**. Your fingers should rest on these keys. When you begin typing other letters in later lessons, it is important to keep at least one finger from each hand on its home row key. If you move your entire hand from the home row, you risk losing your place on the keyboard and making mistakes.

The diagram on page A-7 shows the correct finger placement for the space bar, return key, shift key, shift lock key, and home row keys.

NOW TRY THIS ⇨ Practice the new keys by typing the lines listed under Home Row Key Drills. You will need to press ⌷RETURN⌷ after each line.

HOME ROW KEY
DRILLS

Warm-up Exercises

A	fff fff ddd ddd sss sss aaa aaa fds
S	aaa aaa sss sss ddd ddd fff fff asd
D	fdsa fdsa asdf asdf fdsa asdf af sd
	dfsa afsd dfsa afsd sdaf dsfa as df
F	ff dd ss aa aa ss dd ff ad add fads

Building Words

s sa sad sas d dad dads a sad dad a

a as a fad a sad ad a sad dad a fad

dad fads a as add sad ad fad dad as

Warm-up Exercises

J	jjj jjj kkk kkk lll lll ;;; ;;; jkl
K	;;; ;;; lll lll kkk kkk jjj jjj ;lk
L	jkl; jkl; ;lkj ;lkj j;kl lk;j lk j;
	;lkj ;lkj jkl; jkl; lk;j lk;j j; kl
:;	asdf jkl; af sk dl f; ;f ld ks jfks

Building Words

jkl; ;lkj a lass asks dad; a fad ad

as ask asks all fall falls fad lass

ask a dad a lad falls a fall ad add

New Keys: G, H

You will also learn the other two keys in the middle row of the keyboard—G and H. In the diagram below, notice that *G* uses the left index finger and *H* uses the right index finger.

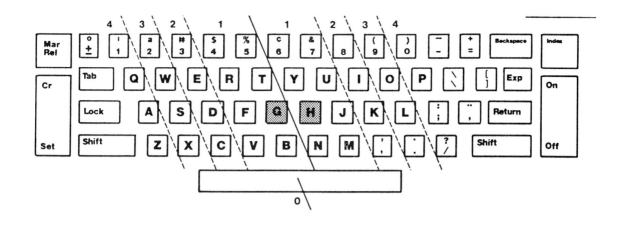

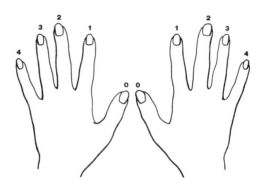

NOW TRY THIS ⇨ Practice the new keys by typing the lines under New Key Drills. Remember to press RETURN after each line.

NEW KEY DRILLS G **Warm-up Exercises**
H ff gg ff gg gg ff gg ff fgf gfg fgf
fg gf gas gal lag sag as a gal gags
jj hh hh jj jj hh jj hh jhj hjh jhj
jh hj has hash halls shall had dash

Building Words
lash shag sash flags gald flask gal
a gal has a flag; a lass shall dash

Ask your teacher for more practice drills using the home row keys.

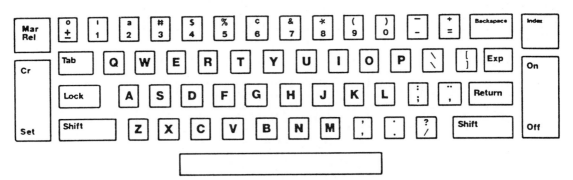

New Keys: Q, W, E, R, T

The first group of reaches stresses the use of the left hand. Remember, when you reach for a key, keep your other fingers on the home row keys. The following diagram shows the correct finger control for typing the letters Q, W, E, R, and T.

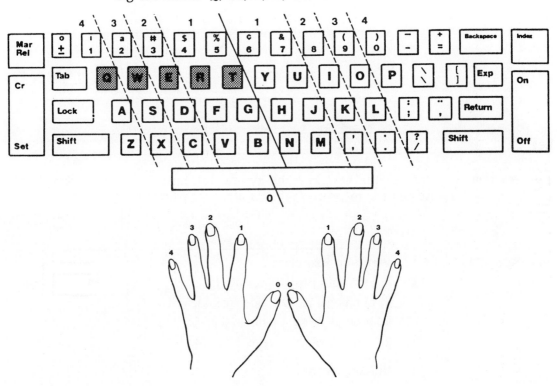

NOW TRY THIS ⇨   Practice the new reaches by typing the lines under New Key Drills. Then try the Review Drills to improve your keyboarding skills. Press RETURN after each line.

NEW KEY DRILLS   [T]   fff ttt ttt fff ft ft tf tf at fast
                              ff tf fat fast hat that all tall at
                [R]   fff rrr rrr fff fr fr rf rf art tar
                              fr rf tart lard raft rash dart hard

                [E]   ddd eee eee ddd de de ed ed deed ed
                              de ed fled sled reared heard leased
                [W]   sss www www sss sw sw ws ws was few
                              sw ws raw was week were saw walk we
                [Q]   aaa qqq qqq aaa aq aq qa qa qaaq aq
                              aq qa waq saq qjk jklq fjaq qasd qa

REVIEW DRILLS   salad talks sleds feed self jaw sea
                        hash get sales safe deal reared red
                        lake left that wars tree were jaded
                        street rest wet hear well jet water
                        Held the lead; We shall see; ledger
                        A faded leaf falls; A desk sale; at

Ask your teacher for more practice drills using the Q, W, E, R, and T keys.

Lesson 4   Right-hand Reaches

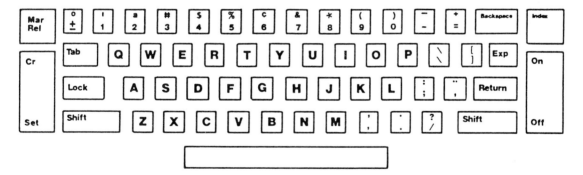

New Keys: Y, U, I, O, P

This group of reaches stresses the use of the right hand. See the following diagram for the correct finger control of the Y, U, I, O, and P keys.

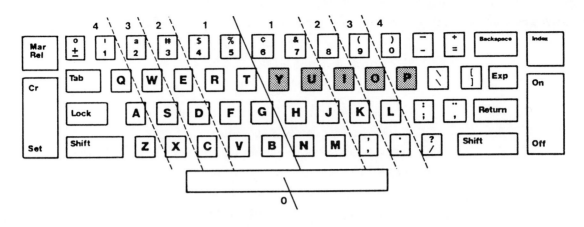

NOW TRY THIS ⇨ Practice the new reaches by typing the lines under New Key Drills. Then try the Review Drills to improve your keyboarding skills. Press [RETURN] after each line.

NEW KEY DRILLS [Y]   jjj yyy yyy jjj jy jy yj yj yes jy
jy yj yet yeast yell say away yard

[U]   jjj uuu uuu jjj ju ju uj uj jug uj
ju uy quart guest guess as quarter

[I]   kkk iii iii kkk ki ki ik ik kid it
ki ik kiss idea sail dish diet it

[O]   lll ooo ooo lll lo lo ol ol log go
lo ol joke yellow jelly doll hello

[P]   ;;; ppp ppp ;;; ;p ;p p; p; pig up
;p p; pillow people power stop pal

A-12

REVIEW DRILLS

goose rose hide quiet hospital ill
ride guard test dropped quilt good
hurt turkey July work short phrase
word jail guide keys food this try
This is easy; Wash your hands; few
See us type; Would you like a gift

Ask your teacher for more practice drills using the Y, U, I, O, and P keys.

Lesson 5   More Left-hand Reaches

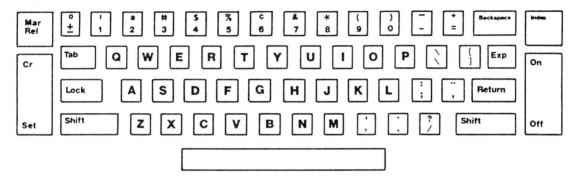

New Keys: Z, X, C, V, B

Next we'll move to the bottom row of the keyboard. In this lesson, the left-hand reaches to the Z, X, C, V, and B keys. Look at the following diagram to check correct finger placement for these keys.

A-13

NOW TRY THIS ⇨ Practice the new reaches by typing the lines under New Key Drills. Then try the Review Drills to improve your keyboarding skills. Remember to press ⌜RETURN⌝ after each line.

NEW KEY DRILLS ⬚B fff bbb bbb fff fbf bfb bfb baby be
fb bf best boat bet but job brother

⬚V fff vvv vvv fff fv fv vf vf van vet
fv vf brave vases driver stove five

⬚C ddd ccc ccc ddd dc dc cd cd cat cap
dc cd scarf police chief crowd cave

⬚X sss xxx xxx sss sx sx xs xs six tax
sx sx exit axe extra fixed sixth ox

⬚Z aaa zzz zzz aaa az az za za jazz za
az za zoo zebra zipper crazy freeze

REVIEW DRILLS size vest effort clue hockey lizard
brought chew froze block view leave
relax library zero video clock cost
space boot glove jacket prize saved
The boat floats; Fix the car; leave
Get a job; Catch a cold; four boxes

Ask your teacher for more practice drills using the Z, X, C, V, and B keys.

Lesson 6   More Right-hand Reaches

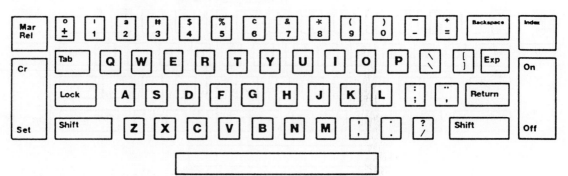

New Keys: N, M, comma (,), period (.), /

In this lesson, you will learn the bottom row keys on the right-hand side. The correct finger placement for the N, M, comma, period, and / keys appears in the following diagram.

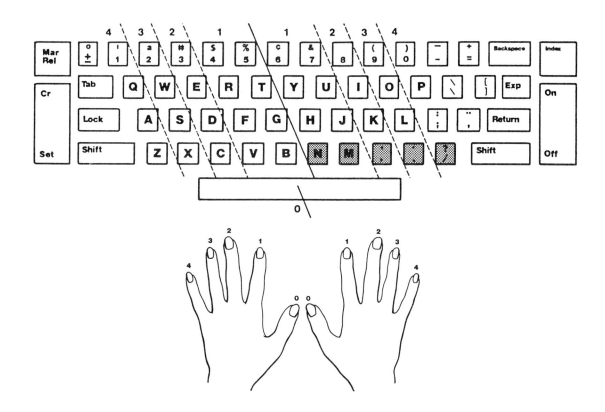

Note: Use your shift key to type the characters that appear on the top half of the last three keys. These characters may vary from keyboard to keyboard (check Section II of this appendix for your specific computer).

NOW TRY THIS ⇨ Practice the new reaches by typing the lines under New Key Drills. Then try the Review Drills to improve your keyboarding skills. Remember to press ⎣RETURN⎦ at the end of each line.

NEW KEY DRILLS   [N]   jjj nnn nnn jjj jn jn nj nj and can
                                 jn nj sand fanned rent kind then in

                    [M]   jjj mmm mmm jjj jm jm mj mj jam mat
                                   jm mj computer drum must dome smoke

                    [,]   kkk ,,, ,,, kkk k, k, ,k ,k Ken, I
                                   k, ,k Jack, to be, on the job, too,

                    [.]   lll ... ... lll l. l. .l .l U.S.A.;
                                   l. .l He is afraid. Type the copy.

                    [?]   ;;; /// /// ;;; ;/ ;/ /; /; chairs /
                                   ;;; ??? ??? ;;; ;? ;? ?; ?; Is she?
                                   ;/ ;? teacher/students Is she next?

REVIEW DRILLS monkey time final candy music piano
concert sunny than dinner magic gun
lunch brown jump point room bank in
win the race, this is fun, big dog,
We work fast. Can you run? counts
They went quickly. Is he sleeping?
on/off start/stop quick/slow rested

Ask your teacher for more practice drills using the N, M, comma (,), period (.), /, and ? keys.

Lesson 7 Numbers and Special Characters

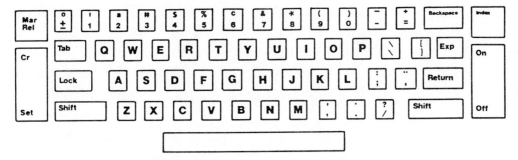

New Keys

This lesson shows the numeric and special character keys. Compare it to your keyboard. See Section II of this appendix for differences of keyboard layout among computers. If any of the characters in the diagram below are in different places on your computer, check your computer's finger placement diagram in Section II.

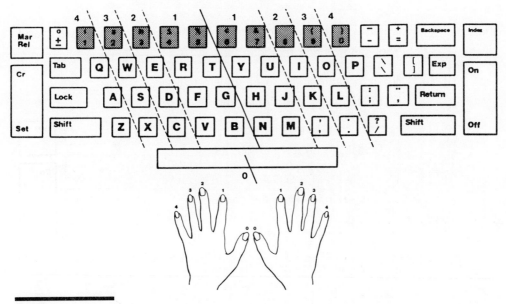

NOW TRY THIS ⇨ Practice the new reaches by typing the lines under New Key Drills. Then try the Review Drills to improve your keyboarding skills. Press RETURN after each line.

NEW KEY DRILLS

| ! | @ | # | $ | % |
| 1 | 2 | 3 | 4 | 5 |

aq1 sw2 de3 fr4 gt5 hy6 ju7 ki8 lo9
;p0 aq1 1qa sw2 2ws de3 3ed fr4 4rf

| ¢ | & | * | (|) |
| 6 | 7 | 8 | 9 | 0 |

gt5 5tg hy6 6yh ju7 7uj ki8 8ik lo9
9ol ;p0 0p; a1 s2 d3 f4 f5 j6 j7 k8
19 ;0 12345 54321 67890 09876 12345

(Remember to use the SHIFT key for special characters)

1234567890 10 29 38 47 56 65 74 83
92 01 123 456 789 098 765 432 13579
24680 156 074 208 519 734 210 19850
aq! sw@ de# fr$ gt% hy¢ ju& ki* lo(
;p) a! s@ d# f$ g% h¢ j& k* l(;) !
123 !@# 345 #$% 456 $%¢ 678 ¢&* 890
() !@#$% ¢&*() (*&¢ %$#@! #%(@%!
$14.92 3 @ 5¢; #00875; M & Ms; .35%
ten (10); **FREE GIFTS**; hi! $15.9

REVIEW DRILLS

Please buy 5 apples and 10 oranges.
Sheila earned $4.25 for babysitting.
The bus stops between 7:10 and 7:20.
Ticket #408 won the sweepstakes!
Deposit checks for $14.28 and $5.90.
Michael scored 100% on the test!
If you buy 5 pens @40¢, you owe $2.

Ask your teacher for more practice drills using these numeric and special character keys.

Lesson 8   More Special Character Keys

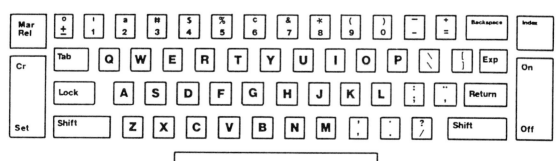

New Keys

This lesson covers the last few special character keys and function keys found on many keyboards. Again, your computer may be different (see Section II of this appendix). The following diagram shows correct finger placement for the keys in this lesson.

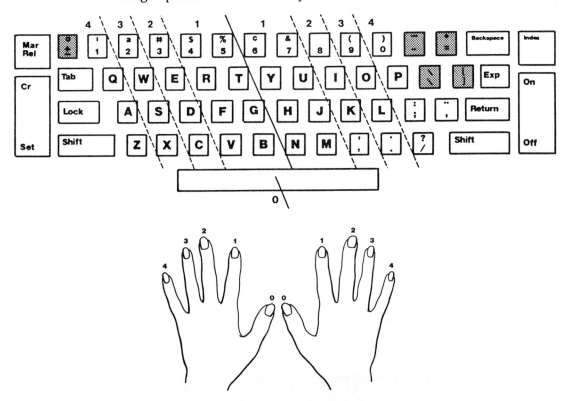

Please note that these are difficult reaches—even for the most skilled typist. Since these keys are not used often, you may want to lift your hand from its home row position and use either finger 2 or 3 for the far reaches.

Keys not discussed in this section are ones not usually found on computer keyboards. If you have questions about any keys, ask your teacher.

NOW TRY THIS ⇨ Practice the new reaches by typing the lines under New Key Drills. Remember to press RETURN after each line.

NEW KEY DRILLS

a± a± a° a° ;- -; ;- -; ;==; ;+ =;
;/ /; ;/ /; ;[[; ;]]; []+=-__+
[/:/+]; try again; ;/ ;] :/ :[; ±1
32 F = O C; left-hand; 352-4931;

Ask your teacher for more practice drills using these special character keys.

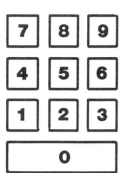

New Keys

Some computer keyboards have a special section similar in design to a calculator. This section is used for entering numerical data.

The following diagram shows correct finger placement for the 10-key numeric pad. Rest your fingers on the middle row.

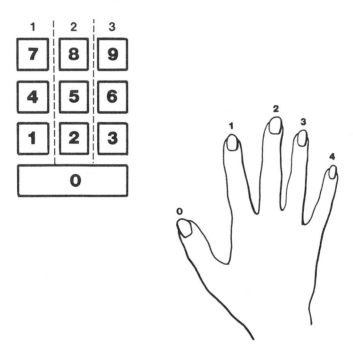

- The index finger is for 1, 4, and 7. (Also any function keys to the left of the key pad.)

- The second finger is for 2, 5, and 8.

- The third finger is for 3, 6, and 9.

- The fourth finger controls any function keys to the right of the key pad.

- The thumb controls 0 and any other keys (for example, a decimal point) on the bottom row.

NOW TRY THIS ⇨ Practice the following drills on the 10-key numeric pad.

PRACTICE DRILLS

44 55 66 456 654 454 654
77 88 99 789 987 787 989
11 22 33 123 321 121 323
47 58 69 474 585 696 400
41 52 63 414 525 636 500
40 50 60 147 258 369 600
12 13 45 46 78 79 15 159
32 31 65 64 98 97 35 357
15 75 57 159 357 951 753
12 56 79 159 753 951 357
70 80 90 708 942 513 845
19 45 24 237 859 631 403
89 62 73 106 473 520 130

SECTION II SPECIAL FEATURES OF MICROCOMPUTER KEYBOARDS

Lesson 1   **The Apple II Plus Keyboard**

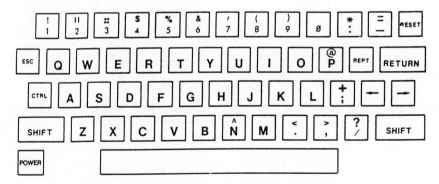

The Apple II Plus keyboard has a slightly different layout than the standard keyboard featured in Section I. Note that some of the special characters (″, $, ′, (, *, and so on) are on different keys. There are also some new keys unique to the Apple II Plus. These keys appear shaded in the following diagram.

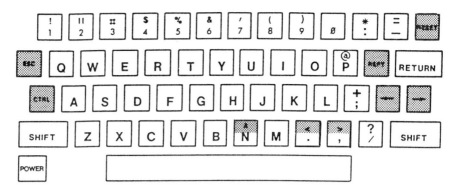

The diagram below shows the correct finger placement for the Apple II Plus keyboard.

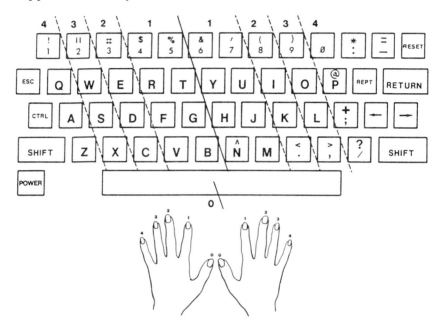

Look at the first diagram. The Apple II Plus keyboard has three symbol keys (∧, <, and >) that are often used in programming. The other new keys are used to do the special functions outlined below.

ESC	This key is used with other keys to control cursor movement.
CTRL	This key does nothing by itself. Along with other keys, it produces additional control characters.
RESET	This key stops program execution, when pressed with CTRL.
REPT	This key causes a character to be repeated when held with a character key.
←	This key moves the cursor one space to the left.

→   This key moves the cursor one space to the right.

Your teacher will provide you with additional information about the features of the Apple II Plus.

Lesson 2   The Apple IIe Keyboard

The Apple IIe keyboard has a slightly different layout than the standard keyboard featured in Section I. There are some new keys unique to the Apple IIe. These keys appear shaded in the following diagram.

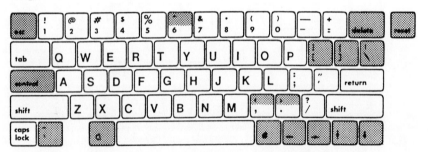

The diagram below again stresses correct finger placement for the Apple IIe keyboard.

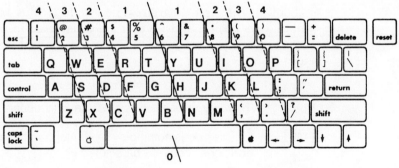

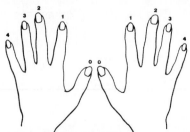

Look at the first diagram. Notice that the Apple IIe has a few new special characters. These charcters include the ∧, {, [, },],| ,\, <, >, ~, and ` symbols. You will use these keys for word processing and programming. The other keys perform special functions and are discussed below.

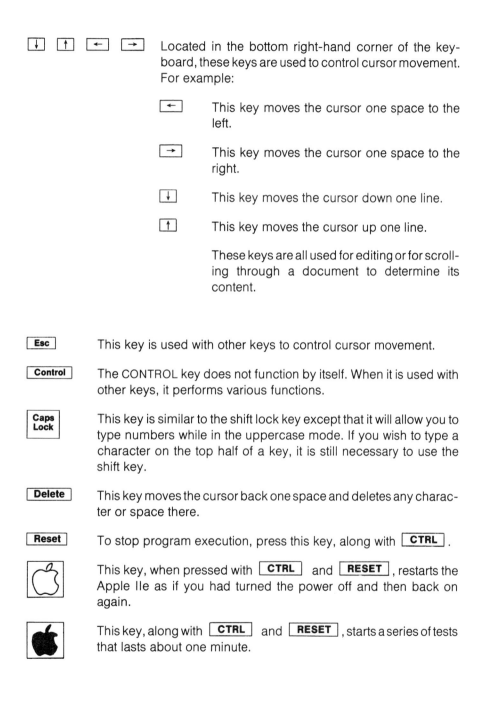

| ↓ | ↑ | ← | → | Located in the bottom right-hand corner of the keyboard, these keys are used to control cursor movement. For example: |

←   This key moves the cursor one space to the left.

→   This key moves the cursor one space to the right.

↓   This key moves the cursor down one line.

↑   This key moves the cursor up one line.

These keys are all used for editing or for scrolling through a document to determine its content.

Esc   This key is used with other keys to control cursor movement.

Control   The CONTROL key does not function by itself. When it is used with other keys, it performs various functions.

Caps Lock   This key is similar to the shift lock key except that it will allow you to type numbers while in the uppercase mode. If you wish to type a character on the top half of a key, it is still necessary to use the shift key.

Delete   This key moves the cursor back one space and deletes any character or space there.

Reset   To stop program execution, press this key, along with **CTRL** .

This key, when pressed with **CTRL** and **RESET** , restarts the Apple IIe as if you had turned the power off and then back on again.

This key, along with **CTRL** and **RESET** , starts a series of tests that lasts about one minute.

Your teacher will provide you with additional information about the features of the Apple IIe.

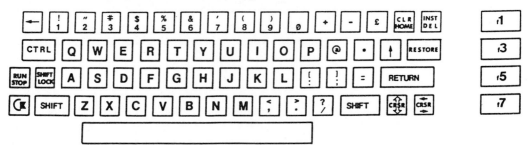

The Commodore 64 keyboard has a slightly different layout than the standard keyboard featured in Section I of this appendix. Note that some of the special characters ('', (,), +, −, and so on) are on different keys. There are also some new keys unique to the Commodore 64. These keys appear shaded in the following diagram.

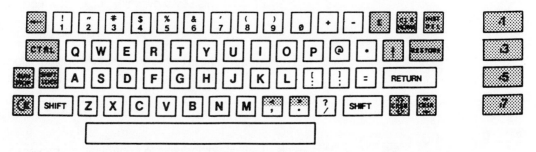

The diagram below illustrates correct finger placement for the Commodore 64.

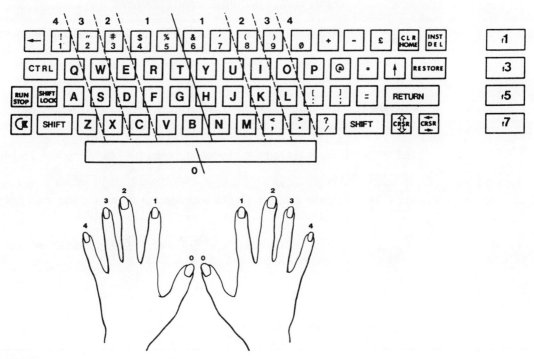

Look at the first diagram. The Commodore 64 has two symbol keys (< and >) often used in programming. You will also find a key with the English pound symbol (£). This symbol is on the keyboard because the Commodore 64 is popular in Europe. The other keys perform the special functions listed below.

⌨ G	This key shifts your work between text and graphic display modes.
CTRL	The CONTROL key changes colors on the display screen. To select a color, press this key followed by one of the color keys (numbers 1-8). Pressing **CTRL** and 9 gives reverse effects; **CTRL** and 0 returns to original colors.
RUN STOP	To stop program execution, press this key.
CLR HOME	Press this key if you want the cursor to return to the upper left-hand corner of the screen (home). If you want to erase your program and start over, pressing **SHIFT** and **CLR/HOME** will clear the screen and move the cursor to the home position.
INST DEL	This editing key adds or removes characters. To delete a character, place the cursor one space to the right of the character and press this key. The cursor will move back one space and erase the character. To insert something, place the cursor where you want to add the character. Press **SHIFT** and **INST/DEL**, and then type the character(s).
RESTORE	If you want to stop a program execution, but keep the program in memory, press **RUN/STOP** and **RESTORE**. This same combination can be used to unjam your computer if it "freezes up."
⇧ CRSR ⇩	This key moves the cursor vertically on the screen. Press this key and the cursor will move down the page. To move upward, press **SHIFT** and **CRSR**.
⇦ CRSR ⇨	This key moves the cursor horizontally on the screen. Press this key and you will advance one position to the right. To move left, press **SHIFT** and **CRSR**.
→	This key is used to print graphic horizontal arrows for prompts in programs.
↑	This is a dual-purpose key. In the standard operating mode, it is an exponential symbol. In the shift mode, it produces the value of Pi (π).
f1 **f3**	These keys can be programmed to handle a variety of user-defined functions.
f5 **f7**	The graphic keys are reached as follows: for the left-hand graphic symbols, use the commodore key (**⌨ G**); for the right-hand symbols, use the shift key.

Your teacher will provide you with additional information about the features of the Commodore 64.

Lesson 4 **The IBM PC Keyboard**

The IBM PC keyboard has a slightly different layout than the standard keyboard featured in Section I. Note that the caps lock key is in a different place. There are also some new keys unique to the IBM PC; these keys appear shaded in the following diagram.

The diagram below illustrates correct finger placement for the IBM PC keyboard.

Look at the first diagram. The IBM PC keyboard has some additional special characters ($\wedge$, $<$, $>$, [,], {, }, ~, ', ¦ , and \ ). These keys are used for word processing and programming. The other new keys perform the special functions outlined below. Note that some of the function keys appear in the 10-key numeric pad section.

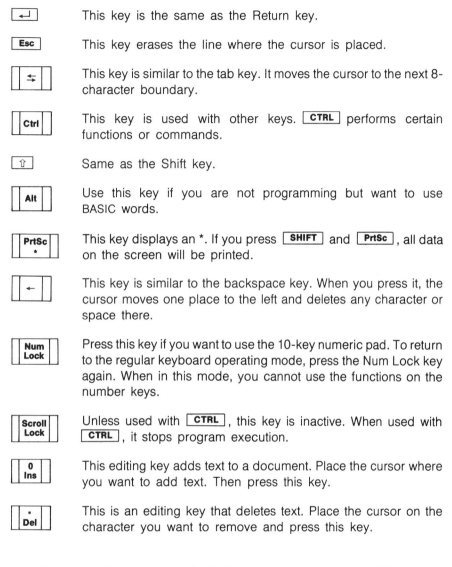

This key is the same as the Return key.

This key erases the line where the cursor is placed.

This key is similar to the tab key. It moves the cursor to the next 8-character boundary.

This key is used with other keys. CTRL performs certain functions or commands.

Same as the Shift key.

Use this key if you are not programming but want to use BASIC words.

This key displays an *. If you press SHIFT and PrtSc , all data on the screen will be printed.

This key is similar to the backspace key. When you press it, the cursor moves one place to the left and deletes any character or space there.

Press this key if you want to use the 10-key numeric pad. To return to the regular keyboard operating mode, press the Num Lock key again. When in this mode, you cannot use the functions on the number keys.

Unless used with CTRL , this key is inactive. When used with CTRL , it stops program execution.

This editing key adds text to a document. Place the cursor where you want to add text. Then press this key.

This is an editing key that deletes text. Place the cursor on the character you want to remove and press this key.

To use the functions on the following keys, be sure the Num Lock key is not depressed.

This key quickly moves the cursor to the last character on a line.

This key is similar to the index key.

This key is used to move the page down.

Key	Description
4 ←	This key moves the cursor to the left one space without deleting anything.
6 →	This key moves the cursor to the right one space without deleting anything.
7 Home	This key moves the cursor to the upper left corner of the screen.
8 ↑	This key moves the cursor up line by line.
9 PgUp	This key is used to move the page up.
F1 F2 F3 F4 F5 F6 F7 F8 F9 F10	These keys perform certain functions. Ask your teacher for a list of these functions.

Your teacher will provide you with additional information about the features of the IBM PC.

Lesson 5   The TRS-80 Models III and 4 Keyboards

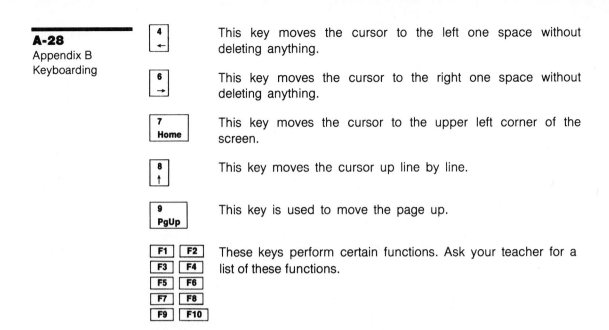

TRS-80 Model III

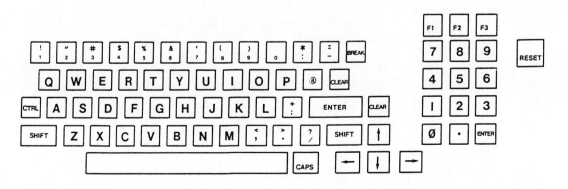

TRS-80 Model 4

The TRS-80 Models III and 4 keyboards have a slightly different layout than the standard keyboard featured in Section I of this appendix. Note that some of the special characters ('', &, ', (,), *) are on different keys. There are also some new keys unique to the TRS-80 Models III and 4. These keys appear shaded in the following diagrams. Notice that although both models have the same unique keys, they are in different places.

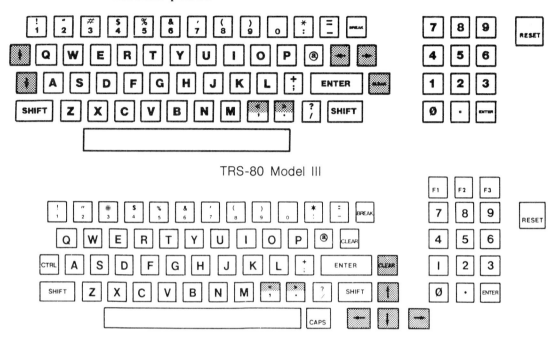

TRS-80 Model III

TRS-80 Model 4

The following diagrams illustrate again the correct finger placement for both models.

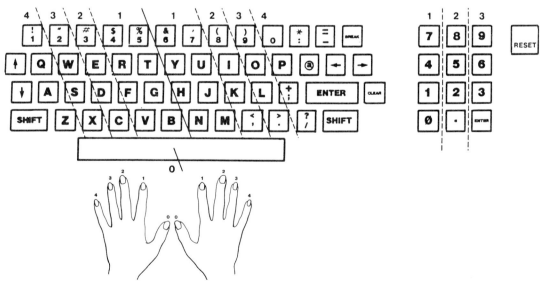

TRS-80 Model III

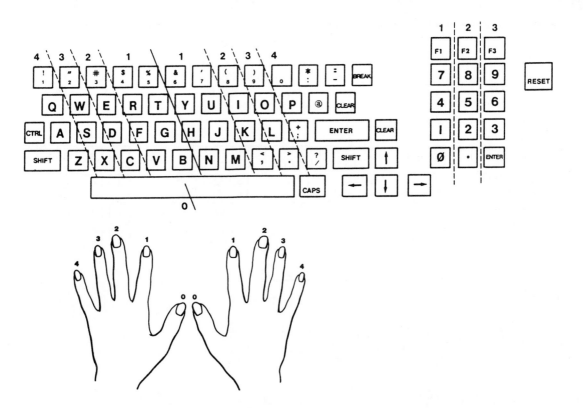

TRS-80 Model 4

The TRS-80 Models III and 4 keyboards have two new symbol keys (< and >) often used in programming. The other new keys are designed to perform the specific functions listed below.

[↑]   This key is used with [ESC] to move the cursor up one line.

[↓]   This key is used for line feed.

[→]   This key moves the cursor to the next 8-column boundary.

[←]   This key moves the cursor one place to the left and erases the last typed character.

The above arrow keys are also used to select information in commercial programs.

[BREAK]   BREAK interrupts any operation and returns control to the cursor.

[CLEAR]   This key erases the display and returns the cursor back to the home position.

Your teacher will provide you with additional information about the features of the TRS-80 Models III and 4.

ENRICHMENT TOPICS

Systems For Corporations

What do we mean when we talk about a system? How do companies put new systems into operation?

Our world consists of thousands of systems, many having nothing to do with computers. A system is a group of related elements that work together toward a common goal. The solar system is a group of related bodies that revolve around the sun, maintaining gravitational pull among each other. Your skeletal system is a group of bones in your body that works toward supporting and protecting the rest of your body. A system that a corporation might use is a group of materials, machines, and people that produce information for the corporation to make decisions about its business. It is often called an information system.

An information system is made up of inputs, processes, and outputs. Inputs enter the system from the surrounding environment as data. These inputs are transformed by some process into outputs. The process occurs by either manual or computer handling. The output is information.

Feedback is another important element of systems. The purpose of feedback is to decide whether the system fills the needs of the people who use it. If not, the inputs or processes in the system may be changed.

Systems that do not work will give misleading, incorrect, or late information. Too much information can present a problem, too. Important facts may be overlooked due to information overload.

A company must study and design a system that will give the right information. Then it must make sure everyone knows how to make the best use of the system. Hundreds of thousands of dollars are at stake. If a company makes a mistake in choosing a system or in putting a system into practice, those dollars could all be wasted.

To design a system and save money, an organized approach called the systems approach is used. The person who studies the system is called a systems analyst. The systems analyst studies how a corporation operates. He or she asks, "What could be done to improve the quality of information and the process of making decisions?"

The analyst offers several solutions to the problem. Once a decision is made, the new system or changes to the old system are put into practice. Errors are corrected and users are trained to use the system.

Even after the system is put into practice, there is an ongoing need to maintain the system so that it continues to provide the needed information. The analyst asks, "Is the information accurate? Is it up to date? Is it complete? Is it available to the people who need it?"

Let's relate the process to the family budget. The bills and paychecks are part of the input. These data may be processed to pay the bills by the due dates, allow cash for irregular expenses, and put the rest of the money in a savings account.

Careful study is needed before the new budget is begun. A system will work only if it is correctly designed and implemented. In addition, if the system costs more in time and money than it is worth to the users, the system will not work. Your family cannot stick to a budget if one or more members spends more money than is allotted. If a new family budget means that one member must work overtime at the expense of family time, the system may not be worth its cost.

Perhaps your parents decide to juggle the various due dates and cash spent to save a little extra money for a vacation. The information output from the budget system helps them to decide that they are able to save enough money toward this goal. Meeting this goal is one form of feedback. Does the system fill your family's needs? If not, what needs to be done to begin a new budget system? Will the new budget system correct the weaknesses of the current system? Will your family continue to evaluate the new budget that is put into place?

Your family will review the budget to see if it is still working well. The feedback from this review determines whether more changes are necessary and whether the system is, in fact, a good one.

Assignments

1. Use outside sources to find the three major steps in systems analysis.
2. Design a budget system for yourself. How do you spend money now? How would you like to spend money? What are the solutions? Are the solutions worth the cost to you?

Communications Software

Communications programs permit you to link your home computer with another computer. The programs are sometimes called terminal software. Once the computers are connected, your computer can do many of the things that you would do if you were actually working on the remote computer.

The connection for home computers is accomplished through telephone lines. Most hobbyists use modems (MOdulator/DEModulator) to change the signals into forms required by the telephone lines and by the computers. Some connect their computers directly through a cable (the wall jack for the telephone).

You will need terminal software to send messages to other computer users, access an information service, such as CompuServe or The Source, and use an electronic bulletin board. Some software allows you to transfer programs between computers. Computer jargon for these transfers is uploading and downloading. Uploading means sending your program or message onto the host computer. Downloading is receiving programs or messages into a form you can use after the communication is ended.

Terminal programs can make your computer into a "dumb" machine or an "intelligent" machine. If the terminal program allows you only to read and not to save the information on disk, then it has turned your computer into a "dumb" machine. If you can save or print information as well as prepare information to be sent to another computer, then the terminal program you are using turns your computer into an "intelligent" machine.

The better terminal programs have several characteristics in common. One of these is that beginners should be able to use the program easily. They can enter a terminal program by choosing from a menu of pictures and words. The simplest way to make these choices is with a joystick or a mouse.

Good terminal programs should have other flexible features. To send data through many other modems, the terminal programs will need both full- and half-duplex transmission, 300 and 1,200 baud, and many other features. Duplex refers to the direction of transmission. In half-duplex, the messages can be sent only one way at a time, although transmission in both directions is possible. In full-duplex, messages can be sent both ways at once. Talking on the telephone is an example of full-duplex. If you and the person you call both talk at once, rather than taking turns, your voices will travel over the phone lines so that you hear both voices at the same time.

Baud refers to the measure of speed at which data are transmitted. A speed of 300 baud is slower than a speed of 1,200 baud. Transmitting data at 1,200 baud is more expensive, but also takes less time. If the transmission requires a long-distance phone call, using 1,200 baud may be cheaper because transmission is faster. Modems of 1,200 baud are becoming more common, so the best terminal programs should have that capacity as well as the 300-baud capacity.

Your screen should be able to show 80 columns. If your screen does not do this normally, you can buy a hardware card or cartridge that will permit the screen to show 80 columns.

Having an alarm clock in the terminal program is useful, too. It may keep you from running up a higher telephone bill than you intended.

The program should also provide a buffer—the bigger the better. A buffer is a memory-holding area where data are stored until you are ready to dump them onto disk, tape, or printer. You also may need a way to tell the host computer to wait while you do something with the data already in the buffer. Sometimes the host computer requires you to wait, too.

Without special characters (usually XON and XOFF) to control the speed of uploading or downloading, you may lose data. Be sure the software has this capability.

Being able to edit the data you receive is important. You may not want to keep all of the data, or you may want to return an answer with part of the orginal data. You should be able to change the data to suit your needs.

Assignments

1. Find out from a computer store the names of terminal programs that you could use with your computer at home or with the school's computer. Find out what additional equipment you would need to complete the telecommunications link.

2. Get in touch with someone who communicates on an electronic bulletin board system. Find out how to link with a BBS, what equipment is needed, and what kinds of things you can do once you have access to the BBS.

How Do You Teach a Robot What to Do?

"The only ones who really appreciate how smart people are are those who try to do some of these things with a robot," says Charles Rosen of Machine Intelligence Company, Sunnyvale, California. Rosen should know. He is a scientist who works with robots.

The processes that seem to occur naturally in humans must be defined exactly for robots. Take opening a door. A child sees the human parents reach out and turn a knob. When the knob is pulled, a door opens. Later, the child simply copies the action to reach the same goal. But try to teach a robot to open a door!

The robot must be programmed to tell the difference between the door and other parts of a wall. Then the robot must stop moving when it arrives at the door. The robot must recognize the knob and know what to do with the knob. When the robot finally can grip the knob, it must turn the knob and pull the door open, let go, and propel itself through the door into another room.

How do you program a robot to do tasks?

There are two basic ways. One way is an on-line method. The on-line method uses the robot and its computer. It is the lead-through method. The programmer leads, or moves, the robot (or robot arm) through the cycle it is supposed to perform. The person who performs the lead-through teaching does not have to know how to program a computer. But knowledge of the actual task is very important. Lead-through teaching can be used to tell a robot how to perform jobs such as spray painting, polishing, or arc welding.

The second way of teaching a robot is by off-line programming. Off-line programming means the program is written on a separate device from the robot and its computer. These programs can be transferred from one robot to another. They tell a robot what to do and govern its touch and sight sensing devices.

For robots to move about freely or handle objects, sensing devices are needed. Otherwise, the robot will continue on a direct path regardless of who or what gets in its way, or the objects it handles may be broken or crushed.

One sensing device is the infrared sensor that detects heat given off by objects. This sensor helps the robot to avoid crashing into objects. Another sensor, a sonar device, transmits a high-frequency sound wave. The sound wave bounces off objects and returns to the robot. The robot's computer calculates how long it took the sound wave to bounce back. Then the robot can figure out its location.

Camera systems help a robot to see. Once it sees an object, the robot must decide what the object is. One way to help a robot to recognize objects is to give it a data base of shapes. Let's see how the robot could know that an object is an airplane. The robot's cameras detect the edges of the object and outline the object. Then the computer smooths out the rough drawing. It rifles through its memory, searching for general shapes. When the shapes are arranged in a pattern, the robot can decide, "Aha, an airplane!"

For the robot, recognizing a doorknob might be more complex than recognizing an airplane. The airplane has a distinct shape, while the doorknob has the same shape as many other round objects. In addition, not all doorknobs are round. Some are handles that are pushed down and then pulled. Some are just handles that are used to push or pull the door open.

Despite the problems of teaching robots, robots can perform many jobs. Today's robots can handle parts as small as the second hand on a watch and as large as equipment weighing a ton. Robots inspect soap flakes and pour dangerous acids and radioactive drugs.

In the future, robots may mine coal, repair and maintain nuclear reactors, do crop dusting for farmers and orchards, and clean the outside windows of buildings. Some robots will perform underwater research. Others will be used in space exploration. Many of these future uses are in trial stages now. In addition, scientists are planning how to direct a robot by voice command. Other scientists are studying ways for a robot to program itself to do a job once it receives a command.

When you see how hard it is to tell a robot to do a simple task like opening a door, you get an idea of the many problems involved in training robots to do more difficult jobs.

Assignments

1. The motions you do to get a can of soda pop out of the refrigerator, open the can, and pour the soda pop over ice in a glass come naturally. List the things a robot must do to perform this task. Limit the list to the job at hand.

2. Name some problems that the robot might have while doing the task mentioned in Question 1.

3. Read the section on artificial intelligence (AI) again. Use other sources to learn more about AI. Discuss how instructing a robot is parallel to the concepts of artificial intelligence.

Computer industry people lose money by illegal copying of their work. Between $200 million and $600 million dollars are lost every year due to illegal copying. Software writers are hurt. They may decide it is not worth it to write good programs.

Even young people like to write computer programs. For instance, teen-aged Cori Grimm helps to create the graphics for programs sold through The Learning Company. How can the hard work of these young people and many other computer programmers be protected from copying?

One way is by registering for a copyright. Software is covered by the U.S. Copyright Act of 1978. The creator of an original work possesses the copyright from the moment the work is fixed in some concrete form. However, following certain procedures protects the creator against loss of the copyright or loss of the right to sue for copyright violations.

A copyright notice protects the owner's copyright. In the notice, the symbol ©, the word "copyright," or the abbreviation "copr." should appear with the name of the copyright owner and the year of the work's first publication. Registration gains for the copyright owner the right to bring suit against copyright violations. Registration can be accomplished by completing a Copyright Office registration form TX, paying a ten-dollar fee, and submitting a copy or identifying portion of the program to the Copyright Office.

What is covered by the copyright? The law makes it illegal to copy a software program except for archival use. Archival use means that one back-up copy may be made.

The copyright also protects the object code by court precedent. The object code is the instructions that actually run the computer. These instructions are in the operating system, applications programs, or ROM (read-only memory). The court precedent is the case of Apple vs. Franklin Computer Corporation with copyright violations for copying the operating system programs held in the Apple II. Apple sought an order to stop Franklin from selling the Ace 100, the computer that combined the copied operating system.

Government officials realize the importance of laws that keep pace with new technology. A bill has passed the U.S. Senate that protects against copying of microchips. Many state laws protect against certain copying procedures.

Will a copyright completely protect these programmers against software piracy? Chances are it won't. That is one reason why computer users need to set up a code of ethics for their own behavior. The code of ethics measures behavior against conscience.

Because they listen to their consciences, many people would not copy a protected disk. And many more people would copy the disks only for back-up or archival use. They wouldn't dream of selling hundreds or thousands of pirated disks.

What code of ethics would you establish for yourself? What code is etched in your conscience? Would you buy a pirated disk, even if you had nothing to do with the copying? Would you make multiple copies of programs in computer magazines? Would you copy from an electronic bulletin board a program that you suspected was pirated? Would you copy software because everyone else does it?

Assignments

1. Use a microcomputer, disk drive, and copyrighted software. Load the program. Look at the copyright information. How is it presented? Should software be copyrighted? Why?

2. Have you ever used public domain software? How does it compare with similar programs that are sold for money? Do you think a fairly good teen-age programmer could write some of the programs that cost $40 or $50?

Choosing a Microcomputer

Buying a microcomputer can be a difficult and time-consuming process. With over 150 models on the market, it is easy for an unprepared buyer to become confused. The purchase of a computer is a major investment for most people, so care must be taken not to make expensive mistakes. Take the time to learn about the different systems on the market before you make a decision. Do not let your computer purchase end up in the closet gathering dust.

Uses

The first step in selecting a computer is to decide just what you want the computer to do. This decision will help you narrow the choices. Computers that cannot perform the jobs you want to do can be eliminated. If you have trouble deciding how you would use a computer, then perhaps you really do not need to buy one.

If your main use for a microcomputer is for playing video games, then one of the less expensive machines will probably work well. More expensive business machines can play games as well as perform jobs like word processing and data management. But unless you will use the higher-priced machine for these applications too, your money will be wasted. If you want a computer that can do several different jobs, make sure that you shop for a machine that can do the jobs to your satisfaction.

Buy Now or Wait?

Changes occur very quickly in the computer field. Technology changes almost yearly. Prices on equipment often drop drastically after a new line of computers has been on the market for awhile. For these reasons people often wonder—should I buy now or wait?

There is no simple answer to this question. Waiting could mean that a newer, faster, better model might appear on the market. It could also mean that the price of a model that you like may go down. Of course, the price could also go up! And time spent waiting could be spent learning how to use your computer. Waiting also keeps you from enjoying the benefits that might be gained by using the computer in a business or at home. Only you can decide which approach is better for you.

What to Look For

There are a number of things to consider when shopping for a microcomputer. Price is one. Other things to consider include the software that you will use and the hardware needed to perform specific tasks.

Price If you are a typical buyer, price will be one of your first concerns. Microcomputers can cost as little as $50 or as much as you wish. The price will be affected by the peripherals you choose to buy with your machine. To a large degree, the price you pay will depend on the use you have decided upon.

Most microcomputers purchased for home or educational use cost between $50 and $2,000. Manufacturers of computers in this price range include: Apple, Atari, Coleco, Commodore, Epson, IBM, and Mattel. Makers of more costly computers include: Apple, Burroughs, DEC, Epson, IBM, and NCR. You can see that some manufacturers offer models in many price ranges.

Be careful of low prices. A low price could mean a lack of support or service in repairing equipment. A low price could also mean that needed peripherals are extra. The additional cost of peripherals could greatly increase the cost of a computer system. Before you buy, make sure that you understand what you are getting for your money.

Software Once you know what you are going to use a microcomputer for, you must determine what software you will need to do those tasks. Computers are powerful, but it is the software that makes computers useful. Software will make a computer do what you want it to do. Therefore, it is important to shop for the software that will perform the jobs you want done *before* buying hardware.

Many software packages have specific hardware requirements. Software can affect the amount of internal memory you will need. It can also determine the kind of operating system that will be needed to run the software. The two most popular operating systems currently in use are CP/M and MS-DOS. Bell Laboratories developed an operating system called UNIX that is also gaining in popularity.

Hardware *The Microprocessor:* The first microcomputers had 8-bit microprocessors. Advances in technology have led to 16-bit and even 32-bit microprocessors. A larger microprocessor means a computer can process instructions at a much faster rate. If you intend to use your computer for jobs like electronic spreadsheet analysis, a larger microprocessor will help perform calculations quickly.

Monitors: Some computers have a built-in video display. Most, however, require the purchase of a separate video display or monitor. There are several things to consider when purchasing a monitor. They include: the screen display dimensions; the color of the display; the monitor's resolution; and the focus, contrast, and brightness control of the display. Microcomputer monitors come in either 40- or 80-column widths and 24- or 25-line displays. If you are going to use your system for word processing, an 80-column screen is more desirable. That is because a standard 8½-inch piece of paper can fit on an 80-column display. This means that you can view the entire width of a document while typing. A 40-column display would require you to use special features to view the full page width.

Monochrome monitors display a single color. The color could be white, amber, or green on a black or gray background. The choice of color depends on personal preference. Some people feel that amber monitors create less eye strain than either white or green.

Color monitors can display full color. A full color display is desirable for playing video games or displaying graphics. There are two types of color monitors. The standard color monitor is similar to a color TV. An RGB (red, green, blue) monitor produces higher quality color displays than standard color monitors.

One of the most important considerations when deciding on a monitor is resolution. Resolution refers to the clarity of the characters displayed on the screen. Characters are created using small dots called pixels. The smaller the dots and the more closely they are packed, the clearer the images on the screen.

Standard televisions are often used as display screens with computers. But TVs have fewer pixels than standard monitors, so they produce images that are not as clear and crisp as most monitors.

Whatever monitor you choose, make sure there is a way to control the contrast, brightness, and focus of the monitor's display. Controlling these factors permits you to adjust the display to suit the lighting conditions of the room in which you are working.

Keyboards: Keyboards for microcomputers can come in one of two forms. They can be attached to the computer enclosure or detached from it. Detached keyboards may either be connected to the computer by a cord or operated by batteries.

The angle of the keyboard is important. Keyboards that are part of the machine's enclosure cannot be adjusted, and typing for long periods of time on these can be tiresome. Detachable keyboards adjust to various angles.

Keyboard touch is another consideration. Most micro-computers have standard touch-sensitive keys. A few offer pressure-sensitive keyboards covered with a plastic film. These may be more suitable for use with young children, for they protect the keyboard from dirt and spills. Pressure-sensitive keyboards are difficult to use for typing. They would not work well for word processing.

Some keyboards come with special features such as repeating keys. Other keyboards have keys that can be programmed to perform special functions. Numeric keypads are useful if many numbers will be entered into the computer.

Secondary Storage: Microcomputers use three types of secondary storage. They are tape cassettes, floppy disks, and hard disks.

Tape cassettes are the lowest-priced form of storage. They are used with less costly systems. Data retrieval with tape cassettes is very slow compared to floppy disks or hard disks. This is because tape cassettes use sequential-access storage. Software such as data managers requires direct-access storage and cannot be used with tape cassettes.

Floppy disks come in three sizes. They are 3½-inch, 5¼-inch, and 8-inch. The most widely used is the 5¼-inch size. One disk can store up to 320,000 characters.

Hard disks are similar to the magnetic disks used on main-frame and minicomputer systems. They provide a good way to store vast quantities of data using microsystems.

Printers: Printers can be one of the most expensive peripherals you can purchase. There are a number of features that should be considered when shopping for a printer. The speed of a printer is measured in characters per second, or cps. Printers can print as slowly as 10 cps or as fast as 100 cps. The number of characters printed within an inch horizontally is called pitch. It is measured in characters per inch, or cpi.

Printers can print from the left side of the paper to the right, or vice versa. They can use either friction feed or tractor feed to pull the paper through the printer. Friction feed is the type of paper feed used by typewriters. Tractor feed requires the use of special paper. The paper has small holes on each side and is fed in as one continuous sheet. Tractor feed prevents paper from shifting while it is being pulled through the printer. Some printers allow both tractor and continuous feed paper to be fed through.

The quality of print available on printers varies depending on the method used to print images. A dot-matrix printer forms images by placing individual dots into groups in the shape of the desired image. The more densely packed the dots, the better the quality of the image.

Letter-quality printers use a daisy-wheel to produce printed output. A daisy-wheel works like a typewriter. Solid characters located on the petals of the daisy-wheel are struck from behind by a hammer. The characters are pressed against a ribbon and the paper, which results in an image on the paper. Solid daisy-wheel characters produce print that is much better looking than the print produced by dot-matrix printers.

A third type of printer is also used with microcomputers. It is called an ink-jet printer. This type of printer forms a character much like a dot-matrix printer. The difference is that ink is sprayed onto the paper by an ink-jet. Ink-jet printers are fast, but the quality of the image produced is not as good as that produced by a daisy-wheel printer. When the ink is sprayed onto the paper by the ink jet, some characters are fuzzy. The primary advantage of an ink-jet printer is its quiet operation.

Other Hardware Devices: Depending on your intended uses and specific needs, your system may require other hardware devices. Some of these devices include: joysticks, modems, light pens, the mouse, graphics tablets, and game paddles. If you think that you may require some of these devices, descriptions of some of these devices and how they work can be found in this text. Also check computer magazines and paperback books for more information.

Other Considerations *Training:* There are a number of ways to obtain training or education in computers after you buy a microcomputer. Community and local colleges offer classes in microcomputers through continuing education departments. Local high schools may also offer classes through adult education programs. Private tutoring is another option to people who can afford to pay for the services of a tutor.

Many software vendors offer seminars that teach you to use the software package and microcomputer that you may want to own. Some local computer stores also offer these services.

Home study is another way to learn about your computer.

Many hardware and software vendors provide tutorials on the use of their products. These tutorials offer the user a way to get hands-on experience while learning. Independent firms are beginning to provide self-teaching educational material that can be used on microcomputers. Check with local bookstores to see if this kind of material is available in your area.

Documentation: One of the most important things to consider when you are shopping for a microcomputer is documentation. As a microcomputer owner, you will want to refer to the user manual occasionally when questions arise. Good documentation should be complete, accurate, and easy-to-use. A microcomputer with poor documentation may be a source of frustration whenever you have a problem.

Where to Buy

Once you have analyzed your needs and decided on the appropriate software, where do you go to buy your computer? There are a number of sources from which you can buy a computer.

Vendors Computer vendors such as IBM, DEC, and Burroughs offer their machines through a direct sales team. Buying a computer this way can be beneficial. The salespeople are highly trained and can help you determine the type of system that best suits your needs. Vendors also offer maintenance contracts and replacement equipment if your sytem should be out of working order for some time. If you use your computer for business purposes, this is a valuable service.

Retailers Many microcomputers are also offered through department stores and computer specialty stores. Buying a computer through a department store has some disadvantages. Often, salespeople do not know about microcomputers and are unable to help you put together the kind of system that meets your needs. Also, these stores to not have service departments and often send machines back to the manufacturer for products they do sell. That is because they purchase in larger quantities and can sell the machines for less than a specialty store. If you know what kind of system you want and service is not a problem, then a department store may be the place for you to buy.

If you want help in selecting a microcomputer and peripherals, a specialty store can be a good place to buy. Most specialty stores have informed salespeople and in-house service departments. The cost of computers purchased from specialty stores will tend to be higher, though. This is because the stores are offering service and support.

Mail-Order Houses Buying from a mail-order house can be a good way to buy a computer, if you know what you want to purchase. Many mail-order houses offer products for less than specialty stores. Before buying a computer this way, however, make sure you know what you can expect in the way of services. For example, if something goes wrong with your machine, will you have to ship your computer back to the manufacturer for service for an indefinite period of time?

Whatever decisions you make about what kind of computer to buy and where to purchase your machine, remember this—when you take your new system home, use it and enjoy it!

Assignment

In the process of selecting a microcomputer you need to decide for what purposes it will be used. Answer the following questions. What will be the expected uses of your microcomputer? What type of software package will best suit your needs? Depending upon your software requirements, what specific hardware will your microcomputer system require?

Looking at Software

Once you have bought a computer and one or two software packages, you will become more aware of the avalanche of software available to use with your computer. All of it will sound attractive and it will be tempting to buy software on impulse. How can you choose software that fits your needs and your budget limits?

You may follow the same steps you would if you were buying clothes or any other major purchase. First, you analyze your needs. Then you shop for items within limits of cost and suitability with what you already have. Finally, you evaluate the available products within those guidelines.

Analyze Your Needs

What do you plan to do with your software? Do you want to play games? Do you want to learn school skills by drill methods? Do you want to acquire thinking skills—analyzing, testing, judging, classifying, or drawing conclusions? Will you do a lot of writing? Do you want to produce graphs, charts, or other pictures to illustrate ideas in a term paper? Do you want to file data about a hobby or a subject you are researching for history class?

Once you have decided what you want to do with software, you must define how you want the software to work and what priority each feature has. Look at software in terms of output, input, and processing.

What do you want the output to look like or do? Do you need certain kinds of formatting features to write that chemistry paper? Do you want to learn about algebra by memorization, or do you want software that will help you analyze problems and arrive at logical solutions? Do you want to be able to use different fonts, draw graphs and pie charts, use different colors, or permit high-quality hard copy?

What kinds of data will you input to the program, and how easy is it to input the data? Can the software handle all the data you input? Are the data entry methods easy or difficult to understand and learn?

What kind of processing is involved in achieving the output? Do you want the program to work very fast? Can you sacrifice speed for some other feature, such as special formatting in a word-processing package? If you need to sort data in files, will you want the software to sort in just one category, or do you want the software to cross-reference other files? Will the software perform the calculations needed to produce the output you expect?

Make sure you allow for future expansion of your software needs. Right now you may need a word processor for short, informal papers. In high school and college, you may need to produce longer documents with footnotes and other special formats. You can handle short informal documents with more advanced word processing software, but you cannot handle long, specially formatted papers on software meant only for memos and two- to three-page papers.

Are other members of your family going to use the software? Have you asked them what is on their software "wish list?"

Determine Your Limits

The biggest limit you are likely to have is money. Your budget may not allow you to buy the program that will do everything you wish. But be careful about letting price be your only guide. Some people believe that if they buy expensive software, it will have all the features they need. This might be true, but studies show that many people who buy higher-priced software use only one-third to two-thirds of the program's capabilities. On the other hand, some people are so thrift-conscious that they buy low-priced software, only to find that they outgrow it very quickly.

Another limit is the hardware you already own. The software you choose must be compatible with your hardware. Your system must have enough memory to support the program and the correct number of disk drives to operate the program. Some software requires two disk drives to operate properly. If you have only one disk drive and do not plan to buy a second drive, then you should not consider that software. Others requires 128K to run, so your 64K machine will not adequately handle the software unless you can add more memory. Does your computer have the correct operating system? Many computers support more than one operating system, so any software you buy must match the operating system, too. Some software requires special equipment or high-resolution screens. The most sophisticated graphics package will not produce high-resolution pictures on a low-resolution screen. For greater detail in your illustrations, you will want to shop carefully for both the software and the hardware. Some software requires the use of a graphics pad, joystick, mouse, or light pen. Check costs on this equipment before buying the software.

Evaluate the Software

Once you have defined your needs and limits, you are ready to evaluate specific software packages. Match the amount of time you spend on the evaluation to the importance and expense of the package. If you are buying a game, you may spend less time in the evaluation stage. But if you are buying an expensive filing program or word-processing software that may last throughout college, you will want to spend more time researching and trying out the products.

Look for reviews of the software in several computer magazines. Ask friends or teachers what they like to use. Inquire at a computer store for demonstrations and information. You should be able to try out more than one program to get an idea of what features are available. When you go to a store, you should have a list of the features you want. In a word-processing package, for instance, you may want to check whether the program reminds you to save your files before starting something new. You should check ease in moving text, merging files, formatting the output, and searching for misspellings.

While you are conducting your research, keep nine factors in mind. First, check the difficulty of the program. Decide how much time you wish to spend learning the program. More sophisticated software requires more time in reading and experimenting, but also allows you to do more. A good program should let you "grow into" the package and not limit you as your experience increases. It should allow you to use the program with several basic commands, yet encourage you to learn more advanced commands as you need them. Be wary when ease of use is chosen as the major selling point of software. It may be easy to use because it is very limited.

Second, you should look for a clear and logical screen appearance when your software is loaded. A screen that is cluttered will take more time to learn. Look at how the program handles movement between program modes—for instance, between the editing and formatting modes of a word-processing package. Movement should be consistent, requiring use of a limited number of keys so you do not accidentally strike a wrong key. Some software supports have pull-down menus that help you format and edit documents. Other programs allow you to display two or more portions of a document in a split-screen format or in pull-down windows. This feature is helpful in using an electronic spreadsheet—you can make a change in one of the windows and see how that change affects data in another window without searching through hundreds of rows and columns of figures.

Third, check the type of command style used in the program. Command style refers to the approach used to command the program. Several approaches are the full menu with explanation, the menu alone, a single command with explanation, or memorization of all commands with no menus available. Although menus are helpful to beginners, experienced users may find that menus slow down the input and processing stages.

A fourth consideration is to be sure help screens are really helpful. A help screen will help you continue in your program if you are puzzled about what step to take next. The most helpful are those that you can call from any point in the program and that then return you to where you left off.

Fifth, examine the program for defaults. A default is a value that the computer assumes when you do not tell it what value to use. For example, many word processors were set up to produce a standard business letter on 8- by 11-inch paper without your having to state this size. Default values make a program more flexible to your needs. Yet they should be easy to change to adapt automatically to the format you use the most.

Sixth, check the error handling capabilities of the software. Find out how you can change errors that you make in entering the data. Also find out how you can recover from a command that you accidentally enter in the computer. For instance, many programs now contain an UNDO command that provides a way to recover material that you might have deleted and want back. Another example involves the SAVE operation. If you are saving material and a "DISK FULL" message appears on the screen, you should be able to replace the disk and redo the SAVE operation without losing any data.

Seventh, be sure your software will handle the amount of data you expect to enter and do what you expect it to with the data. Check the number of pages of text a word processor can work with, or the number of columns and rows in a spreadsheet, or the number of files a data manager will support. If the word processor will handle only 10 pages of text, can you merge that file with another to print out a 20- or 30-page paper? If you have 1,000 records to file and the data manager allows for only 800, the package will be of very little value to you. Look for the kinds of calculations, documents, and graphs the software will support. Can you merge text with a graph done on graphics software? Will the data manager file data by many topics or just one topic?

Eighth, the question of copy protection can be important to users. Being able to copy a program allows a great deal of flexibility. If the software cannot be copied, you may not be able to use it with a hard disk, local area network, or electronic disk simulator because you cannot move the copy from a floppy disk. You should also be able to make backup copies of the program.

Finally, review the documentation. The quality of the documentation can mirror the quality of the software. Look for thorough, well-written manuals that are organized logically. When you are testing the program, look in the manual to see if you can easily run some aspect of the program using only the instructions provided. Step-by-step instructions in tutorials will also guide you in using the software. Cards for quick reference to a program's commands while you use the program are helpful, too.

Remember, the old saying "Let the buyer beware!" applies to software. Know your needs before purchasing software. Purchase from a reliable vendor. Find out the policy if the software is updated, or if there are programming errors in the software. Talk with a users' group or computer club to learn more about the software you are considering. Look into the programs offered by public domain.

Assignment

Prepare a review on some software you own or have used. Evaluate it in terms of this Enrichment Topic. Several reviews can then be collected into a software review paper for your grade or school.

Graphics That Move

Designing pictures with graph paper can be fun and result in some interesting surprises. Once a simple design is completed, you can transfer it to computer by plotting points as you would with X and Y coordinates in algebra class. With some ingenuity, you can even make a picture move across the computer.

The BASIC statements needed to produce graphics are easy to master. They just require some prior thought to decide how to plot the design on the computer's "grid." The methods described here can be used on the Apple II computers. Check the user's

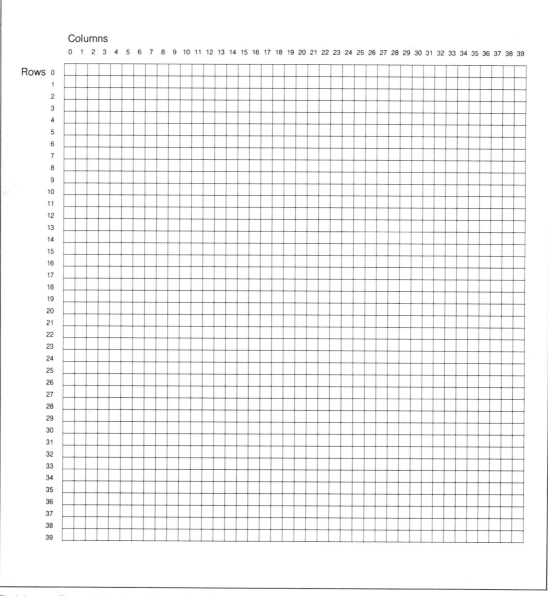

Enrichment Figure 5-1. *Low-Resolution Graphics Screen*

manual for the graphics capabilities of other computers. Then ask your teacher to help you adapt these methods to the other computers.

The new statements you will use are GR, COLOR, PLOT, and SPEED. The GR statement will allow you to enter the low-resolution graphics mode in BASIC. Using the material from the graphics portion of chapter 6, you can guess that low-resolution means that the points of light, or pixels, will be larger than in a higher resolution mode. To enter the low-resolution graphics mode in BASIC, type the following statement:

40 GR

This clears the entire screen except for four lines of text at the bottom, where commands can be typed. The rest of the screen is divided into 40 columns and 40 rows. Each point is named by giving column and row addresses. The point appears as a small rectangle on the display screen. Think of the screen as a sheet of graph paper containing 40 rows and 40 columns (see Enrichment Figure 5-1). There will be 40 x 40, or 1600, points that can be addressed.

Each point can be assigned a color. The COLOR statement tells the computer what color to assign the points in the low-resolution graphics mode. Enrichment Table 5-1 lists the 16 colors available and the corresponding numbers from 0 to 15. These numbers are used in the COLOR statement to set the color. The format of the COLOR statement is:

line# COLOR = color #

For example, the following statement sets the drawing color to pink:

40 COLOR = 11

If a color is not selected, the Apple automatically chooses black, or COLOR = 0, as the current color.

LOW-RESOLUTION GRAPHICS COLORS   Enrichment Table 5-1

Color	Number	Color	Number
Black	0	Brown	8
Magenta	1	Orange	9
Dark blue	2	Gray 2	10
Purple	3	Pink	11
Dark green	4	Light green	12
Gray 1	5	Yellow	13
Medium blue	6	Aqua	14
Light blue	7	White	15

The PLOT statement places a small dot (actually a rectangle) on the display screen. The format of the PLOT statement is:

line# PLOT column,row

The column and row addresses tell the computer where to place the dot. Think of the graph paper with 40 columns and 40 rows. To place a dot at the center of the screen, type:

40 PLOT 19,19

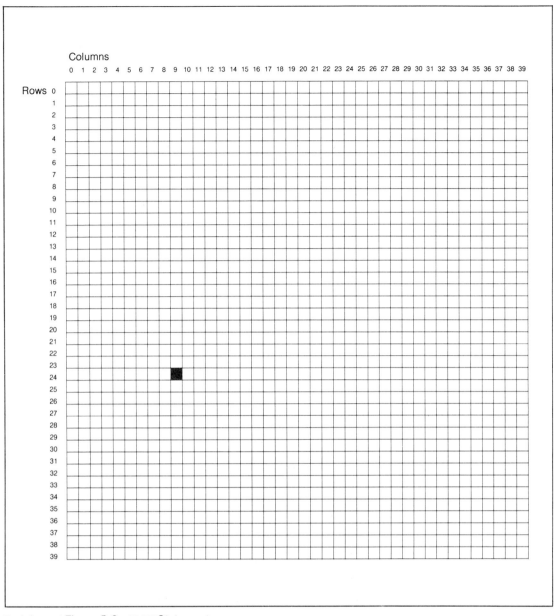

Enrichment Figure 5-2. *PLOT Statement*

This places a dot at the intersection of column 19 and row 19. The reason 19 was used instead of 20 is that both the rows and columns are numbered beginning with 0 instead of 1. Each column address must be a value from 0 to 39, and each row address must be a value from 0 to 39. If you use a greater number, in a PLOT statement, an error message is displayed and the program stops. To produce a dot at the tenth column and 25th row (see Enrichment Figure 5-2), type:

```
10 PLOT 9,24
```

Now draw a square that moves across the screen. You cannot actually make the square move. But if you turn on and off the squares in the low-resolution graphics mode, the squares appear to move. This is done by "coloring" the squares.

Try this program. (To stop the program, press CTRL and C .)

```
100   GR
110   FOR H = 0 TO 39
120   COLOR= 11
130   PLOT H,20
140   COLOR= 0
150   PLOT H,20
160   NEXT H
170   GOTO 110
```

In this program, H stands for the columns across the screen. Line 120 colors the first column pink. Line 140 colors it black— the same color as the background. Essentially, line 140 "erases" the first square. When the FOR/NEXT loop returns, the next column is colored, and then it is erased, and so on across the screen.

Now, with these BASIC statements, try plotting some points of your own to draw a picture and try the assignments, too.

Assignments

1. Use the concepts in this enrichment topic and the FOR/NEXT loops to move a square diagonally across the screen.

2. Use graph paper to draw a very simple picture of an airplane or car. Then write a program to see what the picture looks like on computer.

3. Can you create a program that will make a square bounce twice across the screen? Hint: Plot it on graph paper first using 39 squares across and 20 squares vertically.

Computer Sounds

Most computers will beep on at least one pitch. The Commodore 64, Apple II, and IBM PC will produce a variety of sounds. On the IBM, sounds other than music also can be saved in a library of sound effects. The information given here is for the Apple II. Consult the user's guide for creating sound on other computers.

To produce a beep on the Apple II, you can use one of two methods. The first method is to press CTRL and G . Each time you press those keys, you should hear the beep.

To produce a beep on the Apple II, you can use one of two methods. The first method is to press CONTROL-G. Each time you press those keys, you should hear the beep.

The second way is to use CHR$(7) in a program. Type in this program line:

```
100   PRINT  CHR$ (7)
```

Now type RUN. What happened?

Can you make the computer stop and beep when it comes to your name in the list of students in your class? Be sure that someone besides yourself could use the program!

Type this program portion:

```
100    INPUT "WHAT IS YOUR NAME?";N$
110    FOR X = 1 TO 10
120    READ STUDENT$
130    PRINT STUDENT$
140    IF STUDENT$ = N$ THEN 160
150    NEXT X
160    PRINT  CHR$ (7)
170    DATA   "NORMA","DONNA","BRIAN","KAREN","RUSS"
180    DATA   "PHIL","KIM","SUSAN","RICK","JULIE"
```

You can also activate the built-in speaker in another way. To use this method, you should know that PEEK lets you read the value stored in an Apple II memory location. When you read location –16336, the speaker will give a brief sound.

Type in this line:

```
50 A =  PEEK ( - 16336)
```

Now type RUN. You will have to listen closely to hear a single click. If you RUN it a second time, you will hear nothing. RUNing it a third time sounds the click.

To get a tone instead of a single click, you must "pluck" the speaker over and over again. Type in these lines:

```
100 A =  PEEK ( - 16336)
110  GOTO 100
```

RUN the program. Press ⎡CTRL⎤ and ⎡C⎤ to stop the program.

Suppose you want to vary the sound. You can INPUT a value that will make the speaker sound repeatedly. Repeating a loop just a few times results in a high pitch, while repeating the loop many times results in a low pitch. Type in this program portion:

```
100    INPUT "PITCH, 1(HIGH) TO 11(LOW)?";P
110 A =  PEEK ( - 16336)
120    FOR S = 1 TO P
130    NEXT S
140    GOTO 110
```

Now type RUN. Enter a number from 1 to 11 when the prompt appears. Press [RETURN]. What happened?

Some Apple user's guides will show you how to create tones of a certain length. They will also show you how to use a machine language subroutine to create a song.

Assignments

1. Create a program that will print your name repeatedly and beep each time your name appears. (Hint: You can create time between each beep by inserting PRINT statements to create "blank" lines.)

2. Create a program that will print "OH, NO! MONDAY BLUES!" and sound a low pitch. Then create a program that will print "OH GOOD! IT'S FRIDAY!" and sound a high pitch.

Fun with Functions

BASIC has several built-in functions that perform specific operations. The functions that perform math operations, such as finding square roots or choosing a random number, are called library, or predefined, functions. By using these predefined functions, the programmer saves time in writing steps that would do those jobs.

Functions that can be used with character strings are called string functions. Instead of handling numbers, the string functions manage the characters in character strings.

Let's examine one library function and two string functions. Probably you know some math puzzles that ask you to pick a number—any number, a number between 1 and 10, or some other limit. The library function RND(X) lets you pick a random number at the computer.

Look at this line of a program:

```
100   LET N =   RND (10)
```

You remember that LET means the computer will store something in an address. It will store RND(10). RND stands for RANDOM. (Random means haphazardly or without any pattern.) RND(10) permits the computer to choose any number from 1 to 10. Type this on the computer:

```
100   LET N =   RND (10)
110   PRINT N
```

Now RUN the program. RUN it several times and see what you get for N each time. RND on some computers, among them Apple, IBM PC, or Commodore 64 computer, picks a number between 0 and 1. The result is a decimal number. Let's see how we can change the decimal number into a useful integer.

If N = RND(10) produced .423451, then multiply N times 10. That will yield 4.23452. Then use the INT function, which changes the number to a whole number, or integer value. Change N to an integer by writing N = INT(N). Then N becomes 4. The digits to the right of the decimal point are deleted. But this process chooses single digits between 0 and 9. What if you want numbers from 1 to 10? Just add 1 to N. The complete statement which chooses a number at random and writes it as an integer is:

```
100   LET N =   INT ( RND (1) * 10) + 1
```

Let's toss a coin by computer. How many choices are there? There are two—heads and tails. So the choice for RND is:

```
100   LET C =   RND (2)
110   IF C = 1 THEN   PRINT "HEADS"
120   IF C = 2 THEN   PRINT "TAILS"
```

Now RUN the program. Remember, if the computer you are using picks random numbers between 0 and 1, you will type line 100 as:

```
100   LET C =   INT ( RND (1) * 2) + 1
```

Write a short program for rolling one die. How many choices must you allow for? (See the end of the enrichment topic for a solution to the die problem and more RND puzzles.)

Now let's see how two string functions work. The two we will discuss are LEN and LEFT$. Remember that to signal a character string, you must use the dollar sign ($).

LEN stands for LENGTH. The LEN function gives the number of characters in a string. The format of this function is:

LEN(string)

Let's count the number of characters in your name:

```
100   LET STUDENT$ = "MARGARET"
110   LET L =   LEN (STUDENT$)
120   PRINT L
```

Now RUN the program. What was the value of L?

For a little fun, let's combine the LEN function with the LEFT$ function. LEFT$ counts the characters from the left side. It returns the number of characters desired. The format is:

LEFT$(string, expression)

"String" stands for the string constant or variable. "Expression" stands for the numeric constant, variable, or expression. How does LEFT$ work? Look at the example below:

```
100   LET STUDENT$ = "MARGARET"
110   PRINT  LEFT$ (STUDENT$,3)
```

When you RUN the program, the result is MAR.

Type in this program portion, which combines LEN and LEFT$:

```
100   LET PHRASE$ = "HIT THE DIRT"
110   LET L =  LEN (PHRASE$)
120   FOR J = 1 TO L
130   PRINT  LEFT$ (PHRASE$,J)
140   NEXT J
```

Now RUN the program. What happened? Try it with your name, or another phrase.

Assignments

Remember to use the REM and END statements as described in the BASIC section of this book!

1. Find a math puzzle that asks you to choose a random number and always results in the same answer. Figure out a BASIC program to perform the puzzle by computer. (Sources would include many puzzle books from the library. Your math teacher might also have one available.)

2. Write a program that will pick a random number between 1 and 25, and then ask the user to input a guess between 1 and 25. If the user's number matches the computer's number, then have the program print a positive message ("That's correct" or something similar). If the user's number does not match the computer's number, then have the program print a negative message ("No, try again!" or something similar).

3. Write a program that will print the names of students in your class with their telephone numbers. The program should print the phone numbers in an even column:

```
Mark Thomas     456-3322
Joan Gregg      456-9991
```

Do you need some hints to start? Use the READ/DATA statements, a dummy value, the GOTO statement, and LEN function.

Solution to die problem:

```
100    LET D = RND (6)
110    PRINT "DIE ROLL YIELDS";D
```

Some computers will require line 100 to read:

```
100    LET D = INT ( RND (1) * 6) + 1
```

Fill a File

Suppose you write a program in which you wish to use information that is stored in a file. You will need two programs: the program that creates the file and the program that uses the file.

Let's look at a program that will read a file of student scores, enter a second score, and compute an average. The student names and both test scores are then written back to the file. The programs are written for the Apple II computers. Persons using other computers should check the user's guides for creating and using files.

Here is the program that creates the file:

```
10     REM    *** CREATES STUDENT FILE ***
20     REM
30     REM    *** VARIABLES ***
40     REM        STUDENT = FILE NAME
50     REM        N$ = STUDENT NAME
60     REM        S1 = FIRST SCORE
70     REM
80     REM
90     LET D$ =  CHR$ (4)
100    REM  *** CREATE FILE ***
110    PRINT D$;"OPEN STUDENT"
120    PRINT D$;"WRITE STUDENT"
130    REM
140    REM  *** WRITE TO FILE ***
150    FOR J = 1 TO 4
160    READ N$,S1
170    PRINT N$
180    PRINT S1
190    NEXT J
200    REM
210    REM  *** CLOSE FILE ***
220    PRINT D$;"CLOSE STUDENT"
230    PRINT "THE FILE IS CREATED"
240    REM
250    REM  *** DATA ***
260    DATA   "J. SMITH",98
```

```
270    DATA    "K. MILLER",78
280    DATA    "L. JONES",83
290    DATA    "F. HARVEY",74
```

In the program, line 90 tells the computer a disk is being used. This line is necessary on the Apple II computers. Lines 110 and 120 create the new file and cue the computer that data will be written to the file. The data are actually written to the file in lines 150 to 190. Notice that PRINT statements are used to write the data into the file. Here the PRINT statements will produce no paper or screen display output. Line 220 closes the file.

Now RUN the program. Did you get the message, "The file is created"?

Now you will want to update the program. This involves writing a new program. Here is the update program:

```
70     REM    *** UPDATE STUDENT FILE ***
80     REM    *** VARIABLES ***
90     REM         STUDENT = FILE NAME
100    REM         S1,S2 = FIRST, SECOND SCORES
110    REM         AV = AVERAGE SCORE
120    REM
130    LET D$ =  CHR$ (4)
140    REM  *** READ FILE ***
150    PRINT D$;"OPEN STUDENT"
160    PRINT D$;"READ STUDENT"
170    FOR J = 1 TO 4
180    INPUT N$(J),S1(J)
190    NEXT J
200    PRINT D$;"CLOSE STUDENT"
210    REM
220    REM  *** PRINT HEADINGS ***
230    PRINT "NAME","AVERAGE"
240    PRINT "----","-------"
250    REM
260    REM  *** COMPUTE AVERAGE ***
270    FOR J = 1 TO 4
280    READ S2(J)
290    LET AV = (S1(J) + S2(J)) / 2
300    PRINT N$(J),AV
310    NEXT J
320    REM
330    REM  *** WRITE TO FILE ***
340    PRINT D$;"OPEN STUDENT"
350    PRINT D$;"WRITE STUDENT"
360    FOR J = 1 TO 4
370    PRINT N$(J)
380    PRINT S1(J)
390    PRINT S2(J)
400    NEXT J
410    PRINT D$;"CLOSE STUDENT"
420    REM
```

```
600   REM   *** DATA ***
610   DATA   89,76,87,79
999   END
```

Review to yourself what each portion of the program does. After the variable names you see that a letter appears in parentheses. The letter creates an array, which saves the data until they are used. The letter must match the letter used in the FOR/NEXT statements.

Also you will see that when the data are written to the file again, all of them are written. If only the new scores were written to the file, the rest of the data would be destroyed.

RUN the program. What happens? Can you write a new program that uses the existing file to add a term paper to the file? Remember, you must PRINT all the existing data back to the file. Use this DATA line:

```
500   DATA   "A","B+","A-","C+"
```

Assignments

1. Create a file that will save the names, birthdays, and telephone numbers of several friends. Use the first file as a pattern. (Use three-letter abbreviations for the months and do not use the year of birth, only the day of birth.)

2. Write a new program that will print the first names, birthdays, and telephone numbers of your friends. Use the print-zone method of lining up the columns. Do you need to write anything to the file? Can you reuse the file this way if you do not change the file in any way? Try it. Run the new program again.

3. Now write a new program that will not only print the first names, birthdays, and telephone numbers of your friends, but that will also add their last names to the file. Keep the last names in a separate column from the first names so that you can continue to use the print zones. Are the names of any of your friends too long to use the print zones? Try a print program that uses the TAB functions! You may need an 80-column card to do this!

Alphanumeric data Data comprised of letters, numbers, and/or special characters.

Analog computer A computer that measures continuous physical or electrical states, such as flow, temperature, or pressure.

Application program A program designed to meet a particular user need.

Application programmer A programmer who writes instructions to solve a specific problem or day-to-day task, such as billing.

Arithmetic/logic unit (ALU) The section of the central processing unit that handles arithmetic calculations and logical comparisons.

Artificial intelligence (AI) The ability of computers to think like humans.

Assembler The language translation program for changing assembly language to machine language.

Assembly language A symbolic programming language that uses abbreviations rather than 0s and 1s; an assembler program changes an assembly language program into machine language.

Automatic word wrap A word-processing feature that lets the user continue typing without pressing $\boxed{\text{RETURN}}$ at the end of a line. The computer automatically jumps to the next line

when the text becomes too long for the line length on the monitor.

BASIC Beginners' All-purpose Symbolic Instruction Code; a programming language commonly used for interactive problem solving by users who may not be professional programmers.

BASIC statement The part of the instruction composed of a special programming command, constants, variables, and formulas.

Batch processing Processing data in groups from time to time.

Binary number system The numeric system, used in computer operations, that uses the digits 0 and 1 and has a base of 2.

Binary representation Using 0s and 1s to represent "off" and "on" electrical states in a digital computer.

Biochips Tiny computer circuits that are grown from living material; they are still in the developmental stage.

Boilerplating A word-processing function that copies the same text into different documents or fills in the blanks in otherwise identical documents.

Bit The smallest unit of information that can be represented in binary

	notation; a 0 or 1 for "off" or "on" electrical impulses; short for *BI*nary digi*T*.
Block diagram	See Flowchart.
Block function	A word-processing feature that allows the user to choose parts of text to save, delete, copy, or move.
Branch pattern	Program logic that is used to skip over certain instructions.
Bug	An error in a program.
Bus	The term given to all of the wires and cables that connect the parts of the computer.
Byte	A group of bits that operates as a unit; generally eight bits equal one byte.
Cathode-ray tube (CRT)	A television-like screen that displays the result of computer processing; also called a monitor.
Cells	The boxes made by columns and rows in a spreadsheet.
Central processing unit (CPU)	The brain of the computer, composed of three sections: the control unit, arithmetic/logic unit, and primary storage unit.
Character string	A group of alphanumeric data enclosed in quotation marks.
COBOL	COmmon Business-Oriented Language; a programming language mainly used for business applications.
Communication channel	A pathway that allows remote input/ouput de-

	vices to communicate with the computer.
Compiler	A translator program for a high-level language such as FORTRAN; translates the statements into machine code all at once.
Computer	A machine with uses limited only by the creativity of the humans who use it.
Computer operator	A person who sets up machines and files needed for a program to run and monitors the run for problems.
Computer output microfilm (COM)	Miniature photographic images of output produced on microfilm rather than on paper.
Computer-aided design (CAD)	The use of a computer by an engineer to design, draft, and test a product using computer graphics at a terminal.
Computer-aided manufacturing (CAM)	The use of a computer by an engineer to simulate the steps of a manufacturing process; the use of a computer to monitor the manufacturing process.
Computer-assisted instruction (CAI)	The use of a computer to instruct or drill a student on an individual or small group basis.
Constant	A value that does not change during a program's execution.
Control statement	A statement that will give control to program statements out of sequence.
Control unit	The section of the central processing unit that directs the order of

operation and governs the actions of the various units that make up the computer.

Conversational mode
A question-and-answer mode in which the user interacts with the computer while a program is being run.

Counter
A variable that changes each time a loop is executed in order to count the number of executions.

Cursor
A mark or notation on the display screen that shows where the next character a user types will appear.

Data
Raw facts that have not been organized; the raw material of information.

Data-base manager
Data management software that builds a data base or collection of data to answer many different questions. A data base should fit the information needs of many users and provide a central location of the data.

Data processing
An orderly set of techniques for collecting, handling, and passing out data to achieve a goal.

Data redundancy
Unneeded data repetition.

Data-base administrator (DBA)
A management-level position with responsibility for control of all the data resources of a company.

Data-base analyst
A person who plans and manages the use of data within the system.

Data-entry operator
A person who prepares data in a form that is suitable for computer processing.

Debug
To locate and correct program errors.

Dedicated computer
A computer that has a special job that is determined by its hardware.

Desk-checking
A method used in both system and program debugging in which the sequence of operation is traced mentally to check the correctness of processing logic.

Digital computer
A type of computer that operates by transmission of data in "on" and "off" states.

Direct (or immediate) mode
The mode of operation of the computer where statements are executed as soon as they are typed; does not require line numbers.

Direct-access storage
A method of storing data so they can be retrieved in any order without reading through the other data in order.

Disk drive
The device that rotates the floppy disk and reads data from and writes data to the disk.

Documentation
The written explanation of the program and its logic.

Dumb terminals
Terminals that cannot be programmed but can be used to enter data into a computer.

Electronic bulletin board
An electronic clearinghouse where messages may be posted or received through a computer.

Electronic data processing (EDP)	Data processing that occurs largely by electronic equipment, such as computers.		the number of times a loop should be executed.
Electronic mail	Messages sent at high speeds by telecommunication and placed in special computer storage areas where they can then be read.	**Format**	To arrange the design of output.
		Formatting	Preparation of text for printing. The page is designed with margins, page numbers, number of lines, and so on.
Electronic spreadsheet	A grid for financial study to use with computers; allows the user to see results of certain calculations.	**FORTRAN**	FORmula TRANSlator; a programming language used mainly in mathematical or scientific operations.
END statement	Causes program execution to stop.	**Gallium arsenide**	A substance that may replace silicon in computer chips.
Ethics	Rules or standards that are used to guide personal conduct.	**Garbage in-garbage out**	A phrase used to show that the meaningfulness of computer output depends on the accuracy of the data fed into the computer.
Execute	To perform.		
Exponentiation	Raising a number to a power.		
Expression	A constant, variable, or mathematical formula.	**General-purpose computer**	A computer used for many applications.
Field engineer	See Technician.	**GOSUB statement**	Transfers control from the main program to a subroutine.
File handler	A type of data management software that imitates a standard filing system in which related records are collected.	**GOTO statement**	A statement that unconditionally transfers program execution to a given line number.
Flexible diskette	See Floppy disk.	**GOTO-less programming**	Structured programming method that avoids the branch logic pattern (GOTO statement).
Floppy disk	Also called floppy diskette and flexible diskette; a low-cost form of external storage made of plastic and used with a disk drive.		
		Graphics tablet	A "pad" that allows the user to create designs on the display screen by drawing with a light pen or a finger.
Floppy diskette	See Floppy disk.		
Flowchart	A diagram composed of symbols representing the processing steps of a program.	**Hard copy**	Printed output; a permanent record of output.
FOR statement	The first statement in a FOR/NEXT loop; shows	**Hardware**	The physical components that make up a computer system.

Hollerith code	A method of data representation named for its inventor, Herman Hollerith; encodes numbers, letters, and special characters by the placement of holes in punched cards.
IF/THEN statement	A statement that gives control of the program to a named line number or calls for a certain task only if a stated condition is true.
Indirect mode	The mode of computer operation in which statements are not executed until told to do so; requires the use of line numbers.
Infinite loop	An error condition in which the computer repeats a step over and over again.
Information	Data that have been organized and processed so they are meaningful; used to increase understanding or make decisions.
Initial value	The beginning value of a loop control variable; shown in the FOR statement.
Initialization	A process in which a beginning number value is set or assigned to a variable with the LET statement; done when something is to be counted.
Input	The step in the data-processing flow in which data are collected and coded for computer use.
INPUT statement	A statement that allows the user to enter data at the keyboard while the program is running; usually in question-and-answer form.
Input/output devices	Devices that can be used for both input and output.
Inquiry-and-response mode	See Conversational mode.
Integrated circuit	Electronic circuits etched on a small silicon chip; allows much faster processing than with the larger transistor technology and at a greatly reduced price.
Intelligent terminal	A terminal with an internal processor that can be programmed to do certain things.
Interactive processing	A processing method in which the user can enter input during processing.
Interpreter	A translation program used by small computer systems to evaluate and change program statements as the program is executed one instruction at a time; used frequently in interactive processing.
Joystick	An input device used with a computer to control the movement of the cursor and to provide certain commands.
Keyboard	The part of the computer with the typing keys.
Kilobyte	A term used to stand for 1,024 bytes; the symbol is K.
Language-translation program	The instructions that translate the English-like programs written by programmers into machine-executable code.

Large-scale integrated (LSI) circuits
Hundreds of electronic circuits closely packed in a single silicon chip.

Laser disk
A platter on which the marks are made by laser beam—a concentrated, very thin light beam.

LET statement
Assigns data values or results of arithmetic calculations to variables.

Librarian
The person who catalogs and maintains computer files and programs kept on storage devices.

Light pen
A pen-shaped object used to draw lines on a visual display screen or graphics tablet.

Line editor
A method built into the computer's operating system in which the programmer can check and correct an individual line of programming instruction.

Line number
A natural number or zero that specifies the order in which the statements are executed.

Literal
An expression consisting of alphabetic, numeric, or special characters whose value does not change during the execution of a program.

Logic diagram
See Flowchart.

Logic error
An error resulting from incorrect thinking patterns in developing the program; the program will not process the data in the expected manner.

Logo
A powerful programming language that allows the user to program effectively by defining new commands and creating graphics.

Loop pattern
Program logic that repeats a group of instructions.

Loop variable
The variable in a FOR statement that is increased each time the loop is executed.

Machine language
The only set of instructions that a computer can execute (run) directly; a code that names the proper electrical states in the computer as combinations of 0s and 1s.

Magnetic disk
Secondary storage made of a platter coated with a magnetic recording material. Small spots are magnetized to represent data.

Magnetic ink character recognition (MICR)
The process that allows magnetized characters to be printed on a source document and read by the computer.

Magnetic tape
Secondary storage made of a narrow strip of plastic tape. Small spots are magnetized to stand for data.

Mainframe computer
A large computer capable of full-scale operation at fast speeds; smaller and slower than a supercomputer, but larger and faster than a minicomputer.

Maintenance programmer
A programmer who changes and improves existing programs.

Management information system (MIS) manager
The person who organizes the physical and human resources of a company so that the company's goals are met.

Memory The part of the computer that provides the ability to recall information.

Menu A list of choices shown on the monitor or CRT from which the user can pick the needed operation.

Microcomputer A very small computer, often a special-function computer.

Microprocessor The "brain" or governing unit of a microcomputer; fits on a small silicon chip.

Minicomputer A computer with the components of a full-sized system but having a smaller memory.

Mnemonics A symbolic name or memory aid; used in assembly language and in high-level computer languages.

Modem A device that changes the impulses sent over communication channels into signals the computer can understand or into signals that that will travel over the channels.

Module A logical segment of a program that completes one function independently of other modules.

Mouse A desk-top input device that controls cursor movement and computer commands; it rolls on a smooth surface.

Nanosecond One-billionth of a second.

Nested loop A FOR/NEXT loop inside of another FOR/NEXT loop.

Network The linkage of computers for sharing messages and information.

NEXT statement The last statement in a FOR/NEXT statement; counts the loop variable and returns execution to the statement following the FOR statement.

Nondestructive testing (NDT) Testing done by electronic means so that breaking, cutting, or tearing the product apart is not needed.

ON/GOTO statement A statement that transfers program execution to one of several listed line numbers, depending on the result of a choice or the evaluation of an expression.

On-line In direct communication with the computer.

Operating system A collection of programs that permits a computer to manage itself and avoid idle CPU time.

Optical character recognition (OCR) The process of recognizing and translating characters printed or typed on paper.

Optical mark recognition (OMR) The process of detecting marks made on paper and evaluating the marks according to their location.

Output Information that comes from the computer as a result of processing.

Pascal A programming language named after Blaise Pascal. It is highly structured and is used to teach programming concepts to students.

Peripheral devices	Input and output devices and secondary storage units outside the main computer.		be performed in a program.
PILOT	An educational programming language used to write programs for computer-assisted instruction.	**Punched cards**	A commonly used storage method in which data are represented by the presence or absence of holes according to a coding scheme such as Hollerith's. Each particular set of holes has a distinct meaning that is translated into machine language for the computer.
Pixels	The individual dots on a display screen that are used to create characters and images.		
Plotter	A special printer used to print graphic images such as charts, graphs, and pictures.	**Random-access memory (RAM)**	Storage that allows data to be quickly stored (written to) or accessed (read from).
Primary storage unit	A section of the central processing unit that holds instructions, data, and intermediate and final results during processing.	**Read-only memory (ROM)**	The part of computer hardware containing items that cannot be deleted or changed by a computer's instructions; the circuitry is hard-wired into the computer.
PRINT statement	Causes the results of program execution to be printed on a CRT screen or on paper.	**READ/DATA statements**	Statements that work together to enter data into a program.
Processing	The handling of data provided as input to produce information; includes calculating, classifying, sorting, summarizing, and storing.	**Read/write head**	An electromagnet used to read data from or write data to magnetic tapes and disks.
Program	A series of step-by-step instructions that tells the computer exactly what to do.	**Register**	A temporary storage area located in the CPU and used for holding instructions or data; material held in a register can be processed very quickly.
Programmer	A person who writes a program.		
Prompt	A message printed during program execution to explain to the user what data should be entered in an INPUT statement.	**Relational symbol**	A symbol that shows the relationship between two items; for example, the symbol > means "is greater than."
Pseudocode	A written description of the processing steps to	**REM statement**	Describes the programming problem, defines variables, or explains

calculations; not an executable statement.

Remote terminals Devices used at another geographical location to enter data and communicate with the main computer.

Reserved word A word that has a special meaning to the computer and cannot be used as a variable name.

Resolution Clarity; detail of a picture.

Retrieve Finding stored information so it can be examined by the user.

RETURN statement Transfers control back to the main program after the subroutine has been run.

Screen editor A method to correct errors by listing a portion of a program and moving the cursor to the incorrect parts.

Scroll The process of moving lines up and down on the terminal screen.

Search and replace A word-processing function; the computer locates words or phrases throughout the typed material and replaces them automatically.

Secondary storage Storage that is outside the main computer or CPU.

Selection pattern Program logic that includes a test; depending on the results of the test, one of two paths is taken.

Sequential-access storage Secondary storage from which data must be read one after another in a

fixed order until the needed data are found.

Silicon chip Solid state circuitry on a small piece of silicon, a material found in quartz and sand.

Simple-sequence pattern Program logic in which one program statement follows another in sequence and is executed by the computer in that order.

Soft copy Data displayed on a television-like screen; not a permanent record of output.

Software The programs executed by the computer.

Source-data automation The use of special equipment to capture data in computer-readable form when and where an event takes place.

STEP value The value by which the loop variable is counted each time a FOR/NEXT loop is executed; shown in the FOR statement.

STOP statement Halts execution of a program.

Storage See Memory.

Stored program Instructions kept in the computer's memory in electronic form; can be executed (run) repeatedly during processing.

Structured programming A method of computer programming developed to make programs easier to maintain and change.

Subroutine A set of statements placed outside the main lines of a program. The statements in a sub-

	routine may be used over and over again without being rewritten.
Supercomputer	An extremely powerful computer that is very fast and very efficient; often used for scientific applications.
Supervisor program	The major component of an operating system; coordinates the activities of all other parts of the operating system.
Symbolic language	Also called assembly language; must be translated into machine language before it can be run by the computer.
Syntax error	An error that occurs when the programmer fails to follow the grammatical rules of the computer language being used.
System command	A command used to communicate with the operating system of the computer.
System error	An error that involves the computer equipment.
Systems analyst	A person who works with the users and programmers to study, design, and put into use computer systems.
Systems program	A program written to coordinate the operation of computer circuitry and to help the computer run quickly and efficiently.
Systems programmer	A person who writes programs that control a system's operations.
Tape drive	A mechanical unit that moves magnetic tape past a read/write head.

Technical writer	A person who writes technical or scientific material in an easily understood form.
Technician	The person who installs, maintains, and repairs computer equipment.
Telecommuting	Computer hookups between offices and homes that allow employees to work at home.
Teleconference	A meeting conducted from two or more locations over communication lines.
Terminal	A device in a computer system where data can enter or exit.
Terminal screen	Also called video display terminal (VDT) or cathode-ray tube (CRT); a television-like screen used to display information.
Terminal value	The value at which a FOR/NEXT loop will stop execution; shown in the FOR statement.
Trailer value	A dummy value added to the end of a data list to show that a loop should stop execution.
Transistor	A type of electronic component used to control the flow of electricity; does not need heat or a vacuum to work and is smaller, faster, and more reliable than a vacuum tube.
Typographic error	An error resulting from mistyping characters into the computer.
Unconditional transfer	A transfer of program control made every time a statement is met,

User-friendly — regardless of what conditions exist.

Easy to use; designed to be accessible to users without much technical training.

Vacuum tube — A fragile glass case that has no air but contains a type of circuitry to control the flow of electricity; heat makes the current flow.

Variable — A value that can change either before or during program execution.

Variable name — A name that identifies the value that can change either before or during program execution; associated with a storage location.

Very-large-scale integrated (VLSI) circuit — Thousands of electrical circuits packed on a single silicon chip.

Visual-display terminals (VDTs) — Terminals that display data on TV-like screens (CRTs).

Voice recognition system — A system that allows the user to "train" the computer to recognize his or her voice and vocabulary.

Window — A display method that shows information in boxes or allows the user to see a portion of a large display.

Word processing — It allows the user to write, edit, format, and print text.

INDEX